WILLIAM FAULKNER

TOWARD YOKNAPATAWPHA AND BEYOND

Cleanth Brooks

WILLIAM FAULKNER

TOWARD YOKNAPATAWPHA
AND BEYOND

New Haven and London
Yale University Press
1978

Published with assistance from the
Kingsley Trust Association Publication Fund
established by the Scroll and Key Society
of Yale College.

Designed by Thos. Whitridge,
set in Baskerville type,
and printed in the United States of America by
Vail-Ballou Press, Inc., Binghamton, N.Y.

Published in Great Britain, Europe, Africa, and
Asia (except Japan) by Yale University Press,
Ltd., London. Distributed in Latin America by
Kaiman & Polon, Inc., New York City; in
Australia and New Zealand by Book & Film
Services, Artarmon, N.S.W., Australia; and in
Japan by Harper & Row, Publishers, Tokyo
Office.

Library of Congress Cataloging in Publication Data

Brooks, Cleanth, 1906–
    William Faulkner: toward Yoknapatawpha and beyond.

    Includes bibliographical references and index.
    1. Faulkner, William, 1897–1962—Criticism and
interpretation.
PS3511.A86Z642   813'.5'2   77-10898
ISBN 0-300-02204-2

Coniugi dilectissimae

Contents

Preface

THE EARLY CAREER of William Faulkner is essentially the story of a young romantic, whose imagination was filled with tales of derring-do, of knights errant and their lovely ladies; with landscapes in which fauns and nymphs danced to the music of the pipes of Pan; and with the search for an infinite beauty and a love too ethereal for this earth.

There should be nothing surprising about this. As a Southern boy, growing up some fifty miles north of Faulkner's home town early in the century, I had my own head filled with such matters. Though perhaps the romantic dream had a special hold on that part of our country, I do not mean to imply that such romantic reading was necessarily confined to the South. John E. Mack in his recently published book on T. E. Lawrence remarks that "the imaginations of the educated [of the time in England as well as America] were filled with Chaucer, Malory, William Morris, Tennyson's *Idylls,* Jean Froissart, the *Chansons de geste,* and the ethic of courtly love." Not every one of the texts Mack mentions was necessarily known to Faulkner; yet to the end of his career references to Guinevere, Lancelot, Tristan, Iseult, Camelot, and Carcassonne attest the thoroughness with which a romantic medievalism had tinctured his imagination. That he had also absorbed the ethic of courtly love is easily verified.

As might be expected, the young Faulkner was also well acquainted with the English poets of the 'nineties such as Oscar Wilde, A. E. Housman, and the early Yeats. What is rather surprising is his interest in the French writers of the middle and late nineteenth century—Gautier, Rostand, Baudelaire, Balzac, Verlaine, and Mallarmé.

One would expect, of course, that he would also be reading the British and American poets and novelists of the second and third decades of this century, and indeed he was. He reviewed several of them and mentioned several others in articles published in the University of Mississippi college newspaper. The pedestrian realism of some of the American authors obviously grated on his romantic sensibility. On one occasion he referred to "Mr. Vachel Lindsay with his tin pan and iron spoon" and to "Mr. Carl Sandburg with his sentimental Chicago propaganda." Yet by the early 1920s Faulkner was expressing in his own work certain anti-romantic attitudes. He had read James Branch Cabell's cynical rehandlings of medieval romance and had absorbed something of Cabell's style and attitude. One finds clear echoes of *Jurgen* in *Mayday* (1926), and borrowings from *Jurgen* recur until almost the end of Faulkner's literary career.

Another twentieth-century anti-romantic, of a very different caliber, exercised an even more significant influence on Faulkner. I refer to T. S. Eliot, whose work Faulkner seems to have discovered even earlier than Cabell's. "Anti-romantic" may seem too absolute a label to affix to Eliot, but one might grant the contention that Eliot has his own strain of romanticism and still maintain the argument I am making here. For Eliot represented an attitude and a method that was almost wholly at odds with what Faulkner had found in the early Yeats or in Oscar Wilde, and though Eliot could and did adopt certain modes from a writer like Gautier, what he borrowed was something other than what Faulkner borrowed from Gautier in *Mosquitoes*.

Faulkner also quite early discovered the work of James Joyce, and Joyce's influence, like Eliot's, ran counter to the old-fashioned romanticism in which Faulkner had been nurtured. If for Faulkner these modernist writers did not obliterate his romantic sensibility, and they did not, nevertheless their work suggested ways in which John Keats's notion of what art should be, an ideal that Faulkner never gave up, could be made to survive even in the modern world. Eliot and Joyce, we may say, provided Faulkner with the proper alloy wherewith to give tensile strength and a cutting edge to what might have proved in its purer state too soft a metal for Faulkner's purposes.

Mention of Eliot and Joyce brings up another and more important aspect of Faulkner's literary apprenticeship. The issue soon became not simply, or even primarily, youthful romanticism versus realism, but localism versus a universal (perhaps in this context best called an "international") literature. Faulkner's invention of Yoknapatawpha County—whether we translate invention as *discovery* or *creation*—was crucial to his career as a writer. His mythical county provided him with a social context in which what was healthiest in his romanticism could live in fruitful tension with his realistic and detailed knowledge of the men and manners of his own land. In Yoknapatawpha, the nymphs and fauns of his early imagination take on flesh and blood. That is one side of the equation. But the other side is indeed of equal consequence: the realistic, earthy life of Yoknapatawpha could be invested with an aura of the imagination, a mythic quality that could give vital import to what otherwise would have proved merely drab and pedestrian.

So much for the importance of Yoknapatawpha County in preventing the young writer's losing himself in a baseless dream world. Yoknapatawpha, however, offered a risk of its own: the risk of turning him into a mere local colorist, exploiting the oddities of a provincial scene for the titillation and amusement of a condescending "outside" world. From this danger the young writer's early and intelligent interest in writers like Joyce and Eliot probably saved him. Faulkner wrote some wonderful comedy and he meant for his reader to enjoy the antics of his more grotesque characters. But he takes his Yoknapatawpha world with entire seriousness. He does not condescend to it, nor does he allow his readers to condescend. The issues dealt with in his Yoknapatawpha novels ultimately concern universal human nature and they have reference to the world of the present. Faulkner uses Yoknapataw-

pha as a special lens that allows us to view with illuminating
magnification and emphasis our own modernity. Thus, the monstrous Flem Snopes is not merely a comic sketch to be laughed at
and then dismissed, as a joke once heard is dismissed. Flem is
funny, but he is no mere joke; he is a sinister deformation of universal human nature and a terrifying version of appetitive man,
modern style.

The first six chapters of this book attempt to take the reader from
Faulkner's earlier beginnings up to his formal entry into his now
famous county. But though most of Faulkner work thenceforward
was to have its setting in Yoknapatawpha County, three of his
later novels (*Pylon, The Wild Palms,* and *A Fable*) do not, and
they are worth discussing on several counts. In the first place, they
reward thoughtful consideration because nothing that the mature
Faulkner ever wrote is without interest, and because all three
novels contain many passages of brilliant writing. In the second
place, these novels, just because they do represent excursions beyond the bounds of Yoknapatawpha County, can tell us a great
deal about its importance to Faulkner's art. It may be illuminating
to see what he lost thereby as well as what he may have gained.

In the third place, the most explicit expositions of Faulkner's
ideas about man, religion, love, the nature of the modern world,
modern war, and the pressure of the machine on man's well-being
occur in the novels discussed in chapters 7, 8, and 9. Accordingly,
in the non-Yoknapatawpha novels the structural ideas can be made
out in their very nakedness. Though we ought to be cautious in
assuming that they represent Faulkner's personal beliefs, the very
prominence that, wittingly or unwittingly, he has given them is a
measure of the importance they held for him. Though it may be
a fault in his art not to have accommodated them more fully to
the drama of the narrative, the reader hot for certainties about
what Faulkner "really believed" may welcome the fault. But if so,
such readers ought to be cautioned: Faulkner, like most other artists, speaks his deepest truths when he speaks as an artist fully
caught up in his art.

My concluding chapter (chapter 10) makes no claim to providing a summary of Faulkner's philosophy. It does, however, deal with two of his major concepts, his special notion of time and of history. In discussing them, it draws upon the totality of Faulkner's work, and not merely on the non-Yoknapatawpha novels. Moreover, it interprets *history* in the most literal terms: it touches not merely upon Faulkner's interpretation of Southern history or of American history in general, but that of Man himself.

Such is the general plan of this volume. Though some years have elapsed since the publication of my first volume on Faulkner, I trust that this second volume will not seem too sharply inconsistent with the first. My hope is that, taken together, the two will provide, except for the short stories, a comprehensive account of Faulkner's verse, miscellaneous prose, and fiction. Readers who would like to follow the discussions in something like the order in which his books were written are referred to pages 429–30, where the contents of the two volumes are listed in chronological order.

During the last thirty years, so many books and articles on Faulkner have been published that few people can honestly claim that they have read and assimilated them all. I certainly can make no such claim. I have done no more than cope with the flood as best I could. A vigorous sampling indicates, however, that much of this vast output of scholarship and criticism is repetitious, that much is peripheral, that some of it is positively wrong-headed and perverse, but that a considerable amount is essential reading for anyone who wants to understand Faulkner's literary work. I trust that I have not overlooked too much of this truly valuable scholarship and criticism.

In the text and the notes in this volume I have acknowledged my indebtedness to specific articles and to more general studies, though I am aware that I have not taken cognizance of studies of the various Yoknapatawpha novels, especially those that were published subsequent to the appearance of *The Yoknapatawpha Country*.

Yet my references to some of their specific articles and books does not do justice to my indebtedness to a number of Faulkner scholars. In particular I would name Michael Millgate, whose *The*

Achievement of William Faulkner was a pioneer work that possesses lasting value; Joseph Blotner, whose monumental *Faulkner* is a storehouse of facts to which I have obviously again and again had recourse; Carvel Collins, who has provided us with so many excellent editions of Faulkner's early work; and James B. Meriwether, who has for some years edited the annual Faulkner number of *The Mississippi Quarterly,* in which much newly discovered Faulkner material has been discussed and in which some of it was printed for the first time.

I wish also to express my thanks for two grants that have very materially helped me to complete this study. The first is a National Endowment for the Humanities Senior Fellowship; the second is a visiting research professorship at the University of South Carolina provided by the Southern Studies Program and the Lucy Hampton Bostick Foundation.

I wish also to express my thanks to those who manage the Faulkner collections located in several of our universities: Joan St. C. Crane, Curator of the American Literature Collections at the University of Virginia, for help in using the great collection of Faulkner MSS there; the late William B. Wisdom, for permission to make use of the unique Faulkner items in the Howard-Tilton Memorial Library at Tulane University, and Mrs. Ann S. Gwyn, who has charge of the Special Collections housed there; and Donald Gallup, Curator of American Literature at the Beinecke Rare Book and Manuscript Library at Yale University, who has helped me especially with dating relevant Eliot and Pound items. With regard to all of the Faulkner manuscript materials, I owe special thanks to Mrs. Jill Faulkner Summers for her permission to quote from her father's manuscripts.

Permission to quote from Faulkner's first two novels has been kindly granted by the Liveright Publishing Corporation (*Soldiers' Pay,* copyright 1926 by Boni & Liveright, Inc., copyright renewed 1954 by William Faulkner; *Mosquitoes,* copyright 1927 by Boni & Liveright, Inc., copyright renewed 1955 by William Faulkner). Permission to quote from Faulkner's other novels, his verse, short stories, and miscellaneous prose has been kindly granted by Random House, Inc. Permission to quote A. E. Housman's poem

XXII from *Last Poems* (1922) has been kindly granted by Holt, Rinehart and Winston, Inc.

My thanks are due also to Chester Kerr, Director of the Yale University Press, and to Ellen Graham, who was an extremely helpful editor. I am afraid that I can't name here specifically all the other encouragers of this work, many of them old friends, who have offered suggestions and provided information, but there are some of these whose names cannot be omitted: Albert Erskine, Lewis P. Simpson, Malcolm Cowley, Louis Rubin, and Robert Penn Warren.

C. B.

Northford, Connecticut
11 August 1977

Editions Cited

WITH REGARD to the novels, the page references are to the first edition unless otherwise specified. In every case, however, the place, publisher, and date of the *first* edition is cited below.

Soldiers' Pay, New York, Boni and Liveright, 1926.

Mosquitoes, New York, Boni and Liveright, 1927.

Sartoris, New York, Harcourt, Brace and Company, 1929.

The Sound and the Fury, New York, Jonathan Cape, Harrison Smith, 1929; Vintage edition cited.

As I Lay Dying, New York, Jonathan Cape, Harrison Smith, 1930.

Sanctuary, New York, Jonathan Cape, Harrison Smith, 1931; ML edition has the same pagination.

Light in August, New York, Harrison Smith, 1932; the Modern Library College edition has the same pagination.

Pylon, New York, Harrison Smith and Robert Haas, 1935.

Absalom, Absalom!, New York, Random House, 1936; Vintage edition cited.

The Unvanquished, New York, Random House, 1938.

The Wild Palms, New York, Random House, 1939; Vintage edition has the same pagination.

The Hamlet, New York, Random House, 1940; Vintage edition of 1961 cited.

Go Down, Moses, New York, Random House, 1942; Vintage edition has the same pagination.

Intruder in the Dust, New York, Random House, 1948.

Knight's Gambit, New York, Random House, 1949.

Requiem for a Nun, New York, Random House, 1951.

A Fable, New York, Random House, 1954.

The Town, New York, Random House, 1957; Vintage revised edition of 1961 cited.

The Mansion, New York, Random House, 1959.

The Reivers, New York, Random House, 1962.

Flags in the Dust, New York, Random House, 1973.

With regard to the short stories, page references are to *Collected Stories,* New York, Random House, 1950, except for *Idyll in the Desert,* New York, Random House, 1931; and *Miss Zilphia Gant,* Dallas, The Book Club of Dallas, 1932.

With regard to the poetry and early prose, references are to the following:

The Marble Faun, Boston, Four Seas Co., 1924.

A Green Bough, New York, Harrison Smith and Robert Haas, 1933.

    (The poems in these two volumes were reproduced photographically from the original editions and reissued in a single volume by Random House in 1965.)

To Helen: A Courtship, unpublished, hand-lettered copy in the Howard-Tilton Library of Tulane University.

William Faulkner: Early Prose and Poetry, ed. Carvel Collins, Boston, Atlantic Monthly Press Book, 1962.

William Faulkner: New Orleans Sketches, ed. Carvel Collins, New York, Random House, 1958.

"Nympholepsy," ed. James B. Meriwether, *Mississippi Quarterly* 26 (Summer 1973) : 403–09.

The Marionettes, reproduced photographically from the University of Virginia copy, the University Press of Virginia, 1975.

Mayday, ed. Carvel Collins, the University of Notre Dame Press, 1977. This work is a facsimile of the unique hand-lettered copy in the Howard-Tilton Library of Tulane University.

1

Faulkner's Poetry

LIKE JAMES JOYCE, William Faulkner began his literary career in the belief that he would become a poet; but he was to discover, again like Joyce, that his richest and most sensitive and fully formed writing—his true "poetry," in short—could best be realized in prose. He referred to himself as a "failed poet," [1] a remark too emphatically disparaging to be taken literally. In Faulkner's early work there are certainly the stirrings of poetry, and who is to say that had he not become intensely interested in fiction, he might not have developed into a very considerable poet? William Butler Yeats, like Faulkner, began as a rather dreamy and ineffectual poet, and did not acquire muscle and power until he was a man in his forties. But speculation about what kind of poet Faulkner might have turned out to be, had he not given his full attention to fiction, is arid. Far more to the point is to trace the development from the poet of *The Marble Faun* to the author of

1. "Interview with Cynthia Grenier," *Lion in the Garden*, ed. James B. Meriwether and Michael Millgate (New York, 1968), p. 217. He told the Virginia students, "I've often thought that I wrote the novels because I found I couldn't write the poetry, that maybe I wanted to be a poet, maybe I think of myself as a poet, and I failed at that, I couldn't write poetry, so I did the next best thing." *Faulkner in the University: Class Conferences at the University of Virginia*, ed. Frederick L. Gwynn and Joseph L. Blotner (Charlottesville, 1957), p. 4.

The Hamlet and *Go Down, Moses,* and to show why the more
ample form of fiction allowed his "poetry" to come to full fruition
there.

One can hardly overstate the fact that Faulkner's early verse is
late Romantic verse. Indeed, one might fairly call it Decadent
verse. The poets who had caught his imagination and whom he
was consciously and unconsciously imitating were the poets of the
'nineties. Like theirs, this young poet's world has grown old and
tired. He harks back to a brighter and ampler day in which the
presence of the gods of the fields and forests could still be felt.
Nature, to be sure, still moves through its beautiful rituals, and
man is able, in imagination at least, to sense what nature must
have meant to an ancient Greek. But a sensitive observer cannot
conceal from himself the fact that the antique world lingers today
only in an occasional nook of sequestered beauty and in the
memory of poets and other dreamers.

Faulkner establishes the special kind of romanticism found in
his early verse by telling us that "at the age of sixteen I discovered Swinburne. Or rather, Swinburne discovered me, spring-
ing from some tortured undergrowth of my adolescence, like a
highwayman, making me his slave." Yet Faulkner, in this account,
is frank to say that he is not sure "to what depth [Swinburne]
stirred me. . . . It seems to me now [1925] that I found him
nothing but a flexible vessel into which I might put my own
vague emotional shapes without breaking them. It was years later
that I found in him much more than bright and bitter sound,
more than a satisfying tinsel of blood and death and gold and the
inevitable sea." [2]

The influence of Swinburne seems to have been general and
pervasive rather than a matter of specific borrowings. True, Faulkner published in *The Mississippian* (26 November 1919) a poem
entitled "Sapphics," which represents itself as a definite response
to, and a further commentary upon, Swinburne's poem of that
title. Faulkner's opening phrase, "So it is," implies that the

2. "Verse Old and Nascent: A Pilgrimage," first published in *The Double Dealer*
for April 1925; reprinted in *William Faulkner: Early Prose and Poetry*, p. 114.

speaker here has just put down Swinburne's poem and is stating his general agreement with it. As the title "Sapphics" implies, Faulkner has imitated Swinburne's treatment of that classical verse form. But as for his attempting Swinburne's heavy alliterations and intricate rhyme schemes, I know of only two examples. They are "Hymn" and "Aubade," the full texts of which appear in *Man Collecting: Manuscripts and Printed Works of William Faulkner in the University of Virginia Library*.[3]

The oddest and most amusing specific trace of Swinburne in Faulkner's extant verse has to do with Swinburne's description of "the breasts of the nymphs in the brake"; more specifically, his rather odd phrase, "Her bright breast shortening into sighs" (from the first Chorus of *Atalanta in Calydon*). Faulkner echoes it, not once but four times: viz., "no shortening-breasted nymph," "Dreams her body . . . Shortening and shuddering into his," "did short to sighs her breast," and "Lies on her short and circled breast."

Much of Faulkner's earliest published verse derives from French rather than British sources. The first poem that he published, "L'Après-midi d'un Faune" (in *The New Republic*, 6 August 1919), is a reworking of Stéphane Mallarmé's celebrated poem of that title. Also from nineteenth-century French literature are Faulkner's four translations from the work of Paul Verlaine. They were published in *The Mississippian* in the early months of 1920.[4]

To refer to them as translations, however, rather overstates the case. "À Clymène," for instance, is a rather free adaptation of Verlaine's poem, and "Fantoches" is very considerably altered from the French original. Faulkner makes his poem end with a line of French, viz., "La lune ne garde aucune rancune": but it corresponds to nothing in the Verlaine poem. In fact, it is lifted

---

3. Charlottesville, 1975, pp. 125–26. Joseph Blotner, in *Faulkner: A Biography* (New York, 1974), p. 40, prints four lines of "Hymn" and the third stanza of "Aubade."

4. See below, Notes, p. 345.

from T. S. Eliot's "Rhapsody on a Windy Night." In Jules Laforgue's "Complainte de Cette Bonne Lune," the chorus of stars sings

> —La, voyons, mam'zell' la Lune,
> Ne gardons pas ainsi rancune.

In remodeling the lines to suit his own poem, Eliot had reversed matters: in his poem it is not the stars who hold no grudge against the moon, but the moon itself who holds no grudge. Faulkner must have borrowed the line directly from Eliot[5] and spatchcocked it onto a poem which purports to be a translation of Verlaine.

I have not been able to trace "Une Ballade des Femmes Perdues" to any French original, but his having chosen a French title, his having used as an epigraph a line from Villon, and the two French tags in the poem proper make sufficiently clear the young Faulkner's interest in French poetry.

In December 1924, Faulkner published his first volume, a long poem entitled *The Marble Faun*. He may have borrowed his metrical pattern (octosyllabic couplets) from William Butler Yeats's "The Song of the Happy Shepherd." Yeats's shepherd—whose happiness, however, seems almost as cool and reserved as that of the character whom we hear speaking in Milton's "L'Allegro"—is not himself a faun. It is rather to, or for the sake of, a "hapless faun" that he sings his "songs" of "old earth's dreamy youth." The faun has perished and is now "Buried under the sleepy ground." Yet the shepherd dreams that the faun still "treads the lawn, / Walking ghostly in the dew," and that he is able to hear the shepherd's song, for the shepherd imagines the faun as "Pierced by my glad singing through."

The situation in *The Marble Faun* is quite different. The voice that we hear is that of a prisoner straining against his bonds. This

---

5. See p. 12, below.

would-be follower of Pan has been encased in marble and set on a pedestal as an ornament for a garden. Though in the sixteenth section of the poem "a blatant crowd" of human beings, dancing "To brass horns horrible and loud," invades his garden, for the greater part of the poem the faun is left to himself to observe the pageant of the changing seasons and to brood upon the marble bondage that prevents his responding to the call of Pan as the god and his followers wander through the landscape.

Actually, Faulkner's faun seems to have come right out of Faulkner's favorite poem, the "Ode on a Grecian Urn," for he is a kinsman of the "marble men and maidens" with which the urn was "overwrought." Keats's ode, of course, stresses the superiority of art to nature. The urn's "maidens loth," the object of "the mad pursuit" depicted there, cannot grow old, wither, and die. The "bold lover," though never allowed to kiss the lips of his beloved, will never become jaded and disillusioned. But in *The Marble Faun* it is the inferiority of art to life that is stressed— "wild ecstasy" that has become frozen into a "cold pastoral," the unaging faun who has been turned into inanimate marble.

Faulkner's marble faun, then, yearns to break out of his stony prison and to become part of the world of movement, where breezes stir, waters "rush and kiss," trees swing "to and fro," nature moves through its cycle of the seasons, and night follows day through all the gradations of light and darkness. Unless we read the poem attentively, we may be misled into thinking that the faun eventually does escape from his bonds, for from time to time he makes statements such as "I pass / To cool my feet in deep rich grass" (p. 25) or "All day I run before a wind" (p. 39). As we read on in the poem, however, it becomes plain that these journeyings occur only in the faun's yearning imagination. For as the poem closes, he tells us that he must forever remain "marble-bound," a "sad, bound prisoner" (pp. 50–51).

The faun's melancholy is a double one. He is saddened by the transience of all mortal things:

> we, the marbles in the glade,
> Dreaming in the leafy shade

5

> Are saddened, for we know that all
> Things save us must fade and fall.
>
> [p. 31]

But he is also saddened by his own imperviousness to change—by the fact that he cannot participate in the ever lovely transmutations of nature. This latter circumstance is, of course, the thesis of Keats's "Ode to a Nightingale," where the poet's human self-consciousness prevents his losing himself in a nature that, just because it does lack human consciousness, is not conscious of impending death. Faulkner had evidently read his Keats well; he has fully grasped the nature of the specifically human dilemma. Art achieves its freedom from the transience of nature only by forfeiting the movement of life, and natural creatures (like the nightingale) attain their *virtual* immortality—they do not know that they will ever die—only through lacking the human being's memory and imagination.

To say as much, however, is not to imply that Faulkner in this poem becomes in anything but aspiration the Keats of the great Odes. *The Marble Faun* is in many respects an awkward and stumbling poem. To mention its most obvious defect: the young poet is hag-ridden by the necessity of finding rhymes, and sometimes is forced into quasi-nonsense in his effort to come up with a rhyme. The meter fares not much better: often a line is metrically broken-backed. Nevertheless, there are occasional passages of authentic poetry, as, for instance,

> content to watch by day
> The dancing light's unthinking play
> Ruffling the pool.
>
> [p. 19]

> the noon will cool and pass
> That now lies edgelessly in thrall
> Upon the ripened sun-stilled grass
>
> [p. 22]

6

While the startled sunlight drips
From beech and alder fingertips

[p. 25]

And like a spider on a veil
Climbs the moon.

[p. 29]

Yet, whatever the limitations and deficiencies of *The Marble Faun* as poetry, it may tell us much about the intellectual as well as the literary development of the young man who wrote it. Lewis Simpson,[6] looking back at it in the total context of Faulkner's work, boldly interprets it as "a carefully constructed exercise in pastoral, ironically implying the rejection of pastoral by modernity, and, I believe, more particularly in his own vision. . . . [The Faun] stands fixed in a dispossessed garden—isolated in his own consciousness; divested of the power of pastoral regeneration and purification; having the ironic capacity to discern his incapacity yet unable to do anything about it, a tortured creature of Pan, locked in himself like Prufrock." But to apprehend the full import of Simpson's brilliant though highly speculative essay, one must read the whole of it.

The verse that Faulkner published in *A Green Bough* (1933) is on the whole much more accomplished than that of *The Marble Faun,* but it ought to be noted that most of the poems in *A Green Bough* were written in the early 1920s,[7] many years later than *The Marble Faun.* The poems collected in *A Green Bough* are, like the couplets of *The Marble Faun,* filled with echoes of Faulkner's reading. There is a good deal of Swinburne's characteristic diction, an occasional borrowing from Gray or Keats, an echo of Faulkner's favorite passage in Shakespeare's *Macbeth,* and even a

6. See his "Faulkner and the Southern Symbolism of Pastoral," *Mississippi Quarterly* 28 (1975): 401–15.

7. See Keen Butterworth's "A Census of Manuscripts and Typescripts of William Faulkner's Poetry," *Mississippi Quarterly* 26 (1973): 333–59. The dates of composition that can be fixed with any certainty fall within the period 1920–25.

7

hint of Tennyson,[8] but the overwhelming influence is that of A. E. Housman. Poem after poem, especially those written in quatrains, acknowledges his debt to Housman.

The opening couplet of poem VII,

> Trumpets of sun to silence fall
> On house and barn and stack and wall

clearly echoes the first line of Poem VIII of *A Shropshire Lad,*

> Farewell to barn and stack and tree.

The last stanza of Poem IX of *A Green Bough* reads:

> . . . and found this peace as he
> Who across this sunset moves to rest,
> Finds but simple scents and sounds;
> And this is all, and this is best.

Compare the last quatrain of Poem VII of *A Shropshire Lad:*

> Lie down, lie down, young yeoman;
>   The sun moves always west;
> The road one treads to labour
>   Will lead one home to rest,
>   And that will be the best.

Faulkner has the mother in Poem XIV say of her son,

> He'll be strong and merry
> And he'll be clean and brave. . . .

The last phrase answers to these lines in Poem XVIII of *A Shropshire Lad:*

---

8. For a detailed account of Faulkner's borrowings from the poets, see below, Notes, pp. 345–54.

Oh, when I was in love with you,
Then I was clean and brave. . . .

Poem XXI brings together phrases from several Housman poems. Line 10 begins "Woman bore you"; compare the last line of Poem XXXV of *A Shropshire Lad,* "Woman bore me, I will rise." Line 11 of Faulkner's poem begins "Life's gale may blow," in which Faulkner is undoubtedly remembering line 14 of Poem XXXI of *A Shropshire Lad:* "Through him the gale of life blew high."

Faulkner begins Poem XXXIV of *A Green Bough* with an elaborate metaphor:

The ship of night, with twilightcolored sails,
Dreamed down the golden river of the west. . . .

Compare the first stanza of Poem IV of *A Shropshire Lad:*
Wake: the silver dusk returning
Up the beach of darkness brims,
And the ship of sunrise burning
Strands upon the eastern rims.[9]

In "Verse Old and Nascent," Faulkner describes the circumstances of his chance discovery of *A Shropshire Lad* and the immediate impact on him.

I found a paperbound copy [of *A Shropshire Lad*] in a bookshop and when I opened it I discovered there the secret after which the moderns course howling like curs on a cold trail in a dark wood, giving off, it is true, an occasional note clear with beauty, but curs just the same. Here was reason for being born into a fantastic world: discovering the splendor of fortitude, the beauty of being of the soil like a tree about which fools might howl and which winds of disillusion and death and despair might strip, leaving it bleak, without bitterness; beautiful in sadness. [*Early Prose and Poetry,* p. 117]

9. For further instances of the influence of Housman, see pp. 345–46.

"Verse Old and Nascent" was published in April 1925, and Faulkner's enthusiastic account of Housman rings with the excitement of a recent discovery.[10] At about the same time (12 April 1925), Faulkner published in the New Orleans *Times-Picayune* a short piece of fiction entitled "Out of Nazareth,"[11] in which *A Shropshire Lad* figures. The leading character in this little story, a young wanderer who has the sensibility of a poet, reveals to a stranger his special treasure. It is a "battered" copy of *A Shropshire Lad* which he had come by among "some old books and magazines" handed to him to throw away. Others might set no store by it, but "he kind of thought it [contained the best writing] he had seen."

A somewhat similar experience is related in Faulkner's first novel, *Soldiers' Pay*, the writing of which again dates from the early months of 1925. There we learn that among the personal effects of Donald Mahon, the faun-like young man who had been presumed to have died in World War I, were found a mummied hyacinth bulb, a woman's chemise, and "a cheap paper-covered 'Shropshire Lad' " (p. 68 of the first edition). Was Faulkner projecting his own recent personal experience onto two of his fictional characters?

In any case, Keen Butterworth's "Census of Manuscripts and Typescripts of Faulkner's Poetry" would seem to confirm the supposition that the echoes of and references to *A Shropshire Lad* in the first months of 1925 reflect a recent discovery. Of the poems that he is able to date, the only two that clearly show a Housman influence are dated 16 October 1924 (Poem XLIV of *A Green Bough*) and 11 November 1924 (Poem XXX of *A Green Bough*). Poem XLII of *A Green Bough* (which has a clear Hous-

10. James B. Meriwether has kindly given me a description of Faulkner's copy of *A Shropshire Lad*, a paperback copy that Faulkner rebound in boards, with a label hand-lettered in the style of the labels on *The Marionettes* (see chap. 2, below), which would suggest a date around 1920. Thus, Faulkner might have acquired his copy in 1918 when he was in New Haven and then, like Donald Mahon in *Soldiers' Pay*, taken it off to war with him—in Faulkner's case, off to training camp in Canada. But whether or not Faulkner's acquisition of the book came earlier, the impact of Housman did not manifest itself until late in 1924.

11. See *New Orleans Sketches*, pp. 46–54.

man reference) occurs also in *To Helen: A Courtship* and is in that booklet dated June 1925. In view of the importance of Housman's influence on Faulkner's poetry—and later on his fiction as well—it is remarkable that Faulkner was so late in discovering *A Shropshire Lad,* which, after all, had been published in 1896, one year before he was born.

Next to Housman's, perhaps the most powerful general influence on Faulkner's poetry was that of T. S. Eliot. Curiously enough, Eliot, who has to be counted a radically unromantic "modern" poet, seems to have made an impact upon Faulkner long before Housman did. The first clear echo of Eliot to be found in Faulkner's verse occurs in *The Marble Faun* (p. 37, lines 19–20):

> To comb the wave-ponies' manes back
> Where the water shivers black.

These lines, as was long ago pointed out, are rather clumsy adaptation of Prufrock's vision of the mermaids toward the conclusion of "The Love Song of J. Alfred Prufrock":

> Combing the white hair of the waves blown back
> When the wind blows the water white and black.

Faulkner dated his composition of *The Marble Faun* "April, May, June, 1919." But if the couplet in question was written in 1919, then one must ask how Faulkner had been able to secure a copy of *Prufrock and Other Observations* (published in London in June 1917). "The Love Song" had been printed in the United States, however, even earlier—in the June 1915 number of *Poetry: A Magazine of Verse.* But one wonders about the likelihood of Faulkner's having discovered the poem in 1915 when he was a youth of eighteen, or even two years later in the rather limited London publication. (The notion that Faulkner first read "The Love Song" in Ezra Pound's *Catholic Anthology,* London, 1915, compounds the problem of early date and remoteness from Oxford, Mississippi.)

11

I am inclined to date the final manuscript of *The Marble Faun* later than June 1919—as late, perhaps, as 1921 or 1922, a date which would have given him time to see the New York edition of Eliot's *Poems,* which was published in late February 1920 and which contained "The Love Song" and several of the other poems from which Faulkner was to borrow.

This suggested solution, I must confess, will hardly solve another riddle concerning the influence of Eliot on Faulkner. I noted above that the last line of Faulkner's "Fantoches," "La lune ne garde aucune rancune," is taken bodily from Eliot's "Rhapsody on a Windy Night," and yet "Fantoches" was published in *The Mississippian* for 25 February 1920. "Rhapsody" does appear, along with "the Love Song of J. Alfred Prufrock," in Eliot's *Poems,* 1920, but since *Poems* was not published until "late February, 1920," [12] there would have been no time for Faulkner to read it, decide to borrow lines from it, and get his copy to the printer. Perhaps Faulkner somehow secured an advance copy. But if he did not, then we are driven back to the possibility that he did know *Prufrock and Other Observations* (1917) after all, for "Rhapsody" is to be found there; or else to such improbabilities as Faulkner's seeing a copy of *Ara Vos Prec,* which includes the poem but which was published in London, and no earlier than the first part of February 1920; or that he saw the July 1915 issue of *Blast,* a very long shot indeed. There is a mystery here, and unless and until more evidence turns up, we can only speculate as to where and when Faulkner discovered Eliot's "Rhapsody." But, as with Housman's *A Shropshire Lad,* once Faulkner discovers Eliot, his borrowings come thick and fast. That very fact suggests that Faulkner knew nothing of Eliot's poetry until late 1919 or very early 1920.

The power of Eliot's influence is revealed in several of the poems that make up an 88-page collection entitled *Vision of Spring,* which Faulkner bound and presented to Estelle Oldham Franklin in 1921. Several of these poems appear in revised form in *A Green Bough,* but most of the poems of this little volume are

---

12. See Donald Gallup's *T. S. Eliot: A Bibliography,* rev. ed. (New York, 1969).

still unpublished. Yet, the passages that Joseph Blotner quotes in his biography of Faulkner indicate a large debt to Eliot (see pp. 307–12). The poem "Interlude" has a line, "The horned gates swing to, and clang," that goes back to "Sweeney among the Nightingales" (cf. "And Sweeney guards the hornèd gate"). "The World and Pierrot, a Nocturne" asks Prufrockian questions:

> Who am I, thinks Pierrot, who am I
> To stretch my soul out rigid across the sky?
> Who am I to chip the silence with footsteps. . . .

Blotner also finds a reminiscence of "Preludes," presumably in the line, "To stretch my soul out rigid across the sky" (cf. "His soul stretched tight across the skies" in *Preludes*).

A long poem by Faulkner entitled "Love Song" apparently follows Eliot's "Love Song" almost obsequiously. It asks such questions as "Shall I walk, then, through a corridor of profundities," and "shall I dare to open [a certain door]." Like Prufrock, the character who speaks the poem is conscious of his necktie and his thinning hair. He even uses Prufrock's phrase: "I grow old." The speaker in Faulkner's poem, again like Prufrock, reflects that he ought to have been something other than what he is—perhaps "a priest in floorless halls," and the poem ends with a reference to an awakening that is in fact a kind of death. Compare Faulkner's "to wake him, and he dies" with Eliot's "Till human voices wake us, and we drown."

The Eliot borrowings seem to be all from poems in the 1920 volume: viz., from "The Love Song of J. Alfred Prufrock," "Preludes," "Rhapsody on a Windy Night," and "Sweeney among the Nightingales." I find none that clearly derives from *The Waste Land* until we come to Poems IV and XXX of *A Green Bough*, which Faulkner dated 27 August 1925 and 11 November 1924, respectively. "The Raven Bleak and Philomel" (Poem XXVII of *A Green Bough*) is a less certain derivation from *The Waste Land*, though Faulkner's use of the form *Philomel* (cf. Eliot's line "The change of Philomel, by the barbarous king") and the parallel between Faulkner's "Philomel, on pain's red root / Bloomed and

13

sang, and pain was not" and Eliot's "Yet there the nightingale /
Filled all the desert with inviolable voice" suggests that Faulkner
is probably remembering *The Waste Land* here. In any case,
Faulkner is certainly closely imitating Eliot's "Sweeney among the
Nightingales," and Faulkner's reiterated reference to the droppings
of the two birds makes the point certain,

In Poem IV the reference to Eliot's poetry is not elaborate or
detailed. It amounts to no more than the speaker's characterization of spring as "wanton" and "cruel." But it was Eliot who
taught the twentieth century that April was the cruelest month,
and the association with Eliot comes clear when we compare his
characterization of the spring season with Faulkner's in Poem
XXX:

> O sorry earth, when this black bitter sleep
> Stirs and turns and time once more is green,
>
> . . . .
>
> April and May and June, and all the dearth
> Of heart to green it for, to hurt and wake.
> What good is budding, gray November earth?
> No need to break your sleep for greening's sake

Faulkner's reference here is more restricted than Eliot's, who
alluded to a general loss of belief and purpose, whereas Faulkner
has specifically in mind the soldiers who died in World War I.[13]
Yet both poems insist on a sense of loss and disillusionment, and
they share more than a little common ground. Thus, though
Faulkner used the last stanza of this poem as the epigraph for
Soldiers' Pay, giving it for title there "Soldier," the poem, nevertheless makes plain by its phrase "all the dearth / Of heart" that
those to whom the dead body is being returned also suffer from
a dearth of heart—are too numbered and shocked by grief to
feel any joy in the annual revival of nature in April, May, and
June.

13. One of the original titles that Faulkner gave this poem was "November 11,"
that is, Armistice Day of World War I. See Butterworth, "Census," p. 345.

14

The Waste Land, of course, takes an opposite tack. In Eliot's poem, although there are plenty of specific references to the end of World War I, a conflict in which Europe had come near to committing suicide, it becomes in his vision simply the most violent specific instance of a more general cultural breakdown. Faulkner's own use of the denouement of World War I to suggest such a breakdown in the total culture is rather fully developed in his first novel, *Soldiers' Pay.* In that novel, as we shall see, the influence of both Housman and Eliot is strong. Though it would be hard to demonstrate that these two poets helped Faulkner solve any of his own problems as a poet, their attitudes toward reality and their insights into the human predicament did influence him a great deal, nowhere more so than in his fiction. He continues to demonstrate his indebtedness to them, in one way or another, until at least as late as *Pylon* (1935).

Perhaps Housman and Eliot could not help him find himself as a poet just because he was too close to them. As we have already seen, Housman's poetry proved for Faulkner so powerful a gravitational field that it captures almost at once any piece of verse that Faulkner points in Housman's direction. Such a poem becomes a direct imitation of Housman rather than a poem in which Faulkner merely embodies what he had learned from Housman.

Much the same thing occurs when Faulkner moves toward Eliot. Faulkner's "Love Song" becomes a patent imitation of Eliot's "Love Song of J. Alfred Prufrock," right down to identical phrasings; and when Faulkner writes a poem in the mood of Eliot's "Sweeney among the Nightingales," he produces not a parallel poem but an obvious parody. (Whether or not Faulkner intended it to be an outright parody—even a travesty—I shall consider later, in the chapter on *Mosquitoes.*)

Readers with a special interest in the development of modernism in poetry may wonder why Housman and Eliot did not cancel each other out. For Housman was in some sense the last of the romantics, and his essay entitled "The Name and Nature of Poetry" (1933) is frankly a rearguard action in the defense of the Romantic Movement. Eliot, on the other hand, counts as an antiromantic—tough-minded, "intellectual," witty, ironic, and almost

belligerently "contemporary." If one is to take seriously Faulkner's history of his own relations to modern poetry in "Verse Old
and Nascent," then Eliot did not count at all. For, though Faulkner refers to Robinson, Frost, Aldington, and Aiken, the name of
Eliot is never mentioned. Though, as he claimed, captured by
Swinburne, he had not been impelled to read poetry as such, and
took no interest in the traditional English poets. Later, he did
become interested in poetry for its own sake through reading the
contemporary poets. But his discovery of *A Shropshire Lad*
"closed the period" of shopping around among the moderns.
Having found in Housman "the splendor of fortitude, the beauty
of being of the soil like a tree," he was able at last to go back to
Shakespeare and the Elizabethans, and to Shelley and Keats.

This account makes sense of the evidence we have assembled in
placing the discovery of *A Shropshire Lad* as relatively late and
as constituting a culmination of his search for a poetry that would
make satisfactory sense of the contemporary world. But, as is plain,
the failure to mention Eliot denies what is an obviously important
aspect of Faulkner's development. It ignores the fact that Faulkner became acquainted with Eliot's poetry very early, that his
poems around 1921–25 are saturated in Eliot's poetry, and that
his fiction acknowledges, from *Soldiers' Pay* to *Pylon,* the themes
and attitudes dramatized in Eliot's *Waste Land.*

Since Faulkner has left out this part of the story of his literary
development, it may not be impertinent here to offer a few speculations. Though Housman is one of the last romantics and Eliot
one of the first of the moderns, their influences were not necessarily antithetical. For in Housman's poetry there is a good deal
of realism and a great deal of wit and irony—the qualities that
one associates with the early Eliot. On this level, the two diverse
influences might well reinforce each other and move the young
Faulkner to a fruitful engagement with the contemporary world—
and with the local world of which he had concrete knowledge.
Since it was Housman's stoicism ("the splendor of fortitude")
that most impressed Faulkner, Housman's most useful influence
was to strengthen Faulkner's acceptance of a world shorn of illusions. In short, Housman helped to beget in Faulkner's poetry

clarity, austerity, and tough-mindedness. But though Faulkner admired Housman's regionalism (his "beauty of being of the soil like a tree"), Housman's rather idealized Shropshire was of no use at all in helping the young poet to anchor himself to a familiar world which could provide him with concrete images and allow him to use his own authentic experience.

A basic fault of *The Marble Faun* is its inauthentic and "literary" quality, and it is this defect that blights too many of the poems that fill *A Green Bough*—including most of the poems in quatrains that derive from *A Shropshire Lad*. Faulkner had not, during the period in which he was writing his poems, discovered Yoknapatawpha County. Since poetry—whatever else it is—is incorrigibly concrete, a landscape taken largely out of books would not do.

In spite of Faulkner's praise of Housman's tough-mindedness, Housman's poetry is itself a poetry of the 'nineties. A major theme is the lost Arcadia. He prefaces *Last Poems* (1922) with a poem that vows

> We'll to the woods no more,
> The laurels all are cut,
> The bowers are bare of bay
> That once the Muses wore.

A Shropshire Lad also is full of desolate shepherds; it emphasizes the fragility and pathos of young love, and at its weakest it verges on prettiness and sentimentality. Housman's influence, then, did not send Faulkner back to his native land.

In the introduction that he contributed to *The Marble Faun*, Faulkner's Oxford friend, Phil Stone, wrote that "the sunlight and mocking-birds and blue hills of North Mississippi are a part of this young man's very being." Certainly this statement is true, profoundly so, but it is misleading if taken with any special reference to the poetry of *The Marble Faun* or indeed to most of the rest of Faulkner's verse. For example, *The Marble Faun* is filled with copses and glades and brakes. Instead of the blue hills of North Mississippi, there are wolds, leas, and downs. On these downs grow heath and gorse and may. The cottages have thatched roofs. The birds that fly about these cottages and out of these brakes are rooks, nightingales, and blackbirds.

If to an American ear these words are disconcertingly literary, to a Southern ear they sound even more outlandish. Though it is true that Faulkner uses the word *glade* in one of his novels, this word is unknown to the common folk; and in Mississippi a *brake* would be inevitably a cane-brake and certainly would not have white-breasted nymphs in it. Nor are downs, thatched cottages, heather, or gorse to be found in Yoknapatawpha County.

Or consider the anomaly of Faulkner's English rooks, European nightingales "Whose cries like scattered silver sails / Spread across the azure sea," and his singing blackbirds. These blackbirds (I have counted at least eight instances of them in Faulkner's poetry) make the point most strikingly. For the blackbirds that sing so sweetly in Faulkner's verse, just as they do in the verse of Housman, belong to the thrush family and so come legitimately by their music. The blackbirds that Faulkner could have known in the Southern states—or elsewhere in America for that matter—can hardly be said to sing at all. They don't belong to the thrush family, and in his *Field Guide to the Birds,* Roger Peterson writes: "The 'song' [of the rusty blackbird] is a split creak like a rusty hinge . . . rather penetrating." The purple grackle's " 'song' [is] a split rasping note that is both husky and squeaky." The cowbird's "Courtship song [is] bubbly and creaky, (*glug-glug-gleeee*) (last note thin, on high pitch)." Even if, to be exhaustive, one includes the redwing blackbird among the possibilities, the case is not helped. Peterson describes the song of the redwing as "a gurgling *konk-la-reeee* or *o-ka-leeee,* the last note high and quavering." Anyone who has heard redwings challenging each other or singing their courtship song near a swamp or pond may find the chorus of powerful *konkarees* very pleasant to the ear, but no one who has ever heard them will associate them with Faulkner's blackbirds with "gold wired throats" or with songs that are "Piercing cool and mellowly long."

If Faulkner as a young poet was finding in *The Marble Faun* the mouthpiece for his own youthful yearnings and poetic imaginings, the bonds that rendered him relatively "mute and impotent" were not marble but literary. Until Faulkner was able to break these bonds, his writing, in spite of an occasional felicitous expression or nicely turned passage, remained empty and sterile.

Yet, though the discovery of *A Shropshire Lad* did not free the young poet for vigorous and graceful poetic activity, *A Shropshire Lad* did represent, as Faulkner saw, the placing of the poem within a known landscape, a device that allowed the poet to use particular and even local materials in which to clothe the universal things that he was moved to say. One remembers too that he had, in his essay "American Drama," asked the American writer to use the "language as it is spoken in America," complaining that in comparison with it, "British is a Sunday night affair of bread and milk—melodious but slightly tiresome nightingales in a formal clipped hedge." [14]

In this general connection it is also worth looking at his short review of William Alexander Percy's *In April Once,* which he contributed to *The Mississippian* on 10 November 1920.[15] Faulkner writes that "Mr. Percy—like alas! how many of us—suffered the misfortune of having been born out of his time. He should have lived in Victorian England and gone to Italy with Swinburne, for like Swinburne, he is a mixture of passionate adoration of beauty and as passionate despair and disgust with its manifestations and accessories in the human race. His muse is Latin in type— poignant ecstasies of lyrical extravagance and a short lived artificial strength achieved at the cost of true strength in beauty." One is tempted to say that writing about his fellow Mississippian, Faulkner is writing more or less consciously about his own situation. One does not mean to claim that Faulkner is here, with cool detachment, referring to his own poetry the deficiencies which he found in Percy's. But surely the passage quoted indicates that this highly intelligent, if still somewhat confused young man is aware of the inherent weakness in his own poetry. And surely there is evidence that Faulkner felt that he too had been born out of proper time, since his poetic heroes are the late Victorians, and

14. *Early Prose and Poetry*, p. 95.
15. *Early Prose and Poetry*, pp. 71–73.

that—at least for his own happiness—he ought to have gone to Italy with Swinburne.

Yet a full realization of the necessity to call his own muse home apparently in time did come to Faulkner. He recalled that during his sojourn in New Orleans Sherwood Anderson once said to him: "You have to have somewhere to start from: then you begin to learn. It don't matter where it was, just so you remember it and aint ashamed of it. Because one place to start from is just as important as any other. You're a country boy; all you know is that little patch up there in Mississippi where you started from." [16]

Faulkner never really took the advice in his role as poet. As a fiction writer, he did not act on it until his third novel, *Sartoris* (1929), unless one admits that the small town in his first novel, *Soldiers' Pay* (1926), though formally set in the state of Georgia, is a reflection of Faulkner's home town of Oxford, Mississippi.

Faulkner needed to call his muse home. But he needed something more. His poetry required a wider context for its proper development. Faulkner needed most of all in that context elements of realism sufficient to purge any sense of effete prettiness and faded romanticism. This is not to argue that had he continued to write verse he might not have achieved the requisite muscular force and power through what appears to most people to be a rather opposite process of condensation and compression. Perhaps he might have; the best of his poems suggest the possibility. Yet, on the other hand, the kind of thing he did so magnificently in the best of his fiction might have been wasted had he persisted in trying to fine down and tighten rather than to expand and complicate and enrich the effects of work conceived on a large scale.

One can illustrate by comparing Poem XLIV of *A Green Bough* with the great prose hymn to nature that occurs in the closing pages of "The Bear." Poem XLIV is, in fact, one of Faulkner's most successfully and completely formed poems. The last stanza has a special effectiveness. No grief is to be expended on him: he will not die,

16. *Essays, Speeches, and Public Letters,* ed. James B. Meriwether (New York, 1965), p. 8.

. . . for where is any death
While in these blue hills slumbrous overhead
I'm rooted like a tree? Though I be dead,
This earth that holds me fast will find me breath.

The final pages of "The Bear" also set forth an experience of this sort. As Isaac McCaslin is walking through the big woods on a June morning to visit the graves of Lion and Sam Fathers and Old Ben, he has an experience of nature's immortality. It comes to him that "there was no death" and that neither Lion nor Sam were "held fast in earth but [were] free in earth and not in earth but of earth, myriad yet undiffused of every myriad part," being now part of the unwearied processes of nature. The statement that Sam Fathers is "not held fast in earth but free in earth" is bolder than what is said in Poem XLIV: "This earth that holds me fast will find me breath." Though it denies the literal fact that a buried corpse is indeed held fast in earth, it is nevertheless more realistic than the poem: the earth will not find the dead man breath, though it will, having taken the man back to itself, by turning him into earth again, allow him to merge into the "immutable progression" of the seasons and the unquenched vitality of nature.

One does not want to claim too much: neither variation on the theme "there is no death" can be taken literally; both of them require a kind of leap of faith. But one feels that Faulkner, in writing the conclusion to his great story, has got his priorities right and has based Ike's exalted vision not on a fancy but on a fact that one can cling to.

Something further should be said of the prose version. The man who has the vision in "The Bear" is a person with whose mind and heart the reader has become acquainted, and whose growing up he has witnessed. Ike's vision of the immortality of nature is plausible—in its time and place and motivation. But the young man who speaks Poem XLIV is not quite real: his ancestry is essentially literary. He is a kind of displaced Shropshire Lad, whereas Ike McCaslin—faults, virtues, and all—is a

Yoknapatawpha boy who demands and gets the reader's belief.

The Hamlet contains some of Faulkner's finest "poetry." In this novel, the idiot Ike becomes a kind of faun, not a wistful marble statue, not a being who is Arcadian in any literary sense, but the human animal, presented in his full animality and so deeply sunk into nature that he is all but without speech, shorn of all the ordinary human refinements.

The marble faun merely yearns to follow Pan over the hills, to feel the pressure of sun and rain on his body, and to move in rhythm to the dance of the seasons. Ike, the flesh-and-blood faun, does move, with his companion and goddess, the cow, through the round of the day, and it is interesting to match some of the "nature" passages in Faulkner's first book of verse with comparable passages in The Hamlet. For example, the marble faun imagines Pan, pausing and brooding

> Beside this hushèd pool where lean
> His own face and the bending sky
> In shivering soundless amity.

These lines constitute no mean achievement, but how much more brilliant is Faulkner's account of how the idiot finds the spring, "a brown creep of moisture in a clump of alder and beech," and scoops out a basin for it, "which now at each return of light stood full and clear and leaf by leaf repeating until [the cow and the idiot] lean and interrupt the green reflections and with their own drinking faces break each's mirroring, each face to its own shattered image wedded and annealed."

If such parallels—they can be multiplied—between bits of description in The Marble Faun and lengthy descriptive passages in The Hamlet seem too vaguely general to indicate Faulkner's later development of his earlier imagery, it will not be difficult to show how certain specific images in the verse are, in the later fiction, amplified and developed to their immense advantage. For example, in Poem III of A Green Bough the poet describes an underwater scene in which "Hissing seas rage overhead," and someone "Staring up through icy twilight, sees / The stars within the water melt and sweep / In silver spears of streaming burning hair." Such an image of bright hair streaming up through water closes an elaborate description in *The Hamlet:*

> The pear tree across the road opposite was now in full and frosty bloom, the twigs and branches springing not outward from the limbs but standing motionless and perpendicular above the horizontal boughs like the separate and upstreaming hair of a drowned woman sleeping upon the uttermost floor of the windless and tideless sea. [p. 277]

In the prose passage Faulkner has accounted for the upstreaming hair: it floats from the head of a woman lying on the sea bottom. This passage in *The Hamlet* also absorbs into itself another image from his poetry. In the tenth section of *The Marble Faun,* Faulkner had described a different tree, a dogwood, shining in the moonlight:

> Dogwood shines so cool and still,
> Like hands that, palm up, rigid lie
> In invocation to the sky
> As they spread there, frozen white,
> Upon the velvet of the night.[17]

Here the analogy is more obvious: the boughs of the tree are likened to human hands lifted in prayer—almost as in one of the couplets in Joyce Kilmer's sentimental masterpiece, "Trees." The developed image in *The Hamlet* is not only more elaborate

17. The reader may find it interesting to compare with the tree image quoted from *The Hamlet* the following series of tree images that occur in *Soldiers' Pay:* "The oaks on the lawn became still with dusk, and the branches of trees were as motionless as coral fathoms deep under seas" (p. 99). "At the foot of the hill a dogwood tree spread flat palm-like branches in invocation among dense green, like a white nun" (p. 158). ". . . a tree near the corner of the veranda, turning upward its ceaseless white-bellied leaves, was a swirling silver veil stood on end, a fountain arrested forever: carven water" (p. 247). ". . . the silver tree at the corner of the house hushed its never-still never-escaping ecstasy" (p. 272). "The sky was bowled with a still disseminated light that cast no shadow and branches of trees were rigid as coral in a mellow tideless sea" (pp. 289–90).

than this earlier image; it is much bolder. It is exotically romantic and unearthly. But isn't the analogy ("drowned woman," "uttermost floor") *too* romantic? Doesn't it give off a whiff of Swinburnian decadence? If the reader met with the elaborated figure in *The Marble Faun* he would probably have to agree that it did.

The comparison occurs, however, in another context, and in these matters, context is all. The spotted horses have just arrived from Texas. V. K. Ratliff is sitting with Quick and Freeman and other neighbors on the porch of Varner's store, talking about the horses and making conjectures as to their true owner. Ratliff opines that Flem Snopes is up to some skulduggery. As usual, he is sharp in his observations on Flem and the Snopes tribe: "A fellow can dodge a Snopes if he just starts lively enough." He rallies his listeners for their interest in the ponies and asks with mock incredulity: "You folks aint going to buy them things sho enough, are you?"

Nobody answers him, and in the ensuing silence Faulkner introduces his elaborate figure of the pear tree. Thus it forms a background for the conversation—the natural scene weirdly beautiful under the moonlight, in sharp contrast to men's petty schemes and picayune rascalities. Ratliff's dry wit and earthy wisdom make the appropriate comment upon them. Indeed, the salt in Ratliff's comments is necessary to keep the "poetic" element wholesome and sweet.

One of the men sitting on the porch does take note of the tree —but not until a bird curves "across the moonlight, upward" into it and begins to sing. Does the tree call up to him an image of the floating hair of a drowned woman? No; his comment is that it's the first mockingbird he's noticed this year. A companion remarks that he's heard one earlier, singing in a gum tree. And the talk goes on from gum trees to willow trees and on to the observation that a willow is not a tree but a weed.

The next night, after the auction of the wild Texas ponies, much the same group of men are again sitting on the same moonlit porch and looking across to the pear tree. "It rose in mazed and silver immobility like exploding snow; the mockingbird still sang in it." This second description of the pear tree incorporates, by the way, another image from *The Marble Faun*. The faun sees "Slow exploding oak and beech / Blaze up. . . ." The foliage of the burgeoning trees seems to surge upward as if there were a blast of green ascending from the ground—a "slow" explosion, the shape of the tree's bursting energy, seen in slow motion, hovering in the air. What the faun sees is lighted by the sun; here the illumination is from the moon ("exploding *snow*") and the image is brought to sharper focus (one tree, not the collective "oak and beech").

The image is again ethereally beautiful, but it is once more in tension with an earthy context. One of the countrymen, Varner, does comment this time on the tree: "Look at that tree. It ought to make this year, sho [that is, it ought to bear fruit]." To which one of his companions replies: "Corn'll make this year too."

Yet the contrast, as Faulkner uses it here, is not simply that between beautiful nature and callous man. We are not necessarily to conclude that because the Yoknapatawpha farmers lack capacity for Faulknerian metaphors they are totally insensitive to the poetry of life. Ike Snopes, as idiot-faun, participates in the poetry of nature. Hard-bitten Will Varner, in his own way, worships the moon-goddess and acknowledges her power over all female kind. For Varner, having remarked about the pear tree's "making" this year, goes on to say that "A moon like this is good for every growing thing outen earth." And he tells a story. He and his wife wanted one more child, a girl child. He remembered what an old woman had once told his mother, "that if a woman showed her belly to the full moon after she had done caught, it would be a gal. So Mrs. Varner taken and laid every night with the moon on her nekid belly, until it fulled and after. I could lay my ear to her belly and hear Eula kicking and scrounging like all get-out, feeling the moon."

Superstitious nonsense? Coarse folk humor? Poetry? The reader will make up his own mind, but if Faulkner is indeed aiming at poetry here, it is poetry of a special kind. Not that of moonlight and magnolias, but a poetry which will everywhere acknowledge the unpoetic, the realistic, and even the ugly, and absorb and digest these into itself. There is a great deal of such poetry in

The Hamlet. The atmosphere is that of an Arcadian landscape but not of the Arcadia painted in luminous colors by a Claude Lorrain. In spite of a "mythic" quality and a pastoral quality— various observers have remarked on it—it is evidently located within Yoknapatawpha County.

For his poetry, Faulkner needed a medium which was at once more and less demanding than that of conventional verse. He needed room to turn around, room for repetition and for expansion generally. Most of all he needed the kind of context which would allow him to set up a real tension between his more purely "literary" tendencies and his sense of a solid and believable world.

One can make what is essentially the same point in another way: when Faulkner gave up his Swinburnian model and came to see that even Housman's was a dangerous one (William Butler Yeats had high praise for *A Shropshire Lad* but went on to say that one more foot in that direction and all would have been marsh)—when, in short, Faulkner did call his muse home, it meant that she had to become homebred, in her rhythms, her language patterns, and everything else that went with a Yoknapatawpha girl. I do not mean to say that Faulkner ever gave up completely a certain hankering for extravagantly literary words and highfalutin allusions. To the end of his life he flirted from time to time with the exotically "literary." But Faulkner possessed a high literary intelligence and his basic literary instincts were dead right. In his great works he writes like the born poet that indeed he was.

Faulkner's last and most nearly successful flirtation with extravagant and highfalutin diction is to be found in Chapter V of *Absalom, Absalom!* This whole chapter, save for the final page, is devoted to Miss Rosa's marvelous nonstop tirade against the demon Thomas Sutpen. It is a remarkable performance. Miss Rosa was not the poet laureate of Yoknapatawpha for nothing. Granted that she was an obsessed woman, educated in an old-fashioned rhetorical mode, and wild with her private grief, her long outburst occasionally becomes authentic poetry. Her extravagance and the highfalutin expressions in the context in which they are uttered are in character and dramatically right. They represent, the reader feels, the way in which Miss Rosa would have expressed herself. Perhaps they also express a side of Faulkner's literary personality that he usually repressed. In this instance, however, using Miss Rosa as a mask, by trying to formulate her volcanic outrage, he also released something about himself. (The reader who would like to see this proposition developed, is referred to the Notes, below, pp. 354–61.

Yet, one may well ask whether this is all there is to say about Faulkner's poetry. Granted that he needed to write about the Yoknapatawpha world that he knew and that his creative genius required the more ample context offered by fiction, did Faulkner learn nothing from contemporary British and American poetry? Had he committed himself earlier to a deliberately regional poetry —what then? Might he not have simply produced anemic local color poems such as had been coming out of the South from the 1870s onward?

Some of the poems published in *A Green Bough* provide answers to the question just put. Poem II, for example, is remarkably good, in concept and line by line. Though it has nothing to do specifically with Yoknapatawpha County, it is contemporary and soundly American. The situation it sets forth somewhat resembles that described in the first section of Wallace Stevens's "Peter Quince at the Clavier." [18] There, the man playing music and "desiring you" feels in himself something like "the strain / Waked in the elders by Susanna." In Faulkner's poem the music played by the woman stirs in the man an emotion that finally becomes an overwhelming desire to possess her. In Stevens's poem the emotion remains cool, elegant, and rather remote, and the poem modulates into an evocation of Susanna's thoughts and finally into a quite impersonal disquisition on the immortality of beauty. Faulkner's poem concludes on a wholly different note. At the end, the

18. I do not mean to imply that Faulkner ever read Stevens's poem, though he might conceivably have read "Peter Quince" in the popular *Anthology of Magazine Verse* for 1915. Faulkner's poem is to be dated as early as the summer of 1921 (see Blotner, pp. 308, 310).

woman has risen from her piano and begins to mount the stair. She stops at the turning of the stair, "and trembles there, / Nor watches him as he steadily mounts the stair."

In an earlier version the concluding lines read: "At the turn she stops, and shivers there, / And hates him as he steadily mounts the stair." The man in the poem is not depicted as an unfeeling brute. The poem has aimed at and succeeds in rendering with psychological realism some of the tensions of married life. Such an interpretation is rather confirmed by the fact that in the earlier version the poem is entitled "Marriage" (Blotner, pp. 310–11).

Poem III is a brilliant fantasia in which actual circumstances (if indeed there are any "actual" circumstances in the poem) are so merged with metaphoric expression that the reader might feel it difficult to know what is going on save for the chance preservation of two discarded titles: "The Cave" and "Floyd Collins." In January 1925, a cave guide named Floyd Collins became trapped in Sand Cave, which is near the famous Mammoth Cave in Kentucky. His plight was soon discovered, but in spite of frantic efforts to free his foot that had been pinned down by a rockfall, he could not be extricated. The vain rescue attempt became a front-page story all over the country for days.

Faulkner's poem can be best described as a very free imaginative presentation of such thoughts and emotions as might conceivably go through the mind of a man trapped underground as Collins was. But there is no pretense of realism—and, one might add, very little notion of narrative or logical structure. It is as if Faulkner loosed his imagination in a process of free association and swept together obsessional images that continued to haunt his fiction for years to come. Thus, we find here "vanquished horns" (cf. *Flags in the Dust*, p. 370), snoring "Kings and mitred bishops tired of sin" (cf. *The Mansion*, p. 436), "Trees of coral" undersea (cf. *Soldiers' Pay*, pp. 289–90), "aimless clouds," cropping the sky-hill "like sheep" (cf. *The Hamlet*, p. 184), and priests walking "on their gray feet" (cf. *Mosquitoes*, p. 335). This may well be the poem that Faulkner said was so "modern" that he himself couldn't understand it (Blotner, p. 459).

Poem IV, dated "Paris, Aug. 27 1925," [19] is almost aggressively "modern." There are deliberately startling phrasings such as "that blanched plateau wombing cunningly" and "brittle sweat." The typography is in the style of E. E. Cummings (e.g., "thos Cook" and "someanyplace"). The poet insists upon ironic couplings of the solemn and the trivial ("decay / makes death a cuckold yes lady / 8 rue diena we take care of that yes"). In sum, this particular poem, the fruit of Faulkner's visit to postwar Europe is a mélange of modernistic styles and devices, and with reference to World War I it reflects the moods and attitudes of poets as radically different as T. S. Eliot, Siegfried Sassoon, and Carl Sandburg.

Despite his discovery of *A Shropshire Lad* possibly as late as 1924–25, Faulkner was clearly aware of what was going on in the poetry of his day and was making experiments in the new modes.[20] But he can hardly be said to have found his own style in verse. Poem II ("Marriage") to me seems the most successful attempt to find his own voice and also (not surprisingly) his most nearly successful poem. Poem VI, also in my opinion highly successful, stands at the other extreme, the adoption of another poet's voice and manner. It is written in Housman's favorite quatrains and its basic metaphor is taken from Housman's "The Immortal Part." But Faulkner's eight-line poem does not seem merely derivative. It has its own identity. What Faulkner learned from Housman, in this instance at least, he has fully made his own. If one were making up a list of successes, Poem XLIV (Faulkner's Epitaph) might claim a place high up in the list—even though I have earlier indicated that the thought embodied becomes more massively rich and convincing as developed in the prose-poetry of one of his stories.

But a graduated list of successes and near successes is hardly to our purpose here. What is important is what the verse can tell us about Faulkner's growth as a literary artist—what weaknesses he needed to overcome and where his real strengths lay. The

19. It was originally entitled "Guidebook"; see Butterworth, "Census," p. 77.

20. For a somewhat detailed list of echoes and borrowings from various poets, see below, Notes, pp. 349–54.

weaknesses turn out to be (1) a lack of authenticity, usually because the poems in question are "literary" and written at a remove
from real experience; and (2) lack of focus. Even the rather
brilliant Poem III ("Floyd Collins"), in spite of some of its powerful imagery, is really unfocused. One way of finding a proper
focus, of course, is for the poet to decide who is speaking and to
whom and under what circumstances. Thus, to locate the poem
in a proper context may provide a means for bringing it into
focus.

Poem I, for instance, which Faulkner originally called "The
Lilacs," [21] is an attempt to dramatize the living death in which
certain badly wounded aviators of World War I are trapped.
Their bodies are technically alive, but, because they are psychically damaged, they are not truly alive. But the poem tends to be
vague and confused. Its method is not so much poetic as fictional;
that is to say, there is no controlling metaphor and no concentrated symbolism emerges. As a consequence, the story of Donald
Mahon, a World War I aviator who returns home as one of the
living dead, as Faulkner told it in *Soldiers' Pay*, is a far more
powerful statement of the theme than is to be found in the poem.
Indeed, Poem I only gathers energy and meaning when read in
the context of Donald Mahon's story. But this means that the
poem cannot stand on its own feet.

The comment just made is true of a good deal of the poetry in
A Green Bough. Such poems seem spin-offs of the novels, or become alive only in the novels. It may be best to postpone further
discussion of them until we come to *Soldiers' Pay* and *Mosquitoes*.
The case of Faulkner's borrowing from Eliot will illustrate: the
most thoroughly Eliotic single poem that Faulkner ever wrote
first appeared in his second novel, *Mosquitoes*, and perhaps
Faulkner's most effective presentation of the theme that he
borrowed from Eliot's *Waste Land* is to be found in his first
novel, *Soldiers' Pay*. This very important influence on Faulkner
comes, then, to its full fruition in the early novels, and deserves
to be discussed in the context of those novels.

21. See Blotner, pp. 261–62.

A number of Faulkner's most interesting poems, written in 1925, have never been published. They are to be found in a little book hand-lettered and bound by Faulkner. The title is *To Helen: A Courtship*. These poems, too, are best discussed within a special context, in this instance that of his personal life, his courtship of Helen Baird; and here again discussion of them will be deferred until that matter can be taken up in the next chapter.

Faulkner's poetic activity seems to have come to its most mature development in the years 1921–26. His best poems date from this period, and indeed it would be difficult to discover any of his poems that can positively be dated later than 1926. But this period of his finest poetry overlaps the beginnings of his work as a novelist. Indeed, the year 1925, as we shall see, was a sort of *annus mirabilis* for the young writer.

2

Early Romantic Prose

THE DEPTH AND QUALITY of Faulkner's romanticism comes out in some of his early prose even more strikingly than in his verse. Considering the fashions of the day, we are prepared for the romanticism in his verse, but are surprised to see the young Faulkner's penchant for writing poetic prose in the style of Yeats's *The Tables of the Law* (1897) or Oscar Wilde's *Salomé* (1893); English translation (1894).

Much of the early Faulkner prose that has been preserved consists of book reviews or essays in criticism. These have their own importance, and have been or will be discussed where the topic has special pertinence to Faulkner's own literary development. But we are here concerned with the rest of Faulkner's early prose, which is of a very different order. It is not workaday discursive prose at all, but the product of his poetic impulse, and in style tends to be poetic—in the derogatory as well as the neutral sense in which we apply the term. It resembles, though at some remove, "that extravagant style" that Yeats tells us he had himself "learnt from Pater." [1]

The Marionettes, the play that Faulkner composed in 1920, and

1. See Yeats's "The Phases of the Moon," *Collected Poems* (New York, 1951), p. 161.

illustrated and hand-lettered in an "edition" of six copies, is an early example of his poetic impulse expressing itself in a cadenced and self-conscious prose. The play also contains further examples of Faulkner's poetry in the form of songs sung by various characters. But these verses raise no special problems. They are indeed verses rather than achieved poems, and rather undistinguished verse at that, mostly in tetrameter couplets like those in *The Marble Faun,* but with occasional repeated lines by way of refrains. I confess that I find it less crabbed and awkward than much of the verse in *The Marble Faun.* Curiously enough, it is far less florid and "poetic" than the prose in which the author describes the scenes, presents the stage directions, and has such characters as the "Grey Figure," the "Lilac Figure," the "Spirit of Autumn," and the character of Marietta herself speak.

Essentially, the play is a static mood piece with very little action. Insofar as it has a plot, it concerns the seduction of Marietta by Pierrot. The virgin Marietta, restless and unable to sleep, has left her bed to walk in her walled garden. She is tempted to bathe in the garden pool. Pierrot, who has mounted the wall, sings her a song to the accompaniment of his mandolin. His song is an invitation to Marietta to come away with him to dance in the moonlight. After some initial reluctance, she accepts and departs with him. Later she returns to what is now an autumnal garden. She is now dressed, not in virginal white, but in a flame-colored robe, and has loaded herself with jewels and bizarre ornaments. She walks around the garden alone, consoles herself with the thought that she is still beautiful, but contemplates her eventual loss of that beauty and her inevitable death.

The fact that Marietta knows that her own mother had, long before, yielded to such an invitation and later returned, on feet that were "slow and sad," to die, presumably in childbirth, gives a cyclic character to the story. Such a view is strengthened when one remembers that Pierrot's foster mother is the moon [2] and that his song succeeds in filling Marietta's head with what he calls "moon madness."

The play is about youthful passion—its delight, its irrational-

2. On p. 7 of the copy published by the University Press of Virginia.

ity, and the sadness that comes after the enchantment fails. On
one level, the tale resembles that told in one of A. E. Housman's
poems:

> The sloe was lost in flower,
>   The April elm was dim;
> That was the lover's hour,
>   The hour for lies and him.
>
> If thorns are all the bower,
>   If north winds freeze the fir,
> Why, 'tis another's hour,
>   The hour for truth and her.

The heartlessness of the typical young male lover is stressed by
the First Figure, who remarks that "It is always someone else with
[Pierrot]. Why do we fly to do his bidding, we who know him for
the white sensual animal he is? For where goes Pierrot, also goes
unhappiness for someone" (p. 43).

Such also is the general treatment accorded to Pierrot in a play by
Laurence Housman and H. Granville-Barker, entitled *Prunella or
Love in a Dutch Garden*,[3] though *Prunella* is given a sentimentally
happy ending in which Pierrot is redeemed by his one true love,
Prunella.

The Marionettes, however, does not lay much stress on the
melancholy of a lorn and possibly betrayed maiden. The Spirit
of Autumn descants on Summer's departure, the garden nymph's
sadness and yearning for him, and her foreboding of disaster to
come. The nymph waiting in vain "among her dried rose stalks"
may suggest Marietta's plight, and the departed Summer may
well be a symbol of the departed and possibly faithless Pierrot.
But Marietta, when she returns to this autumnal garden herself,
never speaks Pierrot's name. Instead, her mind is preoccupied
with change. Her first exclamation is, "How this garden has
changed! . . . Ah, I know, it is autumn that has changed the

3. For parallels between *Prunella* and *The Marionettes,* and conjectures as to
whether Faulkner was indebted to it, see below, Notes, pp. 361–63.

34

garden" (p. 42). But in the next breath, she says, "But I am not changed." What she voices is really fervent hope rather than an assured fact, for her next sentence becomes a question: "Am I changed very much, I wonder?"

The First Figure and the Second Figure extol her beauty: "She is like an ivory tower builded by black slaves, and surrounded by flames," etc. "She is like a slender birch tree stripped by a storm," etc. (p. 43). Whether or not Marietta hears the voices of the two Figures, she seems to become more confident: "No, I am not changed, but how my garden is changed! The leaves fall without sound and lie like wearied hands upon the pool. The leaves are dead. . . . But my hands are not dead leaves, my hands are still beautiful" (pp. 46–47).

Time cannot be arrested. "O fearful meditation! Where alack / Shall Time's best jewel from Time's chest be hid?" Marietta has no answer to Shakespeare's question, though she evidently regards her own body as indeed Time's best jewel. She has adorned it with all manner of ornaments—"jade on my finger nails, . . . hair . . . heavy with gold," even, like Oscar Wilde's Salomé, with gilded eyelids.[4] She has become something brittle and artificial as she walks the garden, weighted down by her "girdle of dull brass" and followed by her "peacocks [walking] in voluptuous precision" (p. 53).

As the play ends there is no reference to Pierrot or any other lover. Marietta has retreated into herself: like Narcissus, she looks constantly into the garden pool. Her peacocks, those birds of vanity and pride, also eyeing their reflections in the bottomless pool, do not love their mistress. She imagines them at her death eating "the jewels from [her] feet and the jade clasps from [her] fingertips" and attracted to her "gilded eyelids . . . while their cold feet mark my body with thin crosses" (p. 54). Marietta is both perverse and morbid. She reveals her secret mind when she exclaims (p. 49) that "nothing save death is as beautiful as I am," and she evidently takes a real satisfaction in imagining her dead

4. Faulkner's copy of *Salomé*, in the library at Rowanoak, was published at Boston by John W. Luce & Co., 1912. It contains the Aubrey Beardsley illustrations and reproduces the English translation done by Wilde's friend, Lord Alfred Douglas.

body lying under the moon and being plundered by her white peacocks.

The narcissistic morbidity of *The Marionettes* may derive in part from the influence of Wilde. His influence on Faulkner's play extends much further than the detail of the "gilded eyelids." The poetic prose, the elaborate descriptive passages, and a concern with the attraction exerted by a perverse and corrupt beauty —all point back to *Salomé*. Thus, Marietta goes from innocence to corruption, not from innocence to maturity. Though Salomé is described as a virgin, she is horrifyingly sophisticated, and though her stepfather Herod has initially found her maddeningly attractive, at the end he turns on her as a repulsive monster.

A comparison of *The Marionettes* and *Salomé* reveals many verbal parallels. Thus, in *Salomé* Jokanaan's body is whiter than "the breast of the moon when she lies on the breast of the sea." *The Marionettes* makes quite as much of breasts: the moon is "like a dismembered breast upon the floor of a silent sea" (p. 6) and Marietta says that her own breasts are "like twin moons that have been dead for a thousand years" (p. 53). In *Salomé* the moon is "like a little piece of money"; in *The Marionettes* the moon is a "Roman coin suspended upon [a woman's] breast" (pp. 5–6). Salomé's feet are like little "white flowers" and her hands like doves or like "white butterflies." Pierrot praises Marietta's "little white feet" and describes her hands as plum blossoms that have fallen within her garden (p. 19). In *Salomé* the moon is like "a naked woman"; in *The Marionettes* the pool is like a "naked girl" (p. 13).

A more important indication of how much Faulkner has borrowed from Wilde is the repetition of "how beautiful" Salomé is, particularly in the first third of the play, and of "how beautiful" Marietta is, particularly in the last third of *The Marionettes*. More important still is the similarity in style. There is a persistent rhetoric of what might be called the piling up of irrelevant circumstantiality. Here is Salomé's description of Jokanaan:

> Thy hair is like clusters of grapes, like the clusters of black grapes that hang from the vine-trees of Edom in the land

of the Edomites. Thy hair is like the cedars of Lebanon, like the great cedars of Lebanon that give shade to the lions and to the robbers who hide themselves by day.

Marietta can be just as extravagant in describing herslf as she walks the paths of her formal garden:

. . . between the pains in my head and the slight pains in my feet will be jewels, and silver and dull gold chased cunningly by an Italian dying of tuberculosis, and the purple on my feet will be thick with rubies to rival the red points of my peacocks' eyes like the eyes of wolves upon a wood's edge. [pp. 49–50]

This luxuriant prose hardly moves forward at all. It is a prose of tranced reverie, involved in its own self-generated proliferations.

What is one to make of this curiously static and over-poetical play? Can one find a justification for some of the ingenious devices employed? For example, the Dramatis Personae lists both Pierrot and the "Shade of Pierrot." Pierrot turns out to be not much more than a stage prop. Though he is visible on stage throughout the play, he does not move. Indeed, he cannot, for he has apparently fallen into a drunken sleep. It is apparently not Pierrot but the "Shade of Pierrot" who sings to Marietta the seductive song that lures her from her garden.

What is one to make of the characters called simply "First Figure" and "Second Figure"? Are they spirits? Can Marietta hear them as they describe her and make their comments on Pierrot? The Spirit of Autumn is somewhat easier to account for. He is a kind of one-man chorus—or perhaps something between a chorus and a character like the Attendant Spirit in Milton's *Comus*.

Faulkner, I have no doubt, meant something by these nice distinctions and refinements. But can one confidently derive from the text of the play what he had in mind? Even if a letter or a note does turn up later to make clear why he called his "Figures" that rather than something else, or why he provided just two and not three, or why he did not give us a Spirit of Spring to balance the Spirit of Autumn—even if such documentation should eventually turn up, I think it unlikely that the reader will be convinced that these devices really pay their way.

Noel Polk has made some interesting conjectures about these matters, particularly as to what may have been Faulkner's purpose in presenting us with a Pierrot who remains silent and inert throughout the play. The interested reader can hardly do better than to consult his article.[5]

If one turns to matters other than the meaning of *The Marionettes* as a literary work and its integrity as such—if one turns, that is, to such matters as Faulkner's obsessive themes or prefigurations of situations and attitudes that appear in his later work—several conjectures can be offered.

As for Pierrot's seduction of Marietta, there is a long literary tradition behind that, and that tradition reflects a constant factor in the real world. In his account of his own beginnings with verse, Faulkner tells us that "It is a time-honored custom to read Omar to one's mistress as an accompaniment to consummation—a sort of stringed obligato among the sighs." [6]

As for the cold and imperious woman—Sidney's "my mistress marble-heart" who is self-absorbed and cruel, either actually so or fancied so by her importunate lover—she too is a traditional figure, going back at least as far as Petrarch. With the Decadents, her indifference takes a perverse twist, and Swinburne's Lady of Pain, or Wilde's *Salomé,* or Mallarmé's *Hérodiade* would have furnished Faulkner with examples apt to his hand. So would Aubrey Beardsley's drawings of women of fantastic and often sinister beauty. (As noted, Faulkner's copy of *Salomé* contained illustrations by Beardsley.)

Whether Faulkner in his personal experience had encountered (or thought he had encountered) the coldly indifferent woman of his dreams, I leave to his biographers. But sensitive young men who possess a literary flair do have—or at least once had—such imaginings. At any rate, *The Marionettes* is a mélange of ideas,

5. "William Faulkner's *Marionettes,*" *Mississippi Quarterly* 26 (1973) : 247–80. See below, Notes, pp. 361–63.

6. *Early Prose and Poetry*, p. 115.

characters, and themes from Faulkner's earliest period—the drawings as well as the prose and the verse. Like so much of Faulkner's
earliest work, this play fails to achieve full focus. Yet it has its
interest as an omnium-gatherum from his reading, and it introduces obsessive motifs that were to fulfill themselves—often in a
very different guise—in the later fiction. Thus, the lonely and
embittered virgin betrayed by circumstances or deflowered by a
faithless lover, such as one sees in Marietta, reappears—but how
changed—as Joanna Burden in *Light in August,* or as Miss Rosa
Coldfield or as Judith Sutpen—and how different these two are—
in *Absalom, Absalom!* Pierrot (or at least the character in *The
Marionettes* called the Shade of Pierrot) having been neatly split
into two, emerges in *Soldiers' Pay* as Donald Mahon and as Januarius Jones.

Since the influence of Aubrey Beardsley is powerful in *The
Marionettes* (Faulkner's illustrations for the play are obviously
derived from Beardsley's drawings) it is interesting to note what
Faulkner had to say about him several years later, in 1925, when
he was writing *Soldiers' Pay.* In introducing Margaret Powers, he
tells the reader that "Had Gilligan and Lowe ever seen an Aubrey
Beardsley, they would have known that Beardsley would have
sickened for her: he had drawn her so often dressed in peacock
hues, white and slim and depraved among meretricious trees and
impossible marble fountains" (p. 31).

Unwary critics have jumped to the conclusion that Margaret is
depraved as well as white and slim. She is not, of course, depraved
in the least, and indeed is the most attractive of all the young
women in Faulkner's early novels. The force of Faulkner's indictment (for it is an indictment) falls on Beardsley and his art.
Beardsley's depiction of human beings aside, he had falsified
reality: even his trees are "meretricious," and his marble fountains
are "impossible." In tracing Faulkner's development, this sentence
is important. It marks perhaps not so much a change of heart
on Faulkner's part as a change in his angle of vision and a shift
from the decadent romanticism with which he began. But this is
not to say that the change began at once in 1921 or that Faulkner
ever gave up entirely certain aspects of the romantic dream. "The

Hill," published in *The Mississippian*, 10 March 1922, will provide an instance of the ways in which his romanticism persisted. Though the prose of "The Hill" is literary—that is, not merely workaday prose, the discursive prose one uses for discussion or argument—it is much better as writing than the mannered and artificial prose found in *The Marionettes*. It represents an attempt to deal with an ordinary person's intuition of transcendence.

The writer insists on the ordinary mind and personality of the young man who climbs the hill. His face has the character of a "slow featureless mediocrity"; [7] he has just finished "a day of harsh labor with his hands" in a contest with "the forces of nature to gain bread and clothing and a place to sleep" (p. 92). Moreover, his transcendent experience is gained in no enchanted garden. The landscape resembles that of northeastern Mississippi. The town with its church spire and the columned courthouse— the columns, by the way are "stained with casual tobacco"—might be some little county-seat town like Oxford, Mississippi.

What conditions make the farmhand's insight possible? Sunset, the end of the day, quietness, solitude. Very important is distance: he is too far away from the little town to see the "piles of winter ashes and rusting tin cans, . . . [nor can he see] dingy hoardings covered with the tattered insanities of poster salacities and advertisements." Distance also hides from his eyes all suggestions "of whipped vanities, of ambition, and lusts, of the drying spittle of religious controversy" (p. 91).

Wordsworth described the setting and occasion for such a moment of benediction thus: "The holy time is quiet as a nun, / Breathless with adoration; . . ." Faulkner on occasion also makes use of nuns, along with other overtly religious imagery. But such imagery would be out of place here; besides, the transcendence which breaks in on the farmhand's consciousness is not Christian at all, but pagan. Yet in "The Hill" there are certain parallels with the Wordsworth sonnet: the end of day, the quiet, the sense of peace and detachment.

There is a further difference, however, and it too is altogether on the side of realism: for the tired farmhand, the sense of the

7. *Early Prose and Poetry*, p. 91.

supernal does not quite break through. Instead, there is a terrific groping of his mind as he strains to apprehend his intimation. He almost succeeds: "for a moment he had almost grasped something alien to him, but it eluded him; and being unaware that there was anything which had tried to break down the barriers of his mind and communicate with him, he was unaware that he had been eluded" (pp. 91–92). Even so, his mind has been "shaken at last by the faint resistless force of spring in a valley at sunset" (p. 92).

Though in such a scene at dusk, the author tells us, "nymphs and fauns might riot to a shrilling of thin pipes," it is clear that the farmhand hears no such music. His consciousness having subsided after its momentary faint disturbance, he prepares to descend the hill. Yet he remains tranced for a little while, standing on the hill crest "far above a world of endless toil and troubled slumber; untouched, untouchable; forgetting, for a space, that he must return" (p. 92).

What Faulkner has done—though at what a remove—is to "translate" here a stanza of Swinburne's "The Garden of Proserpine":

> Here, where the world is quiet;
>   Here, where all trouble seems
> Dead winds' and spent waves' riot
>   In doubtful dreams of dreams;
> I watch the green field growing
>   For reaping folk and sowing,
> For harvest-time and mowing,
>   A sleepy world of streams.

The term "translation" used here is justified. Faulkner has managed a translation into his own language, one accommodated to the vision of one of the actual "reaping folk." It was only at some such level as this that Swinburne could provide any real nourishment for the fiction writer-to-be.

"Nympholepsy," which came to light recently as one of a number of manuscripts and typescripts acquired by the New York

Public Library, was apparently written early in 1925,[8] during the period when Faulkner was living in New Orleans. As several people have noted, it can be regarded as an expansion and elaboration of the theme of "The Hill." The season, however, has been changed from April to the time of the wheat harvest, presumably in late summer. But the protagonist is again a farmhand, again one who is tired out from working in the fields all day, and the scene is once more a valley between two steep hills, and the time is late afternoon, sunset, and dusk.

This farmhand too has his transcendent experience—perhaps one could even use the term *adventure*—as he makes his way alone down the hill, across the valley stream, on his way to his boarding house in the small town. But whereas in "The Hill" he has, or almost has, a sense "of something far more deeply interfused" in nature, "whose dwelling is the light of setting suns," in "Nympholepsy" the intimation of the supernatural takes on a more immediately personal and even sexual character—hence the title that Faulkner has used.

"Nympholepsy" literally means to be caught up by a nymph. The *OED* definition reads: "A state of rapture supposed to be inspired in men by nymphs; hence, an ecstasy or frenzy, especially that inspired by something unattainable." The word is of rare occurrence. Where did Faulkner come upon it? The most obvious sources are Browning, Swinburne, and Byron. Yet it seems to me completely unlikely that if Faulkner had indeed ever read Browning's "Nympholeptos," he could have been influenced by it. It is one of the most confusing poems that Browning ever wrote, and the "explanation" of it that he furnished at the request of the Browning Society is, if anything, more difficult to understand than the poem itself. I think that we can safely eliminate Browning's poem as a possible source.

Remembering Swinburne's early impression on the young Faulkner, one would suppose that it was Swinburne's long poem entitled "A Nympholept" that became the main source of Faulkner's prose-poem. It is possible: Swinburne's poem celebrates the

8. See *Mississippi Quarterly* 26 (1973): 403–09, where it is published with an introductory note by James B. Meriwether.

felt presence of Pan, the god of Nature, "the supreme dim god-head, approved afar, / Perceived of the soul and conceived of the sense of man." But the nymph of the title scarcely appears any-where in Swinburne's poem. The speaker is filled with rapture, but it remains a rather solemn and diffused kind.

The nymph as a feminine personification of the unattainable ideal appears much more clearly in Byron's *Childe Harold* (canto IV, stanza xcv; Faulkner knew Byron's *Don Juan* and pre-sumably also knew *Childe Harold*). The stanza in question is a tribute to the fountain nymph, Egeria:

> Whate'er thou art
> Or wert, a young Aurora of the air,
> The nympholepsy of some fond despair;
> Or it might be, a beauty of the earth,
> Who found a more than common votary there
> Too much adoring; Whatso'er thy birth
> Thou wert a beautiful thought, and softly bodied forth.

The nympholeptic experience described by Byron is, by the way, very close to that attributed to Januarius Jones in *Soldiers' Pay* (see chap. 3, below).

The "woman or girl" first sighted afar off by the farmhand in "Nympholepsy" is, however, clearly "of the earth," for though the sight for a moment stirs him with "an old sharp beauty," his "once-clean instincts become swinish" immediately as he lurches into motion after her. Yet a little later he will wonder "whether it was copulation or companionship that he wanted." Later still, something very curious occurs: on his way to the town, as he walks the footlog across the stream, he slips and finds himself thrashing about in the water. Then all sorts of things begin to happen: ". . . beneath his hand a startled thigh slid like a snake, among dark bubbles he felt a swift leg; and, sinking, the point of a breast scraped his back. Amid a slow commotion of disturbed water he saw death like a woman shining and drowned and waiting. . . ." [9]

9. Compare this with the vision of death at the end of *Mayday* (see pp. 50–51, below).

As he treads water, the young man sees the woman—whoever or whatever she really was—"swing herself, dripping, up the bank." He gets out of the stream and pursues her, but she remains well ahead of him and finally disappears from his sight. In his despair, he throws himself on the ground, but "I touched her! he thought in a fine agony of disappointment." Once her "troubling Presence" is gone, however, he gradually recovers himself and indeed forgets her altogether in the thought of "a relaxed body in a sorry bed, and waking and hunger and work." The everyday world encloses him once more. Days of sweaty labor lie ahead. There will be other girls, but the next one will be clad in "calico against the heat." As he descends the hill and enters the town, the moonlight has transformed the world of ordinary objects, but dust clings "to his yet damp feet."

I have mentioned Byron. Two other Romantic poets, Shelley and Keats, also recorded nympholeptic experiences in their poetry. In Shelley's *Alastor, or the Spirit of Solitude,* the hero dreams of a veiled maiden whom he attempts to embrace. When he wakes, obsessed with her beauty, "He eagerly pursues / Beyond the realms of dream [her] fleeting shade" to his eventual death. John Keats describes similar experiences in "La Belle Dame Sans Merci" and in *Endymion.* In the former poem, the strange lady, "a faery's child," whom the knight-at-arms meets in the meads, first looks at him "as she did love," and finally lulls him to sleep. But when he awakes, she is gone, and he is left to sojourn "On the cold hill's side." For the hero of *Endymion,* however, the quest has a happy ending, though the hero first experiences many frustrations and disappointments. One of these frustrating incidents is remarkably like that in which Faulkner's hero suddenly feels "beneath his hand a startled thigh." In the second canto, Endymion, having thrown himself down on a mossy bed and having stretched "his indolent arms, he took, O bliss! / A naked waist"; but his beloved "Unknown" eludes him and it is only some thousands of lines later that he can finally clasp her to his breast.

A later Romantic, William Butler Yeats, in "The Song of the Wandering Aengus," recounts the same experience under the guise of Celtic legend. Aengus catches a little trout and lays it on the floor of his cottage in preparation for cooking it. But as he blows up the fire on the hearth, he hears something rustling on the floor. When he turns, he finds that the silvery trout

> . . . had become a glimmering girl
> With apple blossoms in her hair
> Who called me by my name and ran
> And faded through the brightening air.

As the song ends, Aengus tells us that though he is now old with wandering throughout the world he means to continue his quest for the girl—the apple blossoms tell us that she is really the Celtic love goddess—until he finds her. When he does find her—and his hope seems unquenchable—the two of them will

> Walk among long dappled grass
> And pluck till time and times are done
> The silver apples of the moon,
> The golden apples of the sun.

I have noted these parallels, not to insist that Faulkner has borrowed from any of them or that he had necessarily even read them, though I think he had almost certainly read the poems by Keats and by Yeats. My point is that the experience of nympholepsy —catching a glimpse of the nymph or the goddess—is traditional in romantic poetry.[10] The idealized woman of the erotic sublime is not merely familiar in poetic folklore but is a recurring experience for the young poet.

A more important point to note is that in providing his own version of the experience, Faulkner has tried to accommodate it to reality. He does not strive for the equivalent of Shelley's visionary landscape, or Keats's romantic notion of the Grecian Arcadia,

---

10. The pursuit of the nymph occurs in Faulkner's own poetry. See, for example, the third section of Poem I in *A Green Bough*, where the aviator in his little "pointed-eared machine" stalks a "nymph" through the "shimmering reaches of the sky" and finds her at "the border of . . . A cloud forest." For some twentieth-century examples of the nympholeptic experience, see below, Notes, pp. 363–64.

or Yeats's Ireland before the arrival of St. Patrick. As in "The Hill," the setting is that of the hill country of north Mississippi, and the man who gains the fleeting glimpse of supernal beauty is no introspective Shelleyan solitary nor Greek prince of pastoral times, but a farmhand whose staff is simply the wooden handle of a pitchfork "worn smooth and sweet as silk to the touch."

The story that Faulkner tells in "Nympholepsy" is, however, scarcely successful either as a realistic narrative or as a poetic parable. At points his account of the experience is labored and awkward. We never learn enough about the young man to believe in him fully or to learn how to "take" his experience. But insofar as we are interested in Faulkner's relation to his romantic background, "Nympholepsy" is a highly interesting document.

Such an experience as Faulkner attempted to dramatize in "The Hill" and, more elaborately, in "Nympholepsy," he also tried to put into verse in Poem X of *A Green Bough*. (This poem, by the way, as Butterworth has pointed out, in one of its manuscript versions bore the title "Twilight.") The poem opens, like "Nympholepsy," with the day moving toward sunset. In the next stanza we read that "Behind him day lay stark with labor. . . . Before him sleep. . . ." In "Nympholepsy" we read: "Behind him a day of labor, before him cloddish eating, and dull sleep. . . ."

In the poem, the night falls, and the farm laborer "who strives with earth for bread" has "Forgotten his father, Death," and been forgotten by "Derision / His mother." In "Nympholepsy," when the farmhand falls into "the dark whispering stream," there is in his fall "death, and a bleak derisive laughter." Stanza 4 of the poem reads:

> Nymph and faun in this dusk might riot.
> . . . .
>
> To shrilling pipes, to cymbals' hissing
> Beneath a single icy star. . . .

which lines recall a passage I quoted earlier from "The Hill": "Here, in the dusk, nymphs and fauns might riot to a shrilling of thin pipes, to a shivering and hissing of cymbals."

46

The last stanza of the poem is powerful but rather enigmatic. Beneath that icy star, the laborer

> . . . to his own compulsion
> —A terrific figure on an urn—
> Is caught between his two horizons,
> Forgetting that he cant return.

What are his "two horizons"? The last paragraph of "Nympholepsy" provides a gloss: "Behind him labor, before him labor. . . ." This interval of peace and quiet in which the moonlight turns a homely silo into "a dream dreamed in Greece" and transforms "apple trees" into "silver like gesturing fountains," seems to have nothing to do with his actual quotidian life of "sleep and casual food and more labor." The transcendent moment is a frozen moment—something cut off from the movement of time—and he himself in experiencing it is like one of those arrested figures carved on Keats's Grecian urn.

If one were following a strictly chronological sequence, one ought to turn next to the "New Orleans Sketches" that Faulkner contributed to the January-February, 1925, number of *The Double Dealer,* and to various issues of the New Orleans *Times-Picayune* from 8 February to 27 September of 1925. But since we are here concerned with Faulkner's romantic prose, it makes sense to proceed to *Mayday,* which was perhaps written early in 1926 (Faulkner dated it 17 January 1926) and which is, in its style at least, the most "romantic" thing that he ever wrote.[11] It also has to do with Faulkner's nympholeptic experience, particularly if we take the term to mean "an ecstasy or frenzy, *especially that inspired by something unattainable*" (italics mine). The nymph in this instance was of flesh and blood, a girl whom Faulkner first

11. *Mayday* was written for, and dedicated to, Helen Baird. Faulkner hand-lettered the text and furnished it with five emblazoned initials at the beginnings of sections or chapters. He decorated the endpapers with black and white drawings, drew a small formal design for an endpiece to follow the last line of the text, and provided three illustrations in watercolor. The binding of the little book he attended to himself. A facsimile, edited by Carvel Collins, has recently been published by the University of Notre Dame Press (1977).

met during his stay in New Orleans in 1925. Soon enough he was to discover that for him she was unattainable. Her name was Helen Baird.

Though *Mayday* is a tale of chivalry with a vaguely Arthurian setting, it is at some points sharply anti-romantic. Some time before 1925 Faulkner had discovered James Branch Cabell's *Jurgen* (1919), and the influence of *Jurgen* on *Mayday* is everywhere evident. One obvious feature is Faulkner's use of such locutions as "And the tale tells how" at the beginning of each new episode of the narrative. Another is the carefully archaic language that ultimately goes back to the style of Sir Thomas Malory, but which Cabell employed as a foil for his own ironic observations on the bemused human animal.

The resemblance between *Mayday* and *Jurgen* even extends to the use of specific details, such as the time of day in which the story proper commences. Jurgen's remarkable adventure begins when the Centaur Nessus conveys him to the Garden between Dawn and Sunrise. So also with Faulkner's Sir Galwyn, who is dreaming of slaying giants and dragons and rescuing beautiful princesses as he ends his nightlong vigil beside his maiden armor. First light has dawned but the sun has not yet risen above the horizon.

Faulkner's imitation of *Jurgen,* however, goes beyond circumstantial detail. Cabell constantly undercuts the romantic expectations of Jurgen's quest with his own ironic observations, or by the intrusion of modern common sense, or by uttering pert cynicisms. Faulkner does the same in his treatment of Sir Galwyn. When Galwyn encounters the Cornish man-at-arms whose master, Sir Tristan, has posted him to bar access to the river pool in which Iseult is bathing, that stout yeoman makes plain his lack of sympathy with the romantically harebrained enterprise in which he has become involved through no fault of his own. He tells Galwyn that it is his opinion that "the sooner this maiden [Iseult] is delivered to King Mark the better for all of us, for I do not like the look of this expedition. I am a family man and must take care of the appearance of things."

Sir Galwyn is, of course, not a family man. He is instead a

48

romantic young knight, obsessed with rescuing maidens whether they want to be rescued or not. So he cuts down the yeoman and, a few minutes later, cuts down Tristan himself in his haste to behold the fair Iseult.

Behold her, he does. She is standing "like a young birch tree in the water." When she realizes that her privacy has been violated, she screams "delicately, putting her two hands before her eyes." She does not flee; she does not even adopt the pose of the Medicean Venus. She is a very cool and forthright young woman. The death of Tristan does not disturb her in the least, and she very quickly makes herself completely available to Galwyn.

Faulkner also follows Cabell in the matter of themes. He too regards man as the victim of illusions. The woman of one's dreams is literally just that: a dream. The women of flesh and blood with whom one falls in love are only shadows of the woman of one's ideal vision. For this reason, all actual women must sooner or later cloy, and the lover will sooner or later discover that he has deceived himself. At the end of his story, Jurgen deliberately gives up three beautiful women whom he has loved: Guenevere, Anaitis, and Helen. Galwyn also abandons—though, unlike Jurgen, he does not at the moment quite understand why—the three beautiful princesses, Iseult, Elys, and Aelia,[12] who have in turn bestowed their favors on him. Satisfaction cloys: the unattainable continues to beckon just because it is unattainable.[13]

Both Faulkner and Cabell find that the great charm of youth is its capacity to entertain illusions; but seen in another perspective, youth is to be pitied for its vulnerability. In any case, youth cannot last. It is indeed "a stuff 'twill not endure," and romantic love, since it is the mere efflorescence of youth, is a stuff even less durable than the young flesh itself. Faulkner's little allegory—for it is indeed that—goes even further: Galwyn's quest for love and fame ends with his acceptance of the fact that death, which St. Francis

12. The name Aelia occurs in a burnt fragment of one of Faulkner's poems. See Keen Butterworth's "A Census of Manuscripts and Typescripts of William Faulkner's Poetry," *Mississippi Quarterly* 26 (1973) : 355.

13. For further examples of the influence of *Jurgen* on Faulkner's fiction, see below, Notes, pp. 364–66.

once referred to as his little Sister Death, is more beautiful than any earthly woman—and death at least *is* fully attainable.[14]

It is in this last matter that *Mayday* differs so decisively from *Jurgen,* for Jurgen, in the end, accepts the loss of youth and all of its illusions and is content to return to his not uncomfortable life as a pawnbroker and to his middle-aged, sometimes querulous wife, Dame Lisa. Faulkner's Sir Galwyn refuses to accept any descent to the humdrum and prosaic life that comes inevitably with one's discovery that the ideal woman is merely a projection of his own idealized erotic yearnings. Having discovered that he is but a shadow among shadows and that all is illusion, Galwyn chooses forgetfulness and final obliteration.

His choice is quite deliberate. The Lord of Sleep demands that he choose one of two alternatives. The first is to repeat his quest through the world, "subject to all shadowy ills—hunger and pain and bodily discomforts, and love and hate and despair," and to repeat this quest knowing "no better how to combat [such ills] than you did on your last journey through the world," for the Lord of Sleep points out that his "emigration laws" stringently prohibit "Experience leaving my domain." The second alternative is to accept the dreamless sleep of death.

Galwyn's conversation with the Lord of Sleep occurs on the banks of a river. The author gives it no name, but it would seem to be the stream of time; yet when Galwyn chooses the second alternative it becomes for him the Lethe of forgetfulness. As he ponders his decision, Hunger and Pain, who had been his constant companions (we must remember that *Mayday* is an allegory) order him to look into the stream, and there he sees "one all young and white, and with long shining hair," who makes him think of "young hyacinths in spring, and honey and sunlight." As he looks on the girl's face, he is "as one sinking from a fever

14. Compare the conclusion of "The Kid Learns" (in *New Orleans Sketches,* p. 91). Just before the Kid is killed by the mobster whom he has offended, the young man is surprised to find the young girl, whom he had left just a few moments ago, now standing "again beside him, with her young body all shining . . . and her eyes the color of sleep; but she was somehow different. . . ." When the Kid tentatively addresses her as "Mary," the "shining one, taking his hand," corrects him: she is "Little sister Death."

into a soft and bottomless sleep," and so steps down into the waters.

This is in effect what Quentin Compson is to do at the end of the second section of *The Sound and the Fury,* and though we do not actually see him descend into the Charles River, we are made to follow his thoughts throughout the day of his suicide. They include a reference to St. Francis's friendly acceptance of death as one of the creatures—that is, as one of his little brothers and sisters; moreover, Galwyn's motive resembles Quentin's. Both are despairing young men who have lost any reason for continuing to live.

There is a larger sense in which Sir Galwyn foreshadows characters and themes in the novels to come. His romantic idealism, his vulnerability, his propensity to be taken in by illusions, are traits to be found in many of Faulkner's later characters. Horace Benbow is a kind of Sir Galwyn; so is Gavin Stevens; and Faulkner's interest in such characters probably accounts for the delight that he took in Don Quixote, that passionately purblind idealist who continually projected his romantic vision on the prosaic world that lay all about him.

Faulkner, as we have observed, began as a romantic, and a romantic he remained to the end, though a reformed or foiled or chastened romantic. One of the most signal demonstrations of his personal experience as a romantic lover and of the frustration of his hopes is connected with *Mayday,* and though the little tale is in itself of minor literary importance it lights up personal experiences which were developed and transformed in his later masterpieces. "Transformed" is the proper term, for Faulkner does much more than use his fiction to record his ardors, yearnings, and heartbreaks. He stands above and outside such experiences. He puts them in perspective. He turns them into permanent literature, not mere episodes in a personal history. But in order to do this, he had to go *through* his romantic passion; that is, to come out on the other side, from which vantage point he could look back and inspect his passion *dispassionately.*

Faulkner presumably met the young woman for whom *Mayday* was written some time in the early months of 1925 while he was living in New Orleans. Joseph Blotner [15] tells us that Faulkner and Helen Baird met at a party given by his friend William Spratling, who had an apartment in the French Quarter. This circumstance agrees with an undated letter from Faulkner to Helen (preserved in the Wisdom Collection) in which Faulkner tells her, "I remember a sullen-jawed yellow-eyed belligerent gal in a linen dress and sunburned legs sitting on Spratling's balcony and not thinking even a hell of a little bit of me that afternoon, maybe already [having] decided not to."

The last sentence would also tend to confirm Blotner's account of their relationship: namely, that Helen Baird regarded Faulkner as "one of her screwballs," and that she told someone that he reminded her "of a fuzzy little animal" (Blotner, p. 438). He was amusing, and different from the other young men she knew, but not to be taken seriously as a suitor. In any case, Helen's mother objected to his disreputable appearance—for instance, his summer attire of white duck pants tied at the waist with a rope instead of a proper belt (p. 437). Nevertheless, since friends of Faulkner's, the W. E. Stones, maintained a summer place on the Gulf Coast at Pascagoula where the Bairds also had a summer place, Faulkner was able to see something of Helen there in 1925 and during the summer of 1926, while he was at work writing his second novel, *Mosquitoes*. This novel he dedicated "To Helen."

Another undated letter from Faulkner to Helen (in the Wisdom Collection) clearly refers to this period. He writes that he is now feeling "like I did when I had no money and no p[ai]r of pants and no shirt in Pascagoula and I would go and visit Mrs. Martin [Helen's aunt] and tell her that I wanted to marry you."

In the summer of 1926 Faulkner presented another small book to Helen. It is entitled *To Helen: A Courtship,* and like *Mayday* it is hand-lettered by Faulkner and bound by him in light boards. He dated it "Oxford–Mississippi–June 1926." [16] The text consists of fifteen sonnets, only five of which have been printed: viz., II, IV, V, VI in *A Green Bough* (1933) and III in *The Double*

15. *Faulkner: A Biography*, p. 419.

16. This unique copy is, like *Mayday*, in the Wisdom Collection at the Howard-Tilton Library of Tulane University.

Dealer (January-February 1925) under the title "The Faun" and with a dedication "To H.L." (This last sonnet has been reprinted by Collins in *Early Prose and Poetry*.)

These sonnets are uneven, but they contain excellent individual lines and audacious figures of speech, some of them successfully brought off. In any case, they constitute some of the most interesting poetry that Faulkner ever wrote. Sir Philip Sidney's celebrated line, " 'Fool' said my Muse to me, 'look in thy heart and write,' " though it purports to contain the Muse's own admonition, is not, unfortunately, a guarantee of authentic poetry. Nevertheless, whether or not many of the sonnets addressed to Helen amount to authentic poetry, they do clearly point to what was going on in Faulkner's heart. Consider, for example, Sonnet V, which in the little booklet *To Helen* has a special title, "Proposal." (As printed in *A Green Bough,* where it is numbered XLIII, it lacks this title.)

A glance at the poem will indicate that the "proposal" is not being addressed to Helen at all, but to her mother. What shall he say to her?

> Let's see, I'll say: . . .

but what really fills his mind at this point is the imagined breaking of Helen's "hushed virginity," a vision that distracts him from the matter of how he will formally ask for her hand. That erotic dream of the fulfillment of his desire must not, of course, have any place in what he should say to the mother; and so he resumes (with line 9) the serious business of framing a proper proposal:

> No: Madam, I love your daughter, I will say

but with line 10 his imagination once more carries him back to his erotic dream which, with the final line, is again interrupted by his realization of what the mother's immediate question would be:

> Sir your health, your money: How are they?

How could he answer questions like these? For he could expect to find no answering poetry in her but only such practical questions as how he planned to support a wife.

Though Faulkner evidently did talk to Helen's aunt about marrying her, it would seem unlikely that he ever dared mention the matter to her mother. Sonnet V makes quite clear that he realized that his case was hopeless. In Sonnet VI, however, he does imagine an answer to her imagined question about his health. The sonnet begins:

> My health? My health's a fevered loud distress:
> Madam, I—

But of course the young lover is not really making a response to the mother's practical question as to his blood pressure readings, the state of his bodily organs, and whether he has a good life expectancy. What the young man can scarcely suppress is his feverish desire for physical union with the girl. So the sonnet at once drifts away into a series of imaginary questions that burst out from the heart rather than from the calculating mind. Those questions—which we can be sure were never actually uttered to Mrs. Baird—amount to an appeal to the mother's memory of her own youthful sensuous nature. Surely, he says in effect, you too were once young and beautiful and felt the desires of the flesh. Surely you must be aware of my yearning for your daughter's body. Can't you imagine—can't you remember—what it was like to be young and in love?

These two sonnets are a very nicely turned pair. They are deft and witty, but not at the expense of a genuine passion. Most important of all, they capture the plight of a young writer who has great imagination and is racked by intense emotion, but who has no financial prospects and who is thoroughly aware of the exact degree of estimation that he can claim in the eyes of the world. Both sonnets are dated "Pascagoula—June—1925."

The novel on which Faulkner was at work at this time, *Mosquitoes,* was, as we have noted, dedicated to Helen Baird, and one of the characters in the novel, Pat Robyn, is clearly modeled on her, at least with regard to her appearance and basic personality. The cabin boy on the yacht belonging to Pat's aunt is greatly attracted to Pat, and one of the guests aboard the yacht, the sculptor Gordon, sees in her an incarnation of his ideal girl-woman—youthful, virginal, epicene. He has carved a headless, limbless torso that resembles Pat Robyn. Pat had seen it on a visit to Gordon's studio and noted its resemblance to her own body.

At that meeting in his studio, their first, Gordon notes "with growing interest [the girl's] flat breast and belly, her boy's body which the poise of it and the thinness of her arms belied. Sexless, yet somehow vaguely troubling." Pat, placing her hand upon the "marble's breast," had asked Gordon, "Why hasn't she anything here?" to which he answers, "You haven't much there yourself" (p. 24). Line 8 of the opening sonnet in Faulkner's *To Helen* sequence is entitled "To Helen, Swimming," and refers to "Her boy's breast and the plain flanks of a boy."

When Faulkner met Helen Baird in 1925 she was twenty-one, though Pat Robyn, the character in *Mosquitoes* modeled upon her, is obviously Faulkner's conception of what she might have been like as a girl of eighteen. What clinches the connection between Pat and Helen are two passages in *Mosquitoes*. Gordon sees Pat as "bitter and new as a sunburned flame bitter and new those two little silken snails somewhere under her dress horned pinkly yet reluctant . . ." (p. 48).[17] The second passage describes Gordon's emotions when he hears Pat's name: "your name is like a little golden bell hung in my heart" (pp. 267–68). Now curiously enough, part of a letter from Faulkner to Helen Baird is preserved in the typescript of *Mosquitoes*. The letter is written on the verso of one of the pages. Inadvertently, one presumes, Faulkner cranked into his typewriter a sheet of a letter that he had written but not mailed to Helen. The letter tells the young woman that she is as "bitter and new as fire" and that her name is "like a golden bell hung in my heart." In comparing Helen's name to a golden bell, Faulkner is remembering what Cyrano de Bergerac told his love, Roxanne:

17. In Poem IV of *A Green Bough* (p. 20), "the breasts of spring" are "horned like reluctant snails within / pink intervals. . . ."

Ton nom est dans mon coeur comme dans un grelot,
Et comme tout le temps, Roxanne, je frissonne
Tout le temps, le grelot s'agite, et le nom sonne.

[Act III]

As Blotner relates in his Notes (pp. 76–77), "bell imagery similar to that in [Faulkner's] letter to Helen Baird appears in Donn Byrne's *Messer Marco Polo*" (New York, 1921). Marco has heard of the great Khan's daughter, Golden Bells, and he longs to meet her; Marco tells his uncle that "there's a ringing bell in my heart." But Blotner goes on to add that "The ultimate source may perhaps be found in Edmond Rostand's *Cyrano de Bergerac*." A passage in *Mosquitoes,* however, makes it quite plain that Rostand's play was in fact Faulkner's source, for two pages after Gordon says to himself that Pat Robyn's "name is like a little golden bell hung in my heart," he asks Pat whether she knows "what Cyrano said once" (p. 269). Clearly Faulkner associates the bell sounding the loved one's name with Rostand's play.[18]

Further evidence of the Rostand influence can be found in a passage in Joan Williams's novel, *The Wintering* (New York, 1971), which is a fictionalized account of the association of Joan and Faulkner in the 1950s. Blotner tells us (p. 1475) that Faulkner took Joan in 1953 to see Arlene Dahl and José Ferrer in *Cyrano de Bergerac.* In *The Wintering* the famous novelist, Jeff Almoner (Faulkner) says to Amy, his young friend and protégée, "Listen. *Ton nom c'est une petite sonnette d'or pendant dans mon coeur, et quand je pense à toi je tremble, et elle sonne.*" Then he translates the passage for her: "Your name is a little golden bell hung in my heart and when I think of you, I tremble and it rings." When Amy exclaims that the sentence is beautiful, the novelist tells her: "That's why one of the great lovers said it to his love, long before I. Cyrano to Roxanne" (p. 229).

In the version that appears in *The Wintering,* three lines of French verse have been thoroughly rewritten.[19] So far as I can

18. Roxanne has the same surname as Pat Robyn; for her real name is Madeleine Robin. It would seem that Faulkner deliberately chose to link the two young women.

19. I have looked up four or five English translations of *Cyrano.* Two of them specify the metal of the bell as gold, though Rostand did not. But all the transla-

discover, there is no possibility of a revised version of the play in which Cyrano speaks the French sentence that the famous novelist speaks to the young woman named Amy. Where did Faulkner (or Joan Williams) find this bit of text? I hazard the guess that Faulkner remembered the line pretty much as it occurs in *Mosquitoes* and then later on translated it into French. Perhaps his seeing the performance of the play in New York brought it back into his mind; but evidently he didn't look up Rostand's French text. Perhaps, like V. K. Ratliff, he preferred to remember it in his own way and simply translated his simpler version into French. Or perhaps Joan Williams did the translation.

Faulkner's implied association of himself with the hapless Cyrano—see the letter to Helen Baird—suggests personal reasons for his appreciation of the play. Cyrano, though possessing a poet's mastery of language, believes that his monstrous nose bars him from any hope of winning the woman with whom he is passionately in love. Moreover, Cyrano feels that he cannot express his love directly to Roxanne—only vicariously through the mouth of his friend Christian. Faulkner, of course, could and did express his love to Helen directly, but his status as a suitor was, as he well knew, quite hopeless. We don't know whether Faulkner was aware that he reminded Helen "of a fuzzy little animal," and it seems extremely unlikely that anyone would have reported to him that Helen had advised her friend Ann Farnsworth not to read *Mosquitoes* because "It's no good" (Blotner, p. 549). Nevertheless, such evidence as we do have, including the letter previously cited and the sonnets contained in *To Helen: A Courtship,* makes it plain that Faulkner was probably aware of how little impression he had ever made upon her.

Faulkner must have felt certain personal affinities with Cabell's failed poet Jurgen as well as with Rostand's Cyrano. Jurgen, for example, loved Guenevere more than any other woman in the world, but "very shortly . . . was to stand by and see her married to another." Faulkner had not stood by in Oxford when Estelle

---

tions that I have seen attempt to preserve the niceties of the heart–bell comparison; and so does Faulkner, of course, if we are to assume that the version spoken to Amy by the famous novelist in *The Wintering* is Faulkner's own.

Oldham had been married to another. Instead he had gone up to New Haven to join his old friend Phil Stone. Now, in 1926, as he was writing *Mosquitoes,* the same thing was about to happen all over again, for in May of 1927 Helen was married to another man; but again, Faulkner did not stand by to witness it. According to Blotner (p. 549), he had not been invited to the wedding.

How convincingly Faulkner's little tale of Sir Galwyn conveys a sense of despair is a matter for literary judgment. I suppose that few will be inclined to disagree with my own estimate that *Mayday* is scarcely an important literary text. But there need be little doubt that Faulkner the man felt a very genuine despair. The fragment of his letter to Helen Baird preserved in the typescript of *Mosquitoes* is embarrassing in its naked hurt and almost abject plea for pity.

In terms of Faulkner's development as an artist, the experience recorded in his letters and sonnets to Helen Baird was very important. Faulkner had begun his career as a romantic, a sensitive, idealistic young man, disposed to project his dreams on the various women with whom he fell in love. But the disappointments that he suffered in losing Estelle Oldham and later Helen Baird substantially modified his youthful romanticism, though apparently neither of these experiences, nor subsequent events, ever succeeded in obliterating it. Though he must have suffered disillusionment, he did not subside into cheap cynicism. In his later fiction he often coldly exposes the bemused lover's blind folly, but he never mocks at the idea of an idealized love. Thus, he is able to maintain dramatic sympathy for Horace Benbow, Gavin Stevens, and the young schoolteacher Labove. Perhaps the fairest way of putting it is to say that Faulkner's earliest disappointments in love developed in him, not cynical scorn, but a certain detachment. Though he preserved a rapport with the enthralled lover, caught up in his extravagant ardors, Faulkner was also able to regard this foolish and vulnerable figure objectively.

To be able to view a dramatic situation from both the inside and the outside is for the artist an inestimably valuable gift—a gift displayed in the novel that followed *Mosquitoes—Flags in the Dust.* The poor-white Byron Snopes is, in spite of appearances, another one of Faulkner's unrequited lovers. He also resorts to writing letters, anonymous ones, to his beloved. Because Byron is so far below Narcissa socially, he is aware that she would not countenance him as a suitor or even as a social acquaintance. But in spite of the fact that Byron can express his longings only in fumbling and obscene letters, he is a backwoods Cyrano after all, the victim of a hopeless love, tormented by the desire of the moth for the star. Faulkner, one should note, is able to give even Byron his due; he does not turn him into a monster; he allows him a certain plausibility and the dignity of genuine suffering.

Faulkner's ability to pierce through the glamor of romantic love is part of a larger and more general emancipation from illusions of all kinds. By 1926 he had attained to a less emotionally distorted understanding of women and to a more realistic insight into his own nature and into that of human beings in general. Yet although he had sloughed off the callow romanticism with which he had begun and had gained a certain realism, we should be wary of the view that Faulkner's early disappointments in love turned him into a misogynist, a view still too widely held.[20] These complicated issues must, however, await more detailed treatment elsewhere. At this point we turn back to the poetry and verse dedicated to Helen Baird and to the other works in which, under one guise or another, she appears.

I have already remarked on Faulkner's rather straightforward account of his plight in Sonnets V and VI of *To Helen: A Courtship.* But *Mayday,* too, though an allegory, renders a harsh verdict against romantic love and additionally against women who play the love game selfishly and cruelly. To be sure, Helen Baird is nowhere called a "jill-flirt," the term that, in the end, Jurgen applies to some of the damsels with whom he had thought himself in love. In the passage in question, Jurgen says to Helen of Troy: "Very long ago I found your beauty mirrored in a woman's face . . . , all my life was a foiled quest of you . . . the memory of your beauty, as I then saw it mirrored in the face of a jill-flirt."

20. It has recently been put once more in a very sophisticated essay by Albert Guerard, Jr., "The Misogynous Vision as High Art: Faulkner's *Sanctuary,*" *Southern Review* 12 (1976) : 215–31. See also his *The Triumph of the Novel* (New York, 1976).

The logic of *Mayday* is much the same: the beauty of every flesh-and-blood woman that Galwyn thought so lovely—all of them jill-flirts—was no more than a memory of the face of the woman that at the beginning of his quest Galwyn had seen in the stream. Only when at last Galwyn has come to realize that she is unattainable does he give up his quest and, almost eagerly, descend into the waters to embrace death. Mere shadows of the true beauty will no longer satisfy him.

Did Faulkner, however, really expect Helen Baird to apply the judgment rendered in *Mayday* to herself? His dedication, which reads "to thee / O wise and lovely / this: / a fumbling in darkness," hardly sounds that way. Or was the work for Faulkner so much a fumbling in darkness that he himself failed to see the full import of this story he had set forth? Such speculations are probably idle. Young men very much in love do not always see the full logic of the situation they have all too clearly described in writing about it. They are prone to believe in miraculous reversals and last-minute recoveries, like the lover in Michael Drayton's sonnet, who, having renounced his mistress and having described in detail the deathbed of the little god of love, nevertheless concludes by assuring his mistress, "Now, if thou would'st, when all have given him over, / From death to life thou might'st him yet recover."

In this matter of what Faulkner intended to say to Helen Baird in his two little hand-lettered books and what he expected her to hear, we ought to be cautious. But plainly, early in 1926 Faulkner had achieved a self-knowledge and an ability to detach himself as artist from a situation in which as a man he was deeply involved. This lesson, learned so early, he was subsequently to put to good use.

"Carcassonne" was published in 1931 as the final story of the collection entitled *These Thirteen*. It is tempting to regard it not as a narrative at all—there is little or no action in it—but as one more example of Faulkner's romantic prose. Its composition may in fact date from about the same time as his other writings of this sort, "Nympholepsy" and *Mayday*. Blotner proposes late 1925,[21]

21. One of the characters in "Carcassonne," a wealthy patroness of the arts, is, in the earliest version of this work, called Mrs. Maurier (rather than, as in the

but it may have been composed years later, much nearer to the date of its eventual publication in *These Thirteen* (1931). Whatever the date of its composition, however, in theme and style it resembles Faulkner's romantic celebrations of the role of the imagination and his reflections on the plight of the artist.

He called the story a fantasy and told the Virginia students that he had always liked it because there, in creating a piece of fantasy, he was "the poet again." Its close relationship to his own poetry is, as we shall see, sufficiently obvious; but he also drew upon two poems not his own. He evidently took his title from a French song by Gustave Nadaud, the burden of which is "I never have seen Carcassonne." The singer is growing old, and he now knows that what has always been his "dearest wish" will never be granted.[22]

Faulkner's fascination with the unattainable appears in his now famous grading of contemporary authors, where he rates Wolfe higher than Hemingway because of "the splendor of [Wolfe's] failure." Though Wolfe had failed, he had attempted more than Hemingway or the rest. "Carcassonne" has to do with failure, but a failure made certain by the magnitude of the ambition.

The other poem that Faulkner levied upon was "The Immortal Part" by his old favorite, A. E. Housman. The poem is a dialogue between what Housman regarded as the truly "immortal" part of man, his skeleton, and "the man of flesh and soul." This second man concedes the ultimate triumph of the man of bones, but insists that until "this fire of sense decay, / This smoke of thought blow clean away" he will assert his mastership over the bones—"the sullen slaves"—that shall survive him. "The Immortal Part" is a prime instance of the stoicism that Faulkner admired so much in Housman's poetry.

In "Carcassonne" also the speakers are the man of flesh and blood and his skeleton, and some of the speeches come right out of

---

published version, Mrs. Widrington). Mrs. Maurier is the name of the wealthy patroness of the arts in *Mosquitoes*, on which Faulkner was working in 1926. See Blotner, p. 502.

22. When asked, Faulkner said that he didn't know the poem (see Gwynn and Blotner, eds., *Faulkner in the University*, p. 22). Perhaps he had never read it, but surely he must have known the theme. I, for example, knew of the theme associated with the word "Carcassonne" long before I ever read the poem itself.

the Housman poem. The skeleton says, for example, "I know that the end of life is lying still. You haven't learned that yet. Or you haven't mentioned it to me, anyway." So also with the man's reply: "Oh, I've learned it. I've had it dinned into me enough. It isn't that." But here Faulkner twists the dialogue to suit his own purpose, for the man continues by saying, "It's that I don't believe it's true" (*Collected Stories*, p. 899).

Housman's stoical man of flesh and soul knows quite well that it is true, and accepts the fact. Faulkner's young tramp-poet [23] has tried to do so, but honestly can't believe it. His urge to dream is too powerful, his own dreams too magnificent, not to believe in their reality. Even so, Faulkner's fantasy, like Housman's poem, amounts to a descant on the curiously divided nature of man, so obviously an animal destined to end up as worms' food, if not even earlier as rats' food, for the young tramp-poet sleeps in an attic where the darkness is sometimes "filled with a fairy pattering of [the] small feet" of the rats.

Nevertheless, man's imagination seems boundless, and man has in the past created a heroic world where a Godfrey de Bouillon or a Tancred can achieve glory. Even in death itself man has found it possible to see his role as heroic, for the young tramp-poet alludes to the tragic endeavors and deaths of a Hamlet and an Agamemnon. Note the resemblances between:

> where fell where I was King of Kings but the woman with the woman with the dog's eyes to knock my my bones together and together [*Collected Stories*, p. 898]

and this passage from Sir William Marris's translation of *The Odyssey* (London, 1925):

> But in mine ears
> Most piteous rang the cry of Priam's daughter,

---

23. The young man whose thoughts we follow in "Carcassonne" is taking his repose in a building that belongs to Mrs. Widrington, the "wife" of the Standard Oil Company, and "With her," our hero observes, "if you were white and did not work, you were either a tramp or a poet."

Cassandra, whom the treacherous Clytemnestra
Slew at my side, while I, as I lay dying
Upon the sword, raised up my hands to smite her;
And shamelessly she turned away, and scorned
To draw my eyelids down or close my mouth.

[XI. 425–31]

Though Faulkner did draw upon this passage, he has obviously not used it literally. Agamemnon, as commander of the Greek host, was a king of kings, but it is Faulkner who has supplied his present title and it is Faulkner who has made Clytemnestra knock her husband's bones together. Faulkner was later to abstract from this passage the words "as I lay dying" for the title of his fifth novel.

The young man would like "to perform something bold and tragical and austere," let the known facts of man's mortality be as grim as they indeed are. But the situation is not promising as he lies beneath a strip of tarred roofing paper and dreams and listens to the rats. Indeed, his material condition and prospects as compared to his high-flying thoughts mirror precisely the contrast between his skeleton and what that part of it called the skull contains—a "humming hive of dreams," as Housman describes it.

Much is made in "Carcassonne" of the tramp-poet's vision of "a buckskin pony with eyes like blue electricity and a mane like tangled fire," and of his memory of the "riderless Norman steed which galloped against the Saracen Emir" and which, having been cut into two by a single blow of the scimitar, still galloped on, heroic and apparently immortal. But the steed that human beings are given to ride is of a very different kind. It is the articulated skeleton itself, and we riders are not always heroic. The young tramp-poet reflects that skeletons might sometimes justly complain of the men whom they have to bear. They might feel "Like bones of horses cursing the inferior riders who bestrode them, bragging to one another about what they would have done with a first-rate rider up" (Collected Stories, p. 897).

In Poem VI of A Green Bough, Faulkner uses just such a steed-rider metaphor. The first stanza reads:

> Man comes, man goes, and leaves behind
> The bleaching bones that bore his lust;
> The palfrey of his loves and hates
> Is stabled at the last in dust.

Horse and rider, body and soul, materiality and dream—all of these oppositions appear in a fugue-like descant on man's evident mortality which ever calls in question but never seems quite able to exterminate his yearning for the high dream.

"The Hill," "Nympholepsy," and even *Mayday* are also treatments of this curious double nature of man. So is Poem X of *A Green Bough* (as noted earlier), and so also is Poem XXVIII (which in one of its manuscript versions is entitled "Wild Geese"). Hearing the call of the geese flying southward in November, the speaker asks,

> Was I free once, sweeping
> Their wild and lonely skies ere I was born?
>
> The hand that shaped my body, that gave me vision,
> Made me a slave to clay for a fee of breath.

This is man's all-but-intolerable situation: capable of responding to, and so yearning for, the freedom of the skies, and yet earthbound, a slave to clay. The speaker goes on to say:

> Sweep on, O wild and lonely: mine the derision,
> Then the splendor and speed, the cleanness of death.

Compare this with what is said in Poem X: at the end of a day of hard work, a farm laborer has a moment of insight in which he has

> Forgotten his father, Death; Derision
> His mother, forgotten by her at last.

Much more could be said about "Carcassonne." The dithyrambic style, the almost free association of thoughts and images, the recurrence of what appear to be obsessive metaphors—all these invite speculation—and indeed sheer guesses, since the author has left so many loose ends fluttering. One complex of images, however, may deserve a brief and concluding comment, not because I can pretend to understand just what they meant to Faulkner, but because elements of the complex continue to turn up in one form or another in his later work. It is the image of a human skeleton or of a body lying on the floor of the sea or in an undersea cave. Thus, the tramp-poet imagines that "Bones might lie under seas, in the caverns of the sea, knocked together by the dying echoes of waves," and he reflects further that "it's better to be bones knocking together to the spent motion of falling tides in the caverns and grottoes of the sea" (p. 897). Again, as he listens to the "fairy pattering" of the rats, "his body slanted and slanted downward through opaline corridors groined with ribs of dying sunlight upward dissolving dimly, and came to rest at last in the windless gardens of the sea. About him the swaying caverns and the grottoes, and his body lay on the rippled floor, tumbling peacefully to the wavering echoes of the tides" (p. 899).

The tramp-poet in his dark attic imagines something very like what Floyd Collins, trapped in his dark cave, is made to imagine in Poem III of *A Green Bough:* "the hissing seas / Roar overhead again, and bows of coral / Whip gleaming fish in darts of unmouthed colors. . . ."

What does the image mean? Peace, quiet, ultimate repose? Hard questions, these. It is easier to suggest where Faulkner probably got the imagery. Noel Polk makes the shrewd guess that Eliot's *Waste Land* is the ultimate source.[24] The tramp-poet does not relish having his bones "cast in a little low dry garret" to be "Rattled by the rat's foot only, year to year." He would prefer to think of "A current under sea" picking "his bones in whispers"— as it did those of Phlebas the Phoenician. (See lines 194–95 and 315–16 of *The Waste Land*.)

The undersea imagery may, however, have deeper associations

24. Polk has many other points to make in an ambitious essay which takes seriously the notion that "Carcassonne" is one of Faulkner's most interesting and accomplished pieces of work. My own account is in debt to this essay, and though I have reservations as to whether Faulkner in "Carcassonne" either intended or accomplished what Polk claims he does, the essay should be required reading for all who are interested in this period of Faulkner's career.

65

still—some that go back to Faulkner's early devotion to Swinburne. In *Soldiers' Pay,* "the branches of trees were as motionless as coral fathoms deep under seas" (p. 99), and the "branches of trees were rigid as coral in a mellow tideless sea" (pp. 289–90.) Years later, in *The Hamlet* (in a passage I quoted earlier), a similar image recurs: the "twigs and branches" of a tree stand "motionless and perpendicular above the horizontal boughs like the separate and upstreaming hair of a drowned woman sleeping upon the uttermost floor of the windless and tideless sea" (p. 277). The tramp-poet imagines his body, not at the bottom of a tideless sea, but rather as "tumbling peacefully to the wavering echoes of the tides." But in either case, the body has been returned to the sea that Swinburne called our "great sweet mother," and whether the sea is tideless or tumbles with the "echoes of tides," both passages convey a sense of safety and rest.

3

A Payment Deferred

(SOLDIERS' PAY)

IN VIEW OF what has been said in the foregoing chapter about Faulkner's romanticism, it would be strange if it did not reveal itself in one form or another in his first novel, *Soldiers' Pay*. For *Soldiers' Pay*, we may need to remind ourselves, was composed during the first months of 1925, which means that it was written at about the same time as "Nympholepsy," and that it actually preceded the composition of such works as *Mayday* and *To Helen: A Courtship*.

One point to note is that the nymphs and fauns that occupy such an important place in Faulkner's poetry and in his romantic prose were not really banished from his realistic novel about life in the United States just after World War I. It is true that in *Soldiers' Pay* Faulkner attempts to bring these minor pagan deities down to earth and to show how they were bound to fare in a twentieth-century world. But he could make the attempt because for him they were not simply "poetic" materials, vaguely decorative, that he had borrowed from Swinburne and the poets of the 'nineties. The fauns and nymphs represented for Faulkner an aspect of human nature that he regarded as important and with which he remained concerned throughout his literary career.

At the risk of considerable oversimplification, one can describe

Faulkner's interest in these Greek nature spirits thus: He was from the beginning fascinated by the oddly divided nature of man. Man was obviously a part of nature like the other natural creatures, equipped with much the same biological mechanisms and subject to animal appetites and needs. Yet he was also—with his memory, reason, and imagination—somehow outside nature as the other creatures were not. One might regard Man as a sort of amphibian, swimming in the sea of nature and unable to live outside it, and yet with his head lifted above the surface of that sea. Man's ability to transcend nature was, of course, supposed to be his glory—and clearly in the instance of a Shakespeare or a Keats it was. Yet it could also be strangely embarrassing, setting man at odds with his natural impulses and sometimes rendering him a morbidly inhibited and even perverted creature.

The more austere forms of Southern evangelical Protestantism might well have made the fabulous pre-Christian world particularly attractive to an imaginative youth. In his reading of Swinburne, Faulkner had evidently paid attention to the line, "Thou hast conquered, O pale Galilean; the world has grown gray from thy breath." Thus, he must have found Greek paganism, as refracted through the Decadents of late nineteenth-century British and French literature, especially attractive. Faulkner's youthful imagination was also stirred by what may at first glance seem an antithetical world: the world of romantic chivalry in the Middle Ages. There is, however, no real contradiction between the two attractions. Medieval romance reflected a world of wonders, not at all a world rendered gray by anybody's breath. To the youthful imagination, it seemed ardent, passionate, and above all colorful. If it had to be accounted "Christian," its atmosphere, nevertheless, was not that of the drab Protestant Sunday-school. It was magically strange. And so, from time to time in Faulkner's earlier work, we have references to priests, nuns, and monks, but the asceticism so implied was exotic—and that apparently redeemed it for his imagination.

In his earliest days, however, pagan primitivism exerted the primary attraction. It provided Faulkner with the faun, a symbol of uninhibited man, freely interacting with nature, a creature of healthy animal instincts, of no morbid inhibitions, and with very little self-consciousness. Faulkner's early preoccupation became an abiding fascination with the faun, and it has a bearing on the meaning of that interesting and highly complicated novel, *Soldiers' Pay*.

Donald Mahon, who returns from World War I badly wounded and who in the course of the novel goes blind and finally dies, represents an aspect of the faun. He possesses—at least before his disabling wounds—the traits of spontaneity, impulsiveness, and a lack of inhibitions and self-consciousness generally associated with natural ("inartificial") man. All of this is made very plain in the various flashbacks to Donald's early life. We are told (pp. 82–83) that he had "the serenity of a wild thing, the passionate alertness of a faun." He is a person who "ought to live in the woods." Social institutions and the other forms of society have no hold on him. He could not be made to attend school or even to tolerate a hat or a coat. He would sometimes stay away from home for two or three days and nights at a stretch. Negroes would find him happily asleep in a sandy ditch.

As faun, he has his companion nymph. With the simple and primitive Emmy, his conduct is that of unselfconscious innocence. He at seventeen and Emmy at fourteen build themselves a swimming pool in the woods. They swim together every day and nap on a worn blanket until they are caught by Emmy's father and she is forbidden to see Donald again. They share no sexual experience, however, until one night Donald calls her from her father's house and they go out to sleep together under the stars.

All this is romantically idyllic. Donald's seduction of Emmy is apparently impulsive. For, after Emmy has been forbidden to see him, he falls in love with another girl, Cecily, and becomes engaged to marry her. That he subsequently has his love night with Emmy doesn't change his plans to marry Cecily. That is, Faulkner observes the limits of Donald's faun nature. The boy feels no responsibility for Emmy, and she, on her part, it should be said, shows no resentment toward him. Emmy tells Margaret Powers (p. 126) that Donald "didn't care much about me: he never cared about anybody." Donald's great virtue is honesty: he "always told his father" about us, Emmy says. He "never lied about nothing he ever did" (p. 125).

If Donald is faunlike in his animal innocence and freedom from all guile and deception, Januarius Jones is a very different kind of goat-man, lusting after every nubile woman who crosses his path. (Jones, to be sure, has a good deal of poetry about him, but it is other people's poetry; it is all in his head, and he uses it as one of his instruments for seduction.) In treating this character also as a pagan goat-man, Faulkner makes a nice but important distinction: though Jones, on viewing Donald's picture, immediately recognizes that he is a faun, no one in the novel ever so names Jones. Instead, he is frankly described by the author as a "fat satyr" (p. 286). His lust is insisted upon over and over again. We are told on at least three occasions that his eyes are "like a goat's" (e.g. p. 83), and twice, with very little variation of phrase, that his eyes are "clear and yellow, obscene and old in sin as a goat's" (pp. 67 and 286).

Faulkner obviously means for his reader to regard Januarius Jones as a thoroughly unpleasant fellow.[1] Nevertheless he makes the character something less than, and also something much more interesting than, merely an embodiment of human lust. Jones is capable, for instance, of experiencing what the author calls a "chaste Platonic nympholepsy" (p. 225) and so is related—at whatever far remove—to Faulkner's other characters who have been caught up by the nymph.

But one must hasten to put the matter into more realistic psychological terms. For Jones, sex is thoroughly intellectualized; thus, quite unlike Donald Mahon, he resembles Molière's or Mozart's Don Juan. (Byron's Don Juan—at least the youthful

---

1. Jones is literally a bastard, as he rather ostentatiously confesses to Margaret (p. 248). Perhaps he does so as part of his defiance of the respectable and conventional world. Such information certainly makes no difference to Margaret. Literal bastardy would stir pity in her, not contempt. Nor could the news affect Joe Gilligan, except perhaps to inhibit any tendency to refer to Jones as "that bastard." Whatever Faulkner meant or didn't mean by having Jones declare himself, his being picked up as a foundling anticipates the case of Joe Christmas in *Light in August*. Did Jones acquire his first name from the season in which he was found, just as Christmas acquired his surname?

hero of the earlier cantos—presents quite another issue, and might even be said to resemble Donald Mahon.) There are some further complications in the personality of Januarius Jones, but they are best deferred to the discussion of the motivations of various characters in this novel.

Between themselves, Donald Mahon and Januarius Jones stake out the opposed limits of human nature as distinguished from mere animal nature. Like all of Faulkner's fauns, Donald exists just at the very edge of the truly human world. He possesses the vitality and unconscious charm that delights us in a healthy bird or animal. Januarius Jones, for all that he is frequently compared to an animal—most often to a goat, but at least once to a cat—is almost morbidly self-conscious. All of his gestures toward other human beings are calculated—deliberate, planned assaults on human dignity. He sees other persons as "things," and usually treats them so. They are there for his exploitation—sexual, if they are women; social and economic, if they are men. We are shown no one in Charlestown that Jones really likes and with whom he is simply happy to be. He can cap quotations from Horace with the Rector, jest with him about literature and history, and make witty comments on the human circumstance, but he has no real respect even for the Rector, and privately calls him an old fool.

In *Soldiers' Pay,* the human dimension is to be found somewhere between a man so "natural" that he is not responsibly human and a man so "unnatural" that he subverts all the ties that unite him with other men. Joe Gilligan, no paragon of human nature to be sure, is nevertheless far more "human" than the artificial Jones; but Joe is also, in spite of Donald's animal "naturalness" and "soft, wild" eyes, more human than Donald.

"Natural" man has for a long time fascinated poets and novelists, especially those who live in the overcivilized and overregimented, overcomplicated modern world. The great Romantics, too, were much concerned with finding a new relationship with nature. In their poems, they often celebrated natural man, and they sometimes experimented in their personal lives with becoming natural men. But Faulkner, in spite of his early romantic bias and the attraction that an Arcadian world held for him, is more realistic than Wordsworth and Shelley. Though Faulkner treats with sympathy his simple woodsmen (like Boon Hoggan-beck) and his latter-day fauns (like Benjy Compson and Ike Snopes), he recognizes that they cannot really cope with the human world, and so quietly relegates them to a special status. Faulkner, I shall claim, in spite of his sharp criticism of our present civilization, ultimately comes down on the side of civiliza-tion and the full community, and he does so almost from his beginnings.

All of this is not to insist that in drafting *Soldiers' Pay* he was thinking in terms so abstract as this, or as moralistic as the fore-going sentence might seem to imply. But whether consciously or not, Faulkner did set forth two aspects of the traditional protest against a bourgeois world of restrictions and sterile respectability. The first is typified in Donald's inarticulate protest of the heart—the uninhibited assertion of the spontaneous and instinctive life of the emotions. The second is typified in Jones's quite conscious protest of the subversive intellect, a protest calling in question all the prohibitions imposed by society and mocking at, or actively flouting, its prohibitions.

As between Donald, the innocent faun, and Jones, the corrupt satyr, there can be, for Faulkner, no real problem of choice. For Donald might possibly have grown up some day and, by the time that wrinkles had formed around his "soft, wild" eyes, might have acquired some sense of responsibility and, with it, some elements of wisdom. There seems to be, on the other hand, little hope for Jones. Presumably his obscene eyes, "as old in sin as a goat's," will get still older in sin. Besides, Jones has in effect gone over to the enemy in cultivating the corrosive intellect at the expense of the spontaneous intuitive life. As W. H. Auden has shrewdly pointed out, the pleasure that Mozart's Don Giovanni takes "in seducing women is not sensual but arithmetical; his satisfaction lies in adding one more name to the list which is kept for him by [his servant] Leporello." Jones does not have a Leporello to keep score for him, but he evidently values spectacular victories far more than what E. E. Cummings called "the he-man's solid bliss."

To bed the unglamorous Emmy, with her work-reddened hands, still smelling of harsh soap from her house-cleaning duties and, to cap it all, to do so in the very hour in which her one true love is being put into the grave—this must have given Jones the satisfaction of having achieved a genuine coup. By seeing to it that Donald and Jones possess the same woman, Faulkner has neatly pointed up the difference between the two men in their attitudes toward love and sex.

As for Jones: Faulkner gives us plenty of hints of the almost perversely intellectualized nature of his sexuality. He is no he-man, certainly, and Faulkner hints as much by referring to him as catlike and several times actually calling him "feminine." Though Faulkner in *Soldiers' Pay* sometimes provides a rather shaky motivation for the actions of his characters, his basic grip on their psychology can scarcely be faulted. The polarization between Donald and Jones is soundly conceived in relation to what I make out to be the theme of the novel.

Faulkner's faun and satyr have, as I have already intimated, their female counterparts, Emmy and Cecily. Emmy is the wood nymph who welcomes the faun's call with wholehearted frankness. One supposes that she derives ultimately from Swinburne's nymphs. Faulkner had certainly not forgotten them: in *Soldiers' Pay,* he is constantly comparing young girls not only to trees but to tree nymphs. In the later novels, characters like Horace Benbow, whose heads are filled with classical literature, indulge in reveries in which nymphs dance to the music of Pan's pipes. But Faulkner's flesh-and-blood nymphs, those like Emmy, know nothing of Swinburne or any other poet. They are unlettered girls who have lived very simple lives in the Southern countryside.

Emmy is typical, but she is not the first of Faulkner's nymphs of the realistic breed. In an unpublished story entitled "Adolescence" (written in the early 1920s) Faulkner tells of Julie, a fourteen-year-old, rather hoydenish girl who, like Emmy, swims naked with her boyfriend in sexless innocence. Theirs, we are told, is the "happy time" of "two animals in an eternal summer." Again, like Emmy and Donald, after their swim they are in the habit of napping together on a blanket spread on the grass. At last they are

73

one day discovered by Julie's grandmother, who outrages Julie by accusing her of having had sexual intercourse with the boy.

Obviously the idyll of an innocent paganism fascinated Faulkner, but Emmy offers little opportunity for the complications of a novel. In *Soldiers' Pay* he gives far more attention to Emmy's antithesis, Cecily Saunders, who, though she is so different from Emmy, is called a nymph too. Though she is constantly compared to various kinds of graceful trees, there is nothing really wild or woodsy about her. It is impossible to imagine Benjy, another of Faulkner's fauns, ever thinking, as he does of Caddy, that Cecily smelled like trees. Yet there is a long literary tradition in applying (or misapplying) the term "nymph" to a girl like Cecily. In the poetry of the English neoclassical period, attractive young women are quite regularly referred to as nymphs, and the custom persists in the *vers de société* of the nineteenth century.

Cecily is all artificiality and self-consciousness. The author tells us (p. 81) that "Cecily never [had] been engaged in an unself-conscious action of any kind." This judgment seems to be accurate. In spite of the fact that Cecily is completely self-centered, she is nevertheless completely "other-directed." Her social image is to her everything, and she whirls like a weathercock at every gust of the winds of public opinion. Though Emmy's actions are spontaneous and almost instinctive, it would be misleading to call them impulsive, if one uses "impulsive" to suggest some momentary and transient emotion. But Cecily's vacillating actions are impulsive in just this sense: she is constantly trimming her sails to take account of every fitful breeze—constantly veering and tacking. But the bewildering changes in her directions ought not to mislead the reader; in spite of her changes of course, she is, from the very beginning, steadily making for a definite port: her own selfish well-being.

The corrupt satyr, Januarius Jones, however, presumably means it when he calls Cecily a "Hamadryad, a slim jeweled one" (p. 77). Cecily's mannered freshness, grace, and fragility appeal to Jones. Taking her hand in his, he feels its "slim bones . . . its nervous ineffectual flesh. Not good for anything. Useless. But beautiful with lack of character" (p. 79). In a later passage he seems to regard her as essentially inhuman—literally nymphlike—for he apparently tells himself that "you knew that . . . her clear delicate being was nourished by sunlight and honey until even digestion was a beautiful function . . ." (p. 80).

There is a curious parallel between this sentence and a passage in the hallucinatory Circe chapter of Joyce's *Ulysses,* in which Leopold Bloom in the brothel finds himself confronted by the apparition of a nymph whose image he keeps in his bedroom at home. The nymph assures Bloom that she has no organs of digestion: "We immortals, as you saw today [Bloom had earlier inspected the statue of a Greek goddess to see whether the sculptor had provided it with an anal opening] have no such place. We are stonecold and pure. We eat electric light." [2]

The associations of sunlight and electric light are shockingly different, as is appropriate to the differing tonalities of the two passages in which they occur. If Faulkner did derive this passage from Joyce, then he has so transfigured it that Cecily's diet of honey and sunlight becomes that of the Greek gods, and Cecily, in Jones's eyes at least, becomes the apotheosis of a mortal, a being who, though divine, is still warmly human; [3] whereas Bloom's nymph, who turns out to be only a reified idea of hypocritical modesty, is discomfitted and finally retreats, "her plaster cast cracking, a cloud of stench escaping from the cracks" (p. 553). She is a whited sepulchre indeed.[4]

A possible explanation for Faulkner's having placed in his first novel two versions of the faun and two of the nymph might run something like this: In the modern world the pagan virtues are no longer viable. Donald Mahon's honesty gives place to Jones's brutal cynicism, and Emmy's spontaneous life of the senses yields to Cecily's calculated poses and gestures. This is not, I repeat, to imply that Faulkner consciously worked out his novel in so

2. *Ulysses,* Modern Library edition, 1961 printing, p. 551.

3. The collocation of honey and sunlight is characteristic of Faulkner. See for instance the passage from *Mayday* (quoted in chapter 2, above) where a girl is likened to "young hyacinths in the spring, and honey and sunlight."

4. For other echoes of Joyce, see below, Notes, pp. 370–72.

programmatic a fashion. Yet clearly there is some sort of continuity between the nymphs and fauns of Faulkner's early work, including his poetry, and their human equivalents in *Soldiers' Pay*. And just as clearly the human equivalents of the fauns and nymphs do not fare well in the world as we know it. If they survive at all, it is only at the price of being corrupted into something that has lost its "natural" quality.

What baleful force has put the fauns and nymphs to flight? Is it Christianity? More particularly, is it an aggressive Protestant-Puritanism? Swinburne makes the charge, and a Faulkner nourished on Swinburne might be expected to agree. There are in this novel hints of such a view. But Faulkner knows that the sickness of the present world goes deeper than can be accounted for in such terms. Christianity itself has suffered the fate of the old pagan nature-religion. Its more attractive traits are ineffectual in the world presented in this novel, and only its delinquencies and distortions thrive. To put matters in more obvious terms, the Christian dream of love and peace has been compromised. The country had been mobilized to fight a war that would put an end to all fighting, but those who crossed the ocean to wage such a war were deluded.

Soldiers' Pay deals with the disappointing aftermath of the war fought to make the world safe for democracy, but the disillusionment with which this novel deals is more general still. The soldiers involved had talked "of dying gloriously in battle without really believing it" (p. 162). Now they have rather ingloriously returned to a world that has become strange and disordered. Some of them, of course, have not returned. Lieutenant Powers, Margaret's husband, had been shot down by one of his own men. Donald Mahon had technically returned, but with a crippled body and with a mind that can remember little or nothing, a *de facto* living dead man.

All this is bad enough, but something worse has happened. Too many of the noncombatants have also been mortally damaged. The culture portrayed in the novel has lost its bearings, and lost its faith in itself and in its purposes. In short, its not too sturdy religion has finally caved in, and though Faulkner is not concerned with religion in any narrow denominational sense, he knows that a loss such as has been suffered is devastating, for historically religion has always been the ultimate base of values for every culture.

Faulkner has quietly made his point by choosing for his focal character an Episcopalian priest, Donald Mahon's father, who is a fine, liberal, tolerant man, respected and loved by the best people of the community, yet not a man of faith. He is a man who badly needs help, and who, rather than supporting others, is in need of their support. That support comes from two fundamentally decent human beings, a man and a woman: Joe Gilligan, "Yaphank," a demobilized soldier who, like Faulkner himself, never got across to the Western Front, and Margaret Powers, whose husband had been killed in France. Joe is neither faun nor satyr, and Margaret is no nymph, either natural and spontaneous or brittle and corrupt. Joe and Margaret occupy the middle ground where live almost all the rest of us. Both have their problems, as we discover when we get into the novel, for both participate in the disillusionment that has settled over the country.

They first appear in *Soldiers' Pay* as good Samaritans. They encounter Donald Mahon as he makes his way home by train, immediately comprehend the situation, and resolve at once to see that he gets safely home. They do better than that: they stay on to cushion for the Reverend Mr. Mahon the shock of Donald's coming death, an event that they divine almost at once and which they suspect the Rector is helpless to cope with.

Faulkner has been careful not to make them plaster saints. Though their concern for Donald is genuine, the truth is that they have no pressing business elsewhere. If they have relatives eager for their return, we never hear of them. They are at loose ends. But Faulkner uses this fact, not so much to undercut their generous sympathy for the wounded man as to indicate that they also are victims of the common disaster, not in the obvious sense that Donald is a victim, but in a deeper sense.

Joe, perhaps for the first time, falls deeply in love with a woman with whom he wants to live for the rest of his life; but he cannot win her, though she is not proud or coy, and though she genuinely likes him. Margaret has received a deep psychic wound through the circumstances of her early impulsive marriage and the sense of guilt left when her husband died before receiving the letter in which she tried to tell him that she didn't love him. She finally offers her body to Joe, but she honestly cannot bestow on him the only kind of love that will satisfy him. She wonders whether she will ever be capable of offering such love to anyone.

For readers who interpret *Soldiers' Pay* as Faulkner's waste-land novel, written directly under the influence of Eliot's poem—and we have had some very elaborate accounts of the Eliot parallels— the characters who most obviously suffer an experience like that of the protagonist in *The Waste Land* are Margaret and Joe, along with the Reverend Mr. Mahon. Though Donald Mahon can be plausibly exhibited as an instance of death-in-life, he actually constitutes a poor example. The inhabitants of Eliot's *Waste Land* are suffering a spiritual malaise, whereas Donald's illness is physical: he is scarcely aware of what is happening to him. Margaret Powers, on the other hand, is well aware of what has happened to her. She feels somehow guilty and enervated.

Nevertheless, it is Mr. Mahon on whom is focused the spiritual malaise. In making him an Episcopalian, Faulkner has chosen his denomination very shrewdly. The Rector is a cultured man, well-read, genial, no dour Puritan, no perfervid hot-gospeller. He is in fact a quite tepid broad churchman who has lost his faith. If this last clause seems too strong, then let me put it this way: Mahon's Christianity has become so dilute that it amounts to no more than a sincere humanitarianism spiced with a dash of stoicism. His real interest, as he tells Jones at their first meeting (p. 61), is to develop a beautiful garden filled with the proper trees, shrubs, and flowers. This is his refuge—the personal Garden of Eden to which he would find his way back.

The point scarcely needs to be argued. At the end of the novel the Rector's spiritual counsel to the disconsolate Joe Gilligan amounts to this: "God is circumstance, Joe. God is in this life. We know nothing about the next. That will take care of itself in good time. 'The kingdom of God is in man's own heart,' the Book says" (p. 317). Joe asks the Rector: "Ain't that a kind of funny doctrine for a parson to get off?" And it is a funny doctrine. Sound counsel or not, it is purely secular counsel. "We make our own heaven or hell in this world," the Rector insists. "Who knows; perhaps when we die we may not be required to go anywhere nor do anything at all. That would be heaven" (p. 317).[5]

The attentive reader would not, however, have to wait for the closing chapter of the novel to learn the truth about Joseph Mahon's real beliefs. The truth comes out in various ways and fairly early. For example, though we do hear twice of the Rector's preparing a sermon (pp. 151, 168), we are given only one fleeting glimpse of him in church (p. 282), and one omission in particular is very significant. In 1919, the year of the action of the novel, Easter Sunday fell on 20 April; Donald Mahon got home on 3 April (see the chronology on pp. 366–70, below). The "action" of the novel takes us through that month and into May, when Donald finally dies; but nowhere is there any mention of Passiontide or Good Friday or Easter Sunday, though the Rector's hopes and fears for his badly injured son are heavily engaged during this period.[6]

It is hard to believe that the author himself was not aware that he had placed Donald's abortive "resurrection" not only within the time of nature's springtime resurgence, but in the season of the Christian year in which Christ's resurrection is celebrated.

5. Sir Maurice Bowra, in *Memories, 1898–1939* (Cambridge, Mass., 1966), describes the head of an Oxford college in the 1930s who had once been a member of "the Aesthetic Movement of the 'nineties and was reported as having said, 'I think that one ought to live beautifully.' Now he was not only an epicure, but so far as a Christian priest can be, an Epicurean. . . . Later he said to me, 'Of course, as a Christian I believe in survival after death, but personally I should much prefer extinction'" (p. 152). The Reverend Mr. Mahon, for all that he lives in a provincial Georgia town, is quite in the mode of the great world outside and, for that matter, in the mode of the cultivated English civilization of the period in which so many of Faulkner's early masters flourished—Swinburne, Wilde, Yeats, et al.

6. The reader's awareness of this strange omission doesn't require that he look up the day on which Easter fell in 1919. It requires no more than what most people already know: that Easter four times out of five occurs in the month of April, and that most churches—including certainly the Episcopal church—make a great deal of the Easter season. The dating of Lowe's letters to Margaret makes it plain that Donald's return—from the dead, as it seems to his father—occurs early in the month of April: see also the chronology in the Notes, below.

But whether or not Faulkner consciously contrived this time scheme, the fact that the Rector never even mentions Easter is bound to strike any sensitive reader with telling effect. When a priest—any priest of any cult—is oblivious to his cult's great day, he has ceased to be a true priest and/or the cult is in desuetude.

Again, those who seek to find in *Soldiers' Pay* parallels with *The Waste Land* will find their strongest argument, not in strained allusions to *The Golden Bough*,[7] but in the fact that Faulkner has put such a rector as Mahon at the center of the novel. He is even more nearly central than his invalid son, Donald; and his passivity is even more telling, for Donald's passivity is a consequence of his physical condition. But the Rector's is a spiritual disability. In losing his faith, he has lost his vocation.

Faulkner has wisely not stated the point, but he has powerfully dramatized it. The priest, who should console the brokenhearted and renew the faith of the fainthearted, is, in this novel, for the most part the object of consolation by others. He is an utterly vulnerable man, apparently quite helpless in his situation. The Rector tells Jones that "Least of all did I teach [my son] fortitude. What is fortitude? Emotional atrophy, gangrene" (p. 68). This is not, of course, to say that Donald himself lacked fortitude. Perhaps he learned it from what appears to have been his favorite book, *A Shropshire Lad*. But fortitude is precisely the virtue that Margaret and Joe fear the Rector lacks. At any rate, they go to extreme lengths to protect him from truths that they believe he may be unwilling or unable to face. Margaret actually goes through a form of marriage with Donald, though she knows that Donald will soon be dead and that the marriage certainly cannot be consummated. Her motive is compassion, not love as between man and wife, and her compassion is rather for the grieving father than for the afflicted son. (She is already acting as Donald's nurse and companion. The "marriage" does not alter nor does it add anything to the relationship already established.) Most of the

7. My argument here is not that Faulkner was unacquainted with Frazer's great book. It is rather that a thoughtful reading of *Soldiers' Pay* is more likely to show us what Faulkner really drew from Eliot's poem than is a searching through the pages of *The Golden Bough* for symbolic meanings that Faulkner might have had in mind. The danger is that we will find not too few meanings but too many.

action in this novel consists of the efforts of Margaret and Joe to prepare the Rector for Donald's impending death.

It is Margaret and Joe who are, like the protagonist of Eliot's poem, conscious that the land lies under a curse, and that meaning and purpose have been lost. Early in the novel Margaret says to herself: "Am I cold by nature, or have I spent all my emotional coppers, that I don't seem to feel things like others?" (p. 39). And a little later, as she talks with Joe about the plight of Donald Mahon, she exclaims: "It's a rotten old world, Joe." But the worst of it, they agree, is not maiming or death. It is an emotional and spiritual deprivation. "Even sorrow," Margaret says, "is a fake now." Later still she says: "Everything is funny. Horribly funny."

What Joe and Margaret have is their honesty. In the 1920s some seemed to feel that honesty was almost the only virtue left. It is this very virtue that keeps Joe and Margaret apart. Margaret won't say she loves Joe when she doesn't, and she refuses to fake it. Joe, on the other hand, will not accept her body, which, out of compassion, she offers him, for he will not accept anything less than love. In a world in which depths of emotion, including sorrow, seem a fake, they cling desperately to their emotional integrity.

The novel ends in the mood that dominates the conversation between Joe and Margaret in the early pages. Donald is now dead and buried, and Joe has watched the train carry away the woman with whom he is hopelessly in love. Out of his despair or perhaps it is out of the goodness in his heart, Joe now offers to stay on with the Rector. But the Rector refuses, saying "This is no place for a young man, Joe" (p. 317). Though touched by the offer and genuinely sorry for Joe, he is able to extend only cold comfort and empty consolation. Now he goes on to address himself more specifically to Joe's plight. "You are suffering from disappointment," he says, but adds that the saddest thing about love is not merely that it cannot last but that even "heartbreak [itself] is soon forgotten." That belief is unbearable, of course, but then the Rector goes on to say, "all truth is unbearable."

As the two men walk along in the dusk, they hear the voices of men and women whose faith has not guttered out. The Rector explains that the Negroes are holding their services. On the ears of the two white men, the music falls with "All the longing of mankind for a Oneness with Something, somewhere." The music is beautiful: "above the harmonic passion of bass and baritone soared a clear soprano of women's voices like a flight of gold and heavenly birds" (p. 319). But the singers' faith is not available to Joe nor to the Rector. As the music fades away, the two men turn townward "feeling dust in their shoes."

Significantly, the singing does not come from the Rector's church and perhaps could come from no white church at all—almost certainly not from a white church *in the city*. The voices are those of unsophisticated human beings who have thus far escaped the blight of modern skepticism. Thus, as the novel closes, Faulkner has quietly put aside his fauns and nymphs as beings whose feelings are natural and spontaneous, and set in their place human beings genuinely imbued with a simple faith. The substitution accords with the fact that this is a realistic novel attempting to deal with the present and not an escape into an imaginary land of fabulous peace.

So much for the prevailing mood and the dominant theme of *Soldiers' Pay*. But since it is an attempt at a novel, one must ask how well it is constructed. Very well, in general, as to such matters as unity of mood, tone, and theme. But one has to concede that the actions of the characters are sometimes hard to believe, and their motivations often problematical. Since the author frankly sets Jones down as a fat satyr, it might well be supposed that Faulkner meant him to be more mythological than human, more of a caricature than a realistic character. Yet Cecily's motivation has probably provoked more debate among Faulkner's readers than that of Jones. And, for my money, it is the Rector whose actions are the least credible of all of the three.

Let us begin with Cecily. Her earlier relations with young Donald Mahon present no real problem, nor do her later relations with George Farr. It is her relationships with Jones and with the Rector that raise questions—and the questions arise in good part because of obscurities in the characters of Jones and the Rector themselves.

Cecily is naturally excited at the news of her fiancé's return from the dead, but faints when she sees his horribly scarred forehead, and quietly resolves that now she cannot possibly marry him. Yet though she resists her father's insistence that she call on Donald at the rectory, if only for the sake of his father, she suddenly reverses her position and does so. She even goes so far as to tell Donald (who, we have learned by this time, probably cannot comprehend what she is talking about) that she "will try to get used" to the scar. But as it turns out she mistakenly utters her promise to Jones, primarily because she is so carefully averting her eyes from Donald that she absurdly drops down at the feet of the wrong person. She then quite illogically, but humanly, blames Donald for her humiliation and goes home "nursing the yet uncooled embers of her anger" (p. 138). She tells her father that she is not ever going back to see Donald again, and when he forbids her, then, to see "that Farr boy, any more" (p. 142), she immediately gets in touch with Farr and arranges for a midnight tryst.

Such vacillations as these can be accounted for as the not unpredictable actions of a spoiled, self-absorbed, headstrong young woman. So also can her behavior at the dance to which Joe and Margaret bring Donald so that he can listen to the music. (Obviously, dancing is for Donald out of the question.) Yet when Cecily hears that Donald is sitting in a car outside the house, she goes out to greet him, provoking in Margaret the thought: "What does she want with him now? Watching me: doesn't trust me with him" (p. 205). Cecily actually gets into the car and kisses Donald on the cheek. But soon she is back on the dance floor again.

Cecily's little brother Robert had earlier reported to his sister a conversation between Joe and Margaret that he had overheard. Margaret had said to Joe: "You think I'm in love with [Donald], don't you?" Misunderstanding the import of the conversation, Robert had warned Cecily to "watch [her] step . . . or she'll have him." Cecily evidently can't bear the idea of giving up her claims to a man whom she does not love and whom she clearly has no desire to marry. Her rapid changes of direction—Joe and Margaret see her as a real whirligig—can thus far be interpreted as the outcome of perfectly understandable, though conflicting, emotions: vanity, physical repugnance, possessiveness, and jealousy. But more complications still are to come.

Having given herself to George Farr on the occasion of her midnight tryst with him, Cecily chooses to leave him dangling, though he is frantic in his desire to see her again. Finally, she does relent, and lets him have a meeting with her at the local drugstore. She will not yield, however, to his importunate appeals to marry him. The glamor of being engaged to a returned war hero is still too attractive for her to relinquish it at once. Cecily even ventures to tease her nearly distracted paramour. She says to him: "Darling, aren't we already married, now? . . . is it only a marriage license will keep you true to me?" (p. 215).

A moment later, however, Cecily's amused complacency suddenly turns into sheer terror when she sees that Jones is at another table and might have overheard the conversation. She quickly dismisses Farr, tries to find out how much Jones has overheard, even bringing Jones home with her to have lunch in her desperate attempt to find out how much he knows. Jones evidently has heard a great deal, and Cecily remains deeply frightened. Next morning, she rushes over to the rectory, embraces Donald, and cries out: "I will marry you, I will, I will" (p. 245).

This is the immediate sequence of events that has caused even one or two very careful readers of *Soldiers' Pay* to conclude that Cecily believes she is pregnant. I am convinced that they are wrong and that if we are to understand Cecily (and the novel itself) the record has to be put straight. For what is at stake is finally the young Faulkner's competence as a literary artist and a psychologist. Granted that in his first novel the young writer is clumsy in handling the delineation of character and motivation, there is all the more reason, then, to try to understand what he was attempting to do.

In Cecily, vanity and easy resentment, pride in her power over men, and spoiled self-indulgence are mingled with a certain timidity and fear of public opinion. It is this mingling that explains her vacillations. Cecily will, for instance, defy her family only up to a point, for she is actually timorous and vulnerable. One doesn't need to bring in an alleged terror of finding herself to be an unwed mother in order to account for her sudden promise to marry Donald after all. Moreover, to assume that such is her motive denies the presence in her of a certain cunning and guile, traits that are essential elements of her personality. Emmy might well have borne a child after her one love night with Donald, but Cecily's is a different case entirely, and that difference is an aspect of the author's comment on Cecily and the world she represents.

Though Cecily is not one of Faulkner's most intelligent characters, she is no innocent; she is rarely overmastered by any strong emotion; and she is quite artful. Is it at all likely that she would have made her first experiment in sex without asking her lover to take "precautions"? If anything at all is clear, Cecily was not on this occasion swept off her feet by a great gust of passion. In 1919 contraceptive devices were known and widely used.

In the second place, is it at all believable that Cecily, had she really been pregnant, would have thought that Donald could provide a plausible father for the child-to-be? Except for the Rector, apparently everybody else in town who looks at Donald regards him as a dying man. Hearing that Cecily does plan, after all, to marry Donald, the wretched Mrs. Burney wonders whether Donald is capable of consummating a marriage, and doubtless other townspeople shared her skepticism. Had Cecily married Donald and then borne a child, one that might well resemble not Donald Mahon but George Farr, tongues would have certainly wagged.

If pregnancy were indeed her concern, why did she not at once marry Farr, who is imploring her to marry him? Jones already knew that she had some kind of affair with Farr. What has terrified her is that Jones might talk about it (see pp. 216–45). The best way to shut Jones's mouth would be to marry Farr—something that a few days later she proceeds to do. Why, then, did Cecily hesitate even for a moment to do so? Faulkner has not provided a clear answer, but he has dropped a number of hints. He has suggested, for instance, that Cecily is herself certain that

Donald is impotent and that marriage to him would be an empty formality. During her colloquy with Jones, when she is trying to find out how much he has overheard from her conversation with George, Jones asks her when she means to be married, adding, "He expects it you know." Cecily's reply is interesting. She asks, "What makes you think he does? He is too sick to expect anything, now" (p. 221).[8]

A possible reason for marrying Donald would be to find a refuge, at least for a time, from sex. Early in the novel, Cecily says to herself: "I wonder if . . . I want to get married at all." After her first sexual experience, she goes back into the house in tears (p. 147). Jones thinks of her as epicene, "Not [made] for maternity, not even for love. . . ." Indeed, it is her epicene quality that most attracts Jones to her. Perhaps, then, after her sleepless night and in her almost hysterical state (p. 244), Cecily sees in marriage to Donald a temporary refuge from her present anxieties. (Besides, in spite of his probable impotence, Donald is a war hero, and to be his widow for a while will be nice.) But if this suggestion has any merit, it rules out Cecily's being pregnant. For if she were really pregnant, the husband would have to be a convincing father of the child on the way."

In any case, and whatever Cecily's motive, her practical mother, who has objected from the first to Cecily's honoring her engagement to Donald, is utterly bewildered that Cecily should now have suddenly made her drastic decision; and when, under sharp questioning, her daughter can do no better than say, "I can't tell you. I have just got to marry him," Mrs. Saunders asks, "Got to marry him? What do you mean?" (p. 260). It is in this scene that, for the first and last time in the novel, an intimation of pregnancy appears. Cecily indignantly denies the intimation, I believe quite truthfully. Just a day or so before, over an ice-cream soda, she had been jesting with George Farr about not having to get married now. It is hard to imagine either that she knew then

8. Jones's ensuing remarks make it plain that he was referring to her marriage with George, not Donald. That fact does not bear upon the point being made here; but it does indicate that Jones has overheard a great deal, including George's belief that Cecily will now marry him.

she was pregnant or that something happened some eighteen hours later to make her now believe that she was.

Cecily's difficulty in knowing her own mind, let alone in explaining to her mother why she simply had to marry Donald, is made very clear by the author on page 262 in a passage in which he sets down her thoughts: "Yes, yes, Donald. I will, I will! I will get used to your poor face, Donald. George, my dear love, take me away, George!" Obviously the poor girl is at this point hopelessly divided and does not really know what she will do. Small wonder that Margaret remarks (p. 273) that Cecily "has changed her mind so often nobody can tell what she'll do." In the end, when Cecily does choose to elope with George, no one (except possibly the Rector) could have been much surprised.[9] In spite of her apparent indifference to George, she in fact would like to depend upon him. When she becomes terrified of Jones, she finds herself actually wishing for George (see p. 220), and, George's virtues aside, to choose him is a way to run away from what has become for her an intolerable situation.

The way in which she acquaints the Rector with her decision, however, does raise several questions. One might have expected her simply to bolt without saying anything to him. Or, one might have supposed that she would offer almost any explanation other than the one that she does give—namely, that she cannot marry Donald because she is no longer a good woman. In a sense, of course, it is Cecily's best moment in the novel. It is in fact almost her only good moment—a circumstance that may make it hard for some readers to accept it. Yet, what she does is not wholly incredible.

Throughout the novel, it has been suggested that Cecily has a special relation to the Rector; he appears to be a sort of second father to her. Obviously, she is in the habit of dropping in to see him in the rectory—and long after she supposes that Donald has

9. The town will certainly not be surprised when it hears the news. There had already been talk about "the way that girl goes on with that Farr boy" (p. 152) and how she runs "around town nearly nekkid. Good thing [Donald's] blind, ain't it?" To which someone adds the comment: "Guess she hopes he'll stay blind, too" (p. 262).

died overseas. Now, having decided to elope with George, perhaps she feels that she must herself tell the Rector that she will not marry Donald; and perhaps she feels that she must give the Rector, at whatever cost to her own pride, an explanation that will carry weight with him and yet will not reflect on Donald. So she bursts out with the truth about herself (p. 276).

At any rate, it is a private confession. Neither Margaret Powers nor anyone else is in the room when she makes it, and Mahon is a gentleman: Cecily knows that he won't tell. (As a priest, he has just heard a confession, and the priest must keep the confession secret. If one felt that Mahon really thought of himself as a priest, that guarantee would be sufficient. One is more confident that he is a gentleman than that he believes in the sacrament of confession.) In this moment of truth, one suspects that had Cecily really been pregnant, she might have given that as her reason. Why not?

When Jones tells Cecily in their conversation at the drugstore that, whatever he has overheard, he will not reveal it, she does not believe him, and one can hardly blame her for refusing to. Yet, should the reader share Cecily's lack of faith? The possibility that Jones is in this instance speaking the truth ought to be considered, for it has an important bearing on Faulkner's conception of Jones's character.

On page 228 Jones asks Cecily what difference does it make what he overheard, and goes on to say: "You can have all the Georges and Donalds you want. Take them all for lovers if you like. I don't want your body." Cecily naturally dismisses this notion as nonsense and tells Jones that she thinks he is crazy. With this judgment Jones agrees: "I know I am," he tells her. When Cecily persists in trying to get him to say what he has heard, Jones tries once more to convince her that he means her no harm. "Listen," he says. "You are a shallow fool, but at least you can do as you are told. And that is, let me alone about what I heard. . . . I'm not going to hurt you: I don't even want to see you again. So just let me alone about it. If I heard anything I have already forgotten it—and it's damn seldom I do anything this decent. Do you hear?" (p. 229).

He doesn't convince Cecily, who persists in her nagging at him.

But again, does Faulkner expect the reader to be convinced? Each reader will obviously have to decide for himself, but the author has provided some significant clues. On page 225, as Jones embraces Cecily, "he refused to feel a bodily substance in his arms . . . not an animal that eats and digests—this is the heart's desire purged of flesh." (He had earlier imagined her diet to be honey and sunlight.) Savoring his emotion of transcendence—Cecily as nymph and not as a mortal being—he says to himself "as much as to her, 'don't spoil it.' " On the same page, Faulkner describes Jones's state of mind as that of "a fat Mirandola in a chaste Platonic nympholepsy," [10] as he shapes "an insincere, fleeting articulation of damp clay to an old imperishable desire. . . ."

Cecily does "spoil it." She continues to press Jones to disclose what he has overheard, and thus breaks him out of his "chaste nympholepsy." For he proceeds, by implication, to reveal that he did hear her arrange another midnight tryst with George Farr. Since she can't "get . . . through [her] beautiful thick head" that he wants not her body but something that it symbolizes for him, then very well, he'll have her body. He will keep the tryst himself. For he tells Cecily (p. 232): "I am coming to-night," and when she asks, "You heard that?" he answers, "I say that."

If the reader still finds it hard to believe that Jones was at any time capable, for however brief a season, of being caught up in a nympholepsy—that is, satisfied to contemplate Cecily as an unattainable nymph—he might remind himself that Jones, in more senses than one, does indeed have his sex in his head; he intellectualizes sex to an almost morbid degree. Later in the novel (p. 283) the author describes as an obsession Jones's desire to bed unglamorous Emmy: "It had got to where, had she acceded suddenly, he would have been completely reft of one of his motivating impulses, of his elemental impulse to life: he might have died" [11] (p. 283). Faulkner clearly set out to make Jones one of his

10. See the discussion on pp. 42–45. Faulkner's association of "nympholepsy" with Platonism and Mirandola would confirm the view, expressed earlier, that Faulkner regarded the nympholeptic experience as one in which the divine idea or form shone through the sensual appearance.

11. Emmy's yielding herself to Jones at the time of Donald's funeral may be hard for many readers to accept. Yet, Emmy's intensity, her bottled-up passion, and her very simplicity make her thoroughly vulnerable to just such a person as Jones.

most complex characters. If he only partially succeeded, one probably should applaud the ambition of his conception.

In suggesting earlier that the Rector is perhaps the least plausible character in the novel, I had in mind more than his passivity,
his vulnerability to hurt, his inability to see what every other
character in the novel cannot fail to see, his general helplessness.
These are traits to be found in many civilized people, including,
I daresay, the clergy. We expect a novelist to heighten and even
exaggerate for a purpose, especially when the heightening is
significant for the novel, and we have already seen that the Rector's deficiences and weaknesses are significant for the theme and
mood of *Soldiers' Pay*.

The Rector, however, says and does things that make no sense
and that do not reinforce the theme of the novel. They are simply
meaningless. For example, can one believe that this gentle and
forgiving man, who doesn't want to hurt any human being,
would in the first ten minutes of conversation with a total stranger
point out that there is "dishonor" in his dead son's face and intimate that the young woman servant, Emmy, has been dishonored
by him? [12] Jones gets the point immediately. Or is it conceivable
that the Rector would have a young Baptist minister perform the
marriage ceremony for Donald and Margaret and also (for this is
the clear implication of p. 295) officiate at Donald's funeral? The
point is not that the Rector should have scorned Baptists. It is
simply that if a very quiet and very private marriage was desired,
the obvious course would have been to perform it himself. The
funeral would have been a different matter, and here, his own
racking grief aside, he would have regarded it as unseemly to carry

---

Unerringly, he knows when to approach her: she will be most accessible just in the
midst of her morbidly intensified emotions as she faces her final loss of Donald.
Jones's conquest of her at the hour of a funeral that she was too grief-stricken to
attend is thus shocking, but it ought to be judged other than a contrived irony.
The young novelist shows a sound knowledge of Emmy's psychology. One might
compare Hero's seduction of Lucile in Jean Anouilh's *The Rehearsal*.

12. It is also difficult to believe that the Rector would have employed Emmy as
a household drudge, to do all kinds of menial work, including scrubbing floors. One
would have expected him to have accepted more responsibility for a girl whom his
own son has "dishonored." In any case and whatever his motives, the presence of
Emmy in the Rector's house as a maid of all work is anomalous.

out this sad service. But surely he would have wanted, if only for aesthetic reasons, to have the Prayer Book service, and the normal thing to do would be to call in an Episcopal priest from a neighboring parish.

It is just possible that Faulkner here knew exactly what he was doing and that he wanted to emphasize how completely lukewarm religion had become for the Rector, how all was merely empty form now, with one denomination of professed Christians differing in no wise from another. Yet it is hard to put down the thought that Faulkner at this stage in his career knew very little about the doctrines or forms of worship of the Episcopal church.

If the Rector fails to be plausible, Joe Gilligan, on the other hand, rings true. I grant that having him rather than, say, Margaret, read to Donald Mahon—and read, of all things, Gibbon's *Decline and Fall of the Roman Empire*—is hard to accept. But the incongruity may be deliberate, and Joe, for all his lack of formal education, is extremely intelligent and has a distinct literary flair. His own speech shows that he has a way with words and possesses the gifts of the imagination.

Margaret's behavior may raise questions in the minds of some readers, but I find no insoluble problems—though there are, to be sure, questions that Faulkner has not chosen to answer in his novel. In the breakdown of values during the War and its aftermath, she has suffered psychic damage. But she is thoroughly aware of it and, though sometimes depressed and puzzled about herself, she has not succumbed to despair. She has not retreated into herself. Most important of all, she has retained kindness and concern for other human beings. She has not come to hate men. She is a disciplined woman of stability and fixed character. She exerts self-control, and she shows a compassionate understanding of other people, even of Cecily. Indeed, she constitutes the best answer to those who hold that Faulkner, in his early novels at least, is a misogynist.

The most curious thing about this generally intelligent and sensible young woman is her failure to see that if Donald has to be married to anyone, his proper bride is Emmy, who has loved him all the time and loves him now. Rather late in the day,

Faulkner allows her to see this. On page 271 Margaret tells herself "that no one had done very much thinking during the whole affair, that it had got on without any particular drain on any intelligence." Had this occurred to Faulkner himself late in the novel? One wonders. Margaret goes on to ask herself: "Why did we take it for granted that he must marry Cecily and no other? Yet we all accepted it as an arbitrary fact and off we went with our eyes closed and our mouths open, like hounds in full cry."

So they did. Margaret at once tries to make up for lost time by asking Emmy (p. 273) whether she would marry Donald, only to be rebuffed. Emmy's pride is hurt: "Me marry him? Me take another's leavings?" But in a moment, as she fights back her tears, she finds herself "waiting for Mrs. Powers to ask her again" (p. 274). But Margaret, for once, isn't sufficiently perceptive. She doesn't ask Emmy again, and after Cecily has rushed in to tell the Rector that she will not, after all, marry Donald, Margaret volunteers to do so (p. 277). It is here that the machinery of the plot creaks most noisily.

A first novel is likely to reveal not only strained and improbable motivation but the overuse of coincidences and other contrived happenings, and the use of gimmicky devices. *Soldiers' Pay* is remarkably free of these. True, it is improbable that Margaret should have come by chance to the hometown of the very soldier who shot her husband, and that she should actually meet that soldier's mother. Faulkner might well have omitted the coincidence, for nothing would have been lost. The fastidious reader can dismiss it, if he likes, as a kind of unimportant excrescence on an otherwise simple and even austere plot.

I find only one episode that partakes of the gimmicky. The doctor has declared that he does not know what is keeping Donald alive. It is as if he is waiting for something to happen. On pages 292–94 we find what he had been waiting for: the recovery of his memory of the day on which he was shot down on the Western Front. Donald relives the experience, recovers his sight as he looks up into his father's face, tells him, "That's how it happened," and now is able to die in the knowledge of what had happened to him and in a recovered recognition of his father's presence.

The passage is rather brilliantly done, and, incidentally, it fleshes out Poem I of *A Green Bough*. With few changes in detail, Donald might be one of the living-dead aviators who appear in that poem. The story of Donald Mahon as told in *Soldiers' Pay* makes convincing sense of the experience that Poem I (originally entitled "The Lilacs") only fumbles at. Yet the episode contributes very little to the novel as a whole. We know generally what has turned Donald into a living-dead man, and the details scarcely have a bearing on the theme of the novel. The incident seems to have had no effect on the Rector. How could it, since Donald's brief remark, "That's how it happened," could hardly seem to be a return to intelligent consciousness on the part of his son, and since the account of what happened is not spoken by Donald at all: the Rector could have got it only through some miracle of thought-transference.

The strength of the novel, then, lies in its evocation of a world that is at loose ends, that has lost its confidence in past values and is caught in a malaise of disillusionment. The best scenes brilliantly dramatize the situation—including some of the comic scenes, for the novel is not lugubrious and never sentimentalizes the pathos of loss.

A further strength of this novel is the quality of the writing. It is written up to the hilt. As one would expect in the early work of a talented young writer, the style is uneven. But in general, the writing shows an enormous vitality. It is never languid or tepid. It reflects a largely self-taught genius and therefore intermingles brilliant writing with instances of the gauche and the maladroit.

A simple illustration is afforded in Faulkner's tendency to manufacture new adverbs. Julian Lowe tells Margaret something "youngly" (p. 52). Margaret's "windy dress molded her longly" (p. 104). Joe sits "brittly in his chair" (p. 39). The moon was "a coin broken palely" (p. 286). This proliferation of -ly forms doesn't matter much, but it is a rather clear indication of experimental awkwardness—or perhaps of a straining for literary effects—as are forced expressions not natural to Faulkner's own speech or to that of his characters. On page 138 we learn that Jones "stood *without* the closed door to the study"; Cecily, on page 217, is described as putting "her hand on the railing, *lest* she fall"; on page 272 we are told that "Night *was* come" (my italics in each example).

There are many repetitions of phrases. Some of these, like "the delirium of the sparrows" in the elm trees (pp. 57, 105, 185, 186), Faulkner clearly intended. But other cases of repetition are probably the result of oversights. A striking instance is his description of "a fanlight of dim-colored glass lovely with lack of washing" (p. 65). The second reference, a few pages further on (p. 78) to "a high fanlight of colored glass" is intentional, for the author has reason to refer to this second fanlight which is, as he tells us, "identical with the one above the entrance." But on page 89 occurs a disturbing, because now meaningless, repetition when we are forced to read once again of a "fanlight of muted color dim with age and lovely with lack of washing. . . ." It is a nice bit of description, but only forgetfulness could account for Faulkner's repeating it almost verbatim. Or is it forgetfulness? For on page 298 he writes: "Outside the window, afternoon became abruptly rain, without warning, with no flapping of pennons nor sound of trumpet to herald it." This sentence is repeated, word for word, one page later.[13] It is hard to believe that a copy editor or proofreader could have failed to call it to the author's attention. But Faulkner's early novels got very patchy editorial attention. On page 57, where passages are quoted from Horace, the word "gravida" is dropped from line three of "Integer Vitae" and a few lines later "quae loca fabulosus lambit Hydaspes" is reduced to nonsense by being printed "quae loac fabulosas" etc.

On page 222, Faulkner describes Cecily as follows: "Light in her hair was the thumbed rim of a silver coin, the divan embraced her quietly and light quietly followed the long slope of her limbs." Four pages later Faulkner, in what must surely be a deliberate repetition, writes that "The divan embraced [Cecily] in its

13. On page 191 he writes: "He was not big, yet there was something big and calm about him: a sense of competent inertia after activity." This sentence is repeated verbatim on page 202.

impersonal clasp. Light like the thumbed rim of a coin about her distinct face. . . ." On page 228 Faulkner uses the figure for a third time: "Her body was a vague white shape as he entered the room again and light was the thumbed rim of a coin about her head."

Faulkner is obviously trying to catch a special quality of light playing about her hair and face as a kind of nimbus. But what of the coin image? Does Faulkner mean that Cecily's head wore a halo something like the rim of a coin which reveals a band of bright silver around the thumb which all but covers it? Or does he mean simply that the coin was "thumbed" to smoothness and luster? The second meaning seems to be that which he was to use a year later in *Mosquitoes* (p. 48): "There was a moon, low in the sky and worn, thumbed partly away like an old coin. . . ." Yet if the second and simpler reading is all that is intended, was the elaboration insisted upon by being thrice repeated quite worth the effort?

Another figure perhaps too elaborate and too consciously striven for occurs on page 225. Faulkner writes: "The golden sand of hours bowled [that is, held as in a bowl] by day ran through the narrow neck of time into the corresponding globe of night, to be inverted and so flow back again. Jones felt the slow black sand of time marking his life away." Golden sand transmuted into black: yet one may fairly ask whether the verbal alchemy quite works. Is the golden sand made black merely by falling into the dark bowl of night? The analogy is blurred: it is not the inert sand resting in the darkened lower bowl that Jones sees as "marking his life away." It is the running sand—which ought to be golden. The young stylist is ambitious, perhaps too ambitious. He has elaborated the figure into a metaphysical conceit, but one that lacks the requisite precision for full success.

Passages such as these do not seem quite worth the effort that the writer has expended on them: his reach does exceed his grasp. But it is not always so. The writing in the novel is usually more than competent; some of it is dazzling, as in the following examples: Someone is "watching the streaming window panes, hearing the gray rain like a million little feet across the roof and in the trees" (p. 121); ". . . then he saw her and all his life went into his eyes leaving his body but an awkward, ugly gesture in unquicked clay" (p. 148); "His yellow eyes washed over her warm and clear as urine, and he said, 'God damn you' " (p. 226).

The last example is a nice instance of an effect carefully built toward and, after due preparation—Jones's eyes have several times been described as yellow and obscene—successfully achieved. In this climactic confrontation of Jones with Cecily, the image of yellow urine suddenly washing over the girl dramatically sums up the look that Jones bestows upon her.

For all its lapses, the style, I repeat, is the strength of the book. Description, atmosphere, mood—these Faulkner could manage very early, but, as one would expect, control of dramatic logic and the development of characters had to wait for artistic maturity.

Particular scenes are often brilliantly rendered. There is, for example, the rectory garden. As the Rector's special hermitage, it forms the perfect backdrop for his rather decadent poetic prose. But it is, as Faulkner renders it, a believable garden, with real flowers and the flicker of genuine sunshine. Or consider such vignettes as those of the small-town drugstore or the courthouse square on a Saturday afternoon with its "monotonous wagons drawn by long-eared mules," crawling along; or the afternoon scene at the depot, where people flock, not to take the incoming train but to watch it arrive, to see who gets on and who gets off and, most of all, simply for the sake of the walk and of something to do.

One of the finest of such scenes is that in which Faulkner describes the dance to which Margaret and Gilligan bring the invalid Donald so that he can hear the music. As Faulkner develops the scene, we sense the effect of jazz—the new music—on the young, who are letting themselves go and pretending to be very blasé about it, and the effect on the older generation, who find themselves disturbed by this barbaric music and a little scandalized by the motions that it sets up in the young. There are the wallflowers sharing their nervous misery in company with each other. There are the returned veterans, feeling out of place. They don't see themselves as returning heroes but as an awkward squad who don't know the new dance steps and, aged beyond their years, are somehow out of touch with the younger crowd. There is the stag line of local boys with their interest in the popular girls and especially Margaret Powers, the mysterious stranger. The young men give her the rush; one after another "breaks in" on her current partner, allowing him to take no more than a few steps with her.

These mood pieces and vignettes do more than provide depth and background for the little that happens in the novel. They are rather cunningly fitted together to reinforce the dominant mood. To those who have been touched by the War and have now come home, home has somehow been lost. The more sensitive feel themselves to be displaced persons.

The world of *Soldiers' Pay* is a predominantly white world. There are no Negro portraits like that of Dilsey in *The Sound and the Fury*. Negroes are to be seen everywhere in the town, but the author offers almost no individual treatment of any one of them. Yet one misreads this novel if he finds in Faulkner's treatment mere unsympathetic stereotyping. Even in his first novel, Faulkner was too good an artist to distort the ways in which his various characters would refer to Negroes. We rather expect George Farr to yell at the Negro boy who approaches him. The boy is bringing a letter, as he quietly explains, thus "shaming [Farr] with better breeding." And Joe Gilligan, though he is treated as essentially a decent person, is allowed to say—what he probably would say— "But here comes Othello" (p. 107) when he sees a Negro pushing a lawnmower.

Later, when Joe goes to the railroad station to see Margaret off, he tosses a coin to a Negro boy who happens to be standing near the platform, telling him to look out for her bags, but then Joe turns to Margaret in exasperation: "Damn 'em, they do what you say, but they make you feel so—so—" When Margaret suggests the word "immature," Joe seizes on it: "That's it. Like you was a kid or something . . ." (p. 302). If Faulkner in his depiction of the Negroes departs from reality, it is in the direction of a kind of black mystique: the Negro, it is implied, is able to see through the white man's distractions and obsessions.

Where is Charlestown, Georgia? It is no more to be found on a map than is Jefferson, Mississippi. In certain ways these two imaginary towns are much alike. In the Jefferson of 1909, Quentin Compson remembers pigeons that "strutted and crooned [around the steeple of the church] or wheeled in short courses resembling soft fluid paint smears on the soft summer sky," and in 1919 in Charlestown, "pigeons about the church spire leaned upon it like silver and slanting splashes of soft paint" (p. 104). Mrs. Worthington of Charlestown has a cousin whose articulation is bad. He had "been struck in the mouth with an ax in a dice game in Cuba during the Spanish-American War" (p. 187). Curiously enough, Major de Spain of Jefferson, Mississippi, is alleged to have suffered a similar injury, inflicted in a dice game in Cuba, in the same year. Evidently the creator of Charlestown and Jefferson had difficulty in distinguishing between them. Thus, though technically *Soldiers' Pay* is not one of the Yoknapatawpha County novels, in setting and atmosphere and in the kind of people to be met with in it, it is not dissimilar.

We usually think of the publication of *Sartoris* in 1929 as marking Faulkner's first attempt to take Sherwood Anderson's advice that he write about "that little patch up there in Mississippi where you started from." But if Charlestown, like Jefferson, is modeled upon Oxford, Mississippi, why not shift the date of that first attempt back to 1926? There are good reasons for not doing so, I think. In *Soldiers' Pay* the regional setting is given no special significance. It is not even seen in full perspective. Joe Gilligan, for example, may have come from almost anywhere. If he does come from outside the region, however, it is curious that he never remarks on the differences in speech and manners and cooking that he finds in Charlestown—neither by way of complaint nor approval, as an outsider might be expected to do, especially a man who is as outspoken as Joe is and as sharp in his powers of observation.

There is something to be said for a writer's being so deeply immersed in the customs and folkways of his own society that it doesn't occur to him there is anything special about them. The wrong kind of self-consciousness leads to "local color" literature and the exploiting of regional peculiarities for the amusement of the outsider. Yet one can't truly know one's own society if he knows nothing else. Besides, an important element in the character of Faulkner's own region is its very consciousness of its difference from the rest of the nation. In a later novel, *Intruder in the Dust,* Faulkner was to indicate how intense this awareness could be by taking us into the thoughts of the boy Chick Mallison.

In writing *Soldiers' Pay,* however, Faulkner makes very little use of that difference. Three years later, in *Sartoris,* the principal events of which also take place in 1919, the malaise of the returning soldiers is set off in part by reference to Jefferson's history, to the Sartoris family tradition, to the continuities of the countryside, and to the relatively unchanged cultural state of the yeoman whites and the Negroes. In *Soldiers' Pay* there are no more than hints of these matters. The principal exception is what Faulkner makes of the black community. He consistently presents the blacks as calmer, wiser, still strong in religious faith, and thus less shaken by the War than are the disaffected whites who have been tossed by the winds of change blowing out of the great world beyond Charlestown. But except for the Negroes, Charlestown, Georgia, might just as well have been Charlestown, New Hampshire, or Charlestown, Indiana.

4

Sketches, Early Stories,
&
an Abortive Novel

FAULKNER'S SOJOURN in New Orleans during the first six months of 1925 produced not merely his more than promising first novel but the collection of sketches and abbreviated short stories that Carvel Collins some years ago assembled and edited under the title of *New Orleans Sketches*. But the *New Orleans Sketches* are, generally speaking, as flat and banal as *Soldiers' Pay* is brilliant and exciting. The reminder that the writing of these works went on at the same time may therefore come with something of a shock.

The obvious way to account for the difference is to say that most of the New Orleans material was written for a newspaper audience, written too, one supposes, in a hurry, and written frankly to make money. Faulkner obviously also hoped to make some money from *Soldiers' Pay,* and there is nothing wrong, of course, in writing for money; that wise observer Dr. Samuel Johnson once remarked that only a blockhead did not write for money. But there is a difference between hoping that a work that one simply had to write will sell and deliberately fabricating a story or article because one knows there is a buyer for this sort of thing. Too much of the prose that makes up the *New Orleans Sketches* is perfunctory.

If this view is correct, it has application to Faulkner's later career—to the stories he wrote in order to pay the grocery bill when his finest novels were not selling and to the trips out to Hollywood to work as a script doctor. Blotner's biography of Faulkner is full of this sort of thing. Thomas L. McHaney has put the matter tactfully but accurately in saying, "Faulkner was a serious novelist who wrote short stories rapidly and skillfully to help earn the money he needed to finance the writing of more ambitious, more difficult novels, which did not sell. Faulkner's stories were just like his work in Hollywood . . . except they were a lot better." [1]

Is it fair, however, to call the material published in *New Orleans Sketches* stories at all? The first eleven of them are certainly not, nor were they written for a newspaper but rather for *The Double Dealer,* a serious "little" magazine that flourished in New Orleans between January 1921 and May 1926. They bear such titles as "Wealthy Jew," "The Priest," "The Cobbler," etc. They could be called impressionistic accounts of men and women. Those accounts represent general types, and in this respect might be defined as "Theophrastan characters." The longer and more fully developed of them do perhaps imply a story. Two of them, "Frankie and Johnny" and "The Cobbler," were subsequently developed into brief short stories, the form in which they appeared in the New Orleans *Times-Picayune.* All of the *Times-Picayune* series have to be judged as short stories, and, however ineffective we may consider them to be, they constitute the first short stories —or indeed examples of fiction—that Faulkner ever published.

However limited, however perfunctory, the works of a man of genius are rarely completely unrewarding. After all, they are the product of the same mind, even it it is running at only half-throttle, that produced the masterpieces. The *New Orleans Sketches,* then, give us echoes of Faulkner's reading and occasional anticipations of themes and images that appear in his mature work.

In his excellent introduction to the *New Orleans Sketches,* Carvel Collins has listed a number of these anticipations. For

1. "The Elmer Papers: Faulkner's Comic Portrait of the Artist," *Mississippi Quarterly* 26 (1973) : 306.

instance, in "Out of Nazareth" there is a reference to the "calm belief" of a pregnant woman "that nature will care for her," a faith that anticipates the confidence of Lena Grove in *Light in August*. In "The Kingdom of God" there is an idiot who has cornflower-blue eyes just like those of the idiot Benjy in *The Sound and the Fury*. Also like Benjy, he clutches in his hand a narcissus flower with broken stem. In "The Liar" a horse runs through a house as one of the spotted ponies does in *The Hamlet*. In "Yo Ho and Two Bottles of Rum" a corpse, obviously decomposing under a hot sun, has, nevertheless, to be carried to a particular burial place, just as was the corpse of Addie Bundren in *As I Lay Dying*. In "The Kid Learns" there is a reference to Francis of Assisi's "Little Sister Death," who as a "shining one" greets the Kid just before he dies. In *Mayday* Sir Galwyn is to see her just before he goes to his death in the river, and though we are not told in *The Sound and the Fury* that such a being beckons to Quentin Compson before he steps into the Charles, Saint Francis's Little Sister Death does come into his thoughts more than once during the day on which he commits suicide. (For other such anticipations that Collins has pointed out, the reader should consult his introduction, pp. xxviii–xxx.)

I can suggest a few additional examples. In "The Cobbler" we are told that "the great stars were loud as bells in the black sky, loud as great golden-belled sheep cropping the hill of heaven" (p. 68). In *The Hamlet* it is the cumulus clouds that (much more convincingly) are compared to sheep. In the sketch entitled "The Longshoreman" (p. 9) there is a reference to the coldness of the stars as contrasting with the warmth of the earth which is "heated by the dead buried in it." Faulkner was to develop this passage in a different way and much more effectively in "The Old People" (p. 186), where McCaslin Edmonds explains why his young cousin had seen the spectral buck. The dead, McCaslin tells the lad, haunt the earth because they hate to leave it. They don't need the sky "where the scoured and icy stars glittered." Here, to be sure, the emphasis is not upon the earth "heated" by the dead, but upon the dead dreading the cold of the astral spaces. But the two passages obviously turn upon the same thought: the warmth of the earth (whether given to the earth by the dead or itself giving heat to the dead) as opposed to the appalling iciness of the heavens. The image of the "sparrows delirious in a mimosa" in "Out of Nazareth" (p. 47) is repeated in four or five variations in *Soldiers' Pay*, but, as we have noted above, this may not be technically an anticipation, since Faulkner was writing *Soldiers' Pay* at about the same time as he was composing the *New Orleans Sketches*.

One of the first things that one notices about the *Sketches* is how "literary" they are. The writer is obviously enchanted with language, and the style is frequently stilted and occasionally high-falutin. Sometimes even the grammar used is archaic, apparently in order to render it more "poetic." Faulkner discovers phrases that please him and uses them more than once. For example, in the little character sketch entitled "Wealthy Jew," Faulkner has his wealthy man say, "I love three things: gold, marble and purple; splendor, solidity, color." In his second novel *Mosquitoes* (p. 340), the curiously named "Semitic man" also says: "I love three things: gold, marble and purple—." Michael Millgate [2] has pointed out that Faulkner's source is Gautier's *Mlle. de Maupin:* "Trois choses me plaisent: l'or, le marbre et le pourpre, éclat, solidité, couleur."

The influence of A. E. Housman, which shows so powerfully in Faulkner's poetry, particularly from the fall of 1924 onward, is, as we might expect, strong in the *Sketches*. For instance, the speaker in Poem XLIX of *A Shropshire Lad* says that " 'tis only thinking / Lays lads underground." In Faulkner's "Home," Jean-Baptiste (p. 28) agrees that "Thinking, indeed, lays lads underground."

In another sketch ("Out of Nazareth," pp. 48–49), as we have noted earlier, Faulkner retells the story of his own discovery of a copy of *A Shropshire Lad,* this time putting it in the mouth of the young Middle Westerner, David, whom Spratling and the narrator encounter in New Orleans. Spratling asks David "if he had read Elizabeth Browning or Robert Frost." He had not— never heard of them. He is not "literary." He has simply come upon, quite by accident, verse that speaks to his own heart.

2. *The Achievement of William Faulkner* (New York, 1966), p. 300.

David has written something himself, which he shyly offers to show to Spratling and his companion. Faulkner quotes this composition in full; it is clearly meant to be the high point of the sketch. The "I" who tells "Out of Nazareth" apologizes for the young man's bad punctuation and misspellings, but he remarks that "to correct it would ruin it," and it is plain that the young Faulkner himself regarded it as a fine instance of natural, straightforward prose, the report of a personal experience by one who possesses the innocent eye. Or was Faulkner partially aware that he had here produced a piece of manufactured primitivism? He has the "I" who tells the story describe it as "blundering and childish and 'arty,' " even though he maintains that it has "something back of it." The atmosphere of David's account is a kind of Whitmanian camaraderie, the fellowship of the open road and of the beautiful trust of the young in life and other human beings. His attempt to express this vision may account for the "arty" artlessness of the style. Whatever one's final judgment of the merit of David's composition, it makes an odd contrast to the often mannered style that Faulkner uses in most of the other sketches.

This mannered style sometimes amounts to "translation prose." "Jealousy," for example, is full of "literary" diction and stilted locutions. The setting for this story is a New Orleans restaurant; the time is the 1920s; the principal characters are of Italian stock. The story opens with the restaurant owner's question to his wife: "Knitting again, eh?" To which his wife replies: "As you see, caro mio." But the characters do not speak broken English or even colloquial English. Their language is right out of Sir Walter Scott, or perhaps some nineteenth-century translation of Dumas. Thus, when the husband reproaches his wife, his rebuke takes this form: "Would you have me pay wages to one that you might sit all day like a great lady, knitting with your gossips?" Not to be outdone, the wife at one point exclaims to her insanely jealous husband: "What would you have? Was it not you who put me here?"

The young waiter, who has aroused the husband's jealous suspicions, uses a lingo just as artificial. He addresses his boss like this: "You are already mad. Had you not been I should have killed you *ere this* [italics mine]" (p. 37). Even those sentences provided by the author himself take on the strained quality of translation English. Thus: "The younger man's body sprang like a poised sword, his fire seemed *to make light the walls* [italics mine]."

In the longer of the two pieces that are entitled "The Cobbler," there is perhaps some justification for the rather affected English. The story begins with a comment by the cobbler: "You wan' getta thees shoe today? Si, si. Yes, I coma from—tella in my tongue? Buono signor." But then the cobbler immediately shifts into a very different sort of English as Faulkner attempts to provide a fitting vehicle for the story of the old man's early life in Italy. The cobbler begins his story thus: "Yes, I come from Tuscany, from the mountains, where the plain is gold and brown in the barren sun. . . ." But at the very end, when he has finished his nostalgic account of life in the old country and of the loss of his sweetheart, Faulkner has him suddenly revert to the dialect that he actually speaks: "You getta thees shoe today. Si, si.

It is possible to see in this device an anticipation of the technique that Faulkner used five years later when he wrote *As I Lay Dying*. The characters in that novel, when they speak their inmost thoughts, shift from the north Mississippi hill dialect in which they ordinarily address one another into a diction far beyond their actual cultural level. It is a defensible convention, and in *As I Lay Dying*, of course, it is used brilliantly. There is nothing particularly strange in a young writer's using a hyperliterary style or in experimenting with various kinds of styles and, in doing so, reflecting his reading or, in the course of his experiments, exhibiting the awkwardnesses that are natural at an early stage of development. The staple of prose in these essays and embryonic stories is on the whole actually rather good, and quite fine passages occur. What are surprising are the lapses in idiom and grammar and certain mistakes in diction—attributable perhaps to the fact that Faulkner was largely a self-educated man.[3]

3. In a very important sense, every first-rate writer has had to educate himself, but Faulkner's rather sketchy formal training made him more liable to lapses which, though not very important in themselves, are more flagrant than might be expected.

For example, in "Sunset" Faulkner writes: "To eat he could not, so he decided to find a safe place to sleep" (p. 81); or in "Yo Ho and Two Bottles of Rum": "Mr. Ayers . . . saw something there that gave him to pause" (p. 126). In "Magdalen" the girl meditates: "I can remember when I found days gold, but now the gold of day hurts my head. 'Tis night only is gold now, and that not often" (pp. 12–13).

Turning from style to structure, one has to say that the sleaziness of the plots of most of the stories hints at their perfunctory nature. Whereas "Out of Nazareth" may well have been founded on something that actually happened to Faulkner in New Orleans —he puts his friend Spratling into the story by name and the narrator is obviously Faulkner himself—most of the stories are gimmicky, with trick endings and contrived surprises. The construction of several of them amounts to no more than the forced exploitation of a specific idea. Although insofar as I know Faulkner never refers to O. Henry's stories, he was certainly familiar with them, just as he was obviously familiar with the stories of another popular, and gimmicky, writer of magazine fiction, Irvin S. Cobb.[4]

Stories like "The Rosary" and "Chance" fairly reek of O. Henry. The latter story tells how a panhandler in the New Orleans French Quarter finds a copper cent in the gutter, how that penny subsequently turns into a five-dollar gold piece and then into $2,000 and, finally, during the course of this incredible day, shrinks again to a copper cent, which the panhandler at last flings into the gutter from which it came.

"Cheest" probably owes something in its situation and the manner of its telling to Anderson's "I'm a Fool," a story that Faulkner much admired; but whereas Anderson's story has poignance and resonance, "Cheest" is cheap and tinny. Faulkner was seeing a good deal of Anderson in New Orleans during the period in which he was writing these New Orleans stories. Perhaps the

---

One must take into account, however, the fact that some of the mistakes in spelling, grammar, and in the choice of diction may have to be laid to the typesetter. There was evidently scanty proofreading or, more probably, none at all.

4. See below, Notes, pp. 375–76.

most successful of the stories influenced by Anderson is "Out of Nazareth," where the narrative supposedly written by the young wanderer seems a serious imitation of Anderson's style as opposed to the parody of Anderson's style that Faulkner did in 1926 in the introduction that he provided for Spratling's *Sherwood Anderson and Other Famous Creoles.*

I should add that the most fully pervading aspect of Anderson's influence on Faulkner was Anderson's notion of the "grotesques." The first section of his *Winesburg, Ohio* is titled "The Book of the Grotesque," and in it the storyteller explains that the moment someone takes "one of the [various kinds of truth] to himself, [calls] it his truth, and [tries] to live his life by it, he [becomes] a grotesque and the truth he [embraces becomes] a falsehood." Anderson's fictive Winesburg numbers a good many such grotesques, and his famous book is a series of their case histories. Faulkner's cluster of *Times-Picayune* contributions thus bears a not too farfetched resemblance to the makeup of *Winesburg.* The little jockey in "Cheest," the pathological practical joker in "The Rosary," and the black man trying to get to Africa in "Sunset" can all be regarded as Andersonian grotesques—and, for that matter, so can some of the characters in Faulkner's later short stories. Miss Emily Grierson, in "A Rose for Emily," and Miss Zilphia Gant, in the story that bears her name as its title, are obvious examples.[5]

Some of these Faulknerian grotesques are believable; others put our credibility to severe tests. There is probably less strain on the reader's acceptance when the writer is trying to explore a character that he has himself known; far more, when he starts with an idea and devises a character to fit it. "Sunset" is rather obviously a story contrived in the process of developing an idea, and it reads as if the idea lying behind it and determining its form and structure amounted to something like this:

Suppose you had a Negro man who thought that Africa would provide an end to all his troubles but who knew no more about it than that his people had come from it originally and that, since

5. Faulkner's attitude toward Sherwood Anderson was complex. I shall have more to say about it in the next chapter.

lions and other ferocious beasts roamed wild there, you had better keep your gun handy. Suppose further that this man had no real notion of where Africa was beyond knowing that you had to get on a boat to go there, and suppose that in his complete innocence he could be made to believe that it was only a few hours' journey away.

What would happen to such a man if he encountered a white man who humored his delusions—either dismissing them as insane, or accepting them as grotesquely funny, or simply taking advantage of them for the small profit involved—and therefore, for a fee, undertook to deposit the black man in Africa? And suppose the "Africa" in question was a bank of the Mississippi inhabited by French-speaking "Cajuns," whose language could only be incomprehensible gibberish to the Negro? What might happen then?

The countryside is alarmed at the presence in their midst of what seems to be a madman. For, in the darkness, believing that he is in Africa, the deluded black man shoots a "lion" (in reality, a cow). Then he shoots at one of the Cajuns and, a few moments later, shoots at a black man who impedes his flight. The National Guard is called out. and the simple black man who believes that he is now in darkest Africa is killed. Thus, the story is one that turns on a series of funny (or tragic) mistakes. It lays too heavy a claim upon our belief in the black man's more than childish ignorance; and, at the end, it makes a blatant appeal to our pity. "The gale [of machine-gun bullets] died away, and all broken things were still. His black, kind, dull, once-cheerful face was turned up to the sky and the cold, cold stars. Africa or Louisiana: what care they?"

What care they indeed? Nature is indifferent, and as for the black man's fellow human beings, presumably including his fellow blacks, one of whom he has wounded or killed, they have put him down as a homicidal maniac, and not a poor deluded human being who simply wants to return to his ancestral home. But what else would the people of any society think? Common sense asserts itself and cancels out the too obvious bid for pity with which "Sunset" ends.

It may be useful here to compare "Sunset" with an accomplished short story that Faulkner wrote only five years later, "Dry September," in which Will Mayes, the black man who dies at the hands of the whites, is thoroughly credible. It could be argued that Mayes also dies, as the hero of "Sunset" dies, as the result of a mistake—of Miss Minnie Cooper's neurotic fancy in supposing that he had made advances to her. But the "mistake" is not any mistake made by him. He does not fire into the dark under the delusion that a cow is a lion and that the human beings he hears are really murderous savages. He owes his death in great part to a social climate, and he is no more responsible for what happens to him on this hot September night than if a black cloud had unaccountably formed and out of it had blazed a thunderbolt that struck him down.

Faulkner has carefully underplayed the reaction of Will Mayes when he is first accosted. " 'What is it captains?' the Negro said. 'I aint done nothing. 'Fore God, Mr John.' " He is surprised, bewildered, and now beginning to be scared. Later, when he has been pushed toward the car, handcuffs snapped on his wrists, and has been dealt a blow by one of the white men, he suddenly "whirled and cursed them, and swept his manacled hands across their faces. . . ." Later still, the Negro appeals once more to the one white man in the car whom he feels he knows and in whom resides his only hope: " 'Mr. Henry. . . . Mr. Henry' " (*Collected Stories*, p. 179).

Instead of insisting upon the actions and outcries of the Negro victim, Faulkner's mode of understatement in this instance provides emphasis. He directs our attention to the forces that move to destroy the Negro: there is the masterfully handled scene in the barber shop in which the lynching fever begins to heat up— rumor, outrage, real or pretended, that a white woman should have been insulted. We hear not only the voices of the local bully boys but also that of an outsider: ". . . you can count on me, even if I aint only a drummer and a stranger."

In Part II of the story there follows a brilliant sketch of the victim of Will's alleged black lust, Miss Minnie Cooper, thirty-eight or -nine, who more and more has come to live in a world of "furious unreality" as she glides through her "idle and empty days." There is as leitmotiv constant reference to the dry September heat ("the vitiated air," "the lifeless air," the "glare beneath the dust") which, if it does not precipitate the lynching, at least comes to seem the appropriate atmosphere for this violent though sterile gesture.

One feature of "Dry September" that sets it apart from most stories about lynching violence is the way in which Faulkner has skillfully and very subtly and quietly taken account of the social backgrounds of the characters in this story. This is an element that is hardly to be found in the New Orleans stories that we have been discussing. Their brevity allowed no room for it, and Faulkner knew that the public for whom he was writing did not want it except in the broadest terms—an obvious French Quarter rat, an obvious Italian immigrant working in a shoe-repair shop, an obvious prostitute.

In "Dry September," to be sure, Faulkner does not explicitly refer to the social background of each of his characters, but allows the background to emerge through the speech and act and gesture of the character. He has, for example, been careful to place "Miss Minnie" in exact relation to the community as we learn about her as an individual. "She was of comfortable people—not the best in Jefferson, but good people enough. . . . She was the last to realize that she was losing ground. . . . That was when her face began to wear that bright, haggard look." Her schoolmates began to tell their children "in bright voices about how popular Aunt Minnie had been as a girl. Then the town began to see her driving on Sunday afternoons with the cashier in the bank. . . . Then the town began to say 'Poor Minnie'" (pp. 173–74). (Her situation is generally analogous to that of Miss Emily in "A Rose for Emily," but how different are the women involved!)

The social context is of course important and meaningful: for the tragedy is in a sense a community action, though only certain elements of the community are directly responsible. But the tendency to treat an individual character in terms of his social and community relationship is a characteristic of all of Faulkner's best fiction. As Eudora Welty once remarked to me: if you can hear a

Faulkner character speak two or three sentences, you can "place" him immediately. (Part II of this story, if treated as a "sketch," entitled, perhaps, "A Spinster," and put beside the sketches that Faulkner contributed to *The Double Dealer*, would make any of those "portraits" look pale indeed.)

Faulkner has extended and intensified the tragedy by a further device. Though "Mr. Henry," the barber, to whom Will Mayes appeals, comes from the same general social class as the other men gathered in the barber shop, he defends Mayes and thus exposes himself to the taunt of "niggerlover." He insists that Mayes could not have been guilty, and his appeal to reason encourages one other member of the group to speak up with words of moderation: "Now, now. Let's figure this thing out. Who knows anything about what really happened?" But the voice of a certain violent young man named McLendon finally prevails, and he leads a party out to get Mayes. Henry rushes out of the barber shop after them in time to get into the car, and members of the lynching party assume that he has changed his mind and is joining them. But, as the car drives off, he still is insisting that "Will Mayes never done it."

Yet when the Negro, being beaten by those trying to put him in the car, strikes back with his manacled hands, he "slashed the barber upon the mouth, and the barber [through reflex action? hysteric compulsion?] struck him also" (p. 178). The barber nurses "his mouth with his handkerchief" and a few minutes later asks to be let out of the car. "Jump out, niggerlover," is the leader's taunt; and after Mayes's last appeal, the barber does manage to get the door open and jumps out of the swiftly moving vehicle. This quasi-hysterical and useless gesture is as much of a protest as the barber can manage, but Faulkner leaves the focus on this gesture and does not try to make us privy to the barber's thoughts as he climbed out of the ditch "onto the road and limped on toward town."

Does the title of this story have a special significance? Is it a fair inference from the story that a dry September triggered the lynching in the same way that, as many newspapers later were to suggest, a "long, hot summer" (another Faulkner title) might trigger a riot in a black ghetto? References to the weather recur through-out the story, and in the opening scene someone in the barber shop exclaims: "It's this durn weather. It's enough to make a man do anything." Even so, Faulkner is too good a social historian and too good a psychologist to identify the climate of lynching with a meteorological condition. Moreover, he is too good an artist to use "Nature" as the compelling cause of human actions.

The "bloody September twilight," the aftermath of "sixty-two rainless days," does exacerbate feelings, does set men's nerves on edge, and demands a release for their pent-up hostilities. But there must first be feelings to be exacerbated and hostilities that de-mand expression. In any case, the "bloody September twilight" will get its emotional quality largely from the human beings who project their states of mind upon it. Only thus will it come to seem the inevitable symbol of a certain atmosphere of menace and violence. Or let us treat "bloody twilight" as a metaphor: like any good metaphor, it partakes of both the terms that it unites. The "blood" in the "bloody September twilight" does not simply smear the hands of the lynchers, nor does it simply receive its sanguine hue from their own thoughts. It is a proper intermediary, bloody in both ways. If we say that the "bloody September twi-light" has received its blood from the "wan hemorrhage of the moon" (p. 177), we are back with the same problem: in what sense is it meaningful to think of the moonlight as a "hemor-rhage"? In any case, whence does the moon get its blood? Faulkner has here simply reinforced his original metaphor by presenting it in variant form. It is almost as if he spoke here of a "lyncher's moon" on analogy with a "harvest moon" or a "hunter's moon."

Contrast the last sentences of "Dry September" with the crude and imperfectly formed "Sunset." "Sunset" ends with the "black, once-cheerful face" of the dead man turned up to the unpitying "cold, cold stars." "Dry September" also ends with a glance at the stars: "The dark world seemed to lie stricken beneath the cold moon and the lidless stars." But how different the effect! In the latter story the face that is turned up to the stars is not unseeing. It is the living, contorted face of the lyncher, McLendon, now re-turned from his mission, standing on the porch of his house. He is sweating, "and, with his body pressed against the dusty screen, . . . panting," tense, unappeased, unfulfilled, in a world in which there seems "no movement, no sound, not even an insect," under the gaze of "the lidless stars."

The reference to the "lidless stars"—staring, accusing eyes, fixed on the black man's murderer—makes a powerful and considered indictment of McLendon, a human being who has killed a fellow human being out of his own distorted and frustrated humanity. By contrast, the reference to "the cold, cold stars" in "Sunset" amounts to little more than a sentimental bid for pity. The victim in "Sunset" dies, in good part, because of his own incredible naiveté. Will Mayes has been done to death through no mistake of his own, and the community has to assume the burden of guilt.

If the reader asks whether it is really fair to compare the fiction included in the *New Orleans Sketches* with a story written some five years later, the answer has to be yes: the comparison provides a striking example of Faulkner's growth. Faulkner, to be sure, wrote better stories than "Sunset" in some of his other New Orleans fiction of the period. "The Liar," in spite of its trick ending, has some good moments in it, and "Episode," save for its somewhat too obvious conclusion, is really quite good. But then "Sunset" is not the worst of the collection either, and it does provide a good example of where and how these stories fail.

Yet, as I have said, it is even more startling to compare the fiction in *New Orleans Sketches* with the fiction that in its composition is exactly contemporary with the writing of the *Sketches*. I mean, of course, *Soldiers' Pay*, which is, with all its faults, a brilliant first novel, written with power and conviction. How is one to account for the difference? I have already suggested that in *Soldiers' Pay* Faulkner was writing with full commitment and pouring into the work his creative energy, whereas the *New Orleans Sketches* were written perfunctorily—written with his left hand. The generating motive was the need to earn a few dollars, and the performance was cursory, even lackadaisical. One may, however, suggest some other ways of accounting for the difference. Though with *Soldiers' Pay* Faulkner did not discover Yoknapatawpha County, in this novel he was at least dealing with familiar material. He could take an insider's view. "Charlestown, Ga.," whatever its exact relation to Oxford, Miss., is clearly a Southern town. New Orleans is in the South too, yet it represents a very special part of the South. It is Latin, whereas most of the rest of the South is Anglo-Saxon; Roman Catholic, whereas almost all the rest is aggressively Protestant; and it possesses a cuisine, an architecture, and a way of life that appear exotic to the Southerner who comes to it from anywhere outside south Louisiana.

The impact of New Orleans on the young Faulkner was powerful and exhilarating. It stimulated him and released his creative energies. One remembers how much writing Faulkner did during the year 1925. But an exploitation of the exotic and the romantic were not to constitute Faulkner's strengths. His genius required another milieu and another challenge: that of exploring the meaning of what to him was familiar and ordinary. He had to be an insider as well as an outsider. Hemingway thrived on writing as an outsider. As the expatriate American wandering through Italy or Spain, he found the proper scene and background for what he had to say about modern man. Not so with Faulkner, and therefore, though the New Orleans experience undoubtedly contributed to his literary development, little of his best fiction has a New Orleans setting. The fault lay not with New Orleans as such, but with Faulkner's lack of roots in what, for him, was an alien culture. Most of the characters in the sketches and short short stories that make up the Carvel Collins collection are, in one way or another, uprooted people: a wealthy Jew, a cobbler who has been born in Tuscany and still had a longing for it; a tourist; an immigrant from France; a young American wanderer, and so on. These were the types that caught Faulkner's eye. (Perhaps the answer is even more simple: they were the kinds of people that the readers of the *Times-Picayune* would consider sufficiently "different" to be worth writing about.)

Faulkner had come to New Orleans in order to take ship for Europe, but in fact had remained there much longer than he had originally planned. Now, with his first novel completed, on 7 July 1925 he and his friend William Spratling finally did sail for Europe on the *West Ivis*. Faulkner's months in Europe were even more stimulating than those in New Orleans, as his letters home and his fiction made evident. Even though his whole European adventure extended only from July to December, he absorbed in those months material that would appear in short stories published years later. But the special fruit of his stay abroad was *Elmer,* an unfinished novel, which not only recounts a young American painter's trip to Europe, but which was written on the scene. That he found or seized upon the time to write so much as he did in days presumably devoted to sight-seeing is itself interesting. Faulkner did plenty of sight-seeing: the pages of *Elmer* and of the short stories are full of scenes observed on his travels. Apparently his superlative energy allowed him to devote a remarkable lot of time to both, and as the pages of *Elmer* show, the sight-seeing and the writing were intimately related. Even Faulkner's brief visit to England, which perhaps lasted no more than a week, furnished the pictures of the English countryside so vividly presented in his story "The Leg" (1934).

By far the most detailed account of the still unpublished novel *Elmer* is Thomas L. McHaney's excellent article (cited above, in note 1). In the discussion that follows, I have relied upon it heavily, not only because of its sound insights and judgments, but because it will constitute for my readers the only readily accessible summary of the plot, description of characters, and compendium of direct quotations from *Elmer.*

Elmer was to be the story of the development of a painter from confused and fumbling boyhood, through growth and adolescence, on up to his marriage in young manhood. Faulkner's general model was clearly Joyce's *Portrait of the Artist as a Young Man.* (For proof that he knew the work early, see p. 132, below.) Just as Joyce takes pains to show Stephen Dedalus's growing fascination with words, Faulkner makes a great deal of Elmer Hodge's sensitivity to colors and the associations that various hues held for him. For instance, as a boy, Stephen felt that "Suck was a queer word. . . . the sound was ugly." He associates it with a time when his "father pulled the stopper [in the lavatory] up by the chain . . . and the dirty water went down through the hole in the basin. And when it had all gone down slowly the hole in the basin made a sound like that, suck. Only louder. To remember that and the white look of the lavatory made him feel cold and then hot."

Faulkner makes quite as elaborate play with Elmer's emotional reaction to the color red. For him it means the "red horror" of the night in which the Hodges' house burned, and the color of the throats of his brothers as they wailed their anguish; but much later on he comes to associate red with something very different: his first experience of sex. He remembers the girl's "full red mouth [was] never completely closed." Only much later still does Elmer finally come to terms with the color and see it as simply one element in a complex relationship of colors, having at last come to realize that "no color has any value, any significance save in its relation to other colors seen or suggested or imagined" (p. 289). Earlier, other colors had their special associations. Elmer associated war, for some reason, with brown and blue, and for a time he had, like Picasso, a "blue" period.

In the matter of Elmer's sexual development, Faulkner's account is more specific and more complicated than is Joyce's account of Stephen Dedalus. Faulkner attempts to take us from the first vague intimations of sex as felt by the boy on up to his first coupling with a girl and his affair with Ethel, whom he impregnates but who refuses to marry him as having no prospects and who chooses another man for husband so as to provide a name for Elmer's child.

From the boy's first childish curiosities about the human body and about sex, Faulkner traces Elmer's passage through several important stages. There is Jo-Addie, Elmer's sister, somewhat older than he, whom he adores and who will sometimes allow him to share her bed, though she refuses to let him touch her. There is also Elmer's crush on a handsome boy who is his classmate in the fourth grade. But the boy makes Elmer the butt of a joke that precludes any advances even if Elmer had been really aware of what he wanted of his classmate. Readers who are looking for an incestuous copulation or a homosexual encounter will be disappointed. In *Elmer* Faulkner is simply suggesting the young child's sexual development from vague, generalized and undifferentiated sexual feelings to heterosexual love.

116

In Elmer's case, the sexual development merges with his development as an artist. When the young Elmer makes drawings, they are of such "phallic" images as smokestacks and armless people of tubular shape, and later he will feel a special fascination in handling his tubes of paint, fingering "lasciviously smooth dull silver tubes virgin yet at the same time pregnant" (p. 291). This is (perhaps unconsciously) to have it both ways. But then the artist usually has to have it both ways, and Faulkner as artist especially: furious motion that is at the same time completely arrested, yearnings to be fulfilled and yet always arrested on the brink of fulfillment, "Bold lover, never, never canst thou kiss, / Though winning near the goal. . . ."

The novel, however, has to do with more than Elmer's sexual and artistic development. There is his later meeting with Ethel and her husband and his seeing for the first time the features of his own son; his experience in World War I; his trip to Italy and Paris in pursuit of Myrtle Monson, a girl with whom he has fallen in love and who is doing a tour of Europe in company with her mother. For Elmer's adventures in Europe, Faulkner drew heavily on his recent voyage from New Orleans to Genoa and his trip to Paris. Such scenes were fresh in his mind; the Parisian scenes lay all about him as he wrote out his novel, and some of these scenes constitute the best writing in the book. But Faulkner was up to much more than a travelogue, and more, even, than a serious treatment of the vicissitudes of a young artist occupied with the problem of finding means to articulate his vision of reality.

Elmer was to be a satiric novel and something of a novel of manners, in which the American tourist and the American female culture-vulture were to be exhibited in a comic light. Mrs. Monson, Myrtle's mother, is cast in both roles. But the would-be artist Elmer was to be treated comically too. In spite of Faulkner's rather sympathetic treatment of his growing up, he meant to make Elmer a somewhat ludicrous innocent abroad. So also with some of Elmer's transatlantic acquaintances, particularly the English nobility, some of the more poverty-stricken of whom needed to marry American heiresses and who in turn were sought out by American women eager to provide titles for their daughters.

117

Faulkner finds such matters amusing, and at times he is able to generate shrewd comic touches from them, as, for example, the passage in which Mrs. Monson receives expert advice as to why it will be more socially advantageous for her to embrace Roman Catholicism than to become an Anglican. Faulkner's English noblemen, however, are farcical characters, arrant humors personified rather than credible human beings. Perhaps because he realized that his portraits of them were literary disasters, he soon abandoned the novel, observing years later to James Meriwether that *Elmer* was "funny, but not funny enough." [6]

We have already observed that Elmer's trip to Europe and the impressions made on him by the European scene come right out of Faulkner's own first visit to Europe. But *Elmer* is autobiographical in less evident ways also. A novel about growing up, about the difficulties of becoming an artist, and about one's successes and failures in love is bound to reflect at some level or other the personal experience of a young man, now twenty-eight, who had not been able to marry either of the two young women with whom he had been very much in love.

To some of these matters we shall return, but having acknowledged resemblances between Elmer Hodge and his creator, it is just as important to note some of the differences. Faulkner has deliberately distanced his protagonist from himself. Elmer is the youngest child of a ne'er-do-well father. The family is continually on the move: Paris, Tennessee; Jonesboro, Arkansas; and Houston, Texas, are some of the way stations in Elmer's migratory life. Moreover, his is a distintegrating family: the mother dies while Elmer is still young; his two brothers drift away early. Finally, the sister, the one person whom Elmer really adores, slips away, never to be seen again save for one moment, years later, when Elmer fleetingly glimpses on a New Orleans street a woman who resembles Jo-Addie.

Elmer's isolation and his rootlessness are underscored. Faulkner designed to have him rise, by pluck and luck, from nothing at all to social standing and wealth. For as Faulkner wrote to his mother: "He gets everything a man could want—money, a European title,

6. *The Literary Career of William Faulkner* (Princeton, 1961), p. 81.

marries the girl he wants—and she gives away his paint box. So Elmer never gets to paint at all." [7] His story was, then, to be the record of an improbable rags-to-riches ascent, a sort of spoof on the American dream; yet he was not to attain the goal for which he set out, fame as an artist. But then artistic fame hardly figures in the typical American dream.

Faulkner was a great comic writer, but his successful satire is essentially a series of asides: it needs reference to a base of established values. His V. K. Ratliff, that comic genius, on occasion can make devastating comments on the state of modern culture, but the comments derive their weight and velocity from his known character and personality. *Elmer* is not very funny (nor is *Mosquitoes,* Faulkner's next attempt to write a novel in the mode of comic satire). Failure that it is, the novel does have two significant features, however. It is another instance of Faulkner's attempt to undercut the romantic dream, and, in spite of his own personal dedication to art, it does portray the plight of the aspiring artist with detachment—and even in a comic light. Joyce exhibits a similar distancing and undercutting in his *Portrait of the Artist.* Compare what Joyce as author tells us about the argument between Cranly and Stephen at the end of the novel and Stephen's own version of the same encounter, and recall Joyce's remark to a friend that he hadn't "let this young man [Stephen] off very lightly." [8] In *Elmer,* however, Faulkner employs farcical exaggeration that goes far beyond Joyce's ironies and his introductions of differing perspectives.[9]

Did Faulkner's willingness in *Elmer* to deflate some of the pretensions of art and to smile at the plight of the artist apply also

7. *Man Collecting: Manuscripts and Printed Works of William Faulkner in the University of Virginia Library* (Charlottesville, 1975), pp. 133–34.

8. Frank Budgen, *James Joyce and the Making of "Ulysses"* (New York, 1934), p. 51.

9. A particularly heavy-handed instance occurs in the short story "Portrait of Elmer," which probably represents a later attempt on Faulkner's part to salvage something from the abandoned novel. In this story, Elmer, suddenly beset by a cramping in his bowels, is forced to use for toilet paper the watercolor which represents his best achievement in art and which he had snatched up a moment before to show the important visitors who are just about to call on him. See McHaney, "The Elmer Papers," p. 309.

to romantic love in all its ardors and anxieties? Here the case is less clear, but it is interesting to note that Elmer is allowed to share Faulkner's own attraction to slim epicene young women. In *Elmer* this ideal type is described as "a fierce proud Dianalike girl" who is "impregnably virginal." We see her again in Faulkner's next novel, *Mosquitoes,* where the young Patricia Robyn is a perfect representation of the epicene and is presumably another reflection of Helen Baird. Elmer's sister Jo-Addie is just such a girl. We are told that "no breasts of Joe's would ever trouble any clothes." Myrtle, the girl whom Elmer follows to Europe, is also a "slim silver Diana, arrogant and virginal and proud." But—another undercutting of the romantic dream—Myrtle begins to get "fat, [though] hating it." Flesh-and-blood Dianas do not necessarily remain virginally slim.

Doubtless Faulkner may have come naturally by his own preference for boyish girls—if these matters are ever really "natural." But it was also the fashion in the 1920s, as the girls drawn by John Held, Jr., attest, and as do Faulkner's own Held-like girls, which he drew for the Ole Miss publications. Yet a more likely influence ought to be mentioned, for it helps account not only for the epicene girl, as she appears in so much of Faulkner's early work, but, as we shall see, for a whole cluster of images and concerns to be found in *Soldiers' Pay, Elmer,* and *Mosquitoes.* The work in question is Théophile Gautier's *Mlle. de Maupin,*[10] which contains elaborate discussions of the significance of love and sex to the artist (as well as such topics as the attractiveness of slim, Diana-like women, the beauty of the hermaphrodite, and lesbianism).

Mlle. de Maupin has a special bearing on *Mosquitoes,* for in *Mosquitoes* the artist *par excellence* is a sculptor, and Gautier's hero insists that he regards women with a sculptor's eye and even affects to prefer a statue to a living woman. The influence of Gautier's novel is obvious throughout Faulkner's work of this

10. A copy of the Modern Library edition's translation into English (Boni and Liveright, 1918) is in Faulkner's library at Rowanoak, and it is apparent that Faulkner was acquainted with the novel before he began writing *Soldiers' Pay, Elmer, Mayday,* and *Mosquitoes.* As I have mentioned earlier, Michael Millgate (see note 2, above) points out an almost verbatim borrowing from *Mlle. de Maupin* in Faulkner's sketch "Wealthy Jew" and in *Mosquitoes.*

period, and it even spills over into his letters. He writes to his Aunt 'Bama (September 1927): "I have something—someone, I mean—to show you. . . . Of course its a woman. I would like to see you taken with her utter charm, and intrigued by her utter shallowness. Like a lovely vase. It isn't even empty, but is filled with somethink [sic]—well a yeast cake in water is the nearest simile that occurs to me. She gets the days passed for me, though. Thank God I've no money, or I'd marry her." This might almost be Gautier's D'Albert writing to his friend Silvio on the subject of women: "I have all my life been troubled about the shape of the flagon, never about the quality of its contents." [11]

Horace Benbow, the decadent poet with his "delicate impractical hands" and his "sick brilliant face," mentions the figure of a lovely vase too. He mentally addresses his sister, whom he adores, as "Thou still unravished bride of quietude," as if she were Keats's Grecian urn itself, and most readers will agree that Narcissa was a relatively empty urn. Apparently Horace dotes on her "fond serene detachment" and that is enough. She tells her brother that she "never knew a woman who read Shakespeare," for "He talks too much." Horace's answering comments indicate that her favorite reading matter was written by Michael Arlen and Raphael Sabatini. Nor does Horace demand intelligence from the woman he is to marry. He says: "I admire Belle. She is so cannily stupid." Horace is admittedly interested in beautiful vessels as such. His ambition is to learn how to blow delicate shapes in Venetian glass (*Flags in the Dust*, pp. 146–73 passim).

No one has yet found much resemblance between Faulkner and Horace Benbow. Perhaps his comment on his Aunt 'Bama was simply a young man's gesture of sophistication. Perhaps, for that matter, D'Albert's insistence that he regards beautiful women as simply elegant toys was also mostly youthful bravado. The point is that Faulkner used that "Bible of Romanticism," as Sainte Beuve called *Mlle. de Maupin,* to explore and test some of the extravagancies of idealized love and the idealizations of extravagant love.

11. *Man Collecting,* p. 113; Théophile Gautier, *Mlle. de Maupin,* trans. anon. (New York, n.d.), p. 134.

Perhaps the two most significant evidences in *Elmer* of the influence of *Mlle. de Maupin* are (1) its suggestion that the individual's fixing upon a heterosexual love is not automatic and not always easy and (2) its celebration of androgyny and of the epicene girl. Unlike *Elmer,* which traces the boy's vague and, for a time, undifferentiated sexual love, *Mlle. de Maupin* tells the story of Madeleine, a beautiful young woman who puts on male clothing and passes herself off as a man. She wants to involve herself in male society in order to discover what men are really like. D'Albert meets Madeleine so disguised and at once finds himself immensely attracted to this young cavalier. He is soon horrified to have to confess that he believes that he has actually fallen in love with a man. Later, having finally guessed that the charming young man is really a woman, he expresses his relief at being thereby "released from the pain of regarding myself as a monster" (p. 192).

D'Albert's mistress, Rosette, also quite definitely falls in love with the handsome, yet rather effeminate cavalier, and Madeleine increasingly feels the awkwardness forced upon her by her pretense that she is male. The awkwardness becomes embarrassment when she is alone with a woman who obviously feels a passionate love for her and yearns for its consummation.

Madeleine, in a letter to her friend Graciosa, is willing to confess that she "did not kiss [Rosette's little outstretched hand] without pleasure." Moreover, in her letters to her friend, she is given to such remarks as "the skirt is on my hips, and not in my disposition," and "It often happens that the sex of the soul does not at all correspond with that of the body" (p. 220). Nevertheless, there is no hint in the novel that matters between Madeleine and Rosette ever went any further than a few kisses, and Madeleine herself remarks that "as they say, the most beautiful girl can only give what she has, and what I had would not have been of much use to Rosette" (p. 222). What she has as a beautiful woman she can and does give to D'Albert, for she allows him one rapturous night of love before she departs from him forever.

When D'Albert awakes, he finds a letter from Madeleine in which she tells him that he will never see her again and that it will be useless to try to find her. Yet he should be thankful to her for ending their love affair in this way. He has realized his dream —something that few men do—and to continue to repeat it could only tarnish by familiarity and satiety this one perfect experience of an ideal love; for Madeleine points out that he has all the time really been in love with a dream rather than with a flesh-and-blood woman.

D'Albert naturally sees matters differently. He feels himself now condemned to a whole life of second-bests. His plight resembles that of Sir Galwyn, in *Mayday,* who prefers not to go on living. It also resembles that of the lovers in Villiers de l'Isle-Adam's *Axel.* When they come to realize that they have found in each other the perfect love and that the actual bodily experiences of it could only be a dimming of the radiance of their present anticipation, they prefer not to live past this high moment. As for living, Axel tells his beloved, "our servants will do that for us," and they commit suicide. I don't know that Faulkner ever read *Axel,* but in *Mlle. de Maupin* he would have tasted a romanticism almost as heady.

I find some corroboration of my notion that *Mlle. de Maupin* made a deep impression on Faulkner from something that Meta Carpenter Wilde sets down in her account of her relations with Faulkner in *A Loving Gentleman* (New York, 1976). She is commenting on how the "imperfections of the beloved . . . are unseen when lovers meet in secret, . . . M. d'Albert transformed in his ardor to godlike grace, Mlle. de Maupin leaving the love bed before the harsh light of morning, each partner moving in an amber glow of ideality" (p. 137; see also p. 279). In the course of her book, Meta Carpenter mentions several of what we know to have been Faulkner's favorite poems. This reinforces my opinion that it was he who introduced her to Gautier's novel and that it was he who made the point about romantic love that she illustrates by referring to D'Albert and Mlle. de Maupin.

Whatever her ultimate sexual preference, Madeleine clearly represents to D'Albert his romantic ideal—the almost perfect androgyne. Dressed in male costume as Rosalind for a performance of *As You Like It,* she had completely captivated D'Albert, who was more than usually susceptible to a young woman dressed in male garments because, as he tells his friend, the "son of Hermes and Aphrodite is, in fact, one of the sweetest creations of Pagan genius. Nothing in the world can be more ravishing than these two bodies, harmoniously blended together and both perfect, these two beauties so equal and so different, forming but one superior to both, because they are reciprocally tempered and improved." And D'Albert goes on to rhapsodize further on the nature of hermaphroditic beauty, though he concludes, rightly it turns out, that in the beardless young cavalier the feminine portion prevails and that he "has preserved [in his bodily makeup] more of Salmacis than did the Hermaphrodite of the Metamorphoses" (p. 144).

Elmer Hodge also acknowledges a special satisfaction in the hermaphrodite. He loves to fondle his tubes of paint. In those "fat portentous tubes . . . was yet wombed his heart's desire, the world itself—thickbodied and female and at the same time phallic: hermaphroditic." Elmer's interest in phallic shapes of all kinds (see also p. 117, above) has led some readers to assume that Faulkner was here drawing upon his knowledge of Freud,[12] and perhaps he was. But it would appear that he owed a prior debt to Gautier. Elmer's fascination with the coalescence of the male and female character in one body may hark back to D'Albert's rhapsodies on this subject. The likelihood that it does is reinforced by the fact that Elmer, like D'Albert, dotes on the epicene, the Diana-like girl, who seems to be of an "impregnable virginity" and of a "slimness virginal and impervious to time."

Helen Baird almost certainly lies behind this obsessive image. But one can assume that *Mlle. de Maupin* contributed to it and, at the very least, reinforced it. That it is an obsessive image is very clear if we remember the appeal that Cecily holds for Januarius Jones in *Soldiers' Pay*, that Jo-Addie and Myrtle exert on Elmer, and, as we shall see, the spell that Patricia Robyn casts upon Gordon in *Mosquitoes*. Since these three characters from Faulkner's early novels have little in common except their liking for the epicene girl, it becomes plain that it is Faulkner, their creator, who is obsessed with this kind of woman and who has projected his own interest in the epicene onto them.

12. For Faulkner's knowledge of Freud, see below, Notes, pp. 376–77.

Faulkner's descriptions of Cecily, Jo-Addie, Pat Robyn (and Narcissa Benbow in *Flags in the Dust,* for she too is called "epicene") make sufficiently clear what the term meant for him. But it should be pointed out that he uses it once or twice in rather special senses. Consider the meanings it has on pages 249–50 of *Soldiers' Pay.* Margaret Powers tells Jones that he has "acquired next to no skill with women," he demands an example of his lack of success, and Margaret instances Cecily. Jones replies: "my dear lady, can you imagine anyone making love to her? Epicene. Of course it is different with a man practically dead, he probably doesn't care much whom he marries, nor whether or not he marries at all" (p. 249).

In this context, epicene appears to mean sexless; [13] that is, Cecily feels no attraction to the male and perhaps arouses no sexual desire in the male. The reference to the half-dead man, Donald Mahon, might seem to clinch this interpretation. Cecily, of course, does excite desire in George Farr, as Jones himself well knows. But we don't expect Jones to speak by the card in this situation in which he is sparring with Margaret and Joe. Besides, Jones, who feels that he is a connoisseur in such matters, would dismiss George's opinion as of no account anyway. Actually, if Jones meant that Cecily was a sexless creature, he was not altogether wrong: George Farr's honeymoon with her was apparently a disaster (see *Soldiers' Pay,* p. 306).

Yet there is the possibility that by "epicene" Jones meant something different still. Margaret Powers (on p. 290) gives her own interpretation of his meaning. She and Joe are still taunting Jones on his ill success in love. In the course of their conversation, Margaret gives a special twist to what Jones had said on page 249

---

13. The definition "sexless" would seem to be a rather late development. *The Supplement to the Oxford English Dictionary, A–F* (1972) does not record it. Though this definition does appear in more recent American dictionaries, it does not appear in all. *Webster's New World Dictionary* (1970) does not include it, for instance, nor *The American College Dictionary* (1953), and though the 1952 edition of *Funk and Wagnall's Standard Dictionary* does, it notes that this meaning is "loosely" applied. Faulkner's use of the meaning (1926) is thus early. I suspect that he picked it up from "Mr. Eliot's Sunday Service," where the worker bees, technically female, but infertile, are referred to as "epicene."

(quoted just above). She tells Joe, "Mr. Jones [has said] that to make love to Miss Saunders would be epicene." And when Joe asks what that means, Margaret proceeds to tell him: "Epicene is something you want and can't get." We may brush aside Margaret's careless syntax. She is here concerned only with stinging Jones's thick hide. But she (or is it Faulkner himself?) has here also abandoned the dictionary meanings. I know of none that defines "epicene" as meaning "unattainable."

The simplest way out of this tangle of meanings is to conclude that Margaret, like Humpty-Dumpty, is here making the word mean whatever she wants it to mean. Curiously enough, however, Jones does not challenge the meaning Margaret attributes to him. He simply stalks off. His failure to say, "That is not what I meant at all. That is not it at all." in itself proves nothing. Yet, on reflection, that Cecily is "unattainable" may be what Jones really meant—and incidentally what Faulkner means by the term as it occurs in *Elmer* and *Mosquitoes*. One recalls how frequently he couples "epicene" with references to an "impregnable virginity" and, in *Elmer,* associates it at least a half dozen times with Diana. If so, Faulkner's idiosyncratic development of the meaning would run something like this: epicene means (1) partaking of both sexes; the effeminate man or, as Faulkner commonly uses the term, the slim girl with small breasts and boyish flanks; (2) not ready for sex, perhaps incapable of sexual love; and (3) arousing not sexual desire but quiet contemplation; in Joyce's terms, not a kinetic but a static emotion; not beauty moving in a world of time but beauty conveying a sense of timelessness and transcendence. The third stage would represent a beauty which is quite literally unattainable as the things that transcend our human world always are. One cannot marry Diana; one does not marry Iseult; one cannot take as wife a dream or a statue.

If epicene can mean something like this, then it has been properly placed in the summary position assigned to it in the long paragraph (p. 224) that describes Jones's state of mind as he holds Cecily in his arms. At that moment she becomes for Jones the "symbol of a delicate, *bodyless* lust. . . . Her long legs [had been created], not for locomotion, but for the *studied completion* of a rhythm carried to its *nth:* compulsion of progress, movement; her body created for all men to *dream after.* . . . Her unseen face nimbused with light and her body, *which was no body,* crumpling a dress that had been *dreamed.* Not for maternity, not even for love: a thing *for the eye and the mind.* Epicene, he thought . . . " (italics supplied). No wonder that on the next page Jones's state of mind is deemed to be a "chaste Platonic nympholepsy."

As has been remarked before, Jones, repulsive as he is, is nevertheless a highly complex character. Whether Faulkner has made him completely credible may be open to doubt. The same question may also be raised regarding Elmer Hodge: can one really believe in him? So it is perhaps with all of Faulkner's nympholepts, including Gordon, in *Mosquitoes.*

So much for the esthetic quality of the early novels. But, turning from the works to the man who wrote them, one thing is quite plain: the epicene girl—define the term as you like—powerfully engaged the imagination of the young Faulkner. She is closely involved with his concept of romantic love and with his concept of the whole realm of romance. It is no accident that in the visionary scene experienced by Elmer in Venice, a piece of prose that Faulkner liked so well that he incorporated some of it in *Mosquitoes,* the epicene girl is made to occupy the climactic position.

This passage (which, by the way, probably owes a great deal to Flaubert's *Temptation of St. Anthony*) is a kind of pictorial symphony of extravagantly romantic images. The pageant there displayed includes a procession of heralds, torchbearers, and barefoot priests; a young naked boy whose skin has been colored vermillion and who carries a crown; someone clad in a long azure robe and a corselet of chainmail as fine as woven silk; a girl wearing an ungirdled robe of amethyst who holds a broken sword; an elephant that bears on its back the naked decapitated body of a black woman placed within a brazen howdah; more black women and more torchbearers and more heralds in black and orange liveries; a bevy of virgins and "flame-clad pages neither boy nor girl" (the hermaphroditic theme again); a young man whose body, enclosed in a glass coffin, is as "still as pale amethyst marble"; and after the passage of three more barefoot priests, there comes the final visual image. The "shadows and echoes and perfumes [swirl] upward slow as smoke [and] gain form, changing, becoming a woman slender as a taper with raised joined hands, taut and proud, fierce and young and sorrowful." Appearing with her in the cloud of shadows and perfumes there is a rosy child.

It's quite a vision that the author has vouchsafed to the likes of Elmer Hodge, a man who looks "a little like a Snopes in his Sunday best, [a man who] wears 'tennis shoes and a stiff-brimmed straw hat' . . . [and who] nurses a 'varnished yellow stick.' " [14] But by making Elmer's imagination responsible for these romantic fireworks, Faulkner has found a way to undercut such a display and so perhaps rather to authenticate it. In either case, the author has found an opportunity to lay on the romantic colors as thick as he liked and as he evidently enjoyed doing. Years later, he was to allow himself a like indulgence in *Absalom, Absalom!* by allowing Miss Rosa Coldfield her wonderful chapter-long tirade in flamboyant rhetorical prose.

14. McHaney's comment in "The Elmer Papers," p. 290.

5

A Fine Volley of Words

(MOSQUITOES)

Mosquitoes is Faulkner's least respected novel and it is very easy to see why. There is almost no story line; nothing of real consequence happens to any of its characters. The novel is "literary," "talky," experimental—even gimmicky in some of its devices. The characters' talk about women, about art, about creativity, about the banalities of human existence, is often highly involved, and some of the verbal byplay that goes on is so oblique that to many readers it will seem pointless and quite incomprehensible.

Only readers who enjoy Faulkner's mature work are likely to be interested in this early misfire, but to those who have regard for, say, *The Sound and the Fury* or *Light in August, Mosquitoes* may prove very interesting indeed, for it offers a fascinating opportunity to observe the young Faulkner's use of literary sources, his adaptation of some of the then new narrative techniques, and, most of all, his zest for language and his power to handle it.

Here is a sample of the sort of writing that one finds: A man opens a door, and twilight runs into the room "like a quiet violet dog . . ." (p. 13). The simile is almost an Elizabethan conceit: mannered, strained, and artificial; and yet the figure makes perfect sense. The violet evening is waiting outside the room, as quietly and as patiently as a pet dog will wait for a door to be opened. Once it is opened, the dog does not hesitate, but immediately slips inside. This simile is, in Coleridge's terms, an effect of the fancy rather than of the imagination. But, then, young, exuberant writers tend to be fanciful. (And if Sandburg can have the fog come in silently "on little cat feet," why can't Faulkner be allowed his light-footed little violet-colored dog?)

To take another example: on this same New Orleans evening the "Pontalba [building] and the cathedral [on Jackson Square] were cut from black paper and pasted flat on a green sky; above them taller palms were fixed in black and soundless explosions" (p. 14)— another conceit, as if an explosion could be arrested as to both motion and sound. *Mosquitoes* is full of this sort of verbal play; some of it successful, some of it awkward and forced. Indeed, *Mosquitoes* may be regarded as Faulkner's *Love's Labor's Lost,* an early effort that is rarely read because it seems literary and artificial, but which for the initiate has a great deal of charm because of the brilliance of its wordplay. Thus, Mrs. Maurier "sails" into a room, "bearing her expression of happy astonishment like a round platter stood on edge," and then proceeds to greet her host "in . . . gushing italics" (p. 22). In her next speech to him her voice "was again a happy astonished honey" (p. 23). Whatever the positive merits of such figurative language, it is at least not tired and perfunctory. It borders on surrealism rather than the cliché.

The wayfaring reader of *Mosquitoes* in 1927, however, encountered a more formidable sort of difficulty, though it, too, derived from the young author's willingness to experiment and his trust in his reader's ability to connect up passages sometimes separated by a hundred pages. Here is one example. Two teen-age girls, Patricia Robyn and Jenny Steinbauer, are guests on a yacht belonging to Pat's aunt, Mrs. Maurier. Pat had overheard Jenny use a strange and exciting expression in addressing a man who had stolen a kiss from her. Pat wants to know what it means. But Jenny honestly doesn't know; it is simply something that she once heard a "fellow" say. Yet the expression, whatever it means, sounds so good to Pat that she asks Jenny's permission to use it some time on her own account, a request that Jenny cheerfully grants. Jenny, in

return, has been impressed by an expression that she has heard
Pat use to her aunt, something about "pulling up a sheet or something." If the reader remembers what was said back on page 59,
he will conclude that what Jenny had overheard was "Haul in
your sheet, Aunt Pat, you're jibbing." Expressions from the nauti-
cal world sound as exotic to Jenny as the pungent phrase that
Jenny brings up from her rather raffish world sounds to Pat.

What that pungent phrase actually was becomes clear only some
hundred pages later (p. 271), when Pat, exasperated because the
sculptor Gordon refuses to sell her the marble torso of a woman
that she fancies looks like herself, decides to use on him the phrase
that Jenny had "traded" her. Gordon immediately lays her across
his knees, "drew her skirt tight across her thighs and spanked her,
good."

> "I meant it!" she cried, raging and tearless, when he
> had . . . set her upright on his lap. . . . "I meant it!" she
> repeated, taut and raging.
> "I know you meant it. That's why I spanked you. Not be-
> cause you said it: what you said doesn't mean anything
> because you've got the genders backward. [Pat presumably
> had called Gordon a "bitch of a son."] I spanked you because
> you meant it, whether you knew what to say or not.

As for Jenny Steinbauer, she doesn't use the expression she had
borrowed from Patricia until near the end of the novel (p. 295),
and, like Pat, she has trouble in getting it exactly right. What she
says to her father, who has been understandably upset by her
several days' absence, is "Haul *up* your sheet. You're jibbing"
(italics mine).

Now it is rather charming to watch this pair of innocents from
different social strata experiment with new vocabularies, but the
sense of what is going on (and with it, the attendant comedy) will
be lost on all but the very attentive reader. (It should be said that
even the vigilant reader may have his difficulties with other passages in *Mosquitoes,* some of which read like private jokes or
cross questions and crazy answers. See, for example, pp. 219–20.)

Aside from the sheer verbal interest of the writing, *Mosquitoes* is interesting, to the devoted Faulknerian at least, for what it can tell about Faulkner's literary sources. Since the young writer has not fully assimilated them, one can observe them quite nakedly. Consider, for example, the following paragraph from page 10.

> Outside the window New Orleans, the vieux carré, brooded in a faintly tarnished languor like an aging yet still beautiful courtesan in a smokefilled room, avid yet weary too of ardent ways. Above the city summer was hushed warmly into the bowled weary passion of the sky. Spring and the cruelest months were gone, the cruel months, the wantons that break the fat hybernatant dullness and comfort of Time; August was on the wing, and September—a month of languorous days regretful as woodsmoke. But Mr. Talliaferro's youth, or lack of it, troubled him no longer. Thank God.

The phrase "yet weary too of ardent ways" represents a very slight reworking of the first line of the villanelle composed by Stephen Dedalus in *Portrait of the Artist as a Young Man*. Stephen imagines the inspiration of that poem to be a woman, a temptress, "waking from odorous sleep . . . [with] eyes, dark and with a look of languor. . . ." "Bowled," as Faulkner uses it here, could derive from the *Rubáiyát*—"the bowl of night"; or more directly from Joyce's *Ulysses*—"[The bay] lay behind him, a bowl of bitter waters," from the "Telemachus" chapter. "Spring and the cruelest months," of course, echoes the first line of *The Waste Land*. "August was on the wing" is a variation on Omar Khayyám's "The bird of time is ever on the wing." So much for literary borrowings and echoes. "Hybernatant" must be Faulkner's own coinage, presumably meaning "causing to hibernate."

Mosquitoes was written by a young man who, if he was sometimes shaky on the spelling of certain words and not always aware of their exact meanings, was nevertheless fascinated by what one could do with them, and who was already conscious of his own real mastery of them. Thus, the writing in *Mosquitoes* is exuberant and inspired, rarely slack and never mechanical. Faulkner is not always careful of the rules, but he is never *careless,* if one means by "careless" that he was not thoroughly intent on what he was doing. He is very much interested in verbal patterns of every kind and in experimenting with literary techniques. A consideration of the very title of his novel will confirm the last point: though mosquitoes hum and bite throughout the book, the word itself does not occur a single time in all its pages. The exclusion of the specific name of the insect is obviously deliberate. Was this fact of circumlocution worth the bother? Perhaps so, perhaps not. That is not my point, which is, rather, that the *author,* thinking it was, was willing to take the trouble.

What, by the way, do the mosquitoes stand for? My guess is that they stand for the unpredictable and annoying aspects of reality that human beings have to reckon with. They are constantly bringing to grief romantic elopements, or puncturing the nice accommodations of society, or breaking into certain exalted meditations on art and the nature of truth.

In their several days of conversation, the people on Mrs. Maurier's yacht take in a great deal of territory; but their talk, whether bantering or serious, circles around two principal topics: art and love, or, more specifically, literature and sex. These are the special concerns in several of Faulkner's obvious literary sources—in Joyce's *Portrait of the Artist as a Young Man,* in much of Eliot's early poetry, and in Huxley's *Chrome Yellow* (if that novel was in fact one of Faulkner's sources). But one does not have to appeal to Faulkner's literary sources: for centuries past such topics have been the burning concerns of almost any young writer.

Having in mind the exposition of such topics, Faulkner evidently selected the characters of his novel with some care. There is a highly intelligent middle-aged New Orleanian who is always referred to as "the Semitic man." (His first name is Julius and his surname may well be Kauffman: on p. 327 he says that "Julius Kauffman was my grandfather.") He has read widely and he is confident in his knowledge of life and of the arts. He has a sardonic humor and a certain strain of cynicism. He particularly enjoys needling a midwestern novelist named Dawson Fairchild who affects a relaxed folksiness and who, critics agree, represents Sherwood Anderson. There is a young poet, Mark Frost, whose infrequent poems are so brief as to have become a standing joke among his friends. It is rather unlikely that Faulkner had ever read Dryden's sarcastic reference to a contemporary poet whose most strenuous effort could "strain from hard-bound brains [no more than] six lines a year," but such is the kind of taunt that underlies several jesting references to what amounts to Frost's verbal constipation.

Another poet in the group is Eva Wiseman, the sister of Julius, who writes an aggressively modernist poetry. She has entitled a collection of her verse *Satyricon in Starlight,* and the phrase aptly suggests the kind of poetry to which she aspires: poems that are almost goonishly obscure, yet nevertheless filled with echoes of currently fashionable poets. Eva's verse evidently does not impress her brother Julius. A second woman artist, this one a painter, is Dorothy Jameson. Her interests are far less intellectual than are those of Mrs. Wiseman. Frankly, she wants a man, and her attempt to seduce Mark Frost provides one of the mildly comic episodes of the book.

Gordon—one has to refer to him by the only name assigned to him in the novel—is a sculptor, a dedicated artist, very masculine and quite close-lipped. He does not talk a great deal about art, but he does create it. Julius says that Gordon is an artist all the time, whereas a man like Fairchild is not at heart an artist at all, merely a producer of novels, and is indeed somewhat muddled as to what art is. Fairchild is, in Julius's words, a "poor emotional eunuch," the "bastard of a surgeon and a stenographer." Julius regards the rest of the people on the yacht as occupying a lower rank still: they simply play at art or play around the real artists.

The person who has brought this company together, Mrs. Patricia Maurier, a wealthy widow, has invited them to spend a few days aboard her yacht on Lake Pontchartrain. For Mrs. Maurier, art is the proper sort of refined activity to which a woman of means can lend her patronage. She knows nothing about art and very little about artists. In the several days that they are aboard her pleasure craft, they prove to be discouragingly human and even distressingly vulgar.

134

The device by which Faulkner has assembled this group of people for several days' conversation is as old as Boccaccio and as recent as a novel by Agatha Christie: you get your mixed group together and isolate them from the rest of the world long enough for a murder to be committed and the murderer found out, or for the required number of stories to be told, or for a theme to be developed through discussion and brought to some sort of conclusion. On Mrs. Maurier's *Nausikaa* nothing so dramatic as a murder takes place, but there are some comic scenes, and, as I shall argue, there is the partial development of a theme.

Faulkner has not made the tactical mistake of limiting Mrs. Maurier's guest list to artists or even pretenders to the arts. It turns out that she has also invited Ernest Talliaferro, a kind of cultural flunky and go-between, who has proved useful to her in putting her in touch with the writers and artists of the New Orleans French Quarter. Talliaferro had been born Tarver, but had decided to treat himself to a more pretentious surname. He knows little more about the arts than Mrs. Maurier does, and, like her, he sees art as a means to an end. For Talliaferro, as Fairchild observes, "art is just a valid camouflage for rutting" (p. 71). Talliaferro's dearest conviction is that the writer or painter, by his very vocation, attracts women, and that his true craft and mystery is the art of seduction. Another member of the party is Major Ayers, the complete stage Englishman. Faulkner draws him with very broad strokes indeed; the Major speaks of his days at Sandhurst and even makes references to "decayed countesses" and to a "second footman."

There is one further category of passengers on the yacht: the young. With Mrs. Maurier are her niece Patricia Robyn and Patricia's twin brother, Theodore. Patricia shows up at the last minute with Jenny Steinbauer, a mere chance acquaintance. Pat has no acquaintance at all with the boyfriend Jenny brings along, Pete Ginotta, whose elder brother is a New Orleans bootlegger. Faulkner makes a point of the casualness of the young. When Mrs. Maurier scolds her niece for, in effect, picking up people off the street, Pat does not go to much trouble to excuse herself: ". . . you said yourself there were not enough women coming."

So much for inviting Jenny. As for Pete, he was Jenny's necessary appendage. "He's her heavy, I gather."

The roles of the young men in the novel are unimportant. Pete does little more than glower at the attention the men give to Jenny and try to keep his precious straw hat from getting lost or crushed. Patricia's brother Theodore, referred to as Josh and also as Gus, is preoccupied with fashioning for himself a special kind of tobacco pipe. Pete and Josh provide little more than a measure of incidental comedy. The two young women, on the other hand, have important roles. They do not add much to the talk about art, since their minds are occupied with other things, but their young bodies are thoroughly relevant to the topic, for, to paraphrase Alexander Pope, their bodies are "at once the source and end and test of art." (Gordon, Fairchild, and Talliaferro, to be sure, would, in this context, interpret *source, end,* and *test* in very different fashions.)

Pat and Jenny are not simply duplicates of each other. Pat is another of Faulkner's many epicene young women. She plays an Artemis to Jenny's lush Aphrodite, and the polarity between the girls bears quite specifically on the theme of love and art and the dual role of woman as inspiration and fulfillment. Gordon, for example, is immensely attracted to Patricia, but to Jenny not in the least, though the commotions that Jenny sets up among the other men cause Mrs. Wiseman, on one occasion, to admonish her: "Darling, you simply must not go where men can see you, like that. For Mrs. Maurier's sake, you know; she's having enough trouble as it is, without any rioting" (p. 203).

Yet one is not to conclude that Gordon is an ascetic or that he is anything other than thoroughly heterosexual. Our last sight of him is through the open door of a brothel, as Kauffman and Dawson, his companions on a walk through the French Quarter, watch him "lift a woman from the shadow and raise her against the mad stars, smothering her squeal against his tall kiss" (p. 339). Though we are given no description of the prostitute in Gordon's arms, she would scarcely be virginal and very unlikely would seem in the least epicene. In fact, Faulkner here seems bent on urging the contrast between the kind of woman that Gordon actually embraces and the woman who represents his ideal love, for just after the words ". . . smothering her squeal against his tall kiss" we get the following passage: *"Then voices and sounds, shadows and echoes change form swirling, becoming the headless, armless, legless torso of a girl, motionless and virginal and passionately eternal before the shadows and echoes whirl away."* Faulkner thus reminds us of Gordon's conception of the ideal female body just at the moment when Gordon enters the brothel.

Is Faulkner's point that Gordon is a hopelessly divided man? The answer would have to be: yes and no. No, in the sense that Gordon is not a special case of such contradiction. Yes, in the sense that he participates in a contradiction that seems rooted in universal human nature—or, if that generalization flings the net too wide, then at least in a contradiction for centuries endemic in the culture of the West. A sentimentalized view could hold that Gordon is being faithful to his Cynara in his own fashion, flinging "roses, roses, riotously with the throng" in order to put his true love's "pale, lost lilies out of mind." But Gordon seems made of sterner stuff than Ernest Dowson—and romantic love itself shows a real tension, a tension that often amounts to an agonizing strain between the urge for physical satisfaction and the yearning for the transcendent, the impossible ideal. Moreover, satisfaction often betrays the ideal, or rather reveals that the supposed ideal is spurious. This is why Keats's "Ode on a Grecian Urn" became one of Faulkner's favorite poems. Though the "Bold lover" depicted on the urn can never kiss the beloved maiden, "She cannot fade. . . ." "Forever [will he] love, and she be fair."

Though the brothel episode occurs late in the novel, and though more remains to be said about Gordon, there is an advantage in turning our attention at this point to a central issue—just possibly *the* central issue—of this ambiguous and somewhat confused work. Romantic love itself is ambiguous, and presents the romantic lover with an apparent contradiction. Though the most intense romantic love generates a sense of the eternal and transcendent, it actually is rooted in a fleshly and temporal experience, and though the transcendent experience seems the antithesis of sensuality, it usually demands bodily fulfillment. The two experiences are apparently antithetical, yet each yearns toward the other. The human being, and especially that most sensitive human being, the artist, participates in both, and may at times feel that he is torn apart by them.

Julius Kauffman would seem to be particularly aware of this problem. It is just after Gordon has gone into the brothel that he remarks to Fairchild (or possibly simply says to himself, p. 339): "Dante invented Beatrice, creating himself a maid that life had not had time to create, and laid on her frail and unbowed shoulders the whole burden of man's history of his impossible heart's desire." The statement is not necessarily meant to be a pointed comment on Gordon's action. Certainly, it holds no censure in it: when Gordon asks him for money, Kauffman at once pushes a banknote into Gordon's hand to pay his brothel fee. But his remark about Dante and Beatrice does apply: there are no emotional ties between Gordon and the prostitute, who is presumably the first woman that he sees when he opens the door. His ideal woman is one that, like Dante's Beatrice, he has created for himself.

The case of Dante aside, the heart of every romantic artist feels such a desire, and though reason affirms that the desire is impossible of realization, the heart cries out, nevertheless, against the judgment of the "dull brain" which, in Keats's fine phrase, "Perplexes and retards." Shelley once called this impossible desire the "desire of the moth for the star." There is hardly need to cite more examples: such romantic doctrine is to be found throughout the nineteenth century and on into the twentieth. My generation, like Faulkner's, absorbed it from our high school and university courses as well as from our general reading.

Faulkner's own romanticism is again worth stressing, for in spite of his early fascination with the innovating writers of the twentieth century, his growth to artistic maturity is largely the story of his taming of his romantic tendencies and his bringing them into fruitful relation with the counter forces emanating from the new literature of the twentieth century. Yet, one ought not claim that Faulkner ever repudiated the romantic vision in its entirety. If the problem of the division of heart and head remained to the end a problem for him—as it remains a problem of our culture generally—the terms in which he saw the problem did change, and concurrently his emotional attitude toward it.

Though a romanticism that emphasized the search for the infinite, love as an idealizing force, and woman as either pure spirituality or else tempting sensuality was endemic in the society in which Faulkner grew up, there were special works that we know he read and which influenced him profoundly. One was Rostand's *Cyrano de Bergerac,* which Blotner tells us was his favorite play; another was Gautier's *Mlle. de Maupin,* which I have discussed at some length in chapter 4.

Gordon is a kind of Cyrano, and he tells Pat Robyn what Cyrano once told his Roxanne, Madeleine Robin: "Your name is like a little golden bell hung in my heart." When Pat asks Gordon whether he wouldn't prefer a live girl to a statue, Gautier's D'Albert could have provided Gordon with an answer: "Sculpture has all the reality that anything completely false can possess. . . . Your sculptured differs from your veritable mistress only in this, that she is a little harder and does not speak—two very trifling defects." [1] Gordon, alluding to the headless, limbless marble torso, might almost be a D'Albert himself speaking when he tells Mrs. Maurier: "This is my feminine ideal: a virgin with no legs to leave me, no arms to hold me, no head to talk to me" (p. 26).

If, however, Gordon owes so much to D'Albert, does he owe anything at all to Faulkner's flesh-and-blood New Orleans friend with whom he sailed to Genoa on the *West Ivis* in 1925? William Spratling was a fine looking man and a sculptor as well as an architect; he once wrote that "In *Mosquitoes,* I believe I also figured as one of the characters." [2] Perhaps so, and if so, the character could scarcely have been other than Gordon. Did Spratling share Gordon's view of the artist? Not necessarily. It may be significant that a possibly apocryphal incident which Spratling claims happened to him is in *Mosquitoes* assigned to Fairchild, not to Gordon. In *File on Spratling* (pp. 14–15), Spratling tells how, as a little boy, on his way to the outside privy, he noticed a little girl of about his age who was also evidently bound for the same place. He entered as he thought unobserved and kept very quiet on his side of the partition. But overcome with curiosity, he put his head through the privy hole to see what he could see. To his complete

1. Théophile Gautier, *Mlle. de Maupin,* trans. anon. (New York, n.d.), p. 193.
2. *File on Spratling* (Boston, 1967), p. 24.

surprise he found himself looking into the face of the little girl who had attempted in the same way to spy on him.

In *Mosquitoes* (p. 234) Fairchild tells this story on himself, describing how, having put his "head down through the seat," he saw "two wide curious blue eyes into which an inverted surprise came clear as water, and long golden curls swinging downward above the ordure. . . ." In *File on Spratling* the corresponding sentence reads: "What met my eyes was a pair of blue eyes and golden curls hanging upside down, about three feet away." Now such an anecdote fits the character of Fairchild much better than it fits the character of Gordon, but since Faulkner is writing fiction and not biography, he makes no bones about transferring the original Spratling (Gordon) material to Fairchild, who is universally regarded as representing Sherwood Anderson. There is no slavish adherence to biographical fact: after all both Gordon and Fairchild are imaginary characters.

A great deal of chitchat, sometimes witty, sometimes tedious, about literature and art is heard on Mrs. Maurier's yacht; nearly all the serious observations, however, emanate from Kauffman, Fairchild, and Eva Wiseman. Gordon is not a man of words. He does his sculpture, but he says little about it or about art in general. Mark Frost, though a poet of sorts, hardly counts in the conversation on art. He is not really interested in literature—only in uttering bright sayings and preserving the image of the compleat sophisticate. Major Ayers and Ernest Talliaferro are obvious clowns, each preposterous in his own way. The young are the young—innocent, charming, outrageous, difficult, selfish, delightful, obstreperous—but in any case, not really interested in anything but themselves.

Kauffman and Fairchild are, of course, very different in background and personality. The former is widely read, urbane, and a very acute critic of literature and the arts. The latter has been bred up in a small town, and though he is an intelligent man and far less simple than he seems, he likes to make an issue of his plain horse sense and country bluntness. His opinion of women, for example, if one is to believe him, is brutally realistic: women are "merely articulated genital organs." Yet he also claims to be "a hopeless sentimentalist" about "young love in the spring, and things like that." In spite of their sharp differences in temperament and in manner of speaking, the two men do not differ on the basic issues as much as one might first suppose. For example, both believe that men write their poems not only about women but in the hope of winning a woman's favor, and both seem to have little more than contempt for obscure modern poetry. Furthermore, each in his own way dismisses prettification, pretentiousness, and moral uplift.

To the reader of the 1970s, probably the most interesting literary judgment in all of Kauffman's talk is his estimate of what is right and wrong with the literary work of Dawson Fairchild, for it is just here that Kauffman may be delivering himself of Faulkner's own 1926 estimate of the worth of Sherwood Anderson. The conversation between Julius Kauffman and Eva on pages 241–43 has specifically to do with Fairchild as a novelist. What they say may be summarized somewhat as follows: Fairchild is "a man of undoubted talent, despite his fumbling bewilderment in the presence of sophisticated emotions." His trouble is that he has "inherited all the lower middle class's awe of Education with a capital E. . . ." Because he is overawed by "the ghosts of the Emersons and Lowells," and because he really fears them, he is provoked into a "sort of puerile bravado in flouting" them. So far Julius.

Eva goes to the defense of the New England of the Emersons and Lowells. Julius tells her that he agrees with her judgment, but that is not his point. The point is that the New England man of letters had something that Fairchild lacks, "a standard of literature that is international. No, not a standard, exactly: a belief, a conviction that his talent need not be restricted to delineating things which his conscious mind assures him are American reactions." Fairchild needs to "forget all this fetish of culture and education which his upbringing and the ghosts of those whom circumstance permitted to reside longer at college than himself . . . assure him that he lacks. For by getting himself and his own bewilderment and inhibitions out of the way by describing . . . American life as American life is, it will become eternal and timeless despite him." Finally, Julius observes that "Life everywhere is the same, you

know. Manners of living it may be different . . . but man's old
compulsions, duty and inclination: the axis and the circumference
of his squirrel cage, they do not change."

Now some of what Kauffman says with reference to Fairchild is
very like what Faulkner had written about Anderson in his Dallas
Morning News article; for example, his statement that Anderson
reminded him of "a lusty corn field in his native Ohio." In *Poor
White,* Anderson had seemed "to get his fingers and toes again into
the soil, as he did in *Winesburg."* But in *Many Marriages,* Anderson had got "away from the land," and when he gets away from
the land, Faulkner had written, "he is lost." If such comments as
these contain praise, they also imply a limitation: Anderson is
forced, at the risk of losing his power, to remain very close to the
cornfields of the Middle West. Yet how could Faulkner, of all
people, regard this attachment to locality a defect? Doesn't Faulkner tell us that it was from Anderson that he learned "that, to be
a writer, one has first got to be what he is, what he was born" and
that

> You have to have somewhere to start from: then you begin
> to learn. It dont matter where it was, just so you remember
> it and aint ashamed of it. Because one place to start from is
> just as important as any other. You're a country boy; all you
> know is that little patch up there in Mississippi where you
> started from.

This is what Faulkner, writing in June 1953 in *The Atlantic
Monthly,* tells us he learned from Anderson. But there is no
essential contradiction between what Faulkner said in 1953 and
in 1925. He did not in 1953 withdraw his indictment of Anderson
in order to pay his dead friend a gracious tribute. Sincere tribute
is paid, to be sure, but Faulkner had not changed his essential
position, for in quoting from his 1953 article I have thus far
deliberately left out one important qualification that Faulkner
there makes. After saying that "to be a writer, one has first got to
be what he is, what he was born," Faulkner goes on to add that

to be an American and a writer, one does not necessarily have to pay lip-service to any conventional American image such as his [i.e., Anderson's] and Dreiser's own aching Indiana or Ohio or Iowa corn or Sandburg's stockyards or Mark Twain's frog. You had only to remember what you were.

Faulkner gives credit to Anderson for teaching him this lesson also, and perhaps Anderson did, but if so, it must have been by negative example.

More important, however, than whether Faulkner learned both lessons from Anderson is that Faulkner did indeed learn them both. Moreover, I press this issue of the two different lessons because I want to stress the overall consistency of Faulkner's estimate of Anderson's virtues and limitations. The opinion expressed in 1953 can live comfortably with Julius Kauffman's judgment as expressed in *Mosquitoes,* nor is it, as I have already indicated, really very different from what Faulkner published in 1925 in the Dallas newspaper.

The testimony of *Mosquitoes* is that at least by 1926 Faulkner had come to recognize that a writer was committed for his materials to what he knew (which means—for the beginning writer at least—the experience of his own locality) but that what he did with his material had to be judged not by local but by universal standards. James B. Meriwether has cautioned us, however, against giving Anderson all the credit for the "great lesson" of starting with "that little patch up there in Mississippi where [Faulkner] started from." Some of the credit, he suggests, might well go to Phil Stone. Moreover, he cautions us not to underestimate Faulkner's ability to learn the lesson for himself. Meriwether points out that in a poem written as early as the autumn of 1924 ("Mississippi Hills: My Epitaph") and in "Verse Old and Nascent," published in April 1925, Faulkner shows that he had already made his commitment to his local region.

Of two special issues, however, there can be no doubt: the first is that in 1953 Faulkner, as he looked back at his early relationship with Anderson, wished to acknowledge a debt for lessons learned. (For what Faulkner owed to Anderson in a more comprehensive sense, the reader is referred to Meriwether's fine essay entitled "Faulkner's Essays on Anderson." [3]) The second issue is this: that very early in their relationship Faulkner gave positive testimony to his regard and even affection for Anderson by dedicating to him his third novel, *Sartoris;* and in *Mosquitoes,* by assigning to Fairchild the celebrated definition of genius as the "Passion Week of the heart," a phrase that was to make its fortune and almost certainly represents Faulkner's own definition of genius. On a later page I shall take this matter up again and try to indicate what Fairchild meant by it (and what I presume Faulkner himself meant). At this point, however, I want to return to Kauffman's estimate of Fairchild's merits and deficiencies, for Kauffman's estimate may reveal Faulkner's own artistic credo as he began his career as a writer.

Assuming that Faulkner's roots were indeed firmly planted in Southern soil and that Anderson's example of such commitment could hardly have been more than confirmatory, Faulkner's very regional commitment must have brought up another issue, for the writers who had first excited Faulkner's literary aspirations were nearly all British—and, moreover, British writers who had themselves been strongly influenced by the French writers of the period. Swinburne and Yeats are examples. Some of these French writers who had influenced them, Faulkner himself had read—for example, Verlaine, Balzac, and Gautier. So the claim upon this young Southern writer almost from the beginning was a double claim, that of a regional art but also that of an international art. Did these claims conflict with each other? Can a novelist be regional and at the same time international?

A great deal of Southern writing in the generation before Faulkner had been "local color" fiction. Local color represents the pitfall on the regional side—the writer's presentation of a way of life because it is *not* universal but merely odd and quaint. Of this pitfall, the author of *Mosquitoes* was fully aware. One way in which he shows it is in having Julius Kauffman say (p. 243): "Details dont matter, details only entertain us. And nothing that merely

3. In *Faulkner: Fifty Years after "The Marble Faun,"* ed. George H. Wolfe (University, Ala., 1976), pp. 159–81.

entertains us can matter. . . ." Regionalism as local color merely entertains.

The pitfall on the other side was, of course, a too immediate appropriation of the universal—the lack of local detail or the misuse of local detail. Faulkner's attempts to rewrite the poems that Housman had published in *A Shropshire Lad* would furnish obvious examples. The landscapes in these poems are arty and contrived; the flora and fauna, unreal. Faulkner's first two novels do not err in that direction. Though they consistently drive toward something beyond local color, they are indeed full of the detail of the Southern way of life. Though *Mosquitoes* has less of it than *Soldiers' Pay*, the reader who knows New Orleans will perceive the faithfulness to local detail even in *Mosquitoes*.

Does the "international element" show itself at all in these novels, and if so, how? In *Soldiers' Pay* the case is clear. Charlestown, Georgia, is an extension into the Southern states of the Waste Land of Western civilization. It has suffered a loss of faith and consequent spiritual aridity. In *Mosquitoes,* the influence of twentieth-century writers like Eliot and Joyce is even clearer, though not so much in theme as in technique. *Mosquitoes* is, in fact, a kind of display case of the verbal, scenic, and thematic innovations of Eliot, Joyce, and their fellow craftsmen. But the themes which one associates with such writers—civilizational collapse, alienation, and the desiccation of the older symbols— have in *Mosquitoes* been somewhat blurred. One can find in *Mosquitoes* the theme of the true artist's alienation from society, but Faulkner here follows a conception of the artist that had been largely shaped by the Romantic writers of the earlier nineteenth century and by the Decadent writers of the *fin de siècle*. Gordon, for example, is closer to the young Yeats's wandering Aengus than he is to Eliot's Prufrock, and closer still to the *poète maudit* of the Decadents of the nineteenth century.

Faulkner may, of course, have been aware that the fissure running through twentieth-century culture, the separation of heart and head, provided the subject matter for Eliot, a separation that had begun to be noticed a century earlier by Romantic poets like Wordsworth and Coleridge. (If Faulkner *was* aware of this continuity, he thereby proved himself more aware than most men of his day.) Nevertheless, the tone of Eliot and Joyce was almost belligerently antiromantic. This difference, Faulkner certainly sensed. Amid such a collision of forces, where did the young Faulkner stand?

The problem comes to a head in the poems that Faulkner offered to the reader as coming from the pen of Eva Wiseman. Faulkner knows enough of the new mode to be able to concoct effective parodies of it. But were they to Faulkner anything more than parodies? To be specific: What did Faulkner really think of his poem entitled "The Raven Bleak and Philomel"? That he had simply neatly skewered Eliot's "Sweeney Among the Nightingales"? Or that his poem had positive merit? That he was to publish it later in *A Green Bough* perhaps does not prove that he was necessarily proud of it; but it does show that he was willing to allow it a life outside the context of *Mosquitoes*.

Or did Faulkner share Fairchild's distaste for another of Eva Wiseman's poems, "Hermaphroditus"? As we have remarked earlier, Fairchild regards it, and modern verse in general, as "a kind of dark perversion." What complicates the problem further is that "Hermaphroditus," unlike "The Raven Bleak," is actually a good deal closer to Swinburne's poetry—for which Faulkner at sixteen had conceived such a passion—than to Eliot's. It may be impossible to give a convincing answer to the questions just raised. My own guess is that when Faulkner was writing *Mosquitoes* he was still more or less the unregenerate romantic. What is important is that he was, nevertheless, thoroughly aware of the new poetry and the new fiction as challenging, not only the techniques but the philosophical assumptions of the older romantic literature, and that he was already convinced that any regional literature that aspired to be a genuine *literature* had to be prepared to be judged in universal terms and in modern terms, which meant compelling it to meet the standards of international literature.

Allen Tate, in a celebrated essay,[4] accounts for the rise of a genuine Southern literature in the 1920s by arguing that then, for the first time, the Southern writer had an opportunity to look at

4. Allen Tate, *Essays of Four Decades* (Chicago, 1968), pp. 577–92.

his region with some detachment. He no longer felt compelled to make a defense of it, a motive that tended to turn poetry into rhetoric and fiction into propaganda. He could at last judge his region and sometimes even quarrel with it. A serious literature comprehending inner tensions thus, at last, became possible. Although Tate was speaking not about Faulkner but in general terms about a whole generation of Southern writers, the argument seems to me clearly to apply to Faulkner, who made this discovery for himself and in his own terms. It is a mark of his genius and his sure literary instincts that he made it unaided and so early in his career.

I have used the phrase "made this discovery," but *Mosquitoes,* of course, is not an essay in criticism nor a literary manifesto. It is a novel in which various characters talk, and sometimes argue, with one another. The fictional mode is faithfully maintained by Faulkner, but this is not to say that he has not recognized the basic problem. In Julius Kauffman's suggestion that the writer—even the regional writer—needs to apply to his work "a standard of literature that is international," we have convincing evidence that Faulkner at least as early as 1925 was moving in the right direction.

Such may be the most important thing to note about this novel, but of course it concerns the *author* and not really the novel itself as a dramatic action. In fact, there is too little dramatic action in *Mosquitoes,* and Faulkner, in solving his personal problem, has found no way of presenting that solution in the novel. It has no very close relation, dramatically or otherwise, to what goes on aboard the yacht. In fact, it has only a rather oblique relation to most of the conversation by Mrs. Maurier's guests.

Readers may or may not find some humor in the constant references to grapefruit, or in Mrs. Maurier's pained embarrassment at the antics of some of her guests. (Her role is delineated in strokes almost as broad as those describing Mrs. Claypool in the Marx Brothers' *A Night at the Opera.*) There are attempts at other sorts of comedy, such as the humors of the young: Josh Robyn's disabling the mechanism of the ship in order to secure a metal rod with which to bore out his special tobacco pipe, or Pat Robyn's dogging the steps of her brother and insisting that she is going to accompany him to Yale in the fall. (None but the more determinedly psychoanalytical, however, will insist upon regarding the relationship of Pat and Josh as incestuous.)

There are the tall tales spun by Fairchild about Al Jackson, that direct descendant of Andrew Jackson, the victor of the Battle of New Orleans in 1815, who bred up a flock of sea-going sheep and whose brother Claude actually turned into a shark. In time, Faulkner learned to tell the tall tale to perfection, but the Al Jackson story is early and crude—not really of vintage quality.

It is scarcely accurate to call the "action" that occurs on the yacht merely incidental, for if someone should ask "incidental to what?" there would be no obvious answer. These bored people are just killing time. Perhaps the one exception to this generalization is Pat's adventure with David West, the young steward. She impulsively suggests that they slip off from the yacht and visit the little resort town of Mandeville. Their journey is a disaster. They are almost devoured by the mosquitoes. They get hopelessly lost. In the end, they come upon a foul-mouthed swamp-rat who owns a boat and whom Pat pays to return them to the yacht. If we see the theme of *Mosquitoes* as a critique of romanticism, then the account of their expedition does have a certain relevance; reality has a harsh way of dealing with dreams—not only with the artist's dream, but with the romantic dream of the innocent young. Pat's Mandeville becomes a tantalizing mirage. She parches with thirst, but though the road runs through sodden swamps, there is no water fit to drink. And the mosquitoes never let up their attacks.

What accentuates the sense of a void in the novel, a monotonous no-action, is the elaborate and carefully articulated framework in which the young novelist has placed it. There is a Prologue and an Epilogue, which have to do with events before and after the voyage of the *Nausikaa*. The voyage itself is partitioned into chapters entitled "The First Day" on through "The Fourth Day": and these chapters are broken up into percisely labeled sections: "Ten O'Clock," "Eleven O'Clock," "One O'Clock," etc. It is likely that Faulkner took these devices from Joyce's *Ulysses*, but whatever their source and whatever their purpose, the effect of this meticulously indicated chronology has to be ironic. Otherwise, why note

148

so precisely hours in which nothing happened? But perhaps this was just the point the author wanted to score.

Earlier I have said that for this young writer the important issue was the tension between the regional and the universal—the arrival at a truth that was true for Lafayette County, Mississippi, and yet also true for the world at large. Whether or not he solved that problem in his first or second book, it is to be counted a sort of triumph if he at least shows that he is aware of it. Faulkner is aware of all the angularities and awkwardnesses of the world of actuality. It is all but impossible to mold the real world closer to the heart's desire. The genuine artist can create his ideal in words or in marble or with pigments on canvas, but he realizes that that vision of perfection is not actually available in this world. To assume that it is available is to become fatuous and absurd; the genuine artist does not delude himself.

So it is with those on the *Nausikaa* who know art best. There is a vein of proper cynicism in Kauffman. Fairchild, in spite of confessing to sentiment, cultivates a bluff earthiness. Gordon, in spite of his idealistic visions, is hard as nails. Yet though they refuse to delude themselves, all three, I should argue, are romanticists. Like the great Romantic poets of the nineteenth century in England, Germany, and France, their concern is with the split between art and nature, the heart and the head, dream and reality. They are hard-bitten romanticists and see little or no hope in overcoming the split, but they can strive, as Kauffman puts it, to create a maiden "that life [has] not had time to create," in order to represent one's "impossible heart's desire."

I have said that Faulkner was at this point still an unregenerate romanticist, but in *Mosquitoes* he nevertheless insists upon undercutting all romantic effusions and exaltations. As we shall see, he does so even when Fairchild is to make a pronouncement in the truth of which Faulkner surely believed. For he refuses to violate the consistency of Fairchild's character in the interest of giving the truth rhetorical emphasis.

Fairchild begins his statement with his usual fumbling as he tries to find words for his vision. Yet what is the "Passion Week of the heart"? If the word "Week" means anything at all, it can hardly consist in "that *instant* of timeless beatitude" with which Fairchild identifies it. But Fairchild is by this time very drunk, and only a pedant would be too hard on him, particularly when his immediate correction does get matters right. In fact, he finally develops his idea quite coherently. There is, for example, no real contradiction in his making his instant "timeless," for the beatitude that comes at such moments partakes of the nature of eternity and thus is really outside the realm of time. "Genius" is here being described, one notes, not as an act of making but as an act of vision, in which we see the discordant "accidents" of life reconciled and brought into harmony. In this process, the brain itself seems to be passive: its only function is to accept this timeless beatitude that is given to it as an act of grace. One seems to look into the heart of things. Such moments are what Wordsworth called "spots of time." As a novelist, Fairchild is presumably aware that, for the writer, even such vision as this is not enough. The writer has to be able to find the words that will convey his experience; but here he chooses—or rather, since I believe he is here speaking Faulkner's own thoughts, Faulkner prefers—to make genius the ability to achieve such insights, not the ability to render the experience in words.

The emphasis is on the poet's heart rather than on his craftsmanship; and yet Faulkner is thoroughly aware of the fragility of such transcendence. Thus, just after Fairchild has delivered himself of this definition of genius and is himself caught up in the experience about which he has spoken, he stares for a moment "into the hushed mad sky, hearing the dark and simple heart of things"—and then begins to vomit. No wonder; he has drunk a lot, and the retching of the body does not necessarily obliterate the sense of "timeless beatitude." Faulkner is making the point that our transcendent visions are dependent upon a thoroughly earthy body which has its own urgencies and makes its own claims.

The series of comic episodes with which the novel ends is presumably an attempt to stress the same point: art is a precious thing, but it achieves nothing. Art butters no parsnips. Art is not of this world. Through Gordon's fingers it can reveal the secret life that lies behind the mask of Mrs. Maurier's face, but it cannot change her life. For most people, it is simply an amusement, a plaything, or not even that—simply an irrelevance.

If we want to poke and probe a little, *Mosquitoes* can tell us a good deal about the young Faulkner's genius and what he thought of his own art. But that is not at all to say that it is a successful novel. It has its bits of brilliance; it can be made to say something. But it is unfocused and at once too easy and too difficult. It demands too much of its reader and yet gives too little in return.

6

First Forays into Yoknapatawpha County

Two of Faulkner's early stories, stories that achieved publication as so many of his early attempts did not, have to do with women who are, if not clinically insane, regarded by their neighbors and acquaintances as quite mad. The neighbors use the word "crazy." One of this pair is Mrs. Jim Gant, whose story is told in "Miss Zilphia Gant," published in June 1932 but written some time before December 1928, and perhaps earlier.[1] The other woman is Miss Emily Grierson of "A Rose for Emily," Faulkner's first published story (April 1930; probably written in the latter months of 1929). These two stories show, among other things, Faulkner's continuing interest in feminine psychology, though neither Emily Grierson nor Mrs. Gant (nor Mrs. Gant's daughter Zilphia) bears any resemblance to Cecily Saunders of *Soldiers' Pay* or to the jill-flirts of *Mayday* or to the Diana-like Patricia Robyn of *Mosquitoes*.

Faulkner has not described in detail the pressures that shaped and perhaps distorted the soul of Mrs. Gant. At almost her first introduction to the reader she is a woman of iron will capable of the swift and merciless punishment that she visits on her unfaithful husband. But Faulkner gives a rather thorough accounting of

---

1. See Blotner, pp. 600 and 631–32.

what happened to Zilphia Gant. Zilphia may well be called the Amazon's daughter, brought up to distrust and fear men because her mother hates males. But Zilphia does not yield to her mother's hatred of men immediately or ever entirely. Faulkner provides an anecdote from Zilphia's life just as she was entering her 'teens. Mrs. Gant discovered Zilphia lying beside a boy under a blanket "in the mutual, dreamlike mesmeric throes of puberty" and was horrified. The incident reminds one of similar incidents in *Elmer* and in *Soldiers' Pay,* but Zilphia is no Faulknerian nymph. And if she ever had that potential, her mother disciplined her out of it.

Like her mother and like Emily Grierson, Zilphia becomes an obsessed woman, and also like them she comes to possess an iron will. Once her mother has died, Zilphia shows the same determination and tenacity in securing for herself what has finally become her obsession—a child of her own to care for and to rear. By the end of the story Zilphia has found a cure for her psychic problems. She is no longer tormented at night by racking dreams. Furthermore, she eventually wins for herself a place in the community. Though people continue to call her "Miss Zilphia," they no longer do so out of "tolerance or pity." She enjoys her food—in fact, she has become plump as a partridge. Her widow's black becomes her, and the ladies who come to her dressmaking shop "never tire of fondling" her child, little Zilphia. If her story is one of abnormal psychology, it is also a kind of success story, in which the victim discovers for herself the proper mental hygiene.[2]

Miss Emily is also a victim. She suffers from the crippling restrictions imposed by an overbearing parent—this time a father—who drives away the young men that come to court his daughter, and thus condemns her to the lonely isolation of an unwanted spinsterhood. Like Zilphia, she makes an effort to resist her father's influence and to secure the husband that she needs and wants. She is willing to defy the censure of the community by accepting the courtship of a man whom the people of Jefferson regard as a coarse Yankee, far beneath her in social standing. But when her paramour prepares to desert her, she refuses to be jilted. She insists on holding him, on retaining his dead if not his living body; and so

2. See below, Notes, pp. 380–82.

she poisons him and conceals his corpse in an upper bedroom, which becomes a macabre bridal chamber.

Miss Emily thus crosses the line that separates a powerful but harmless obsession from homicidal mania. Miss Zilphia, of course, does not go that far, but doubtless she too breaks the law in achieving her will, though the author does not specify what falsehoods she must have told and what misrepresentations she made to the civil authorities.

Having waited for six months after her mother's death to see whether her husband will return to claim her—her mother had separated her from her husband before the marriage could be consummated—Zilphia gives up, and actually feels a measure of relief that this period of hopeless waiting is over. She has secured a partner for her dressmaking shop and her business is prospering; yet within the year she begins to make timid efforts to find her husband through letters that she places in various newspapers. Meanwhile, she scans carefully all the wedding notices, until one day she finds an account of her former husband's marriage to another woman in the nearby city of Memphis.

Apparently she makes no further effort to communicate with him, but she does arrange with a Memphis detective agency to keep her informed of every significant change in his life. Through her weekly report from this agency, she learns of his new wife's pregnancy, then of her death in childbed, and of the husband's death when hit by a car as he attempts to cross the street to the hospital where his dead wife lies. The next day, we are told, Zilphia arrived at the Memphis hospital to take charge of the newborn child. What Zilphia told the authorities in order to get possession of the child and how she settled matters with the relatives of the dead parents—surely one or the other had some relatives—we never learn. All we do learn is that in three years' time, Zilphia returns to Jefferson, in widow's weeds, with a wedding ring and a three-year-old daughter. Her accomplishment in bringing off this coup implies a passion, a determination, and a resourcefulness that recall her mother's.

The mother, one remembers, when she learned that Jim Gant had left her for another woman, immediately borrowed a neighbor's pistol, left her child Zilphia with a friend, and departed to dispose of the guilty pair. When she came back to her child, she returned the pistol without a word of explanation to its owner and without even taking the trouble to eject the two exploded cartridge shells. She is evidently an excellent shot and obviously fired no needless bullets into dying flesh. She is perfectly economical and businesslike in the whole matter and, thenceforward, just as thorough in protecting Zilphia from all contact with males.

Zilphia, in spite of her desire to flee from her mother, has been too completely repressed to leave her mother's house with the itinerant house-painter whom she has impulsively married.[3] Indeed, in the end she comes to resemble her mother. The last glimpse we have of Miss Zilphia provides a repetition of the scene depicted pages earlier when Mrs. Gant walks to school holding Zilphia's hand. Now it is Zilphia walking to school holding little Zilphia by the hand. She is even dressed as her mother used to dress, with a "sewing apron of black oil cloth, and the straight thin glints of needles in her black bosom and the gossamer festooning of the thread."

So Miss Emily, as she grows older, takes on the traits of her domineering father. She insists upon her own version of things (e.g., that her taxes in Jefferson have been remitted); she commands what she wants (e.g., she compels the druggist, by sheer force of character, to sell her the arsenic without telling him for what purpose she means to use it); she is completely rigid and inflexible in purpose. Though her father kept her from marrying any of the eligible young men who came courting, Emily, nevertheless, clings to her father's memory. His crayon portrait, placed on "a tarnished gilt easel before the fireplace," dominates Miss Emily's parlor. When he dies, Miss Emily refuses to let the body be taken out of the house for burial. For three days she even denies that he is dead. The narrator of the story observes that "We did not say she was crazy then. . . . . we knew that with nothing left, she would

---

3. Blotner suggests (pp. 600–01) that Faulkner may have been remembering here the ending of one of Joyce's stories in *Dubliners* in which Eveline, at the last minute, finds that she is unable to break away from her unhappy home to leave for South America with her fiancé. I think Blotner's suggestion is sound.

have to cling to that which had robbed her, as people will." This is sound psychology, and in spite of the violence, improbable events, and gothic horrors, "A Rose for Emily" embodies psychological truth.

Mrs. Gant, Zilphia Gant, and Emily Grierson are all grotesques in Sherwood Anderson's special sense. (See p. 107, above.) Each has taken a partial truth to be her whole truth. There are differences to be sure, between Faulkner's three women and the several characters whose stories are told in *Winesburg, Ohio*. A little later I mean to discuss some of the differences between Winesburg and Jefferson, Mississippi. But first, one ought to point out that none of these women, neither Faulkner's nor Anderson's, are merely regional freaks. There is a relationship between them and conditions in the world at large. For example, one of the stories in *Winesburg, Ohio* has to do with Alice Hindman, whose early love affair had come to nothing. Now at twenty-seven, she says to herself, "I am becoming old and queer." One rainy night, Alice, having undressed, impulsively runs downstairs naked and out into the rain. As she feels "the cold rain on her body," she is possessed by a "mad desire to run naked through the streets. . . ." She almost succeeds in attracting the attention of a man to whom she calls out, but she resists her impulse to run up and embrace him, and she gets back safely into her room, where she falls on her bed and weeps broken-heartedly. "What is the matter with me?" she thinks. "I will do something dreadful if I am not careful."

In Part II of *The Waste Land* the woman in the rich room exclaims in her frustration and loneliness: "I shall rush out as I am, and walk the street / With my hair down, so." She and Alice are sisters of the age, both suffering from the same general malaise. So is Zilphia Gant. After her mother's death, and after she is sure that the man with whom she has gone through a marriage ceremony is not going to come back for her, she tells herself that the Virgin Mary conceived a child without the help of a man, and Faulkner describes how, rousing up at night, "furious, [with] her hands clenched at her sides, the covers flung back and her opened thighs tossing," she would tell herself, "I will conceive! I'll make myself conceive!"

156

Though in Emily Grierson the malaise of the age becomes clinical insanity, readers who interpret the story as a horrifying tale of necrophilia, aimed merely to shock and titillate, have missed the point. Yet to see that Miss Emily's story has general significance will require us to understand how she stood in relation to the community in which she had grown up and to understand what the inhabitants of Jefferson must have made of her life and death. For her horrible act to acquire universal meaning, it will have to become "localized." [4] That is to say, the reader will have to come to understand that her act had significance for a particular group of people—the participants in a culture to which she and they belong. Otherwise, her murder of her lover and her retention of his body become simply one more bizarre case history, one more item for the daily newspapers, the sort of thing that catches the reader's eye and produces a momentary smile or a grimace of horror.[5]

In *Winesburg, Ohio* the community is hardly visible. It is really a society of "others"—presumably people who are insensitive or indifferent to the misfits and grotesque characters in the little town, the very characters who interest Anderson and whose stories he is concerned to tell. This is not to say that Anderson ignores the community at large—or despises it as Sinclair Lewis, say, comes close to despising Gopher Prairie. But it is to say that the other people in *Winesburg* remain simply rather conventional and uninteresting "squares." They have no story worth telling: their basic function is to serve as a rather featureless backdrop for those curious and sometimes pathetic people whose stories are worth recounting.

Something like this state of affairs obtains in "Miss Zilphia Gant." Mrs. Jim Gant lives in Yoknapatawpha County, in Frenchman's Bend, some three days' journey by wagon from Memphis, Tennessee. After despatching her husband, Mrs. Gant moves to

4. No real paradox is involved in this assertion. Monstrous acts which occur in a vacuum—which have no significance to the people who make up the community in which they occur—can scarcely have any real significance for mankind in general.

5. See below, Notes, pages 386–87, for some instances of similar stories reported in newspapers.

Jefferson, where she spends the rest of her life and where Zilphia grows up. But we learn almost nothing about the community or Mrs. Gant's relation to it. The town authorities do eventually require Mrs. Gant to send Zilphia to school, and we learn, from time to time, of the town's views: there is pity for the little girl whose face is seen peering out of a barred window. The townsfolk mildly deplore Zilphia's falling in love with a house-painter, since house-painters tend to be ne'er-do-wells. They regard Mrs. Gant as most eccentric, and some interpret her strange actions as proof that she is downright crazy.

Yet the author keeps the community at arm's length—pretty well at the length at which the community keeps Mrs. Gant. Significantly, there is in the story no representative of, no spokesman for, the community. Section II of the story does open with a sentence that reads: "They told me in the town how she and her daughter, Zilphia, lived in a single room," etc., and this would imply that there is a narrator of the story. But James B. Meriwether has pointed out that "me" does not occur in the typescript and actually is a mistake made by the typesetter, or else an editorial intrusion.[6] (This questionable "me" is the only reference to a narrator in the story.)

In "A Rose for Emily," on the other hand, there is a narrator who, though he never identifies himself, clearly speaks for the community. For example, he never says "I thought," or "I knew," or "I believed," but speaks rather of "our whole town"; he says that "we were not pleased" at certain happenings; he remarks that "We did not say [Miss Emily] was crazy then"; he tells his listener that "the next day we all said"; and so on. This anonymous speaker never insists on his individual judgments. (The community is a true community and he is clearly its voice.)

This is not to say that there are not subgroupings within the community, including different generations. They have their differing emphases and even differing ideas of what is proper. Colonel Sartoris, for example, belongs to an older generation, with a paternalistic ethic, a certain elaborate courtliness of manner, and

6. In an introductory note to *Miss Zilphia Gant,* mimeographed and privately circulated.

a good many old-fashioned beliefs. It was he who, undoubtedly with the approbation of his peers, concocted the fiction that Miss Emily owed no real estate taxes because of an arrangement made years before between her father and the town. The new generation, blessed with more up-to-date ideas, insists that she pay taxes like everyone else, that she should attach the new street numbers to her house, and so on.

The narrator is presumably not one of the remaining Civil War veterans—notice in what terms he refers to them—and he is probably younger than the generation of Colonel Sartoris (who must have died a good many years before Miss Emily's death). But the narrator is not a member of the younger generation either, or if he is in actual years, he is far from sympathetic with their ideas and he does not identify himself with them. He has not only a sense of community but also a sense of history. I think of him as a man in his fifties or sixties at the time of Miss Emily's death.[7] Though he is immersed in the customs and beliefs and values of the Jefferson community, he has, nevertheless, a good observer's detachment. He is also an accomplished story-teller. He knows how to build toward an effect, how to hold up a disclosure in the interest of suspense, and how to heighten dramatic impact. He is, however, much more than a tricky rhetorician. He is concerned with the deeper meanings of the story he has to tell, and though he is no glib moralist (as all too many of those who have written on Faulkner's works are) he never lets his auditor forget that Miss Emily is a human being.

It is interesting to see what he does not do. He eschews, for example, the use of psychological explanations, though this literate narrator of the mid-1920s may have known something about them. (Freud and Havelock Ellis are at least mentioned in Faulkner's

7. Some commentators on this story have badly confused matters by speaking of a "plural narrator" or of making the narrator one of a small band of Miss Emily's former suitors who helped her hide the body of Homer Barron in a sealed room and were thus accomplices after the fact to Miss Emily's crime of murder. The symbol-mongers have also had a field day with the story: Miss Emily represents the Old South; Miss Emily's necrophilia "suggests the necrophilia of an entire society that lived with a dead but unburied past," etc. For further discussion of some of these mares' nests, see Notes, pp. 384–88.

first two novels, and Jung, at least by implication.) The narrator is plainly not interested in exploring Miss Emily's aberrant actions in clinical terms. Mad as she has evidently become, he is willing to see her as not only a pathetic but even a tragic figure.

The narrator begins with the conclusion of his story,[8] with Miss Emily's death and funeral, a matter that allows him to comment quite naturally on her relation to the community in which she lived and died, and to its history. Almost at once, the narrator spells out the terms of the relationship: She "had been a tradition, a duty, and a care; a sort of hereditary obligation upon the town . . ." (*Collected Stories*, p. 119). The last phrase allows the speaker to present, by way of illustration, the first of the several brilliant scenes into which he disposes Miss Emily's story. In the first scene we are inside Miss Emily's rarely opened parlor, and listen to the polite and even overawed deputation sent by the Board of Aldermen to talk to Miss Emily about the taxes that she had not paid for years. We witness how Miss Emily, by refusing to accept their authority, "vanquished them, horse and foot." She owes no taxes. Colonel Sartoris had remitted her taxes years before. Let the delegation see Colonel Sartoris. In this scene we are also given the first clear hint of Miss Emily's madness, for the narrator tells us that the Colonel, whom she suggested the deputation see, had been dead for nearly ten years.

This victory of Miss Emily's brings to the narrator's mind another such victory that she had won over the town authorities some thirty years earlier. Two years after her father had died and a short time after the man "we had believed she would marry" had left town without marrying her, her neighbors had complained of a bad smell emanating from the Grierson residence. But the mayor had pointed out that you can't "accuse a lady to her face of smelling bad," and the matter was attended to quietly and privately by four men, under cover of night, throwing lime around the house and into the cellar, to enter which they had to break open the door.

The narrator observes that it was at this time that people began to feel sorry for Miss Emily, people who had heretofore resented

8. For a chronology of the story, see below, Notes, pp. 382–84.

the Grierson's pride and self-assurance. Now that Miss Emily was thirty, still unmarried, and facing a life of genteel poverty, now that her father was dead, she had become somehow humanized. As the narrator puts it, "we were not pleased exactly, but vindicated; even with insanity in the family she wouldn't have turned down all of her chances if they had really materialized." The mention of the strain of inherited insanity offers an opportunity to mention Miss Emily's refusal to let her father's body be buried.

The narrator (we are now in Section III) mentions her long illness after her father's death, the coming of Homer Barron, the "rustling of craned silk and satin behind jalousies" and the scandalized whispering: "Do you suppose it's really so?" Then follows the incident with the druggist when Miss Emily buys the arsenic. The word about her purchase of poison must have leaked out almost at once, for in Section IV the narrator tells his auditor: "So the next day we all said, 'She will kill herself'; and we said it would be the best thing." For Miss Emily is a lady. The town is confident that, mad or not, as a lady she will not suffer a stain on her honor. But Miss Emily turns out to be not a Southern lady; she is a Clytemnestra, a figure out of tragedy. As she retreats more and more into herself and defends her privacy, she refuses even the routine ties with the rest of the town. She does not allow the town authorities to "fasten the metal [street] number above her door [or to] attach a mailbox to it. She would not listen to them." And so she lives out her life and dies in a downstairs room of her decaying house.

In the foregoing paragraphs I have been stressing the masterly fashion in which the narrator has organized his tale into a few powerful dramatic scenes. But the narrator has been doing something more: he measures Emily Grierson's exercise of will at every point against the counterforce of tradition, convention, decreed usage, and received moral law. Her struggle to assert herself has, especially after her father's death, found the force against which it must exert itself in the community of Jefferson. But the community is not simply a monolithic block, a cold and anonymous force that does not even comprehend such resistance to its inertia. The town of Jefferson is human (often all too human) and it is fascinated by Miss Emily's behavior. If it is often envious, titillated, exasperated, and at times outraged, it can also be sympathetic, pitying, admiring, and from time to time overawed. Even those townspeople who were disposed to resent Miss Emily's pride and disdain found themselves emphatically on her side when two of her female cousins from Alabama were summoned to attend to a Grierson woman who had probably stooped to folly.

If the reader of Faulkner's story is properly sensitive to the way the community responds to the various events in which Miss Emily figures, he ought to be able to see what is meant when Miss Emily is said to have "passed from generation to generation—dear, inescapable, impervious, tranquil, and perverse" (p. 128). The terms are contradictory; some are laudatory, others derogatory. But there are perfectly obvious senses in which every one of them fits Miss Emily's case.

What did the narrator feel when the upstairs room was forced open and he looked on the bridal bed? What did the community make of the total history of Miss Emily, taking into account everything, including the final gruesome details? Well, a community of folk is not a fully articulate organism. Doubtless few individuals in the community would have been able to find the words that form some of the narrator's observations, but I don't believe that even the narrator's analogies would have been lost on them. When he found in Emily's face "a vague resemblance . . . to angels in colored church windows—sort of tragic and serene," they would have accepted her aura of detachment and serenity, even if the serenity was in part the calm of madness. Moreover, some of them would have apprehended his comparison of her face to a "lighthouse-keeper's face." The keeper's is a public function. His light serves to warn ships off the dangerous rocks on which his lighthouse is built. But he pays a price: he lives apart from the rest of humanity in lonely isolation, and the light that he maintains offers no light to him. He himself peers out into blackness.

The members of the community, having heard some of these observations uttered, might well say, "That's about right." In short, the community might experience feelings and attitudes that its various members could not themselves put into words. As for the total meaning of Miss Emily's story, let me try to articulate what many of the more sensitive Jeffersonians may have felt. Most, I believe would have been wiser than to see the story of Emily Grierson's life as a mere cautionary tale (don't consider yourself better than other people; don't try to shut yourself up in the past; do accept change as the law of life). After all, even the stories of Oedipus and King Lear when pared down to cautionary tales become pretty small potatoes.

The members of the Jefferson community might well have felt that in some sense Emily Grierson was more sinned against than sinning. She had not willed the great warping of her life; it had been imposed upon her. They would have felt, too, that her insistence on meeting life on her own terms had something heroic about it. Indeed, in a world growing more and more timid and conformist, Miss Emily's insistence on having matters on her own terms has something exhilarating about it. Even madness can sometimes be meaningful. It can throw light on man's heroic energy as well as on the distortions of his values.

With "A Rose for Emily," Faulkner has clearly entered into Yoknapatawpha County, and the advantages to be gained thereby are in that story set forth in bold relief, especially when we compare "A Rose for Emily" with another story of this period, "Idyll in the Desert." "Idyll" is told by a narrator who knew the principals of his story well, though, like the narrator in "A Rose for Emily," he has no real part in the story itself. (I have suggested earlier that Faulkner might have adopted this narrative device from Irvin S. Cobb.) But this tale of a woman's sacrifice for a man who was not worth the sacrifice is set forth in a kind of cultural vacuum. The man and the woman are from the East, but are living in Arizona, where he has gone to try to cure his tuberculosis. The narrator is a Westerner who rides the post route and who thus has the opportunity to observe this not very idyllic affair. The tuberculous patient is eventually cured and goes back East. The woman who has faithfully nursed him to health and who has abandoned her husband and two children in order to come West with him, remains in Arizona, having herself contracted the disease; but she waits in confident expectation that her lover will return. He never does, and years later, when he does glimpse her, quite by accident, at a railway station, he does not recognize her. He is on his way to Los Angeles on his honeymoon; she is lying on a stretcher on the way to her death in a hospital in the same city.

The narrator of "Idyll" is a good observer and can tell a good yarn, but he is in this story too much the outsider. The woman's love for the faithless man and her confidence maintained for eight years that he will return to her violates all the probabilities. She does an "insane" thing, but lacks Miss Emily's madness or even Miss Zilphia's mad obsession that might allow us to accept it.

A comparison of "A Rose for Emily" with "Miss Zilphia Gant" reveals the importance of the Yoknapatawpha setting even more sharply. The story of Zilphia Gant is technically a story of people living in the County. Mrs. Gant moves with Zilphia from French-man's Bend to Jefferson, where most of the action actually occurs. But in this story the community never really comes alive. In "A Rose for Emily" it is the narrator-interpreter who makes it come alive, and he can do so because he is the spokesman for a living community. "Miss Zilphia" loses heavily by lacking such a nar-rator. To be specific: both Miss Zilphia and her mother remain curious isolates, as Miss Emily, for all her aloofness from other people, does not. It is what is aberrant about both the Gant women that holds our attention—not traits and qualities which, however shocking, have some general significance. The early warping of Miss Zilphia is developed even more elaborately than is the early warping of Miss Emily, but Miss Zilphia remains odd and pathetic, never universal and tragic, as Miss Emily is.

The early commentators on Faulkner were wrong in assuming that he was aiming at sociology. Instead of exclaiming, "Look, how dreadful Yoknapatawpha County must be that hath such monsters in it," they would have exhibited more discernment by noting that, through locating certain strange and sometimes depraved ex-pressions of the human spirit in an authentic community, Faulk-ner made their occurrence more nearly credible and endowed them with universal significance. In short, Faulkner's very interest in the strange and excessive required a full cultural context, not the reverse.[9]

In 1929 Faulkner published *Sartoris,* a revised and shortened form of *Flags in the Dust* (which itself was not published until 1973). *Sartoris* is usually regarded as marking Faulkner's entrance into his special domain, Yoknapatawpha County. For that reason, I included a discussion of *Sartoris* in my *William Faulkner: The Yoknapatawpha Country;* but since the preceding chapters of the present volume are concerned with the early Faulkner and his development, it seems in order here to include some remarks on the original version of *Sartoris,* that is, *Flags in the Dust.*[10]

Faulkner probably began work on this account of the Sartoris family in the fall of 1926; he had completed it by September 1927. Thus, when writing "A Rose for Emily," he had enjoyed the advantage of having already explored what was to become his special fictional world, and of having fully and richly exploited it. Because of the short story's finish and compactness, it illustrates better than does *Flags in the Dust* the immense value of the setting, especially in making credible some of the psychological issues with which the young Faulkner was so much concerned, things such as Miss Emily's madness or Mrs. Gant's obsession.

Such problems are very important in *Flags in the Dust.* Indeed, in moving into the Yoknapatawpha country, Faulkner did not abandon his interest in madness, psychic aberrancies, or sexual complexities and ambiguities. Nor did he show any falling off of interest in the compulsions and inadequacies of the romantic dream. Narcissa Benbow, for example, is fearful of men. She

9. In this connection one might remember the division of labor worked out by Wordsworth and Coleridge in putting together the *Lyrical Ballads.* Wordsworth was to "give the charm of novelty to things of every day," by awaking his reader to the wonders to be found in ordinary experience. Coleridge was to deal with "persons and characters supernatural, or at least romantic," yet to give these incredible or out-of-the-way materials "a human interest and a semblance of truth." Faulkner's role in much of his early writing seems to me closer to Coleridge's role than to Wordsworth's.

10. For the relationship between the novels, see below, Notes, pp. 388–91.

sometimes declares that she hates them, and yet she has a quasi-morbid dependence on her brother Horace. Horace himself is a born romantic, an aesthete and a dreamer. (Matters such as these were played down somewhat when *Flags in the Dust* was trimmed down and revised into *Sartoris.*)

The "epicene" woman who figures so prominently in *Soldiers' Pay, Elmer,* "To Helen," and *Mosquitoes* sets foot on Yoknapatawpha soil too. Faulkner applies the term to Narcissa (p. 47), and Horace constantly thinks of his sister as a woman of "inviolable virginity." For him, her virginity is quite literally inviolable, for though he dotes on Narcissa, she *is* his sister, and Horace has not the slightest intention of committing incest. He is content to hold her hand occasionally and to tell her that she is "the bride of quietude," as if she were a kind of animated Grecian urn. But Narcissa, in her fear and distrust of men, is also epicene in the sense of "sexless." The adjective is accurate in this instance, for though she is to bear Bayard Sartoris a son, her marriage with him is a disaster.

Faulkner accords Narcissa very sympathetic treatment in *Flags.* Narcissa is shy and fearful; Bayard is unfeeling. Most girls would find it impossible to deal with the problem that he sets for her. In *Sanctuary* and in "There Was a Queen," Narcissa's character goes downhill rapidly. She becomes the abject slave of mere respectability. Though it can be argued that such deterioration might well occur to the psychically bruised woman presented to us in *Flags,* one must concede that the woman who bears her name in the later fiction seems to be a thoroughly different person. More than once in his novels Faulkner has radically changed the personality of a fictional character. It is difficult if not impossible to reconcile the Henry Armstid of *The Hamlet* with the Henry Armstid of *Light in August.* In fairness to the Narcissa of *Flags in the Dust,* it ought to be noted that the men in her life, the brother whom she had promised her dying mother to look after and the young man whom she was eventually to marry, both failed her dismally. Horace betrayed the special relationship that he bore to her, not by just marrying but by marrying a woman whom Narcissa quite properly regarded as completely unworthy. She sees that Belle Mitchell is shallow, crass, and morally dirty, and though Horace concedes that Narcissa's judgment is true, he proceeds, nevertheless, to marry Belle.

Bayard Sartoris is so restless, so filled with guilt, so incapable of tenderness of any kind, that Narcissa, even after her marriage, can establish no real relationship with him. Finally, because he is unable to face the family after he has, by his reckless driving, killed his grandfather, Bayard simply abandons his wife and their unborn child without a word. After these two experiences Narcissa might be forgiven for believing that men are by nature untrustworthy.

One ought to keep in mind that Bayard and Horace, for all that they are antitheses, are both "romantics," the one, an intense activist to whom a racing car or an airplane provides release for a pent-up nervous energy; the other, an intellectual, a dreamer, a man who finds his release by retreating into some ideal world of his imagination. Neither man can bear to face the reality of his life. They both have recently returned to north Mississippi from the war zone in France—Bayard as a reckless fighter-pilot; Horace as a noncombatant, a YMCA secretary in the army. Whether Horace has been directly damaged by his war experience, it is difficult to say, but clearly Bayard has been. He is one of the airmen of whom Faulkner said: "they had exhausted themselves psychically. . . . they were unfitted for the world that they found afterward." Bayard is a perfect example of this thesis. It could be argued that Horace was from birth temperamentally unfitted for the world; that is, if we mean the world of choice, decision, and action—though Horace did attempt to act unselfishly in *Sanctuary* and deserves more credit than he usually gets from Faulkner critics and scholars.

In a sense, then, one might regard *Flags in the Dust* as one more work in which Faulkner applies the test of realism to the cult of romanticism. Since Faulkner's women are typically better realists than men, one index of a man's sense of reality is the conduct of his relations to women. Obviously, both Bayard and Horace fail the test. Yet to draw parallels in this fashion may be to force the novel into a kind of diagrammatic pattern. Faulkner almost certainly did not consciously have in mind such a scheme. He clearly sees the world of the 1920s in much the same way that T. S. Eliot (and others of Eliot's generation) saw it: as a troubled world that was confused about its values and purposes and which, by and large, had not been able to come to terms with the new forces that were convulsing it.

In fact, all the basic themes and situations met with in *Soldiers' Pay* are to be found in *Flags in the Dust;* even some of the speeches made by characters in the first novel might well come out of the mouths of some of the characters in Faulkner's third. Thus, the Reverend Mr. Mahon, an Episcopal clergyman, says that he refused to teach fortitude to his son Donald, for "What is fortitude? Emotional atrophy, gangrene" (*Soldiers' Pay*, p. 68). Horace Benbow, who for a time thought of becoming an Episcopal clergyman, writes to his sister that "Perhaps fortitude is a sorry imitation of something worth while . . ." (*Flags in the Dust*, p. 340).

Donald Mahon had been an airman, and comes home so broken in body and mind that he cannot be called fully alive. But the dead body of young Bayard, as Faulkner observed in his comments on all such World War I aviators, might as well have been sent home to be buried; for he wrecks his car several times, kills his grandfather, and later, as a test pilot, flying a tricky, experimental plane, succeeds in killing himself. Why? Specifically, because he believes himself guilty of causing his twin brother's death. But as his own account indicates, John Sartoris invited his own death by undertaking a foolhardy mission, and it is difficult to see how anyone could have prevented it. Bayard's special sense of responsibility— he was by some minutes the first twin to be born—allows him to feel guilty for not having prevented his brother's daredevil act. But, of course, Bayard is not a reasonable being at this point. He is continually courting danger and death under some completely irrational compulsion.

Bayard seems most calm when he is associating with some of his hunting companions who live in the backwoods, the admirable but eccentric McCallums. Though he acts wickedly in scaring the wits out of his grandfather's black butler, Old Simon, he is also, on the whole, more sane and sensible with the blacks. He is at his best on the Christmas Eve when he stops over with a humble black family and next day shares their Christmas dinner. But generally, Bayard is a neurotic—almost psychotic—case. He is uncomfortable with his peers and with his own family. His war experience has completely unfitted him for living in a small town and in an old-fashioned society.[11]

The matter of the "old-fashioned society" is important. One notices that Faulkner has rather carefully removed one generation from the scene. Bayard's father and mother have been dead for some years. His family has been reduced to his grandfather, "Old Bayard," and his great-grandaunt, Miss Jenny. (The parents of Horace and Narcissa are also dead, and their grandparents and other relatives of that generation have not survived.) Thus, the World War I generation (Bayard, Horace, and Narcissa) are in unmediated contact with a generation that experienced the Civil War (Old Bayard and Miss Jenny Du Pre). One can easily show the significance of this fact by noting that early in the novel Miss Jenny tells the story of the younger of her two brothers, Bayard Sartoris, who was a daredevil, something like the twentieth-century Bayard and his brother John. Her brother Bayard had charged into a Union army encampment to secure some coffee. The element of surprise, his unbelievable derring-do, and a good deal of luck had allowed him to get back to his own side unhurt. But hearing that there were anchovies to be had in the Federal camp, he immediatetly rode back to get them. Once more he almost got by with it, except for the chance that an army cook "who was hidden under the mess stuck his arm out and shot Bayard in the back with a derringer" (p. 19).

The recklessness of Miss Jenny's brother and of his commander, Beauty Stuart, move a captured Yankee major to observe that this sort of thing is not "bravery: it is the rashness of a heedless and headstrong boy." And of course the Yankee major is right—though it is plain that he has to admire, in spite of his common sense, such incredible daring. Miss Jenny herself, though berating the wild

11. The fact that Bayard is more at home and more comfortable with the simple and unsophisticated poorer whites and blacks of the countryside may give some hints as to the nature of his spiritual malady.

folly of the Sartorises, obviously can't help being proud of her brother's feat. She ends his story by remarking that General Stuart "always spoke well of Bayard. He said he was a good officer and a fine cavalryman, but that he was too reckless" (p. 19).

Now Faulkner has deliberately countered this story of the Bayard Sartoris who died in 1862 with a story about the John Sartoris who died in 1918 and his brother Bayard who is daily risking his neck in an automobile driven much too fast over country roads. Young Bayard tells Narcissa the story of John's death. He had tried to keep John "from going up there, on that damn Camel." But John was drunk and hell-bent on going. When Bayard had tried to head him off in the air, John had actually shot at him. The German planes jumped him and one got on his tail. Later, Bayard explains how he tried to fight the German off, but every time "I got my sights on him, John'd barge in the way again." Finally, John's plane took fire, and John, looking straight at Bayard, swung "his legs outside. Then he thumbed his nose at me like he was always doing and flipped his hand at the Hun and kicked his machine out of the way and jumped . . . feet first" (p. 239). Bayard tried to dive under him to pick him up but of course failed.

The Civil War Bayard Sartoris and the twentieth-century John Sartoris are merry and nonchalant in their recklessness. Both die with a flourish—a wave of the plume—and their bravery in both cases may be more accurately named a devil-may-care recklessness. Yet there may be a difference, after all, not in the young men, but in the circumstances. The twentieth-century war was more mechanical and had an even smaller place for heroics than did the nineteenth-century conflict. To go up in a notoriously inferior plane, and to attack clearly superior aircraft present in large numbers lengthens the odds even beyond those that attended the other Bayard's foray for the anchovies. Faulkner has, however, tried to be very fair in this matter. When General Stuart offers to go back and capture a mount for his prisoner, the Yankee major, the major asks Stuart whether he would jeopardize his safety and that of his men and his cause to provide for "the temporary comfort of a minor prisoner of his sword." Stuart replies "haughtily" that

"No gentleman would do less"; to which the major observes: "No gentleman has any business in this war. There is no place for him here. He is an anachronism, like anchovies" (p. 18).

The major is right. In some sense, the American Civil War was the first modern war. It was the first in which the capture and retention of rail lines was of strategic importance; the first that introduced armor-clad naval vessels and observation balloons and even submarines. But some of the soldiers, particularly cavalry officers, insisted on fighting it as if they were paladins of romance. The Bayard Sartorises and General Stuarts were indeed anachronisms. The old heroics were—though those bent on heroism were unwilling to admit the fact—passé. But in World War I, they were a full half-century further out of date.[12]

Herman Melville was aware of a touching if foolhardy nonchalance exhibited in the Civil War: in one of his poems he observed that all "wars are boyish and are fought by boys"; youth had "to lend its ignorant impulse" for any war to be possible at all, though that ignorance was bound to receive "enlightenment" from "the vollied glare" of murderous rifle fire. But if the Civil War left little room for the heroics of the paladin, World War I allowed very little place for the virtues of the brothers Sartoris— even though they occupied such little space as was left for heroics, being themselves single-combat knights of the air. John Sartoris was able to summon up a gesture of light-hearted defiance as he died; the brother who survived was in worse plight: alive, but emptied and living in an emptied world.[13] Yet this aspect of the matter is only one element in a deeper malaise, essentially a deeper disillusionment and a more inward sickness, one that could affect even a Horace Benbow or the Reverend Joseph Mahon of *Soldiers' Pay*.

Miss Jenny, on the other hand, had been a part of that vanished heroic world. It is true that she constantly scoffs at heroism and the follies of men in general, and Narcissa is an easy convert to the view that Miss Jenny and all women suffered in the Civil War

12. See below, Notes, pp. 391–93.
13. In this matter of the relationship of the two brothers, see below, Notes, pp. 393–95.

much more than the men, who at least had vainglorious dreams to buoy them up. Yet it is plain that Miss Jenny, for all her scoffing at male folly and that of her bull-headed Sartorises in particular, is secretly very proud of their daring and their bravery. It is Miss Jenny, after all, who tells the story about General Stuart and her brother Bayard and the anchovies, and in finishing her narration, "her voice was proud and still as banners in the dust" (p. 20).

How much did the Civil War really differ from World War I? A great deal; in any case, Faulkner's characters believed that it did. They saw the Civil War as having been a defense of the homeland,[14] and it had been fought on the soil of the homeland, not, as in World War I, across the ocean and for what very quickly showed itself to be an abstract issue. By 1920 it was hard to believe that the conflict just past had been a war that could put an end to all war, or that it had made the world safe for democracy. The disillusionment is a matter of record, and the disillusioned were not merely Americans, but the whole Western world. Yet the sense, on the part of the Confederate veterans, that theirs had been a heroic struggle is a matter of record too. To see that this is true for Faulkner's Southern characters, one need only consult his fiction as a whole. Perhaps the most telling example is Isaac McCaslin. Isaac is no Bayard Sartoris, no daredevil or fire-eater. He regards slavery as a curse and rejoices that it has been ended as a result of the War. But he is proud of the fight that his people put up against overpowering forces, and, like Miss Jenny, he is proud to recount the exploits of "Jackson in the Valley and three separate armies trying to catch him" and "Stuart riding his whole command entirely around the biggest single armed force this continent ever saw in order to see what it looked like from behind" and "Morgan leading a cavalry charge against a stranded man-of-war" (*Go Down, Moses,* p. 288).

In *Flags in the Dust,* as we have seen, Bayard is brought up squarely against two of the survivors of a heroic age, his grandfather and his grandfather's aunt. If Bayard is consciously aware

14. Old man Falls "chewed his tobacco for a time, quietly retrospective, reliving in the company of men now dust with the dust for which they had, unwittingly perhaps, fought, those gallant pinched-bellied days into which few who now trod that earth and drew breath, could enter into with him" (*Flags in the Dust,* p. 214).

of the contrast, he makes no comment upon it; but then he is the man of action, not of words, and this is, of course, part of his problem. He cannot express to himself what his problem is, but feels the more intensely that he has no cause and can find no purpose in living. He muses: "Three score and ten years, to drag a stubborn body about the world and cozen its insistent demands. . . . And he was only twenty-six. Not much more than a third through it. Hell" (p. 144).

Horace Benbow is a man of words, but his words are arty and "literary" in the worst sense, and his purpose is to live in a pleasant dream. One of the problems of the modern world is just such a polarization—ideas which do not lead to action and mindless activity that is itself as much a narcotic as the escape into dream.

If the heroic world of Miss Jenny points up her much younger relative's frantic restlessness and rootlessness, it does the same for Narcissa Benbow, the girl whom Bayard is later to marry. Miss Jenny's sense of who she is and her firm confidence in the traditional values blind her to the plight of this younger generation. She apparently really believes that marriage will solve Bayard's problems and Narcissa's too. Miss Jenny apologizes later for her part in promoting the marriage, for though she would like to see the Sartoris line carried on with the birth of a child, she had not meant simply to use Narcissa.

The difference between the two women and the values that they embody comes out most obviously, of course, in the matter of the obscene letters that Byron Snopes had sent to Narcissa before her marriage. Narcissa was ashamed that someone would address such letters to her, and said she felt soiled, but at the same time she was titillated and vaguely excited. Miss Jenny, knowing that she herself had not encouraged or sanctioned such attention, would not have felt at all sullied by it. She would burn the letters at once or else turn them over to some man in the family in the hope that they would provide clues for finding the sender and putting a stop to his writing. Miss Jenny is practical, assured, and confident of her own integrity. Narcissa is not. She is afraid of sex but also thrilled by it. She keeps the letters.

It would be simplistic to say that Narcissa, Horace, and Bayard are all, in their various ways, representative of the modern world, its "sick hurry and divided aims." Moreover, even if it seems reasonable to believe that Faulkner was using the Civil War generation to point up the distempers of the modern age, we are not to conclude that Faulkner meant the reader to regard Old Bayard and Miss Jenny as paragons of virtue. They have the defects of their virtues. Miss Jenny has become a rather tart and vinegary old lady, and her views on color and caste and politics have the limitations of the earlier day in which she grew up. Her nephew has become a testy old gentleman, well set in his ways. Old Bayard refuses to buy an automobile, although he does ride with his grandson. But he rides with him only because he hopes that he can keep him from driving too fast. Miss Jenny, on the other hand, rather enjoys having Bayard drive too fast. She has not completely closed her mind against the new. (To see what Old Bayard and Miss Jenny were capable of in their own finest hour, one must view them over a half-century earlier in "An Odor of Verbena.")

What happened to this new generation who date from about the 1890s? What went wrong with Bayard? With Narcissa? With Horace? Readers who take the Compson family as entirely typical of the planter families of Yoknapatawpha County will be inclined to put it down to the degeneracy of the Southern ruling class. Some readers will add that this pretended aristocracy was bogus from the first and that the freeing of the slaves and the collapse of the older economy of the South simply exposed the sham; they were, from the beginning, ruthless and greedy people and underbred people to boot. Other readers may take seriously Miss Jenny's old-fashioned ideas about blood lines and agree with her that the Sartorises were a feckless lot from the beginning, a truly doomed family. The author himself at times encourages this notion when he lets the name "Sartoris" inspire a purple passage like this: "For there is death in the sound of it, and a glamorous fatality, like silver pennons downrushing at sunset, or a dying fall of horns along the road to Roncevaux" (p. 370). In expressing such sentiments, Faulkner shows himself to be the still unregenerate romantic—though in an earlier sentence of this passage he seems to concede that Sartoris is now the name of an outmoded "game," no longer playable in the modern world.

Let me, however, return to the question of what happened to the generation of Bayard Sartoris and Horace Benbow. What happened to them was not precisely what happened to Quentin Compson. Bayard's death was a kind of suicide, granted, but courting danger is very different from putting flatirons in one's pockets and deliberately submerging oneself in a river. Even Horace, who, like Quentin, is an intellectual and a dreamer, does not try to take his life, though he obviously ruins it with his marriage to Belle. In any case, the special collapse of the Compson family, a breakdown that ultimately accounts for Quentin's death, has not ocurred in Bayard's family or in that of Horace Benbow.[15]

Unless one believes as seriously as Miss Jenny does that blood will tell and that the Sartoris family is somehow doomed, one will have to seek out a more credible reason for the malaise that affects the twentieth-century Sartorises. In any case, a family curse won't account for what happens to Horace and to Narcissa. It would seem to be the general disorder and disillusionment that came with the end of World War I. Eliot, Pound, Joyce, Dos Passos, Hemingway, and even Yeats, to a lesser degree, reflect it. It was a general condition, then, not peculiar to the Southern states of America, though it could be argued that because of the old-fashioned and highly conservative character of Southern society, the cultural shock upon the Southerner may have been greater.

It should be pointed out that the black culture of the South was at this period little affected by it. Neither were the poorer whites and the plain people generally, though those who had actually gone overseas had been jolted. So had the young, especially those living in the towns and cities, who did respond to the new music, the new fashions, and the new styles.

Such is the general picture that we get in *Soldiers' Pay* and *Flags in the Dust*. (*Mosquitoes* provides a glimpse of the new

15. The relatively early death of their parents and the lack in both cases of a large extended family of cousins, aunts, and uncles may have had a deleterious effect on Bayard and on Horace; but if it did, Faulkner makes no special point of it and, in any case, the movement toward the nuclear family is not nowadays usually regarded as a mark of family degeneracy.

ideas as expressed by that very special class, the intellectuals and the artists.) The alleged Southern decadence hardly comes into the picture, though Southern conservatism does, and *Flags in the Dust* powerfully conveys the difference between the older members of a traditional society, still sure of itself and possessing a clearly defined code of manners of conduct, and its younger members who have been jarred loose by the new ideas, events, and experiences.

The reader's judgment of the Old South will seriously affect this estimate of the conflict between the old and the new as represented in Faulkner's novels. It will affect the meaning of the novels themselves. To be blunt about it: if the reader begins with sufficient prejudice against the Southern planter class because they were former slaveholders or the descendants of slaveholders, then he is likely to applaud automatically every rebel against the old ways and to dismiss every holdover from the old society as irrelevant because anachronistic. My own experience in teaching Faulkner's novels bears out this supposition, but the reader may test it for himself by examining the books and articles on Faulkner written during the last forty years.

Faulkner is not easy on his planter folk. In *Flags in the Dust* he is not easy on Old Bayard or even on Jenny Du Pre. He describes in detail the hard ruthlessness of John Sartoris, the Old Colonel,[16] who established the Sartoris family in Yoknapatawpha. But there is a difference between a realistic account of one's characters and a blanket condemnation of a whole order of a society. To refuse to see that Faulkner found some admirable virtues in the leaders of the Old South, or that he himself saw the Civil War as a kind of heroic age, is to distort the meaning of many of his stories and novels. It will, for example, make rather meaningless the contrast in *Flags in the Dust* between the generation of Miss Jenny and that of Narcissa Benbow, between Old Bayard's experience of the Civil War and Reconstruction, and young Bayard's experience of World War I.

Yet if Faulkner himself does make the distinction in his fiction, why not let the reader find it there for himself? A good question,

16. See *The Unvanquished,* particularly "An Odor of Verbena."

and the sensitive and unprejudiced reader, I would maintain, can indeed be left to find it for himself. But who of us is really unprejudiced? Most readers come to Faulkner from reading books and articles about Faulkner, too many of which, to my mind, are biased on the very issues in question.

In 1963 I fondly believed that where the ordinary reader's understanding needed to be corrected was with regard to the landless whites and the whites with small holdings. Accordingly, in *William Faulkner: The Yoknapatawpha Country,* I included a chapter entitled "The Plain People." In 1977 I think that an equal misunderstanding occurs with reference to the other end of the social scale. Hence I have added an appendix on the planter class as represented—or *not* represented—by Thomas Sutpen (see appendix A, below).

7

People Without a Past

(PYLON)

FAULKNER TOLD THE STUDENTS at the University of Virginia that he wrote *Pylon* "because [he'd] got in trouble with *Absalom, Absalom!* and . . . had to get away from it for a while so [he] thought a good way to get away from it was to write another book. . . ." [1] But one wonders whether just any book would have served his purpose, and it is tempting to suppose that in writing *Pylon* Faulkner was escaping not merely from the special problems of writing *Absalom, Absalom!* but also seeking a holiday from Yoknapatawpha County—and from the Southern past. At any rate, *Pylon* is Faulkner's first considerable fiction since *Mosquitoes* to have its setting completely outside the Yoknapatawpha country.

Pylon must have given Faulkner a sense of freshness and even release, for it was written very rapidly. He began it in October (Blotner, pp. 865–75) and sent the last chapter to his publisher in December of 1934. It reads like a book written on a surge of creative energy, something rather different from a book hurriedly put together and showing the obvious marks of haste. Though I do not find *Pylon* a rich or ultimately satisfying book, Faulkner's

1. *Faulkner in the University,* ed. Gwynn and Blotner, p. 36.

178

writing, sentence by sentence and scene by scene, includes some of his very best.

The movement away from Yoknapatawpha, whether a calculated escape or not, was certainly thorough. The barnstorming nomads of the air, four adults and a child, have nothing to do with Faulkner's mythical country. They are predominantly—perhaps totally—from the Midwest. Shumann was born in Ohio; Laverne, his wife, in Iowa; Jiggs, the mechanic, has left behind a wife and two children in Kansas. Holmes's natal state is not specified. The child Jack was born in an airplane hangar in California. At his birth, Shumann and Holmes rolled dice to decide which one would assume the role of father and marry Laverne. Shumann won (or lost, depending on one's point of view), and he and Laverne were at once married by a justice of the peace.

Yet far more important than their place of birth is their general rootlessness. These people really belong to no place, and Faulkner's description of them as they walk the streets of New Valois (New Orleans) is brilliantly apt: they have the same air "which in Jiggs was merely oblivious and lightlyworn insolvency but which in them was that irrevocable homelessness of three immigrants walking down the steerage gangplank of a ship" (p. 79).

These nomads of the air, moreover, have no ties with the past. Quentin Compson, the principal narrator in the novel on which Faulkner was also at work while he wrote *Pylon,* is hag-ridden by the past. Most of the other characters in that novel are figures summoned up out of a time long since gone. But to most of the characters in *Pylon,* past is as alien as place. Faulkner told the students at the University of Virginia that the air people of *Pylon* "had no past"; that "they had escaped the compulsion of accepting a past and a future"; that they lived purely in the present, a life that "was frenetic." He said that it seemed to him "interesting enough to make a story about [them], but that [his real impulse was] just to get away from a book that wasn't going too well, till I could get back at it."

The Reporter, who is our chief source of information, makes the same general point, but prefers to stress the air nomads' lack of a place, a place "where you were born and have to go back to . . . now and then even if it's just only to hate the damn place good and comfortable for a day or two" (p. 46). The Reporter sums the situation up in saying to his editor: "they aint human like us; they couldn't turn those pylons like they do if they had human blood and senses and they wouldn't want to or dare to if they just had human brains" (p. 45). Nevertheless, the Reporter is utterly fascinated by them.

Faulkner was also obviously fascinated by aviators all his life. He had tried to become a fighter pilot in the Royal Air Force, but "they stopped the war on him" before he got his wings. Later, he did learn to fly and owned his own plane. In his fiction, particularly in a number of his early stories, the flyer is the hero. We shall misunderstand *Pylon,* however, if we assume that all the airmen that Faulkner personally knew were daredevils, taking hair's breadth chances just for the hell of it. Vernon Omlie, his friend at the Memphis airport, was not such a man, nor was James R. Wedell, who designed planes as well as flew them, and on whom the Matt Ord of *Pylon* is modeled.

In *Pylon* Faulkner is interested not in airplane pilots as such, but in a special type of human being. That type of person was prefigured in *Flags in the Dust* in the account of the twin brothers, John and Bayard Sartoris. John is shot down over the Western Front in World War I. Bayard survives the war, but dies in the crash of an experimental plane that he is testing. Indeed, the circumstances of Bayard's death closely resemble the circumstances of Roger Shumann's death in *Pylon,* for though Shumann crashes in the course of a race, he is fully aware of the chance that he takes in flying his tricky and dangerous plane.

Whether Roger Shumann and Bayard Sartoris are really very much alike in their makeup and motives, will be discussed later. The Reporter, had he known Bayard Sartoris, might have regarded his case as different from Roger Shumann's. He thinks of Shumann as almost a machine, with cylinder oil for blood; the Reporter would have had to admit that Bayard, on the other hand, did possess the sort of human ties that Shumann lacked, and he would have to add that Bayard did have a place to go back to, though Bayard evidently had come to hate that place and ended up by repudiating it.

The soundness of the Reporter's judgments may be properly questioned. Since it is through him that we learn most of what we know about these gypsies of the air, it behooves us to know how acute his perceptions are and something about his psychic makeup. Clearly, he is a kind of psychological freak, of a sort that Faulkner apparently delighted to depict in his fiction. His ramshackle gait, his loose-jointed air that reminds one of a "halfgrown highbred setter puppy," and his "wild bright" face with its look of "worn and dreamy fury," call forth endless amused comments from the barnstormers whom the Reporter is trying to befriend. Even if we make all the necessary subtractions for overstatement by Jiggs and Holmes, the Reporter is a very queer-looking bird indeed. The novel suggests that he is also queer-acting in many ways.

As for the quality of his mind and imagination, the Reporter is obviously of the company of Faulkner's feckless romantics. He is prone to project his own aspirations and dreams upon Shumann, the aviator, and Holmes, the parachute jumper, and the woman who is their common paramour. He finds them endlessly interesting and finds their *ménage à trois* not their least interesting aspect. In spite of his editor's warning, a warning spoken as by an adult to a child, "Why dont you let these people alone?" the Reporter simply cannot let them alone. He is torn between two ways of viewing them—as merely passionless machines or as heroic supermen. (The two notions, let it be granted at once, are not necessarily in complete contradiction.) In any case, the air people are not of Adam's ordinary breed or, if they are, have managed somehow to transcend humanity's usual claims and limitations. Moreover, the Reporter resembles the barnstormers in at least one important regard: like them, he is a creature with no biding place in the human world. We are told that it was difficult to believe that he had actually been born of human parents, and his mother, when she turns up later, is, if certainly human, herself a freak.

The Reporter's specialized world is, in its way, almost as far from Yoknapatawpha as is that of the aviators to whom he attaches himself. Indeed, a main difficulty for most readers has been just this lack of solid "human" reference points. The editor, Hagood, whose usual barking at the Reporter is so much worse than his bite, hardly serves as a human base line. Besides, the look on his face in most of the glimpses that we get is of chronic outrage—occasioned by the Reporter's follies or the Reporter's accounts of the incredible doings of the inhuman creatures of the air who have taken the Reporter in thrall. In short, the world of *Pylon* is presented as a strange and even nightmarish place in which the fabric of humanity is put to its hardest test. The answer as to whether it passes the test is reserved for the close of the novel. One of the persons most concerned with the results of this test is the Reporter himself.

We have already remarked the presence of the daredevil aviators in both *Pylon* and *Flags in the Dust*. But the two novels have more in common still: *Pylon* repeats with variations the pattern discerned in *Flags*: the unreflective man of action played off against the inactive man of words. Like Bayard and John Sartoris in *Flags in the Dust*, Shumann and Holmes are reckless of life and limb, but do not regard themselves as glamorous. Like Horace Benbow in *Flags*, the Reporter is the dreamer and would-be writer, who participates only vicariously in what he sees as heroic action.

An observer less romantic than the Reporter might not regard the life of Shumann or Laverne as glamorous in the least, but Laverne, with her grease-stained forehead, with her body clad in man's dungarees, is for the Reporter sexually overpowering. We ought not, provided we have read Faulkner's earlier novels, to be in the least surprised to discover that Laverne turns out to be for the Reporter an "epicene" woman. She is oddly boyish. She wears the same kind of clothing that her men wear, and even when she dresses for the street, she puts on a "sexless" trenchcoat. She has a "hard boy's face that looks like any one of the four of them might cut her hair for her with a pocket knife when it needs it . . ." (p. 49). She is "epicene" also in Faulkner's special meaning of "unattainable." The Reporter has no real hope of sharing a bed with Laverne, but he derives a kind of satisfaction from remembering that her body has touched the sheets of the bed in the apartment in which he lives and which he has invited the homeless group to share.

Yet the Reporter's principal interest in the group is essentially unselfish and compassionate. He is genuinely concerned that they get enough to eat and find a place to sleep. He quickly discovers that they are practically penniless and that, though Roger Shumann, by brilliant and daring flying, has taken second prize money in Thursday's race, none of it will be paid him until Saturday.

In their own eyes, the members of Shumann's group do not seem in the least romantic. They are hard-bitten, pragmatic, utterly realistic. They could not survive otherwise. For them, every day offers one more test in survival. Theirs is a hand-to-mouth existence, a brutalizing existence. Their glamor is projected upon them by the public at large and in a more intense way by the Reporter. Yet glamor may not be quite the right word to describe the quality with which the Reporter's imagination has invested them; perhaps "awe" would be more accurate. The Reporter is drawn to them as if to a magnet, for they seem to be a new breed, or in any case members of the old breed who have dared to break loose from the old rules, conventions, and human values.

What is it that makes the barnstorming aviators behave as they do? It is not the money, as the Reporter tells himself over and over. In terms of the risks they take, their pay is very small. They are poor economists indeed if they hope to become rich. Yet if their motive is not fame, glory, adulation, or money, as I think the novel makes plain, then what are their motives?

Theirs would seem to be no rational motive at all, but rather an urge, a need. They are like compulsive drunkards, who know what they are doing to themselves and yet cannot put the bottle down. They are hooked on speed, and they could not kick the habit if they tried. We are not told in detail how they became hooked but we are given some hints. The life they led before they became involved in flying was apparently monotonous and ultimately unsatisfying. At the end of the novel we get a glimpse of Roger Shumann's father and a hint of what Roger's childhood must have been like. His father is a country physician who worked hard, dutifully made the rounds of his patients, and was ill-paid by those whom he treated. He seems to be a kindly, decent, conventional man who had been deeply wounded by his son's refusal to go to medical school and follow in his father's footsteps (pp. 274–76). Roger Shumann evidently found nothing in his father's life to induce him to accept it.

We have a glimpse of Laverne's life too—which was far worse than Roger's. She was a drudge in the house of her married sister, a woman nearly twenty years older than she. She was eventually seduced by her brother-in-law, who gave her just a taste of a life of color and excitement. Finally, Roger Shumann, the young and handsome aviator, came into her life like a god descending from the sky. But there was for her—and presumably for him—in their new life more than a mere escape from dreary monotony and numbing drudgery. There was a positive fulfillment in speed and danger.

Laverne's preparations for her first parachute jump react on her as a powerful aphrodisiac. In the most *outré* passage in the novel, Faulkner describes how, clinging to the inner bay strut of the wing, ready to jump, she suddenly makes her way back to the cockpit in which Shumann is piloting the plane. To his amazement, she climbs in with him and up on his lap. He tries to fight her off for a while, since he has to give some attention to flying the plane, but she has her way with him and at the end it is only through "some blind instinct out of the long swoon" into which he has fallen that he remembers to "roll the aeroplane toward the wing to which the parachute case was attached" and the next moment sees "the parachute floating between him and the ground" (p. 196). The two excitements—the sexual orgasm and the shuddering thrill of the parachute jump—almost merge. One experience moves without break into the long climax of the other.

The Reporter's obsessive fantasies about an almost continuous sexual activity going on in the air nomads' *ménage à trois* may have some basis in fact. The danger met and faced earlier in each day is itself a sexual incitement, and the real possibility that one's next coupling may be the last he will ever experience exerts, every night, its own compulsion. For Shumann and Holmes, the admonition to eat, drink, and be merry for tomorrow you may die is immediate. The chances of their dying tomorrow are high.

The various pressures of their commitment to their insecure, dangerous, hand-to-mouth, day-to-day life have stripped from the flyers most of the manners, customs, and principles of traditional morality. The nurture of children, the maintenance of a home, marriage, even fidelity to one's love, are luxuries that the troupe can scarcely afford even if they had any special concern for them. The repudiation of the traditional role of spouse and parent bears most heavily, of course, on the woman, who has been immemorially the special custodian of sexual morality and the one most directly concerned with the nurture of children. Primitive tribes, though they may have different sexual codes, are pretty much at one in insisting that the woman identify the father of her child and thus see to it that the tribe is not saddled with children whose support devolves upon the whole tribe rather than on the men responsible for begetting them. The traditional morality has therefore, on any showing, seriously lapsed when the woman does not know who the father of her child is. Laverne, however, is not at all the usual wanton, not simply a whore or a mistress. In some deep sense, she obviously wishes for a home, and in some curious way is in love with her husband. She does not lead this life for money; there is precious little money in it and a great deal of hardship.

The nearest analogy might be to a female camp-follower, who is so much tied to her man that she is willing to endure every kind of discomfort and difficulty in order to share his life. But in this case Laverne has not one man but two. There can be no doubt that Faulkner is emphasizing the special dislocation of values represented by these outlaws from conventional society, and Laverne provides the most emphatic testimony to such a dislocation. Her repudiation of the role of wife and mother is radical. Her clothing and her hair style are "unisex"—forty years before the term became current and fashionable. She honestly doesn't know whether it is Shumann or Holmes who is the father of her child (though she is confident that it is Holmes who has fathered the child she is now carrying). Apparently it makes no difference to her which is the father; hence the men can roll dice for the rather empty title. It is she, by the way, who has taught the six-year-old Jack to fight anyone who asks him, "Who's your old man?" As a cruel joke? [2] As a way of toughening the boy? As part of his training to face the world in which he must live? In any case she has taught him to resent the question as a slur. He is to attempt to knock down the person who asks it.

Laverne also seems as hard as nails when she leaves the child with his grandfather, not having prepared him for what she means to do or even kissing him goodbye. Yet she seems terribly moved by her husband's death. She keeps an unceasing vigil during the many hours in which an attempt is made to recover his body. She bitterly reprehends the Reporter for his part in securing the plane in which Shumann met his death. Later, however, she confesses to Shumann's father: "Maybe I could have stopped [Shumann from attempting to fly the dangerous plane]. I dont know. . . . But I didn't. I didn't try, anyhow" (p. 309). Would Laverne have mourned the death of the parachute jumper with equal intensity? Laverne's character remains an enigma—not only to the Reporter but probably to the reader also.

Faulkner has not, however, tried to turn Laverne into a monster, or even to unsex her. He has even allowed her to retain a residual domesticity. For instance, the Reporter's cleaning woman at once notices the neatly made bed in which Laverne had slept the night before. She still can provide the touch of a woman's hand in spite of her daily life as a grease monkey in the hangar. At least once in the novel Faulkner allows her to express her longing for some permanent habitation: she tells Shumann, ". . . all I want is just a house, a room; a cabin will do, a coalshed where I can know that next Monday and the Monday after that and the Monday after that . . ." (p. 165). Is this really what she wants? Or is her outburst no more than a temporary resurgence of her nesting instinct? As with other aspects of Laverne's char-

2. Jiggs suggests that the Reporter ask the child, "Who's your old man," and see what happens. Jiggs, it seems, habitually puts the question to the child.

acter, it is difficult to find a convincing answer. But whatever the correct answer, Laverne, because of the very fact that she is a woman, exemplifies as the most poignant instance of all the general rootlessness that characterizes the group.[3]

In *Pylon* the airplane becomes the prime symbol of rootlessness. As such, it is the perfect symbol, for it literally lifts man away from the sustaining earth. It compresses time and almost eliminates place. For many human beings its promise to free man from his terrestrial limitations has a positive attraction, an attraction that Faulkner himself strongly felt. In fact, if the airplane did not appeal to human beings, its threat of becoming a force disturbing to the human enterprise would be nil.

The best proof that in *Pylon* the plane is regarded as one more, though an especially dangerous, aspect of the generally dehumanizing mechanizations of human life is to be found in the author's comments on another and far less spectacular piece of modern machinery, the motor car: "a machine expensive, complex, delicate and intrinsically useless, created for some obscure psychic need of the species if not the race, from the virgin resources of a continent, to be the individual muscles bones and flesh of a new and legless kind . . ." (p. 87).

Other aspects of the machine-made character of modern civilization come in for comment. The period from 1915 to 1935 is referred to as "a sudden and vicious double decade" (p. 86). The food at a short-order joint, the plates on which it is served, and even the waitresses who serve it, are regarded as synthetic: "the heaped indestructible plate and the hand scrubbed, with vicious coral nails, the hand too looking as if it had been conceived formed and baked in the kitchen, or perhaps back in town and sent out by light and speedy truck along with the scrolled squares of pastry . . ." (p. 143).

What is under attack in all these examples are the dehumanizing aspects of modern civilization: the lack of community, the dullness and uniformity, the exploitation of human beings. The people who comprise the troupe of air nomads that Shumann leads are at once the proponents and victims of such crimes against

3. See below, Notes, p. 400.

187

humanity. The Reporter sees them, however, primarily as victims.

A closer look at some of the relevant parts of the novel will yield examples. We see (pp. 60–61) Shumann and the other air gypsies waiting in the lobby of one of the hotels in the city, along with many other transients. There are, for instance, the salesmen who "in the old lusty days called themselves drummers; [we see them] among the brass spittoons of elegance and the potted palms of decorum, legion homeless and symbolic: the immemorial flying buttresses of ten million American Saturday nights, with shrewd heads filled with tomorrow's cosmic alterations in the form of pricelists and the telephone numbers of discontented wives and highschool girls. 'Until time to take the elevator up and telephone the bellhop for gals,' the Reporter thought."

What comes even more sharply under attack is corrupt politics. In *Pylon* the most scathing remarks are directed at an individual, Colonel Feinman, who is depicted as a crooked politician, who has developed sufficient wealth and influence to have the new lakeside airport named for him and who has set up the airshow to celebrate its dedication. His status and qualifications are, on an early page, put succinctly in a conversation between Jiggs and a bus driver. Jiggs, a stranger to the city, suggests that "This Feinman" must "be a big son of a bitch," to which the New Valois bus driver replies: "He's a son of a bitch all right. I guess you'd call him big too." The driver has another laconically eloquent answer to Jiggs's suggestion that Feinman "gave you guys a nice airport, anyway." It is: "Somebody did."

Feinman, however, is presented as more than the ordinary crook, more than the usual corrupt politician. He is cheap, mean, small-minded, and absolutely without sympathy for the barnstorming aviators who are providing the thrills for his air circus. For example, when, on the first day, Lieutenant Burnham cracks up and is burned to death, it is decided to print new programs for the next day's events, programs that will of necessity omit Burnham's name. Feinman decides that the cost of this new printing is to be taken out of the prize money for the next day's events.

Other aspects of the times are touched on, though more lightly.

There is the cute crassness of the press which can concoct the following headline for the story describing the death of one of the aviators: "Burnham Burns." Even the Mardi Gras festivities hover on the edge of commercial exploitation, as the description of some of the decorations on Grandlieu Street show, and as Faulkner's descriptions of the carnival night parades hint: for example, the floats are described as bearing "grimacing and antic mimes dwarfed chalkwhite and forlorn and contemplated by static curb-mass of amazed confettifaces . . ." (p. 53). The flaring torches provided to light up the scene have not endowed it with warmth and gaiety. Those riding on the floats have been reduced to dwarfed mimes with chalkwhite skins, and the faces of the specta-tors have been transformed into the impermanent and inhuman fragility of Mardi Gras confetti.

The floats in the Carnival parade had been meant, one sup-poses, to conjure up a fantasy, a kind of fairy-tale world, and with it an atmosphere of mirth and hearty laughter. It is not so. The revellers on the floats seem "forlorn" and those who watch them have been frozen into a "static curbmass." In short, the loneliness and rootlessness of the air nomads find their reflections in what can be seen in the hotel lobbies and also out on the streets.

The Reporter is almost as rootless as are the air people. We are never told where he came from, just as we are never told his out-landish name. But he is presumably not a New Orleanian. Though he has a host of acquaintances among the other newsmen, photographers, and policemen, he seems to have no friends. He is unmarried. The newspaper editor, Hagood, has a special relation-ship with him. He fiercely bawls him out, "fires" him on occasion; yet always takes him back, and, when the Reporter pleads for help, always advances him what are really considerable sums of money. Hagood sees the Reporter as a special case who needs to be scolded for his own good, but who, nevertheless, stands in need of protection from the outside world and from his own personal folly.

On page 167 the author makes a curious and enlightening com-ment on this character. The gangling, unusually tall Reporter is condemned to look down at most of the people he speaks with. He is evidently regarded as either genial or forbiddingly fresh. His fate is to endure, or at the least pass the time "until that day when time and age would have thinned still more what blood he had and so permit him to see himself actually as the friendly and lonely ghost peering timidly down from the hayloft at the other children playing below." The Reporter is a loner, a child not invited by the other children to take part in their games. He would like to be accepted by the barnstorming air people; and in their own curious terms they are honestly grateful for his efforts to help them, but they cannot accept him and they do not. He is too innocent to enter into their world. It would appear that he is also too innocent to belong to the everyday world in which he does assume he has a place.

If Shumann and Holmes (in spite of major differences) generally resemble Bayard Sartoris, then the Reporter resembles (at least vaguely) Horace Benbow; he is called the "patron (even if not guardian) saint of all waifs, all the homeless the desperate and the starved" (p. 183). This is precisely the role that Horace tries to assume in *Sanctuary*. Moreover, Horace is even less understood by Lee Goodwin and his common-law wife Ruby than the Reporter is understood by Laverne and her two lovers and companions. The Reporter, Faulkner tells us, had "that air of worn and dreamy fury which Don Quixote must have had." There is something of Don Quixote in Horace too. The Reporter is a tender-hearted man. When he is told the story of how Laverne was treated by her brother-in-law he suddenly retches and begins to vomit (p. 278). So does Horace Benbow when he thinks of Popeye's rape of Temple Drake.

The Reporter has absolutely no sense of money. Editor Hagood is aware of this, as is the Reporter's mother. During the years that her son has been on the payroll of a New Orleans newspaper it turns out that she has continued to send him an allowance. Even Hagood is astounded when he discovers this. He had assumed that it was the other way around—that the Reporter had been sending regular remittances to her (p. 96). The Reporter's very cleaning woman knows that he is incompetent to handle money. When she discovers him asleep, lying in the alley outside his apartment—he has accidentally locked himself out—she reaches into his pocket and abstracts the two bills of currency that she finds there. She explains to herself: "If he found any of hit left hit wouldn't learn him no lesson. Laying out here in the street, drunk" (p. 133). Later, when he discovers that all his money is gone, he says to himself: "It's all right. It aint nothing but money. It dont matter" (p. 139). That is the one trait that he believes he shares with the air people. They don't think money matters either. They are not stuffy materialists.

For the Reporter is not only a romanticist; he is an idealist. Here again he resembles Horace Benbow. Though he keeps telling his fellow journalists and his editor that the flyers simply "aint human," he still wants to believe that they are honorable and will not lie or steal. Thus it goes hard with him to have to believe that the air nomads whom he had rescued from the streets and brought into his apartment the night before had rifled his pockets while he lay in drunken sleep. They had, as a matter of fact, taken his money, though they had been careful to leave him two bills—a five and a one—which the cleaning woman later takes. The Reporter doesn't begrudge Laverne and her friends his money, but he cannot believe that Laverne would not acknowledge having taken it. Throughout the morning he keeps telling himself: "That's all [Laverne] would have to do. Just tell me they. . . . It aint the money. She knows it aint that" (Faulkner's ellipses; p. 142). Much later, evidently to his intense relief, Laverne does decide to tell him: "Listen. We took some money out of your . . ." (p. 161). He assures her that "It's O.K.," but she goes on to specify the amount, $6.70, and asks, "How much did you find in your pocket this morning?" The Reporter lies like a gentleman, assuring her that the rest of the money was all there.

Because the Reporter has offered his apartment to the troupe for another night and now proposes to help them secure a plane to replace the one that had cracked up earlier that afternoon, Laverne, shamed by his continuing generosity, brings the matter up once more. "About that money. That was the truth. You can ask Roger and Jack." To which the Reporter replies: "It's all right. I would believe you even if I knew you had lied" (p. 166).

The will to believe can go no further. The Reporter not only has to believe that they have a sense of honor; he yearns to receive a measure of gratitude and not have them treat him as a mere convenience. His wish in the end comes true. Even Holmes, who had begun by thoroughly disliking him, ends up by apologizing for hitting him and commissions him almost solemnly to help him discharge a debt of honor. Even the brutal and contemptible Jiggs pawns his precious boots as his only way of realizing money to contribute to the now widowed Laverne.

As for Holmes, Shumann, and Laverne, a sense of honor is about all that they have left, and under crisis they do respond. Though Shumann knows that the child Laverne is now carrying is not his, he risks his life to win the two thousand dollar prize that Laverne's welfare demands. Jack Holmes, too, is highly sensitive to the claims of honor. When Shumann suggests that, because of his hurt leg, he sleep with Laverne in the one bed that is available to them, Holmes refuses: "I'll sleep in a cuckold's bed but not in a pimp's"—which makes a smart retort, but doesn't really answer to the circumstances. In this menage the application of the term cuckold becomes pretty much interchangeable, and pimp is an empty epithet. But Holmes will later make the honorable gesture in a more substantive way.

Before he leaves New Orleans with Laverne, he seeks out the Reporter and gives him the $22 that Shumann had told him he owed the Reporter. Then Holmes hands the Reporter an additional $75. This is to pay for shipping Shumann's body back to his father in Ohio. He promises to supply more money if more is needed, but the body must *not* be sent collect. Holmes insists that the Reporter actually pronounce the words: "I promise." Moreover, should the Reporter discover that $75 is not enough to pay for sending the body to Ohio, and should he conclude that he cannot trust Holmes to make up the difference later, then he must promise to bury Shumann in New Valois. The one thing he must not do is to make Dr. Shumann, the old father, pay.

In an essay entitled "Pulvis et Umbra," Robert Louis Stevenson insists that honor is everywhere "the ensign of man's ineffectual goodness." I have no idea whether Faulkner ever read that essay, but he would have approved of this assertion. Stevenson insists that one can find honor maintained in the most unlikely places and under the most hopeless conditions. He discovers honor in human beings "under every circumstance of failure, without hope, without health, without thanks, still obscurely fighting the lost fight of virtue, still clinging, in the brothel or on the scaffold, to some rag of honor, the poor jewel of their souls. They may seek to escape, and yet they cannot; it is not alone their privilege and glory, but their doom. . . ." Faulkner probably would have been skittish of aspects of the Victorian rhetoric in which Stevenson put the matter, but the word "doom" would have pleased him and certainly it applies to his hard-bitten air people.

They don't even pretend to virtue. If they boasted at all, it would be of their realism and their ability to take whatever comes, and yet the most practical of them all, the woman member of the small band, knows that there are certain things that you cannot do; you can't, for instance, rob a man whose guest you are. In case of dire necessity, you can "borrow" from him, but then you must tell him later that you did and how much you took.

A principal theme of *Pylon,* then, is the incurable humanity of human beings. (This will, of course, surprise no reader of Faulkner's work.) Faulkner apparently did not believe that man was naturally good. Rather, his characters are constantly stunned to discover the depth of depravity in their fellow human beings and, sometimes, in themselves. Yet Faulkner celebrates again and again man's power to rise above himself and is quietly confident that man can never become either a mere animal or a mere automaton. I am inclined to interpret the Nobel Prize Speech in this way: that Faulkner is not insisting that man will ever create a utopia on earth or that the human race is capable of permanent improvement. What he does wholeheartedly believe is that the qualities that separate man from the other creatures, the qualities that truly make him man, will endure and prevail over his tendencies to relapse into the mere beast.

Yet the members of Shumann's troupe are a far-gone lot. In their repudiation of marriage, normal family life, and participation in any genuine community, they have given up a great deal.

Faulkner has been perfectly willing to present scenes of physical and moral squalor in the old-fashioned world of Jefferson and in the outlying precincts of Yoknapatawpha County, yet life in Yoknapatawpha County is never inhuman, whereas the life led by the members of the air troupe sometimes is. The air people themselves recognize that they are different from other human beings. This is precisely what Holmes means when he tells the Reporter: ". . . take a tip from me and stick to the kind of people you are used to after this" (p. 261).

Such advice points to the other principal theme of *Pylon:* the almost paralyzing discovery of evil and the realization of how terrible the life of men and women can be. In urging the Reporter to stick to his own kind, Holmes appears to be touched by the Reporter's vulnerability. Certainly he is trying to comfort the Reporter when he tells him: "Don't take it too hard. You never made [Shumann] try to fly that crate anymore than you could have kept him from it. No man will hold that against you, and what [Laverne] might hold against you wont hurt you because you wont ever see her again, see." Since the Reporter is desolate because he knows he never will see Laverne again, Holmes is unwittingly proffering him cold comfort. But Holmes means it to be kind, and surely his reasoning is based on hard common sense.

We must not overlook the vulnerability of the Reporter if we are to understand *Pylon.* The Reporter is not at all the tough newspaperman of *The Front Page.* In the first place, he is younger than most readers take him to be. (He confesses to twenty-eight years on p. 301.) His mother can't quite believe that he really holds down a job. She asks the editor "to sort of look out for him. Because he is a fool, you see. I dont know whether he is a newspaperman or not. Maybe you dont know yet, yourself. But he is the baby" (p. 93). As we have seen, the editor does try to look out for him, by scolding him, by threatening to fire him, by occasionally doing just that, but then making a special trip to his apartment to rescind the dismissal, and finally by advancing him money to help him out of the difficulties that his philanthropies have got him into.

Faulkner was from his very beginnings interested in the idealistic romantic and the difficulties that such a man encounters, not merely in coping with, but in simply believing, the fact that many other human beings are cruel, callous, and malicious. In *Flags in the Dust* Horace is attracted against his better judgment to Belle Mitchell, and marries her though he certainly has some notion of what she is really like. In *Sanctuary* Horace, out of kindliness and idealism, serves as attorney to a bootlegger falsely charged with murder. But he is confounded by the callousness of his own sister when she objects to his taking the case of disreputable people; touched but also shocked by the bootlegger's wife's offering her body in payment of legal fees for which she has no money; and absolutely blasted by the lying testimony given by Temple Drake, testimony that results in his client's death.

Gavin Stevens is a man who in many respects is very different from Horace. But he too spends a good deal of his life being surprised and sometimes shocked by the depths of depravity that he finds in other human beings. (One concedes that it is also true that he is occasionally exhilarated by discovering unexpected virtues.) But, as with Horace, it is most of all womankind that Gavin cannot understand. He utterly misreads the character of Eula Varner Snopes, whom he worships from afar, and though he believes that he has "formed the mind" of Eula's daughter Linda, he is completely unprepared for Linda's toughness, resolution, and willingness to be an accessory before the fact to a murder.

The differences between the Reporter and Gavin Stevens and Horace Benbow are very great indeed, but a certain pattern does emerge. No wonder that Faulkner regarded *Don Quixote* as one of the greatest books, and says that he reread it every year. It is impossible, of course, to separate his fascination with that book from his fascination with the character who so utterly dominates it, the Don himself. Faulkner evidently felt a compulsion to explore the encounters, usually comic but sometimes tragic, in which the idealist comes up against an unyielding actuality. Faulkner does not spare his idealists: one thinks of the shock that Horace felt when, after all her promises to testify for Goodwin, Temple turns up in the company of the Memphis lawyer. One remembers Gavin standing like an embarrassed schoolboy before Judge

Stevens (*The Town*, p. 99), and of the Reporter's various gauche attempts to establish some rapport with Laverne.

These three characters are not only idealists and romantic dreamers. They are all "literary." Horace is, in aspiration at least, a decadent poet of the 1890s. Gavin has his preposterous scheme to translate the Septuagint version of the Bible into classic Greek. The Reporter is a journalist, but he obviously yearns to write a more exalted prose.

Were these three romantics ever really tamed, jolted, and disciplined by a reality that they could not escape? There is no evidence in Faulkner's fiction that they ever were. Even after Gavin has married, rather happily one supposes, and has become less inclined to quixotic adventures, he proves in *The Mansion* that he can be painfully shocked by the unpredictable conduct of a woman he thinks he understands.

Was Faulkner himself a tamed romantic? I would say yes. The best evidence is his handling of Horace, Gavin, and the Reporter; that is to say, Faulkner was enough of a romantic himself to have a thorough knowledge of the type, but in spite of his sympathies with them, he does not himself become ensnared by their delusions. Though these characters may delude themselves, their creator is well aware that the road of the romantic idealist is hard, sometimes sorrowful but, often enough, actually comic.

At this point we may well ask: what is Faulkner's final attitude toward the characters that he presents in *Pylon*. It is complex, obviously. But is the complexity so great that no resolution occurs at all? Are we left in the end with only a kind of bleak, clinical detachment? Problems of this sort come to a head in the last chapter of *Pylon,* which Faulkner calls "The Scavengers."

Who are the scavengers? The sergeant of police and his crew who are dragging the lake bottom with grappling irons in an effort to recover Shumann's body? Or the five newspapermen who are trying to retrieve from human disaster additional bits of human interest, gruesome details, or shreds of gossip for the great many-headed public to read the next day? Or is the real scavenger the Reporter, who would reclaim, if he could, a residue of glory, a moral victory, or even just human meaning from this blotting out of a human life? Whether or not this question can be answered, there are other related questions that are troubling. In what does the unity of the novel reside? In the final development of a theme? In an implied judgment on certain actions? In a new conception or redefinition of what is essentially human?

As the Reporter listens to the other journalists speculate on what the wife will now do—one of them cynically remarks that when Shumann's plane dived into the lake, Laverne's thought must have been, "Thank God I carry a spare [husband]"—the Reporter rouses himself to try to find out what indeed Laverne means to do. He is able to track down the mechanic Jiggs and learns from him that Shumann has a father back in Ohio and that Laverne plans to take her child there and leave him with his grandfather. Immediately (p. 302) the scene shifts [4] to the little town of Myron, Ohio, where Holmes, Laverne, and the child are just arriving at the railroad station. Holmes decides to wait in the station, and Laverne gets a taxi to drive her and the child out to the Shumann farm. There ensues a conversation between Laverne and Dr. Shumann. If she leaves the child with him, she is to promise never to try to see him until the Shumann grandparents are dead. Laverne makes the promise without demur and prepares to go back to the station. She does not wake the exhausted child, who is now sound asleep. Dr. Shumann is obviously surprised that a mother could leave her young child without an explanation or a kiss of farewell, but when Laverne asks him whether he can think of a better way, he admits that he can't.

Laverne is being eminently practical: she is not sure that she will be able to feed this child, and she is expecting another. When Dr. Shumann asks whether she knows that the child in her womb is not Roger's, she gives him this assurance, but she cannot assure him that little Jack, whom she is leaving with him, is indeed Roger's son, though the grandfather begs for this assurance: "If I just knew that he is Roger's! . . . Can't you give me some sign? . . . Any little sign?" Laverne is an honest woman. She can't and she doesn't, but with Dr. Shumann's insistence that he wants the

---

4. The original publishers of *Pylon* would have helped the reader if they had introduced a one-line space to signal this abrupt change of scene.

child anyway, she goes out to the taxi and presumably out of his life forever.

Yet if I read this difficult novel correctly, Dr. Shumann does get his little sign after all. The child is asleep with his toy airplane on the pillow beside him, but Dr. Shumann takes him by the shoulder and begins to shake him. The child wakes, and when he asks where Laverne is, Dr. Shumann says: "You're at home, but Laverne is gone. Gone, I tell you. Are you going to cry?" Is the old man beside himself, or has he waked the boy deliberately to test whether he will burst into tears?

Whatever the grandfather's motive, the boy does not cry. Instead, he asks about his toy plane: "Where's my new job? Where's my ship?" And then Dr. Shumann, with "a grimace of gnomelike rage," seizes the toy and hurls it at the wall and begins to stamp on it. The little boy makes only "one sharp sound." He does not weep. The money that the Reporter had hidden in the toy plane for the child's benefit comes fluttering out, and Dr. Shumann at once puts it in the stove as the wages of sin of which he wants no part. But while his attention and that of his wife is thus for the moment diverted, the little boy has gathered up his clothes and the ruined toy plane, and with his cap already on his head is preparing to walk out of the house into the snow.

Dr. Shumann shouts to his wife: "It's our boy. It's our boy, I tell you." Was the requisite sign the little boy's refusal to burst into tears; his manliness; his tough-minded composure; his devotion to his plane? We don't know, just as we don't know whether the child's preparation to leave the house—something that Dr. Shumann had apparently not yet observed when he cried out, "It's our boy," has furnished an additional hint to the reader that Jack is indeed Roger's son and is already exhibiting the qualities that made Roger rebel against his father's plans for him to become such another country doctor as himself. It would be pleasant if one could assume that old Dr. Shumann had indeed received the little sign for which he yearned, but it is hard to believe that Faulkner would bother to tack a happy ending of sorts onto this somber novel. It would be, in any case, a happy ending only for the Shumanns.

Faulkner's real reason for adding this scene may be that he felt that in order to understand Roger Shumann fully the reader needs to get a glimpse of the world against which he had rebelled, and also a sense of what price his parents had had to pay for his release into the life that he craved. Perhaps also Faulkner wanted to give the reader a further measure of Laverne's nature. Surely the giving up of her child cost her something? Or did it? Had she simply become numb? Is the Reporter's estimation of her (and the others) correct after all: that she and her paramours belong to a new breed? The episode at the Shumann farm ends with Dr. Shumann having buried his head in his wife's lap, weeping—with tears of joy? Relief? Or just emotional exhaustion?

The reader could use here, too, some typographical help in the form of extra space, for in the sentence that follows we are back once more in the city room of the newspaper for which the Reporter works. He has left on Hagood's desk a paragraph about the abandonment of the search for Shumann's body and about Mrs. Shumann's departure for Ohio. It is a factual account, of the sort that Hagood had earlier insisted that the Reporter should aim at, but the ironic tone of the passage makes it plain that the Reporter is disgusted with these constrictions on his style as well as with his inability to come to grips with the story that he senses has somehow escaped him. The copyboy discovers crumpled in a wastepaper basket the discarded first draft of the Reporter's story, and in this version the copyboy finds "what he believed to be not only news but the beginning of literature." Doubtless this is what the Reporter also believed, for like so many journalists he was a frustrated novelist.

The Reporter has also left on Hagood's desk, to serve as a paperweight for his copy, an empty whiskey bottle and a note saying, "I am going down to Amboise st. and get drunk. . . ." The experience of the last four days has been a little more than he can contain.

Thus the novel comes to an end in a scene that stresses the Reporter's reaction to the hectic events of the last four days. Is he, after all, the central character of the novel? Is it finally *his* story rather than that of Roger Shumann and Laverne? (The question resembles, not too remotely, a similar question in *Ab-salom, Absalom!* Is the story told that of Thomas Sutpen or of Quentin Compson?) In *Pylon,* at least, the difficulty in saying whose story it is points to a central difficulty in the novel; one has to ask whether the novel really has a proper focus. We may have to press this issue further still: what is the novel really about? Is it a biting satire on aspects of twentieth-century America, the bit-terest indictment of modernity, with the possible exception of *Sanctuary,* that Faulkner ever wrote? The contemptible selfishness of the corrupt politician, Feinman, the sleaziness of a machine-made culture, the indifference and cynicism of the world of the press and the public relations men, the advertisers, and the slogan-makers—all come in for a scathing treatment.

Faulkner does not sentimentalize the flyers. Their fate is in good part of their own making. They choose, for reasons ap-parently compelling to themselves, to become gladiators who pro-vide blood sports as entertainment for trumped-up public spec-tacles. Nevertheless, it is their bodies that are at risk, and even when they survive physically, the psychic damage they suffer is brutally severe. If their residual humanity does triumph in the end, small thanks are due to the civilization around them. They have no ties with it. They have pulled up whatever roots they had in it. Certainly the individuals who make it up—in this novel mostly faceless and anonymous—conceive of them as oddities, as freaks, perhaps even as pariahs. Their constant mobility insures their complete rootlessness. Yet their mobility is simply a special and extreme instance of the increasing mobility of the culture at large. The flyer's rootlessness points to a rootlessness that is be-coming general.

If *Pylon* is a bitter indictment of modernity and its worship of speed, what is the base line from which modern aberrations are defined and judged? For if everything is nightmarish, then the nightmare would have to be counted normal. Who in the novel stands outside the nightmare to proclaim it for what it is?

As a matter of fact, a few individuals do stand outside. Hagood is basically a kind and decent man who feels the need to protect the Reporter from his follies. He does not know the air people first-hand, and does not want to know them. Yet in the end, he becomes their vicarious benefactor, for he keeps advancing funds to the Reporter, though he is pretty sure that those funds will end up with the air people. There is also the madam of a French Quarter brothel who rents the nomads a room on credit and takes care of the child while the adults are trying to collect the prize money Shumann has won. There is, most of all, Ord, from whom the Reporter, through a trick, gets the fast but unsafe plane for Shumann. Later, Ord does his best to prevent Shumann from flying the plane because he knows that it is unsafe. (Ord would have succeeded except for Feinman and his tricky legal secretary.) After Shumann's death in the plane, Ord voluntarily burns the promissory note for $5000 that Shumann and the Reporter had signed in his favor, and offers his house as a temporary refuge for Laverne and the child.[5] "Get her away from here," he tells the Reporter at the airport. "Just put her in a car and come on over home" (p. 244). New Valois can boast at least four good Samaritans. And when the journalists, waiting out at the lakeside for the possible recovery of Shumann's body, begin to make some jokes about the sexual arrangements of the *ménage à trois,* one of them exclaims: "You dirtymouthed bastards. Why dont you let the guy rest? Let them all rest" (p. 290).

These instances, however, are probably an insufficient makeweight to the prevailingly bleak account of the nomads who have no friends and can exert no claims on the society. But in saying this, are we not leaving out a character who is a powerful makeweight since he does dominate the book—the Reporter? Has not

5. Faulkner has rather gone out of his way to imply that a man who knows and loves and flies planes does not have to be the romantic daredevil. The description of the cozily middle-class furnishings of Ord's house is significant. In it we see the "new glow of two rose-shaded lamps which looked like the ones that burn for three hours each night in a livingroom suite in storewindows dressed by a junior manclerk. . . ." A few sentences further on there is a reference to the "livingroom of Ord's new neat little flowercluttered house, . . . with the newmatched divan and chairs and tables and lamps . . ." (p. 168). Ord has recently come into money as an airplane designer: that is one point made through the description. But a more important one is this: a first-rate flyer may find American middle-class life quite compatible with his life as an airman. The Shumann-Holmes troupe may be a special case.

the author specified that the Reporter is the patron saint of waifs and strays? Indeed he has, but that circumstance hardly affects the dominant theme of the novel, for the Reporter, as we have already seen, turns out to be almost as decisively cut off from society as are the people whom he tries to befriend. If he is a "friendly ghost" (p. 167), he is a "lonely ghost," and most of all a ghost, not really part of the world about him. His friendly overtures to the air nomads are almost embarrassing in their blundering ineptitude. *Pylon* is thus dominated by black sheep and lost sheep, and the categories can and do coalesce in the novel.

In fact, the more one thinks of it, the more evident it becomes that the general situation stressed in *Pylon* greatly resembles that in *Sanctuary*. In the earlier novel, Horace Benbow, the idealist and romantic, tries to befriend those outcasts from society, Lee Goodwin the bootlegger, Ruby his common-law wife, and their sickly child, but fails to save Goodwin. The cards *are* stacked against him. The air people are not precisely outcasts of society, but to the crowds who have come to see their feats, they are remote—larger than life as momentary heroes or maybe just as curious puppets, and finally not human at all. In describing them to a group of students, Faulkner went much further than I have. He said that "they were outside the range of God, not only of respectability, of love but of God too." [6]

The world of Quentin Compson, particularly as revealed to us in *Absalom, Absalom!*, is a world suffocated by its past, and many readers have regarded it as a horrifying world, a world of nightmare. It certainly does contain its horrors. But the world of the barnstorming pilots would seem to be more horrible still, truly a nightmare. For granted that the past can become oppressive, in having no past at all one risks losing one's status as a human being. Shumann's gallant gesture makes it plain that he hasn't lost all of his. So also does Holmes's pledge of funds to insure that Shumann's body not be returned to his father, C.O.D. What about Laverne? Is her renunciation of her child also an example of self-sacrifice for the good of the child? Or a precious gift to the old

---

6. *Faulkner in the University*, p. 36.

man who has now learned that he has lost his son? Or is Laverne simply morally lobotomatized? It's a real problem. Perhaps Laverne's heart is wrenched apart by what she does, but there is no hint that this is so. Yet it is always harder to present the woman as the complete stoic. That role seems peculiarly male.

If a dominant theme—perhaps *the* theme of *Pylon*—is alienation, would Faulkner have gained by setting his novel in Yoknapatawpha rather than in New Orleans? Would he have found an advantage in making Dr. Shumann a Jefferson physician and Roger, his son, a Yoknapatawpha boy who had highschool classmates there who remembered him, and friends and relatives in the countryside who had known him as a child? He would have gained certain obvious advantages of the sort that are evident in *Flags in the Dust*. In that novel, there are Suratt (Ratliff) and the McCallums and Bayard's Aunt Jenny to deepen the contrast between Bayard's present life and the older way of life that he has repudiated. But Faulkner probably wanted to depict an alienation deeper still. Even if Bayard has repudiated his past, it exercises claims upon him nevertheless. But the people Faulkner described in *Pylon* have, as he has himself told us, somehow "escaped the compulsion of accepting a past."

Yet, one can say this: in Faulkner's more accomplished treatments of the theme of alienation, the Yoknapatawpha setting is demonstrably important. One may illustrate from "A Rose for Emily." Miss Emily's isolation from the community and the consequences of her being cut away from it give substance as well as definition to her story. Or to illustrate from a major work: there is *Light in August,* in which we gradually come to understand how Joe Christmas was, from very babyhood, warped away from any human community, to appreciate the heroic elements in his defiance of the community as he tries to find out what he is, and ultimately to accept as inevitable the consequences of his dogged adherence to a moral isolationism.

Yet one must acknowledge that there are limits to what the Yoknapatawpha setting as such can provide. *Sanctuary* falls short of being one of Faulkner's greater achievements in spite of the fact that it is set in Yoknapatawpha and in spite of the fact that it embodies some of the most brilliant writing, paragraph by paragraph, that Faulkner ever did. *Sanctuary* is somber and bleak, but most readers, I venture to say, have found *Pylon* bleaker still.[7]

7. For further discussion of Faulkner's attitude toward the air nomads, see below, Notes, pp. 401–05.

8

A Tale of Two Innocents

(THE WILD PALMS)

AFTER FAULKNER had marked out the boundaries of his imaginary county, his first considerable departure from it, *Pylon,* had been written, he has told us, as a relief from writing the greatest of his Yoknapatawpha novels, *Absalom, Absalom!* The situation dramatized in *Pylon* is indeed the antithesis of that presented in *Absalom, Absalom!* (see p. 202, above). In the latter novel, the past is a portent and a menace, overshadowing the present and holding a mortgage on the future. In *Pylon* the past is a nothing—a vacuum (though, of course, a vacuum can be lethally destructive too).

The bifurcated nature of *The Wild Palms* apparently stemmed from the same sort of impulse that caused Faulkner earlier to have two novels going at the same time. He made this very clear in an interview in 1955:

> I did not know it would be two separate stories until after I had started the book. When I reached the end of what is now the first section of *The Wild Palms,* I realized suddenly that something was missing, it needed emphasis, something to lift it like counterpoint in music. So I wrote on the "Old Man" story until "The Wild Palms" story rose back to pitch. Then I stopped the "Old Man" story at what is now its first section,

and took up "The Wild Palms" story until it began to sag. Then I raised it to pitch again with another section of its antithesis, which is the story of a man who got his love and spent the rest of the book fleeing from it. . . .[1]

In an interview in 1939, however, he had given a different account:

[I] wrote one story and thought it was good but not enough. So [I] wrote another and slipped the chapters of the two in between each other like shuffling a deck of cards, only not so haphazardly. I played them against each other. . . . Contrapuntally.[2]

The best authorities on *The Wild Palms* accept Faulkner's 1955 account rather than that of 1939. Thomas L. McHaney, who has produced the most elaborate study yet made of *The Wild Palms,* makes an excellent case for Faulkner's having deliberately worked out, as he went along, the contrapuntal relations between the story of Harry Wilbourne and Charlotte Rittenmeyer and the story of the Tall Convict.[3] Even in the 1939 account in which Faulkner says that he "slipped the chapters of the two [stories] in between each other," one remembers that he admitted that he did so not "haphazardly" but "contrapuntally."

Pylon's antithetical partner is to be found in a separate book, one set in Yoknapatawpha County. But in *The Wild Palms* the Yoknapatawpha element is the novel's other hemisphere, an integral part—in claim, at least—of the same fictional organism. Is the tale of the Tall Convict, however, really related to Yoknapatawpha? In terms of the general purpose it served for Faulkner, I would have to answer yes. For if the Tall Convict is not precisely a Yoknapatawpha boy and if no familiar Yoknapatawpha names appear in the Convict's story, he is nevertheless the kind of person who might have been bred and brought up in Beat Four. His

1. *Lion in the Garden,* ed. Meriwether and Millgate, pp. 247–48.
2. Ibid., p. 36.
3. *William Faulkner's "The Wild Palms": A Study* (Jackson, Miss., 1975).

language and his outlook on the world fit with it perfectly. Perhaps Faulkner felt that in a novel which would have to do with an urban world, a bohemian world, and an almost completely emancipated world, he needed a base line of this sort.

Even that other world, the non-Yoknapatawpha world, in *The Wild Palms* was not wholly unfamiliar territory. Much of the action in the story of Harry and Charlotte takes place on the Gulf Coast near Pascagoula, Mississippi, or in New Orleans. And though neither of these places possessed for Faulkner the imaginative resources that Yoknapatawpha held, nevertheless, they were places with which he was moderately well acquainted and which had for him some pleasant as well as painful associations. Aside from a few of his early short stories that have a European setting, Faulkner's only major invasion of foreign parts was to come later on, in *A Fable,* though even there he felt it necessary to touch base with his native South somewhere, as he does in the episode about the three-legged racehorse.

Though Faulkner makes the story of the Tall Convict and the story of Harry and Charlotte end in the state of Mississippi, the stories do not take place in the same time span nor do the characters in the one ever come into contact with the characters of the other.[4] But when we turn from the matter of time and place to situation and theme, the two stories do lock into each other at once, for *The Wild Palms* is a tale of two innocents, or, more precisely, it is two tales, each with its own innocent hero (or victim), yet so truly parallel that they constitute a consideration of what is essentially the same basic human situation and thus the dramatization of one theme.

Man's innocence obviously fascinated Faulkner. I have here more in mind than the general experience of growing up. *The Unvanquished,* for example, is the story of Bayard Sartoris's development from the age of thirteen to twenty-six, when he

---

4. McHaney makes the half-serious conjecture that the physician who talks to the Tall Convict on the rescue boat may be the same man to whom Harry Wilbourne ten years later appealed for help when Charlotte began to hemorrhage. Maybe so. But if so, the connection amounts to little more than a private irony on Faulkner's part: this minor character scarcely "connects" the stories.

makes his great moral decision and enters upon a disciplined maturity. *Intruder in the Dust* is a novel about Chick Mallison's development toward maturity. But the innocence of which I speak here is more special: a quality of stubborn idealism and ingrained romanticism that continues to leave its human possessor puzzled, shocked, or even "outraged" (to use one of Faulkner's favorite words) with the recalcitrancy of reality.

In Faulkner's earlier work, obvious examples of such innocents are Sir Galwyn of *Mayday* and Horace Benbow of *Sartoris* and *Sanctuary;* later, there is the Gavin Stevens of *The Town* and *The Mansion;* and in a more technically specialized way, there is Thomas Sutpen of *Absalom, Absalom!* Perhaps one should add Quentin Compson of *The Sound and the Fury,* and there are traces of such innocence in many of Faulkner's minor characters— particularly when it comes to their knowledge of womankind. One thinks of Labove and even Mink Snopes in *The Hamlet,* for in understanding women, most of the male sex in Faulkner's novels display incorrigible innocence. Harry Wilbourne and the Tall Convict obviously belong to this not inconsiderable company.

To start with Wilbourne: Faulkner begins his novel by insisting on Wilbourne's lack of experience and his general naiveté. Faulkner makes it clear that Harry at twenty-seven has never slept with a woman; he is quiet, methodical, unadventurous in any sense, and performs without rebelliousness or even any inward repining his work as a medical student who is serving the last months of his internship in a New Orleans hospital. Harry is to learn much in the course of the months that lie ahead, but even after he has apparently changed his life utterly, his Chicago journalist friend can tease him for his gullibility, and his mistress can call him a "damned home-wrecking boy scout." Right up to the end, Harry shows himself inept in dealing with people. For example, in his desperation, he goes to a brothel to see whether he can secure a drug that will make Charlotte abort the foetus she is carrying. But he is so awkwardly self-conscious that the madam immediately becomes suspicious of his true mission, summons the bouncer, and has him literally thrown out of the house. We are told at this point that Harry "was indeeed learning fast the things he should have known before he was nineteen years old" (p. 214). Faulkner perhaps risks overreaching himself here, and so rendering his hero incredible; yet Harry never becomes merely a comic caricature. He arouses our pity, not our laughter. Faulkner has, however, played so close to the line that it is a remarkable tribute to his narrative skill that he has succeeded in maintaining Harry's dignity as a man.

Yet, how could this stolid, conventional, completely correct young man suddenly throw up his internship and utterly change his whole way of life? How could one evening at a party given by some arty people in the French Quarter effect so thorough a re-direction of his career? Faulkner does not try to cushion the reader's shock. This love at first sight must be accepted as a *donné* of the novel. We begin with it: given such a situation as presented in the first chapter of *The Wild Palms,* the author asks us, what would happen to the young man? to the young woman with whom he fell in love?

It is the woman, of course, who in this instance makes the advances, and, granted Harry's innocence, that would have to be the case for the affair to have begun at all. Charlotte Rittenmeyer has been married for some five years to a successful New Orleans businessman and is the mother of two little girls, aged four and two. When Charlotte meets Harry, the unprepossessing medical student, it is apparently love at first sight for both, a passion that is overpowering, irrational, and unpredictable. As the story develops, one sees that the effect on each other of this so very different pair of people resembles nothing so much as the accidental drinking of the love potion by Tristan and Isolde. We see no evident meeting of minds and not even an obvious and mutual physical attraction. Yet the man and the woman are immediately committed to each other, totally.

The drinking of the love philter does constitute an explanation of sorts in the Tristan story, but none at all is offered in *The Wild Palms.* It just happened inexplicably, as sometimes in real life such things do happen. Later, as we read on into the novel, we can pick up some clues that may partially account (but only partially) for this startling instance of love at first sight. It may be that Harry's very innocence was the attraction for Charlotte, for she may have interpreted it as a lack of involvement in the ordinary, middle-class world of success and respectability that she had come to loathe.

Charlotte, as we quickly find out, is simply aching to break away from that bourgeois world. Though the two cases are by no means identical, there is a certain amount of Madame Bovary in Charlotte. She has an intellectual lust for a world of pure romantic love as she conceives it—a love that scorns all compromises, that demands all or nothing, that will burn forever with a hard and gem-like flame, or, failing that, at least disappear in some final flash. She is dissatisfied with domesticity and respectability. Even the bohemianism of the New Orleans French Quarter is much too insipid for her.

Did Charlotte, like Madame Bovary, get her ideas about the nature of romantic love from reading romantic books? Probably. At one point she mentions the notion of love conveyed by books: ". . . the second time I ever saw you [Harry] I learned what I had read in books but I never had actually believed: that love and suffering are the same thing . . ." (p. 48). In any case, she wants to experience life so intensely that it will burn and hurt. She is now convinced that real passion does cause one to suffer.

Let me put a different, though related, question: did Faulkner derive Charlotte Rittenmeyer from *his* reading, specifically from his reading of Flaubert's *Madame Bovary?* We can only speculate, though we know that *Madame Bovary* was one of his favorite novels. In any case, Charlotte and Emma are both restless, willful women, who find that their married life is dull and depressing, who yearn for love, want to live, and believe that to be truly alive is to be passionately in love.

We can with a considerable measure of confidence name the actual woman from whom Faulkner derived Charlotte's physical appearance and certain traits of personality. Joseph Blotner has seen in Charlotte a reflection of Helen Baird, and Thomas McHaney concurs. Like Charlotte, Helen had been badly burned as a child, and still bore the scars, which, like Charlotte, she disdained to conceal. Again like Charlotte, Helen made little figurines, very much like those that Charlotte made for sale in Chicago. (See Blotner, pp. 438, 982). I can add one more point of resemblance—one that I think clinches the identification. In *The Wild Palms* Faulkner constantly speaks of Charlotte's eyes as yellow, "not hazel but yellow" (p. 39). He also saw Helen Baird's eyes as yellow. (I have quoted in chapter 2 from one of his letters to Helen Baird: "I remember a sullen-jawed yellow-eyed belligerent gal," etc.)

We first see Harry and Charlotte at Pascagoula, and it is there that Harry sees her for the last time. Faulkner had good reason to associate Helen Baird with that part of the Mississippi Gulf Coast. I see no reason, however, to assume that she was a model for Charlotte in more than her physical appearance and her strong will. In fact, I suppose Charlotte to be a personality largely made up in Faulkner's own head, although Thomas McHaney believes that Faulkner might have derived a good deal of Charlotte's character from Sherwood Anderson's second wife, Tennessee Mitchell.[5] McHaney also suggests a number of close similarities between *The Wild Palms* and Anderson's *Dark Laughter* (in which Tennessee Mitchell figures as one of the characters). "These links [of *The Wild Palms*] to Anderson through his second wife have gone unnoticed," McHaney remarks, and he is surely right. Again, I believe that I can add one more link connecting Anderson with *The Wild Palms*. The decisive event in Harry's life, as it turns out, is his finding a leather wallet containing $1278 in bills—by sheer accident and in a most improbable place, a public garbage can. His finding the wallet enables the lovers to escape from New Orleans and to consummate their passionate love for each other.

Earlier on the afternoon on which Harry was to find the wallet Charlotte had agreed to meet him in a cheap hotel, but she looks around the room and cannot go through with it. She exclaims, "Not like this, Harry. No back alleys." Since her husband will not give her a divorce, and since they do not have the means to go away together, their situation seems hopeless. It is only a few minutes

5. *William Faulkner's "The Wild Palms,"* pp. 10–12.

after Charlotte has left for her home by taxi that Harry discovers the wallet. It contains cards that identify the owner and provide his address. Harry's first impulse is to return the money to the owner, and he has actually boxed the wallet for mailing when the telephone in the interns' dormitory rings. The call is from Charlotte. She is preparing to tell Harry goodbye forever. She has talked to her husband and evidently has assured him that the affair has now been completely terminated before it had ever really begun. This unexpected call tips the scales in Harry's mind. Suddenly he knows that he is not going to return the money. Instead, he tells Charlotte that he has $1278 and the next day the lovers depart for Chicago.

Now something remarkably like this happened to Sherwood Anderson. In the winter of 1920 Anderson went to Mobile, pretty much on impulse, not having any special reason to visit that city —just putting his "finger on the map." But once there, having got into "a dirty poorly lighted street," his foot struck something on the pavement. It was a pocketbook, and in it a billfold holding $140.[6] Anderson tells us that it didn't occur to him that the money belonged to someone else. "It seemed sent to me by God." It struck him as providential, for it meant "two or even three months more of freedom," time to get on with a novel that he had been meaning to write. In the next several pages Anderson goes on to talk about his happiness that night, his "great sense of relief, of tension taken off. . . ."

The first publication of Anderson's *Memoirs* was in 1942, some three years after the publication of *The Wild Palms*. But I think it very likely that Anderson had told Faulkner about the incident during the time that they were in New Orleans together. Though the sums contained in the two wallets differ vastly, the circumstances that neither finder made any serious effort to return the money, that they even looked on the windfall as heaven-sent, and, more important still, that the money made a decisive impact in the subsequent life of the finder—all persuade me that Faulkner here adapted a real event in Anderson's life to his own purpose.

6. *Sherwood Anderson's Memoirs*, ed. R. S. White (Chapel Hill, N.C., 1969), p. 354.

He may even have felt that the obvious improbability of Harry's good fortune was lessened somewhat by his knowledge that this sort of thing had actually happened to someone he knew.

Improbability in fiction is not, however, necessarily redeemed by the possibility that it could happen, or even by the knowledge of an instance in which it did happen. Fiction has to find other justifications. Yet, as we have seen, *The Wild Palms* begins not merely with one event difficult to accept, but with two: there is not only the miraculous provision of the money, but the almost equally improbable love at first sight.

The general mode of *The Wild Palms* is in keeping with these first incidents. Though there is plenty of realism in the story, the tale itself is not realistic. It is more accurately called a romance—filled with ironies. It begins, one might say, almost like a fairy tale. The lady is bored with her tiresome life. The man is so benumbed with routine that he cannot even conceive of passionate excitement. Then a good fairy waves her wand and brings them together and they sense immediately that each can give the other a life of true passion. But they are penniless, and so their potential for passion cannot be fulfilled. Then, when all again seems hopeless, the good fairy once more waves her wand and the couple are allowed to seek their joy together. Granted such fortune, the teller of the tale then appears to ask: will they live happily ever after? Grant me these improbable opening circumstances, he implies, and we shall see. Such is the implication of the fairy tale. Yet, since *The Wild Palms* is much more than a fairy tale, there may be further complications. Was the giver of these gifts a kind of fairy godmother or a wicked witch? Were the gifts a blessing or a curse?

The companion story, the story about that other innocent, the young hillman who is serving a long sentence in the state penal farm—is it by contrast a realistic story? Again, it certainly has a great deal of realism in it, but it too is filled with events that put a strain on our capacity for belief. It begins with a most improbable premise: we are asked to believe that a young man was so naive as really to think he could pull off a train robbery on the basis of what he could learn from a periodical called the *Detec-*

tives' *Gazette,* and that he actually purchased by mail order such necessary supplies as a "dark lantern in which a candle burned and [a] black handkerchief to wear over the face." Such is the young man's notion of what is romantic and heroic. But his attempt at heroics, the train robbery, turns out to be a fiasco, a comic failure.

Later on he does accomplish some truly heroic actions, but he seems unaware that on these occasions he is being heroic. Even here his adventures have their comic side. Furthermore, if we are truly to understand the tale of the Convict's adventures, we shall have to be aware of his unconscious humor and the author's thoroughly conscious (and complicated) comic spirit. Since the story of Harry and Charlotte is also an account of almost preternatural events, yet also larded with humor, unless we take into account the tone and mood of both stories, we shall scarcely understand how cunningly they are made to counterpoint each other.

To return to the human situation presented in *The Wild Palms:* we have a woman obsessed with her own notions about romantic love, a love which must be kept chemically pure, never compromised, never sicklied o'er with dull domesticity; and man who is obsessed with this woman. What is the notion of romantic love that Charlotte holds? I have discussed it at some length in *William Faulkner: The Yoknapatawpha Country,* particularly in the chapter entitled "Passion, Marriage, and Bourgeois Respectability" (pp. 192–218).[7] Let me here summarize briefly. In romantic love (or, as Denis de Rougemont calls it, chivalric love) the lovers discover a transcendent element. Neither is interested in simply possessing the beloved one's body; nor is his or her desire fulfilled and exhausted in the sexual act. The loved one has become unique and infinitely precious, and the proof of the purity of one's devotion to her or him is the fact that the lover has no worldly end in view. For the sake of the beloved, the lover dares to defy all prohibitions. Lancelot's love for Guinevere or Tristan's for Isolde exemplify the type.

7. There I have drawn principally on Denis de Rougemont's *Love in the Western World* (New York: Anchor Books, 1957) and *Love Declared* (New York, 1963).

In a day when men and women were mated as a means to titles or power, or to add a province to the kingdom, or to assure an alliance, the institution of marriage became tarnished by material gain and worldly power. The truly pure love, chivalric love, stood above and beyond such considerations: it was often a hopeless love, with no prospect of consummation, or with consummation to be achieved only in defiance of convention, law, and the received codes of morality.[8]

The concept of romantic love persisted long after the age of chivalry, and had its disturbing effect on bourgeois life in the eighteenth, nineteenth, and twentieth centuries. Domesticity and everyday living threaten to dim the clear flame of romantic love. Madame Bovary longed for a love more ardent and exciting than could be offered in the humdrum life in which she was associated with her sobersides husband. Charlotte Rittenmeyer, having abandoned her comfortable home and thoroughly respectable life with her financially successful husband, tells her true love, Harry, that for the two of them "it's got to be all honeymoon, always. Forever and ever, until one of us dies" (p. 83).[9] Any falling off from this point of intensity would constitute a betrayal.

Under the circumstances, Charlotte's declaration is understandable and dramatically appropriate. She makes her demand upon love with transparent sincerity. But in making it she begins to hammer on the iron doors of reality. Hers is a brave but hopeless resolution. If she means to carry it out, and she does, she has sentenced herself and possibly her lover to death.[10] And there is more than a hint that Charlotte is half in love with death. Early

8. Harry himself alludes to the "romance of illicit love" which attracts men, and he describes it in almost precisely these terms. He calls it "the passionate idea of two [lovers] damned and doomed and isolated forever against the world and God and the irrevocable" (p. 82). Compare Quentin Compson's desire to be isolated with his sister Caddy forever in some corner of hell (see *The Sound and the Fury*, p. 144).

9. The Faulkner of *Go Down, Moses* (1942) passes judgment on the impossibility of such a desire. He calls it "that brief unsubstanced glory which inherently of itself cannot last" (p. 326).

10. In his *Love in the Western World*, Rougemont argues that the romantic lovers are really in love with death. They demand a union, each with the other, so absolute that their very bodies become a hindrance. The perfect consummation of their desire, therefore, can come only in death. The rapturous love death of Tristan and Isolde in Wagner's opera is the perfect example.

in the novel she tells Harry where she would like to die—in water. "Not in the hot air, above the hot ground, to wait for hours for your blood to get cool enough to let you sleep. . . . The water, the cool, to cool you quick so that you can sleep, to wash out of your brain and out of your eyes and out of your blood all you ever saw and thought and felt and wanted and denied" (p. 58). Her speech sounds the true note of chivalric love: what one yearns for is not to attain the desired goal, but to be rid of the desire itself. One's ultimate desire is not so much for an intense realization of burning life as for peace—for the cool relief of death. Charlotte, to be sure, will later on insist that she hates dying, and wants to live, and there is no reason to argue that in such utterances she is insincere. But this earlier speech about death by water, a speech made to Harry just before they consummate their passion, may provide a glimpse into a deeper truth about Charlotte, one of which she herself may not have been aware.

Rougemont's account of romantic love also indicates why the chivalric lovers so often are at odds with society yet not necessarily fully aware of what their defiance entails. Charlotte at least partially realizes that she is impelled toward Harry because she is hopelessly bored with her role in society, her stodgy husband, and her secure position. She may not, however, be fully aware that Harry is glamorous to her because he is a man *outside* society. His very poverty and innocence render him romantic. Rougemont comments that the romantic lovers need society to set up barriers and to frown upon (if not actually punish) the attempts to cross over those barriers. Complete permissiveness is the real threat to romantic love. Harry and Charlotte again and again cry out against the soulless society that makes no allowance for their love and, through its insistence on money and respectability, intends to extinguish it. And yet, if Rougemont is right, had the lovers been able to live quite outside the framework of society and had they never been menaced by its prohibitions, their passionate love would have withered.

This essential point is clearly made in *The Wild Palms*. After Harry and Charlotte have gone away to the cottage in the Wisconsin woods, after their last neighbor has bade them goodbye, they are apparently free of society at last, free to enjoy, undisturbed, their private Eden. Charlotte underlines their blessed solitude by addressing Harry as "Adam." But Harry is a fallen Adam living in a fallen world. Obviously he cannot sustain the burden of Edenic bliss, and, surely enough, in good time, he realizes that he is "bored . . . bored to extinction." (Milton himself had his difficulties in providing Adam and Eve even before the Fall with a convincingly rich and meaningful life.)

There is another difficulty for post-Adamic man. Though man cannot live by bread alone, neither can he live without bread. Harry discovers, moreover, that he needs to *earn* his bread—needs a vocation. He further discovers that he needs to return to the world of time. He can no longer endure "the sunny and timeless void into which the individual days had vanished" (pp. 113–14). His immediate concern is to know what day of the year it is, and he proceeds at once to construct a calendar and thus locate himself once more in time.

The endeavor to live only for love and by love having failed, they return to Chicago, but find again that they are being corrupted by the world, reduced to the abhorred status of middle-class husband and wife. Yet when they flee once more, to the mine camp in Utah, they find that their plight is even worse than it was in the Wisconsin cottage. There, though starvation and the cold of winter were threats, they did have solitude. Now in Utah, they have enough food, but the cold becomes so intense that their solitude is threatened. Their sleeping place, even with the gasoline stove burning constantly, becomes so cold that they are forced to bed down with the Buckners, the only other English-speaking pair in the mine. The Buckners advise them that it is warmer to sleep with the mattresses on the floor, and when the temperature drops from fourteen below zero to forty-one below, the two couples "moved the mattresses together and slept as a unit." The earthy Buckners are not in the least inhibited by this arrangement, and their vigorous and noisy couplings occur almost nightly. But Harry and Charlotte are too fastidious for that. Their eroticism is no mere matter of the glands, but of the mind and the imagination as well. And so, like the Phoenix and the Turtle in one of Faulkner's favorite poems, they spend this winter at the mine in "married chastity." The passionate lovers, who have fled to the wilderness to keep their love pure and unspotted from the world, find that they have taken the world into bed with them.

Faulkner's use of this episode constitutes perhaps the sharpest irony that he directs at his chivalric lovers, but this is not an isolated instance of such ironic judgment. Back in Chicago, the lovers had found themselves in almost equally absurd plight. Charlotte had found a job in a store where she dressed windows and display cases. Harry produced for the "confession magazines the stories beginning 'I had the body and desires of a woman yet in knowledge and experience of the world I was but a child' or 'If I had only had a mother's love to guard me on that fatal day' " (p. 121). Harry thus mechancially cranks out vapid stories about "love," mere "moron's pap," "sexual gumdrop[s]," tawdry parodies of the high mystery to which Harry believes he has been called. Charlotte, for her part, spends her nights, not in the arms of her lover, but dressing and undressing female mannikins displayed in the shop windows. During this period, usually "he was awake mostly while she slept, and vice versa." This is the way they find themselves spending the perpetual honeymoon to which Charlotte had vowed them.

If the reader ignores the ironic light so steadily beamed on Harry and Charlotte, he will certainly miss the import of this novel. Though Faulkner does not turn the lovers into comic figures—they suffer too much, they are too seriously pledged to their cause for that—he is certainly not easy on them. In fact, to grasp his precise attitude toward them constitutes one of the more difficult problems encountered in this truly complex novel.

On the other hand, Faulkner clearly holds no brief for a crass society, the enemy of the lovers and the prime threat to the integrity of their love. He does not, of course, speak out in his own person, but he powerfully dramatizes the issues at stake. Harry's diatribes against the state of civilization are ably reinforced by McCord, his journalist friend. The world, Harry insists, has eliminated love—the need for it and the possibility of attaining it. Respectability is all. Harry is savage in his castigation of respectability—the habit of playing safe, of wearing the proper blinders, of dampening down the fires of passion, of conforming to what a cowed society regards as good and proper. In Faulkner's novels—from the early ones on—respectability always comes off badly. The saint and the hero refuse to have anything to do with it. Faulkner apparently always had an admiration for the autonomous and high-hearted spirit, and a loathing for the person who was herd-minded (The technical term would be, I suppose, "other-directed.") Even Flem Snopes may just possibly elicit a kind of grudging respect until in the end he capitulates to respectability; that, for Faulkner, is the truly unpardonable sin.

A civilization so far gone in its worship of respectability that it takes public relations seriously and can acquire its preferences and aversions from an advertising agency—such an ultimately mass-minded society has no room for the heroic, either in love or war. The old-fashioned society scorned "a laggard in love and a dastard in war"; but modern society, Harry feels, would regard either the true hero or the chivalric lover as insane. There is a certain accuracy, therefore, in Harry's insisting that modern society has "got rid of love at last just as [it has] got rid of Christ" (p. 136), though in saying this Harry may be more than a little mad. (On page 112 he has admitted that he is mad. It could be argued, however, that it was the sterile rationality of the society that had pushed him over the line into madness.)

What attitude does Faulkner mean for us to take toward Harry and toward Charlotte? As I read the novel, he expects us to acknowledge their folly. They are pursuing an impossible goal; they ask of human life a great deal more than it can provide. Yet Faulkner surely expects us to be sympathetic with their repudiation of a world that is not fervently committed to anything. Instead of thinking of Harry and Charlotte as having, like Tristan and Isolde, drunk a love potion, it might be more accurate to say that they behave like people to whom a revelation—some blinding truth—has suddenly been given, and that their story is that of people who, in spite of every difficulty, have somehow kept the faith and been loyal to the truth vouchsafed.[11] Yet the "truth" that calls forth such loyalty may be a half-truth or even a false dream.

11. Faulkner's original title for *The Wild Palms* was *If I Forget Thee, Jerusalem.* For the source of the original title, see below, Notes, pp. 406–07.

Heretics, along with orthodox martyrs, have often suffered bravely for adherence to their beliefs.

In *The Wild Palms* Faulkner has played very fairly indeed. If he has sometimes represented the lovers as having acted absurdly, and even fanatically, he never really violates their tragic dignity. Whatever the aesthetic merit we finally accord to *The Wild Palms,* we shall have to agree that Faulkner's attitude toward Harry and Charlotte is very complex, perhaps too complex for the good of the novel. Faulkner takes them very seriously, but he does not fail to judge them, even severely.

Since this is a double novel, we now turn to the story of the other innocent, the Tall Convict. (He obviously has a name, but Faulkner never considers it important to tell us what it is. The Convict, it is implied, is a sort of Everyman.) The Tall Convict is, in general, Harry's antithesis: he is not an educated man, not given to meditation or lucubration or even to much self-conscious reflection. This is not to say that in his own way he is not as "romantic" as Harry. His reading, such as it is, has filled his head with ideas of adventure. He has studied long and hard how to pull off a great train robbery. He is even the romantic lover, for he attempts the robbery primarily in order to win the admiration of a girl, a girl with "ripe breasts and a heavy mouth and dull eyes like ripe muscadines" (p. 338). Yet how different are his and Harry's experiences with, and their attitudes toward, the women with whom they are blessed (or condemned) to spend the months before they enter (or reenter) the penitentiary. Charlotte is borne to Harry on a flood of passion that breaks through all the dykes of convention and morality. But the Convict is borne to the woman perched in the tree on a literal flood—that of the lower Mississippi River in 1927, which inundated hundreds of thousands of acres.

In contrast to Harry's goddess, who has unaccountably condescended to give herself to him and for whom in turn he unhesitatingly gives up his career, the woman who climbs down into the skiff seems to the Tall Convict to have been dumped upon him almost as an obscene jest. He had vaguely hoped to rescue some fabled Helen or "living Garbo" if he had to rescue anybody, but the woman he finds in a tree is not only a rather homely girl dressed in a calico wrapper and wearing a pair of "man's unlaced brogans"; she is heavily pregnant. The Convict sees her as a nuisance, an encumbrance, a sheer liability. True, he does not rail at her or complain about her to her face. He treats her with grudging courtesy, for, as we shall see, he has his own code of honor. He does better than that: later he makes superhuman efforts to protect her and he succeeds in saving her and her newborn child from the perils of the flood. Yet his motive for saving her has nothing to do with her romantic charm or sexual attraction.

No more than Harry does the Convict want to assume the role of husband, though he has no reason to fear what Harry dreads, that he will come to be "exactly like any husband with his Saturday pay envelope and his suburban bungalow full of electric wife-saving gadgets . . ." (p. 132). There are no gadgets of this sort on the sodden mound alive with snakes on which the Convict desperately beaches the skiff barely in time for the woman to bring forth her child. There is not even a pocket-knife to cut the navel cord: the sharp edges of a crudely opened tin can will have to serve, and do.

The flood-drowned world in which the Tall Convict and the woman find themselves is not respectable, but heroic; not bourgeois, but barbaric. In attempting his great train robbery with mail-order props and according to methods swatted up from the pages of the *Detectives' Gazette,* the youth who became the Tall Convict was caught up in a silly, romantic dream of heroism. But on the raging Mississippi, he meets up with the real thing and answers with heroic action.

The story of the Tall Convict's epic adventure and how he accomplished it has, for most readers, proved to be the obviously attractive part of this novel. Early readers responded to it at once and readers continue to respond. As a consequence, the Convict chapters were early split off from the rest of the novel and published as a separate story entitled "Old Man," the nickname of the Mississippi River on whose swollen waters the Convict performed his heroic actions. Certainly the "Old Man" half of the novel contains some of Faulkner's most brilliant writing, and for that very reason one can afford to say the less about it here. It offers solid but quite obvious rewards to the reader, and it presents far fewer problems than does the story of Harry and Charlotte. But if we seriously ask just what is the relation of the Convict's story to the rest of the novel, aside from providing a few quite obvious contrasts, problems do emerge, and they may be well worth discussing.

"Old Man" tells how a man and a woman were pushed to the uttermost limit of their powers. The Convict is again and again shocked to discover how much he can accomplish or endure. (We learn less of what goes on in the woman's mind, but her few remarks suggest a being of Spartan valor and stoical calm.) The two face preternatural happenings: rivers suddenly run backward, pushing down upon them a wall of water and debris; the one bit of planking that has to serve for a paddle is lost, and though there is to hand a tree limb to provide the substance for another, the Convict lacks an axe, a hatchet, or even a pocket knife with which to fashion something he can use to steer the boat. Circumstances are as dire and fresh catastrophes as numerous as in any Tall Tale out of the Old Southwest; the events narrated are almost as outsized and as outrageous as those we find in a tale told by Davy Crockett.

To say this, however, is not to imply that the Convict didn't perform what the novel reports he did. Most of his story is actually told in the third person by an omniscient author, though the Convict, after his return to the prison camp, does tell his fellow convicts about his strange wanderings. Faulkner's reasons for letting the reader hear parts of the story in the Convict's own words are obvious. He is able thereby to dramatize the Convict's modesty about his own exploits, his laconic way of talking, his "innocence." A good example is the way in which the Convict delivers himself up to the officer at the Parchman Penal Farm. During the flood, he had been given a boat and told to rescue a woman perched in a tree and a man who had taken refuge on the roof of a cottonhouse. Now, after seven weeks, the Convict has returned, mission accomplished. He says, "Yonder's your boat, and here's the woman. But I never did find that bastard on the cottonhouse" (p. 278).

What attitude are we expected to take with regard to the Tall Convict? He performs heroic actions, but is he really a hero? Can there be a somewhat dim-minded hero? Or an unintentional hero —one who is unaware that he is making and abiding by heroic choices? Can one, in short, become a hero "on instinct," as Falstaff, on one celebrated occasion, became a coward on instinct? To specify a particular action: need the Convict have insisted on bringing the skiff all the way back to the Penal Farm? Or couldn't he in New Orleans have turned the woman over to one of the Red Cross workers that were at the camp in numbers and have her sent home as a refugee at government expense? Most puzzling of all, why did he himself insist on returning to the Penal Farm? Why didn't he simply get lost. He had been presumed to be dead by drowning. If he had assumed a new name and gone to another section of the country, even some other part of the South, the chances were excellent that he would never have been detected.

The truth about the Convict's conduct would seem to be that even a very simple man may possess a personal code of honor that both prevents his doing certain things he would like to do (such as getting rid of the woman he rescues by throwing her out of the boat) and requires him to do other things he would rather not do (such as returning voluntarily to the Penal Farm, not only with the woman entrusted to his care, but with the rest of the State property in his keeping: the skiff and his prison uniform, now freshly laundered). One must not scold a literal-minded man who has a sense of honor for interpreting it in a literal-minded way.

By many people, such quixotically gallant actions will be dismissed as folly, as they were by the officials of the Penal Farm. But if we feel compelled to agree with the Penal Farm officers, then we will have to regard the "Old Man" section of this novel as very grimly sardonic indeed. That interpretation would imply that heroism sometimes is not to be separated from dull-witted folly. But does the Convict forfeit his claims to our applause by his gross stupidity and his sheep-like docility? I have put the case in extreme terms to make a point, but I am not trying to turn the

Faulkner of *The Wild Palms* into the Swift of *Gulliver's Travels*, coldly seething at the folly of mankind as well as at the corruption of all human societies. He does not push matters to such extremes. This novel is essentially the story of two innocents and what they learned (or failed to learn) from their experiences—the one adrift on the flood of passion, the other adrift on the flood-swollen river.

As a foil to the story of Harry, the story of the Convict answers to nearly every relevant aspect. Both men are snatched from their secure places of refuge, Harry from his interns' dormitory; the Convict, from the Penal Farm. The flood on which the Convict is borne away sometimes seems to possess a human intelligence, actually playing with him, mocking him with an individual's malice. On the other hand, the flood of human passion which tosses Harry about sometimes resembles a natural force as impersonal as wind and wave. Eventually, after terrific strivings, each man reaches safe harbor—the same harbor. The Convict wins his struggle against nature. But over what does Harry win victory? Indeed, is either man a victor? And if so, in what terms can we describe his triumph?

Such reflections invite one to look more closely at the *nature vs. human nature* contrast as set forth in this novel, for this contrast is an important aspect of the contrapuntal system that Faulkner has attempted to set up. The natural forces against which the Convict struggles are external to himself: the great river against which he contends, or the hawk that he scares off the carcass of the drowned rabbit so that he may have the food for himself and the woman. Even the men who, noticing his prison stripes, fire at him to prevent his landing, are in a real sense external forces. With these he can try to cope, and does cope with a good deal of success. There is, however, one natural force with which he cannot fight and with which he can only hope to comply. That is the force that will expel the child from the pregnant woman's womb. This force cannot be denied nor can its chosen time be altered by anything that the Convict can do.

It would be unfair, however, to say that the Convict does not also have to struggle against human nature—largely, his own wishes, habits, and desires. He had to put down not only his impulse to drown his woman companion but later any temptation to make sexual advances toward her. After his return to prison, he is forced to admit that "there were times, seconds, at first when if it had not been for the baby he might have tried." The admission is made to one of the other inmates who refuses to believe that he could really have abstained from bedding her. We go on to read, however, that his temptation lasted "just seconds because in the next instant his whole being would seem to flee the very idea in a kind of savage and horrified revulsion . . ." (pp. 334–35).

In sum, though the struggle with the natural elements is difficult and barely won, he seems to win his struggle with his own nature rather easily. Not so with Harry. His struggle is only incidentally with nature, though as we shall see nature is ultimately involved. But Harry's basic contest is with human nature—specifically with a romantic dream which is not like the Convict's boyish fantasy of cops and robbers but is deadly and serious. That dream of chivalric love will exploit the body for its own ends. It is a dream that has all the formidable power of a centuries-old religion with power to consign its devotees to death. In short, it transcends the flesh.

Harry is aware of this fact of transcendence. He regards it as a breaking through the realm of time; he describes the sexual orgasm as a moment when you are "present in space but not in time" (p. 139). Time is then suspended or perhaps simply ceases to exist. The experience constitutes "one single abnegant affirmation" (p. 138). What is affirmed, of course, is life itself. But it is also, he says in the same breath, a surrender of "volition, hope, all —the darkness, the falling, the thunder of solitude, the shock, the death, the moment when, stopped physically by the ponderable clay, you yet feel all your life rush out of you into the pervading immemorial blind receptive matrix . . ." (p. 138). This is an eloquent piece of nature worship which describes the individual ego's gladly pouring itself out and losing itself in the totality of nature, dying back into that which can itself never die.

But Harry also gives a naturalistic account of the matter, one that is disconcertingly at odds with the foregoing mystical celebration of nature. He tells his newspaper friend that, as for himself, he ought to have had his first sexual experience at fourteen or fifteen. Instead, he had waited too long: "twenty-seven is too long to wait to get out of your system what you should have rid yourself of at fourteen or fifteen" (p. 137)—which seems to imply that his present commitment-to-the-death version of romantic love is a consequence of arrested development. Perhaps Harry really thought it was, or perhaps he just didn't want to speak so solemnly in the presence of his rather skeptical journalist friend.

The problem of the flesh is an especially difficult one for Harry, for though he is the chivalric lover—Charlotte is for him an absolutely unique woman and no woman could conceivably be substituted for her—he often talks as if the flesh were all. This exaltation of the flesh reaches naked intensity in the last words that we hear Harry utter (p. 324). After Charlotte has died and Harry has been sentenced to life imprisonment as her murderer, Charlotte's husband comes and offers him the cyanide that Charlotte had made him promise to convey to Harry,[12] for she has had a foreboding that the abortion she has compelled Harry to perform on her will end in her death. Charlotte, horrified to think of his being hanged or languishing for years in prison, has obviously believed that Harry would accept gratefully this opportunity to make a quick ending of his life.

Harry, though grateful to Rittenmeyer (and to Charlotte), decides not to swallow the cyanide. He wants to continue to live and for a special reason: so that he may go on remembering his nearly thirteen months of life with Charlotte. That experience must be somehow preserved; it is too precious to be allowed to disappear into mere nothingness—to be lost to the meaningless black void. "There's the waste," he says to himself, and is appalled.

Harry had told McCord once that it was Charlotte who had taught him "to be alive and know it." Presumably, in the years before he met her he had not been truly alive. Now he must hang on to that life if only in memory, and even if memory has to be the function of a living human body. With Charlotte's death the

12. See below, Notes, pp. 410–11.

potential for preserving that memory has already been halved. So *"if I become not,"* he says to himself, *"then all of remembering will cease to be.—Yes,* he thought, *between grief and nothing I will take grief"* (p. 324). This is why he has to concede that *"it is the old meat after all, no matter how old."* Yet the flesh is to be kept alive only as a means to an end, only because it supports a dream. In fact, it is just because Harry is resolutely naturalistic —he is certain that there is only the biological mechanism—that he drives the flesh so hard. It must endure the long years in prison, which will be years of grieving, because he is resolved to preserve as long as he can the memory of a dream. The chivalric lovers are indeed hard on the poor old flesh.

To say this is neither to glorify Harry nor to mock at him, only to understand him. He stakes all on transcendence, though it is a desperate and finally hopeless kind of transcendence. He cannot even promise himself to give his love such immortality as is conferred by art. His remembering her is a highly private sort of thing and just as mortal as Harry's own body. To get some perspective on his plight (or heroic stance, if one prefers to describe it so), one might compare him with the speaker in a lyric by Walter De la Mare. The speaker is remembering a beautiful lady, now dead. She was the most beautiful lady "That ever was in the West Country."

> But beauty vanishes; beauty passes;
> However rare—rare it be;
> And when I crumble, who will remember
> This lady of the West Country?

His point is much the same as Harry's: the memory of the lady is for the speaker a sacred trust. When he dies, a special beauty will have winked out and been lost forever. But of course De la Mare's poem is merely wistful, whereas Harry's statement is desperate and instinct with an almost violent personal responsibility. His desperation reflects the cultural situation in our time when the ethos of romantic love is increasingly under fire (for bad as well as for good reasons), and the pressures of naturalistic secularism have become increasingly powerful. Comparison of Harry's response to his situation with the way in which Shakespeare, John Donne, or Andrew Marvell dealt with similar situations [13] will lend emphasis to that point. Harry and Charlotte are children of our century.

In 1939 Faulkner was already far into the burden-of-consciousness problems that have come in for so much attention in the literature of recent decades. The Tall Convict has no real burden of consciousness and so by contrast calls attention to the weight of the burden under which Harry groans. This is not to say that the Convict has no consciousness. As we have seen, he is no mere animal. But he does not think too narrowly on the event. He can act—almost, it would sometimes seem, by reflex action. Harry acts spasmodically, clumsily, and sometimes is not able to act at all. Faulkner underscores the difference almost excessively when he allows the untrained Convict to make a successful delivery of the child, whereas the medically trained Harry botches the abortion he performs on Charlotte. Faulkner underscores another difference between the two men. Harry has elevated his woman into a high priestess of love, if not a goddess herself, whereas the Convict, in the last sentence of the book, dismisses the whole sex with one curt obscene word.

What have the two innocents learned? Has the Convict failed the course and Harry passed it with flying colors? Such an answer would surely be too simple. The Convict obviously gives up too easily and accepts too tamely his insulated life as a prisoner. He is the burnt child who forever after dreads the fire. But his flood-time adventure has proved that there was good stuff in him. His return to the prison for ten more years does indeed represent, to use Harry's word, a *waste*.

Harry is also the child who has been burnt by the fire, but he actually cherishes the burning. It stung him into life for the first time. He chooses to cherish and perhaps even to nurse the pain. Is this a noble martyrdom? Or is it a morbidity—and unhealthy aspect of the hyperconsciousness of our day in which we

13. For a few concrete illustrations, see below, Notes, pp. 411–13.

feel that our triumphs and our defeats have to be internalized? [14]

I suppose that most of us will say that of the two Harry takes the nobler course. Book-reading people, at least those who read books like *The Wild Palms* rather than the *Detectives' Gazette,* will at once award the palm to Harry. We value a highly developed consciousness, as we should do. We read the novel badly, however, if we assume that Faulkner asks us to choose between the young convict and the young doctor. Both men are in part victims of the societies which produced them, and of the age in which they grew up. In both cases there was a wastage. Our culture seems to offer little scope for the heroism latent in the naive young hillman, or the almost ascetic dedication to passionate love latent in the young sobersides intern. These are propositions which the Convict probably did not learn and the young physician may have learned only partially. Nevertheless, they constitute Faulkner's judgment on our time.

14. This matter has relevance generally to the bleak world view that Faulkner presents in *The Wild Palms:* pain is better than mere nothingness and better than the numbed death-in-life from which Harry believes Charlotte had rescued him.

9

Man's Fate and Man's Hope

(A FABLE)

IT IS NOT EASY to be fair to this novel. It was a work that evidently
meant a great deal to Faulkner; he put much of himself into it,
and his early hopes for it were high. He evidently believed that it
was going to be his major work, one that would successfully embody much of what he wanted to say about man and about man's
place in history. Yet from a very early period *A Fable* was adjudged
a failure—at best a noble failure. There is some evidence that
Faulkner himself eventually came to regard it so.[1] One must be
careful, however, not to justify a negative verdict by hinting at the
author's own concurrence. If the author's judgment of his success
may be wrong, his judgment of failure may be wrong too. In any
case, the critic must take responsibility for the judgment he
renders and must try to base his verdict on the quality of the work
itself.

The principal difficulties in *A Fable* derive from its being
fabulous—or, rather, from an unsuccessful mingling of fabulous
and realistic elements. One way to put this is to say that the reader
does not know how to take the story. Is it a fable through and
through? Or is it the realistic novel that at so many points it seems
to be? We could perhaps accept it if *A Fable* were either one or

1. See Blotner, p. 1506.

the other. But it is often not clear where the fabulous leaves off and the realistic begins.

Ivan Karamazov's story of the Grand Inquisitor is a kind of fable. (Ivan insists that it is, especially when his brother Alyosha fumes and frets at some of its implications.) Let's imagine, Ivan asks his brother, that Christ did appear again on earth: how would He fare? How would His own Church—at least the Church that claims to be His—receive Him? In Ivan's fable, Christ is the divine Son of God, the Christ of the Gospels and of the Church's teaching. He is not demythologized, not reduced to a simple, kindly, Spanish peasant of the sixteenth century. The miracle that He performs is thus accounted for, and so also the Grand Inquisitor's dramatic reaction when he confronts Him and recognizes at once Whom he faces and Whom he now has in his power.

The reader knows precisely what kind of assent to give this story, and the fable makes its point powerfully. In fact, it carries full conviction even to the agnostic or atheistic reader. For if such a reader accepts the divinity of Dostoevski's Christ only provisionally, only for the sake of the story to be told, nevertheless he can accept fully the indictment made of the ecclesiastical institutions condemned by the returned Christ. Yes, he probably says to himself; if Christ really did exist and did return to earth, such would be the kind of reception that He might receive at the hands of the very institution that claims to worship Him as the Son of God.

Now Faulkner knew and admired *The Brothers Karamazov,* and I think that there is no doubt that the meeting between the Corporal and the Old Marshal in *A Fable* was heavily influenced by the story of the meeting of the returned Christ and the Grand Inquisitor. Faulkner, however, has carefully demythologized his "Christ." He is to be taken literally as a young man, simple, uneducated (he cannot even read), pure-hearted, courageous, and filled with a profound faith in the ability of men to act with love and kindness toward their fellows and even to die for their sakes. Though this young man, who has become a corporal in the French Army during World War I, is presented as Christ-like, he claims no special relation to God, and actually never mentions God. His career simply presents a series of parallels with the life of Jesus Christ.

So far so good. Nearly all our great fiction has to do with characters presented as actual human beings. That such a man as the Corporal might attempt to stop a murderous conflict which he considered senseless is thoroughly conceivable. That, and many actions like it, have been undertaken throughout human history. If some men recognize the Corporal's life as exhibiting the Christian virtues, again well and good. History will yield other examples of such human beings.

Faulkner, however, has not left it up to the reader to discover for himself the Corporal's Christ-like qualities. There is an almost tedious insistence on parallels with the life of Christ, items that are not at all necessary to the Corporal's story nor inherent in his particular situation. Thus, the Corporal is made to gather around himself disciples, not to the number of seven or nine or fourteen, but precisely twelve. Two women closely associated with him have names that are the French equivalents of Mary and Martha. The Corporal has his Judas, who will later in the novel fling on the floor exactly thirty coins. The Corporal is condemned to die and is executed between two thieves. After being buried, his body strangely disappears from the grave in which it was laid and, by a wildly improbable coincidence, suffers a "resurrection" of sorts. Finally, it is buried in the tomb designed to hold the corpse of the Unknown Soldier.

Why the rather forced insistence on parallels between the Corporal and Christ? Clearly, they have been introduced to make a point, and the point would seem to be that Christ was just a man after all, and that he did not need the supernatural claims made for him to become a beacon light to man. This would account for the author's demythologizing the Christ-like Corporal while at the same time dressing him in unmistakable Gospel trappings. To this matter I shall recur on a later page.

The question I would raise at the moment, however, has to do, not with theology, but with aesthetics. Some of the events that we are to take literally are as hard to believe—because quite as fabulous—as the fantastic events we would expect to find in something that was frankly identified as a fable. Therefore, why the scrupulous demythologizing, presumably done for the benefit of the wayfaring twentieth-century reader, if that reader is expected to believe in such marvelous coincidences as the Corporal's dead body found wearing a crown of thorns (actually barbed wire) just after he was executed? The author suggests that the stake to which the Corporal was bound "may have been flawed or even rotten because . . . the corporal's body, post bonds and all, went over backward as one intact unit, onto the edge of the rubbish-filled trench behind it" and "the plunge of the post had jammed it and its burden too into a tangled mass of old barbed wire, a strand of which had looped up and around the top of the post and the man's head . . ." (p. 385). How many times would you have to try that feat with a dummy tied to a post to execute this particular chain of events which would end up with the dummy's wearing its crown of barbed-wire thorns?

Even what would seem to be the most realistic and down-to-earth episode in the novel, the story of the racehorse that broke a leg and yet won race after race in the back country, makes impossible demands on our credulity. Dogs can run—at least for a while—on three legs, but a horse cannot: I have the word of the chief veterinarian at one of our big Eastern tracks that it is impossible for a horse with only three good legs to run, let alone to win a race. He says that he has heard once or twice of farm horses that had broken a leg and yet were able, after the leg had healed, to hobble around a little. But such horses could not run.

So I must regard the story of the unbeatable racehorse as another one of Faulkner's Tall Tales, a genre of which he was a past master. In certain contexts, such a story would be thoroughly appropriate, and as V. K. Ratliff would tell it, it might be wonderfully compelling. But what is this account of a string of equine miracles doing here? It's either a kind of improbable yarn, told and to be accepted in that spirit, or else, if told with straight face and serious intent, a miraculous happening that obscures and confuses the general process of demythologization. The anomaly is calculated to promote a certain queasiness in the serious reader.

The problem, however, is not that *A Fable* contains so many improbable happenings and highly unlikely coincidences. If the tone of the novel were really that of a fairy tale or a piece of science fiction, or a rousing Tall Tale out of the Old Southwest, we might accept even impossible happenings with a willing suspension of disbelief. The events that dominate *A Fable* are, however, far too serious and momentous to be treated either as playful fantasies or as lusty, full-blooded tales of the sort that grow out of the folk imagination. The tradition from which the episodes of *A Fable* derive is just as ancient and as deeply rooted in the folk mind, but it makes a different appeal and satisfies a very different need.

The unlikely and sometimes incredible events recounted in *A Fable* are presented with such circumstantiality and in such realistic detail that the problem of the reader's belief is compounded. Are we reading a kind of modernized miracle play? Or some kind of religious allegory? In any case, it soon becomes plain to the reader that he is being asked to believe in these improbable happenings for the sake of a point the author wants to make. Incidents in which the reader cannot believe literally are to be justified because they are psychologically or morally significant. Thus, the victories of the three-legged horse serve to indicate what a will to win can accomplish, and the extraordinary events that remove the Corporal's body from its original grave to its final resting place in the honored tomb of the Unknown Soldier provide symbolic vindication of the Corporal's cause: truth crushed to earth will rise again, and has risen to its proper place of honor. (Of course the French populace is completely unaware of the Corporal's body having arrived at a place of honor. Only the reader *of A Fable* is let in on the secret.)

Authentic novels, however, are not built out of naked ideas. Even allegorical building blocks are too flimsy to be of use in most fiction. The normal procedure is for the novelist to tell a story that involves certain characters who act in given situations. If the author is sufficiently an artist, his narrative will quietly come to embody the meaning that he wishes to present, and the competent reader will find the meaning himself as the tale unfolds.[2]

2. This is not to say that some excellent writers of fiction have not worked effectively with thinly disguised ideas or built up allegorical structures. One thinks

The method of *A Fable* seems to go quite contrary to the procedure I have just described. The characters and events are too obviously summoned forth at the behest of an idea, and the basic drama of the novel is to be found in an almost naked contest of ideas.

One is tempted to say that *A Fable* was flawed at its very inception. Faulkner generously acknowledged that he owed "the basic idea" for the novel to two Hollywood friends who were working for Warner Brothers at the time.[3] Great novels incorporate ideas, but the testimony of many writers would suggest that the germ of authentic novels and poems is not an idea, whether borrowed or not, but an obsessive image, a scene that haunts the author's mind, a concrete incident lodged deep in his unconscious, which demands its fulfillment in a process that entails the writer's exploration of its meaning. The "idea" does not determine the narrative exposition; rather, the narrative, when fully articulated, yields the idea.

Such was the genesis of some of Faulkner's greatest novels. For example, he has told us more than once that *The Sound and the Fury* began as an image of a little girl's muddy drawers as seen by the other children as she climbed a tree. Though the muddy drawers would seem to be an obvious symbol of defilement of some kind, the idea in this germinating image proved to be very dense and compact. Faulkner's own testimony is that though it was for him mysteriously compulsive, he did not know what the obsessive image meant, and consequently was compelled to write *The Sound and the Fury* in order to find for himself the total meaning. The image, in short, did not predict its significance even to the author.

Different works of art may, of course, begin in very different ways. One must not lay the failure of *A Fable* to the fact that

---

of Kafka, for example. But they tend to make frank use of fantasy or fable or legend, and are skillful in setting the tone that is appropriate to fantasy or fable. Faulkner's great triumphs are in another mode.

3. Perhaps "the basic idea" had to do with what would happen if Jesus Christ returned to the modern world, but in a letter of 4 February 1954 to Saxe Commins, Faulkner says, "[William] Bacher and [Henry] Hathaway approached me in Cal. with the idea of a moving picture script based on this idea—that is, who the unknown soldier might be" (*Selected Letters of William Faulkner*, ed. Joseph Blotner, New York, 1977, p. 361).

Faulkner first borrowed the idea from friends. In any case, if *A Fable* is deemed to fail, one has to make good the judgment of failure by an appeal to the work itself. Unless the failure can be demonstrated to exist there, speculations about why the author allegedly failed are finally idle and irrelevant.

The main plot of the novel is easily told. During World War I, after the long stalemate of the trenches has brought about a virtual deadlock of the warring powers, a mysterious corporal serving in the French Army comes to the notice of the authorities. The Corporal and his followers have been bringing to their fellow soldiers a message of hope and peace. If the men fighting on both sides would simply refuse to kill each other anymore, the war would necessarily end. The Corporal and his disciples are able to win to their way of thinking not only soldiers on the Allied side but soldiers on the other side as well.

The Corporal, however, has his Judas, who betrays him to the high command. The generals on both sides conspire to stop the peace campaign and to keep the war going. Throughout the novel the high command is thoroughly diabolical. For example, they arrange for a contingent of the French Army under the command of a General Gragnon to make an attack which is designed, for their own sinister purposes, to fail.

The Corporal's challenge to the military machine is doomed to fail too. After having been betrayed to the high command, he is arrested and taken before the Old Marshal, the generalissimo of all the Allied armies. Though the Marshal is aware that the Corporal is his own son, he shows no fatherly softness nor does he appeal to a son's filial respect. Instead, he tries to persuade the Corporal to abandon the cause of peace. He offers him magnificent rewards if he will do so and threatens him with death if he declines. When the Corporal remains resolute, he is executed by a firing squad, and his body is turned over to his sister for burial. The war goes on; the Allies win; and the Corporal's sacrifice has apparently come to nothing.

The Corporal is not the only idealist to be found in the novel; idealism abounds in such people, some of whom figure in the elaborate subplots. There is the young British airman, Levine, who is

willing to die for what he regards as a sacred cause and who believes in military glory and honor. When he discovers that his own
command had arranged to have a German general's plane arrive
scatheless behind the Allied lines, he commits suicide in disillusionment. There is the old black preacher who heads his own
movement for universal brotherhood. He "bears witness," not for
God, since he declares that God needs no witness, but for Man,
who does. His testimony is that Man, in spite of appearances to
the contrary, is capable of goodness. The old preacher is an ally of
the Corporal and dies with others to vindicate the Corporal's
cause.

There is a British battalion runner who takes measures to be
demoted from his rank as an officer and, having become a private,
joins actively in support of the French Corporal's mission. Even
one officer of the highest rank, the Quartermaster General, a close
friend of the Old Marshal, is stirred by the Corporal's action and
tries to aid him. The Quartermaster General had for a long time
idolized the Old Marshal, confident that he beheld in him the
future savior of France. Though shocked by some of his friend's
actions, the Quartermaster General continues to trust in him, until
he discovers that the Old Marshal means to execute the Corporal.
He confronts the Marshal, but proves to be no match for the
Marshal's logic. Furthermore, he lacks the courage to break with
him. Thus, though he has resolved to throw up his commission and
cut all his ties with the Army, in the end he does not. It is left for
the Corporal to stand up to his father's logic, to refuse all the
temptations offered, and finally to die almost cheerfully for his
cause.

From the beginning, in spite of its subplots and digressions, the
novel steadily gravitates toward the scene in which the Old
Marshal and the Corporal, father and son, come face to face. This
is the crucial scene of the novel, the scene in which the theme of
the novel comes to a head.

In view of the importance of the confrontation of these major
characters, it is a pity that we have by this time learned so little
about the Corporal. We have had some glimpses of him in the
company of his disciples. He seems to be a sincere, confident,

honest man, who exhibits no self-consciousness, no posing, no flaunting of a prophetic charisma. All of this is to his credit, and we have already observed that, given his purposes, Faulkner wants to play down anything like supernatural virtues. Yet, if the Corporal is to constitute a real threat to the whole military establishment, the reader must be convinced that he is truly formidable. He must be seen to possess the power to stir men's minds and emotions. We are told that he does, that his fellow soldiers believe in him. But though we are asked to accept the fact that others believe, the reader himself probably does not believe. He has to take this power on hearsay, for there is no scene in which we hear him talking to others about peace or about how to stop the war.

The Corporal and his disciples have actually crossed over to the other side of no-man's-land. They have spent some time with the German soldiers and have evidently won their minds and hearts. Granted the multiple lines of trenches, the barbed wire, watchful German officers, the fact that neither their leader nor any of the rest of them speak German, the exploit is most remarkable. One must suppose that the Corporal's very presence conveys something awesome. Yet this too, the reader must take on faith, and in this instance the requisite faith is hard to come by. Faulkner has devoted a good deal of space to explaining how much effort was required (with full cooperation of the high commands on both sides) to fly one German general over to the Allied side. It is difficult, therefore, to see how the Corporal, with apparently no outside help at all, has got himself and his twelve associates over to the German side and safely back again.

The contrast between the influence claimed for this illiterate corporal and his rather ordinary words and deeds as actually dramatized for us puts a strain on the reader's faith. True, in his interview with the Marshal, the Corporal does comport himself well. He refuses the various temptations in simple, manly fashion; his steadfast composure and quiet questions and answers are impressive. Yet even in this scene we learn less about the Corporal than we need to know. He says so little; he is so self-composed, so laconic in his questions and replies that we hardly know what is going on in his mind. What is his faith? He believes in Man. That is quite clear, but beyond that, very little is clear. His world view and his faith really have to be deduced by negatives—by his refusal of the various things that the Marshal proposes.

By contrast, the world view and the ultimate faith of the Old Marshal are set forth in great detail, but his rhetoric and the abundant detail with which he makes his points raise troublesome questions. If the Corporal says too little, the Old Marshal says too much. Moreover, what he says at one moment cannot always be squared with what he says at another. Questions are raised in the reader's mind. Are the contradictions real or only apparent? Do the complexities of his argument spring from a wise comprehensive view of man and reality, or from a confused mentality?

In order to answer such questions, we shall have to examine not merely the Marshal's rhetoric, but the actions that he has taken and the further actions that he proposes to take if the Corporal refuses to desist from his campaign for peace—or as the Marshal will have to regard it, his campaign of subversion leading to the troops' refusal to obey orders. It is difficult to understand some of the things that the Marshal does, or to see the logic of some of the things that he proposes to do. Why does he find it necessary to call in a representative of the German high command to a conference with the Allied high command to consult about how to deal with the Corporal's peace effort?

A good deal of space is devoted to the way in which this conference was managed. A German general is to fly over the lines at a predetermined point and at a particular hour, and land at a British air base. To get him across safely, blank anti-aircraft shells have to be supplied to certain batteries and blank machine gun ammunition to British fighter squadrons patrolling the sector in question. The German plane lands safely, and the German general, who is all ruthless efficiency, at once shoots his pilot: that mouth is shut permanently. But we learn that at least one British soldier notices the delivery of the blank anti-aircraft shells, and that the fighter pilot Levine, having seen his tracer bullets hitting full on target on the German plane, gets suspicious, makes a careful check later, and comes to realize what has happened. His consequent suicide is fortunate for the generals; another man having made the discovery might have talked. The plot forces the high command to take risks like this. It takes even larger risks at the conference itself, where, in addition to the Old Marshal and the heel-clicking German general, there are representatives from the British and American armies. The Marshal's confidence in their silence is remarkable considering the magnitude of the scandal that disclosure surely would have caused.[4]

We don't learn what the generals said to each other about ending the menace of the Corporal's peace effort, and we wonder why any German cooperation was ever considered necessary. For if the Old Marshal meant all along to offer the Corporal certain rewards for desisting from his peace efforts, he didn't need German permission or aid for that. If, on the other hand, he was pretty sure all along that he would have to have the Corporal executed, he didn't need any German help for that either. What the Marshal finally did (ordering the execution of the Corporal) apparently proved effective. The war went on unhindered by threats of peace and ended just about as the Marshal intended for it to end. (See pp. 433–37.)

The only actual contribution made by the Germans to suppressing the peace movement was their part in the barrage which destroyed almost all of the British contingent that tried to walk unarmed across no-man's-land to join in friendly handclasps with the German soldiers in the opposite trenches. Yet even here German artillery fire was scarcely needed. One side, if it means business, can be pretty efficient about killing its own men. Moreover, the Allied command might with a good deal of confidence have left it up to the Germans (whom the Old Marshal praises as the finest soldiers in the world, p. 344) to manage to wipe out their own peace-minded soldiers. And if they didn't? If the German

4. In Faulkner's *Letters* (p. 247) we read: ". . . the villain [in *A Fable*] is historically the French army or all the allied armies of 1918, and the principal ones are (still historically though to me fabulous and imaginary) Foch, Haig, Pershing, et al." This passage explains something of Faulkner's ire and why "fabulously" at least he would put nothing past them. (Compare the last sentence of Faulkner's story "Turnabout" quoted on p. 392, below.) But if this letter of 1947 gives some hint of Faulkner's personal attitude toward high commands in general, it scarcely solves the problem of the novel, for however wicked we may believe the Old Marshal (along with his compeers) to be, the novel goes to pieces if we are forced to think of him as a foolish man who takes unnecessary risks.

command did allow its own troops to throw down their arms instead of killing them off as the Allies promptly killed off their own mutineers, the German command's forbearance would have allowed the Allied armies to push through the collapsed German lines into the heart of Germany—entirely to the Old Marshal's satisfaction. On reflection, it seems rather odd that the Old Marshal was ever concerned to warn the Germans about peace mutinies.

There is another and perhaps still more difficult problem. Why does the Marshal need to offer the lordship of the earth to the Corporal? In view of the ease with which the Marshal says that most men can be deceived, why offer this pleasant and innocent and very simple young man power over the whole earth? If the Corporal can be made a world emperor, would not almost any stand-in—any decently personable young man, furnished with the proper speech writers and public relations men—be made to serve adequately? Thus, unless the author can really convince us that the Corporal does have a unique power over men and a peculiar ability to speak to their hearts, we are bound to wonder why the Corporal was in the least necessary for the Old Marshal's plan, and why the Marshal did not, on the Corporal's refusal, proceed at once to try it with someone else taking the Corporal's place.

If the Marshal was aware that he did not need the Corporal, what then? Was he simply testing the resolution of his son? More hateful still, was he simply playing a game, cynically amusing himself? If the colloquy between the two men is to generate dramatic power, we need to believe that real issues are at stake, that the Corporal does pose a powerful threat to the values to which the Marshal is committed, values in which he profoundly believes quite apart from any narrow self-interest. We have to believe also that the Marshal at the end sees no possible way to protect those sovereign values except by decreeing the Corporal's death. If circumstances force him to choose between two goods—or two evils— and if the difficulty in choosing is heightened by the knowledge that the Corporal is his own son—then the Marshal might well exemplify what Faulkner regarded as the great theme: the human heart in conflict with itself.

But the Marshal exhibits no agony of choice; he remains remarkably cool and detached. The reader has the uneasy feeling that the detachment springs less from the Marshal's Spartan control over his feelings than from Faulkner's failure to dramatize the issues presented. What evidence is there of a father's concern for his son? If the Marshal had been racked by the thought of killing his son, might he not have looked for possible alternatives? If, instead of having his son shot, he had put him in prison for the duration of the war, would the Allied cause have suffered thereby? The quiet disappearance of the Corporal would have blighted his peace mission as effectively as his disappearance by death actually did. We hear some talk about the propaganda effect of martyrdom, and the Old Marshal himself hints of its power (p. 349). But news of the martyrdom of the Corporal, if it ever got to the troops, apparently did nothing to provoke further mutinies. One searches vainly to find what overwhelming consideration compelled the Old Marshal to destroy his son. In sum, since the reader has no reason to believe that the Marshal was torn apart by an agonizing decision, the big, crucial scene lacks poignance and drama.

I have earlier commented on some of the difficulties in understanding the Old Marshal's mind and character. It would appear that Faulkner thinks of him as a perverted idealist, a man resembling the brilliant Mr. Kurtz in Joseph Conrad's "The Heart of Darkness." The career of either man would illustrate the notion that the very worst represents a corruption of what was potentially the best. The Old Marshal obviously began his career as one of the very brightest and best. As a young man he refused to take advantage of his powerful family and social connections and of his brilliant record as a student. He spurned the obvious means to promotion, insisted on being assigned to the most difficult and least desirable posts, later abandoned his military career altogether and withdrew for thirteen years into a Tibetan lamasery. Worldly success was not important compared to the attainment of truth and the purification of his soul.

In the upshot, however, neither Kurtz nor the Marshal believes that man possesses a soul. Kurtz had gone to Africa to bring light to the Dark Continent. Marlow, who relates Kurtz's story, happens on one of Kurtz's early pronouncements on his African mission. It is a high-minded and eloquent statement of what can be done for the African peoples. But Marlow notices that Kurtz had later added a postscript. It consists of a brief statement in the imperative: "Exterminate all the brutes."

In his colloquy with the Corporal, the Old Marshal would appear to speak of mankind in very different terms. Man will not only endure—he will prevail. But this prophecy amounts to something quite different when read in its full context. What the Marshal seems to be saying is that it is really impossible to exterminate the brutes, desirable though that might be. Like some primitive form of life, human beings have turned out to be virtually unkillable. Their stubborn tenacity can even evoke from the cynical old soldier something like grudging admiration.

I find in the Old Marshal, however, more of Dostoevski's Grand Inquisitor than I do of Conrad's Kurtz. The Inquisitor is also a perverted idealist. What remains of his religion is an aggressive fanaticism combined with a genuine and abiding pity and sympathy for the generality of human beings. He has to be cruel to certain individuals in order to be kind to the masses. He will sentence Christ to the stake, not out of hatred but to avoid the future disappointments and suffering of men in general. Likewise, the Old Marshal will send the Corporal to the firing squad for the general good of the human estate. (The Inquisitor does eventually relent: Christ is simply told to go away. The Old Marshal is made of harder metal. His death sentence is allowed to stand.)

What is common to Kurtz, the Inquisitor, and the Old Marshal is their pessimism with regard to man's ability to take care of his own interests and to learn to live decently if not virtuously. The Inquisitor says that Christ had asked too much of mankind. How could men really hope to follow His example? It was cruel of Him to expect them to do so. It was cruel of Him also to force on mankind the perilous gift of free choice. Men are not free, and they are not capable of freedom. They need an established order that will take into account their weakness, one that will treat them like the children that they are and, through a system of rewards and punishments, keep them in some sort of order, flatter their delusions that there is an afterlife for them, and in general help them get

243

through the difficulties of this world with as little pain and anxiety as possible.

The Inquisitor concedes that it was all very well for Christ in the Wilderness to reject the Devil's temptations, but, with reference to ordinary human beings, the Devil, in the Wilderness encounter, was completely right. Men need someone who can turn stones into bread, or at least makes them believe that he has that ability. Moreover, what a man really wants is "someone to worship, someone to keep his conscience, as some means of uniting all [men] into one unanimous and harmonious ant heap, because the craving for universal unity is the third and last anguish of men."

What the Grand Inquisitor says to the returned Christ markedly resembles what the Old Marshal tells the Corporal: that men are not free, and need to be controlled for their own good, since they would otherwise fall into riotous confusion. If the Corporal would only be willing to let the Marshal proclaim him as his son and would accept his help in gaining control of the world—something easily attainable—he would be able to do much for mankind, for the Corporal would be God, "holding [man] forever through a far, far stronger ingredient than his simple lusts and appetites: [holding man] by his triumphant and ineradicable folly, his deathless passion for being led, mystified, and deceived" (p. 349).

Like the Inquisitor, the Marshal is speaking in the interest of an institution. Like the Church, the Army is necessary: without it, mankind would fall into chaos. Like the Church, the military establishment is international. On page 316, the Runner says "that the biped successful enough to become a general had ceased to be a German or British or American or Italian or French one almost as soon as it never was a human one. . . ." The Marshal does not say this himself, but this is the principle upon which he acts, for obviously the plan to fly the German general across the Allied lines for a conference of the generals of both sides assumes an interest that transcends any single national concern. The Marshal's argument owes a great deal to the Grand Inquisitor, but it lacks the Inquisitor's coherence and internal logic. The Inquisitor, for example, says nothing about mankind's enduring and prevailing.

One more source of Faulkner's temptation scene—perhaps a

surprising one—ought to be mentioned. It is to be found in James Branch Cabell's *Jurgen*.[5] The "brown man" has just told Jurgen that Jurgen is worthless, a being of absolutely no consequence. Jurgen, though terrified, replies as follows:

> "None the less, I think there is something in me which will endure. I am fettered by cowardice, I am enfeebled by disastrous memories; and I am maimed by old follies. Still, I seem to detect in myself something which is permanent and rather fine. Underneath everything, and in spite of everything, I really do seem to detect that something. What rôle that something is to enact after the death of my body, and upon what stage, I cannot guess. When fortune knocks I shall open the door. Meanwhile I tell you candidly, you brown man, there is something in Jurgen far too admirable for any intelligent arbiter ever to fling into the dustheap. I am, if nothing else, a monstrous clever fellow: and I think I shall endure, somehow. Yes, cap in hand goes through the land, as the saying is: and I believe I can contrive some trick to cheat oblivion when the need arises," says Jurgen, trembling, and gulping, and with his eyes shut tight, but even so, with his mind quite made up about it. "Of course you may be right; and certainly I cannot go so far as to say you are wrong; but still at the same time—" [pp. 139–40]

I concede that *Jurgen* is an unlikely place in which to find the core of Faulkner's faith in Man's endurance, a trait that he couples with Man's immortality. But here it is, and for good measure we have in the brown man's reply a hint of the Old Marshal's admiration and perhaps partial agreement, for the brown man says: "Now but before a fool's opinion of himself, the Gods are powerless. Oh, yes, and envious, too." The brown man, whatever else he may represent,[6] is, like the Old Marshal, a realist. Jurgen, in rejecting

5. New York: Robert McBridge & Co., 1919. (All subsequent printings have the same pagination.)
6. The brown man tells Jurgen: "I am everything that was and that is to be," i.e., reality itself. The Old Marshal proclaims that he is "champion of this mundane

the truth of what the brown man has shown him, calls it "the degraded lunacy of a so-called Realist." It is something that Jurgen "choose[s] not to believe." It is what the Corporal refuses to believe, and the Corporal's faith as he states it seems to be based on nothing more substantial than Jurgen's. Apparently, like Jurgen, the Corporal simply knows in his bones that he will endure.

Since I have frankly expressed my misgivings about the literary effectiveness of the encounter between the Corporal and the Old Marshal, it is only fair that I should say that Faulkner has added a second temptation scene, which I think is very effective. Since the Marshal does not give up easily, he has sent a priest to the Corporal's cell, ostensibly to give him his last Communion before he faces the firing squad the next morning. The priest's real purpose, of course, is to try once more to persuade the Corporal to give up his mission. The power of the state has failed; now the attempt will be made by a representative of organized religion.

The priest proves to be a good advocate for his cause. He makes an eloquent plea for the Erastian church, the church whose function is to keep order, to supplement the police force, and to serve as the other arm of the state. After all, the priest argues, the Church was not really founded by Christ or even by Peter, the rock on whom Christ claimed to have founded it. It was founded by Paul. Paul was a Roman citizen and, being partly Roman, was only "one-third dreamer." Paul knew how to organize, and he knew that organization was necessary if the Church were to be available and useful to men. The Corporal ought to render, then, to the State what properly belongs to the State. Christ himself said that Caesar was to be rendered his due, and the Church owes much to Caesar. Without his help the Church would not exist.

Yet, skillful though he is, the priest gets nowhere with his arguments. The simple and honest young man turns them all aside. He does more: he converts the evil counselor. The priest suddenly drops to the Corporal's feet and says: "Save me too." The Corporal replies: "Get up, Father," but the priest, still on his knees, fumbles for his missal and begs the Corporal to read "The office for

---

earth," whereas he regards the Corporal as the "champion of an esoteric realm of man's baseless hopes and his infinite capacity . . . for unfact" (p. 348).

the dying." As we shall realize in a moment, he is asking the Corporal to act as priest and read the office for him, since he has resolved to kill himself. (It is a nice touch: the representative of official religion bowing to a higher and truer priesthood.) But he has forgotten that the Corporal cannot even read.

In a few moments the priest goes out, borrows a bayonet, and impales himself on it. In hopelessness? In complete despair at his betrayal of true religion? Perhaps, but not necessarily, for his last words seem to indicate that he believes that what he is doing is done in imitation of Christ's own crucifixion. Thus he insists to himself that the blade must pierce his *right* side, though "I'm right-handed." And he tells himself as the bayonet enters his side: *"But He was not standing either. He was nailed there and He will forgive me."*

Whether the priest dies in hope or dies in despair, his rejection of the mission on which the Old Marshal had sent him is absolute. Can his act be regarded as a representation of Judas's suicide? Just possibly it can. If so, he is a far more effective Judas figure than the actual betrayer of the Corporal, who later on will throw precisely thirty—count them—coins down on the floor of the Corporal's sister's kitchen.

Most of this chapter has gone to a discussion of the Corporal and the Old Marshal, and their views of Man and his possibilities. In devoting so much attention to this episode, I have left out of consideration many other things, some of them really rather fine. I am thinking, for instance, of the adventures of the detachment of soldiers sent to bring back an unidentifiable corpse from Verdun to be placed in the tomb of the Unknown Soldier. These feckless clowns, interested only in drink and women, are thoroughly out of keeping with the patriotic idealism of their mission. They are not impressed with the idea of placing in a tomb of honor a French soldier whose name is known only to God. Any old corpse will do, is their attitude—which literally, of course, fits the terms of their mission; but whereas the intention of the French nation is to exalt even the humblest *poilu* who had died for France, reverence and tender regard are emotions furthest from their minds.

A moment's realistic reflection will make one agree that such would be the attitude of almost any set of body snatchers. *We* know whose body they have finally secured after selling off the first one. But we are reminded that the Unknown Soldier might very well have been a soldier exactly like any one of them, and that the idealization of the common man that we find in the notion of a tomb for an Unknown Soldier makes assumptions that are unrealistic. In erecting a tomb to the Unknown Soldier, is the state indulging in what amounts to fraud? Carrying out a publicity stunt? Advertising that all its soldiers died bravely *pro patria?* Really hoping to honor its heroic dead, no matter what the rank or condition? In short, in this little episode, a valid symbolism emerges, one pertinent to the complicated issues presented in *A Fable.* A "meaning" is not imposed on the episode. The event, which is plausible and credible, generates its meaning: the Marshal and his compeers naturally are buried in illustrious tombs. But since the state can't afford such for everybody, it provides in effect such a tomb as a lottery prize for the rest. A lottery ticket is secured by getting killed and in the process losing your name tag.

Another brilliant scene is that in which General Gragnon is shot by a detail of three American soldiers. The detail is composed of an Iowa farm boy, a black man from Mississippi, and a Brooklyn-born future gangster and bootlegger. The high command has decided, for its own purposes, that Gragnon must be shot, and that the wound received should indicate that he died leading his men in an attack on the German lines. This means that he has to be shot with a German pistol and from the front. The need for these precise details is not made entirely clear. Is it at all likely that French newspaper reporters will demand to see the body and have it examined by a small-arms expert? One would expect that the high command could easily have got its fabricated version of Gragnon's death accepted by the public. Who could have suspected what actually happened? Indeed, the most implausible part of the fabricated story is that a major general had been killed while leading his troops to the attack. That just wasn't done in World War I. Besides, death by a machine gun or rifle bullet would be a thousand times more likely than a wound inflicted by a German officer's sidearm.

Never mind. Granted these highly unlikely circumstances, the episode does give Faulkner an opportunity for some of his most compelling writing. There is the implacable French general, utterly unafraid and determined to foil the attempt to shoot him from the front. He knows that he is being executed by his own side, and he wants to make certain, by a last minute twist of his body, that the bullet shall enter the back of his head.

Consider the three Americans. The farm boy, when he realizes what he had volunteered to do, refuses to help. There is the rather fastidious black man who plans to be an undertaker and finds himself with his first case on his hands. There is the wisecracking gangster, hard as nails, seeing the whole enterprise as simply another job to be done. None of the three speaks French. They represent America in its diversity, in its lack of homogeneity, in its innocence and in its corruption.

The setting is a "cubicle fierce with whitewash and containing [a] single unshaded electric light and a three legged stool." Here again, the symbolism is not forced on from the outside but rises as an exhalation from the scene itself. Corruption and betrayal: the high command chooses, perhaps inadvertently, a proper executioner, an American gangster-to-be, an executioner as professional and impersonal and corrupt as the high command itself is. Deviousness and secrecy: the German pistol is handed to the gangster just before the party makes its way to the soundproof cell. Inhuman detachment: death at the hands of a stranger, a man who has never seen his victim before, acting not out of a passion, but for reward: a three-day pass to Paris.

Gragnon himself contributes his own ingredient of sardonic meaning to the incident. He is the complete military officer. He lives by discipline and courage. He is also ruthless; he had wanted to have his whole division shot for refusing to leave their trenches and attack. Even the Old Marshal saw that this would not do, that Gragnon is intolerably stiff and inflexible. But his discipline and his courage are genuine. When his assassins enter his cell, he is every inch the general, even though he is wearing "the plain G.I. tunic and trousers which a cavalry sergeant would have worn." In spite of their efforts to hold him in position for a shot from the front, he manages to have his own way after all.

The Gragnon execution furnishes one further element of significance: the nature of World War I as Faulkner conceived it. There is the sense of unreality, there is the artificial relation of the high command to the soldiers who do the actual fighting. There is even a glance at the *abstract* character of the American involvement in the war. All of these come into focus in this account of Gragnon's death. The episode constitutes a model of the right way for a novelist to make his symbolic points.

By contrast, the last scene of the novel is not the right way. The scene is not without a certain poignance, but it carries an air of contrivance in such items as the Old Marshal's pompous funeral cortege, the perpetual flame burning over the burial place of the Unknown Soldier, the Quartermaster General's face suffused with tears, and the maimed Runner's act of hurling the Medaille Militaire at the dead Marshal's coffin. In that scene there is a coming together of almost naked ideas rather than of any action of dramatic characters. The English Runner has been almost reduced to an idea, for he is described as a "mobile and upright scar." He is only half a man, possessing "one arm and one leg." One "entire side of his hatless head [is] one hairless eyeless and earless scar." As the novel closes, even that scar of a man has just been beaten up by the crowd because of his gesture of contempt for the dead Marshal. Yet he is indomitable, and apparently—fabulously?—unkillable. Through his bloody mouth and shattered teeth, he is still able to shout defiance: "Tremble. I'm not going to die. Never." Men die. Ideas do not, and what speaks here is an idea, an idea very thinly clothed in human flesh and blood.

10

Faulkner on Time and History

MUCH HAS BEEN WRITTEN about Faulkner's sense of place—and properly so. His very creation of Yoknapatawpha County underscores the importance he attached to place. A writer had to write about what he knew, and if his "own little postage stamp of native soil" was what he truly knew, he must write about that. The area did not need to be large or famous; even in its obscurity and ordinary character it could serve his purposes as a writer, for, as Faulkner insisted in his various interviews, in all lands and throughout all epochs men are essentially the same. You could find even in Yoknapatawpha County a sufficiently full representation of the human predicament, examples of man's virtue and of his baseness. So much, for my present purposes, for Faulkner's abiding concern with place.[1]

Something more needs to be said, however, about Faulkner's concept of time. Though various writers have had perceptive remarks to make on this subject, much of what has been written seems to me misleading or confused. Moreover, what Faulkner, on one occasion or another, is quoted as having said about time needs to be put into its proper context. In particular, his acknowledgment of his debt to Henri Bergson stands in need of clarification.

1. I touch upon the subject again in Appendix C, where I discuss the resemblances between Faulkner and W. B. Yeats.

In an interview with Loïc Bouvard, Faulkner apparently did say:

> There isn't any time. In fact I agree pretty much with Bergson's theory of the fluidity of time. There is only the present moment, in which I include both the past and the future, and that is eternity. In my opinion time can be shaped quite a bit by the artist; after all, man is never time's slave.[2]

As stated, however, this is a rhetorical, not to say poetic, utterance. That it is poetic in character does not, of course, mean that it is necessarily false, but the assertion as given may need to be translated and expanded. In any case, the passage quoted comprehends at least three propositions, which in this compact statement are not so much related to each other as simply pressed together.

Before beginning our examination, it might be best to compare with the statement to Bouvard another that Faulkner made some ten years later. (This later one, by the way, occurs in the very paragraph in which Faulkner spoke of his "little postage stamp of native soil.") Speaking of the characters who are made to inhabit his mythical county, Faulkner says:

> [the fact] that I have moved [them] around in time successfully . . . proves to me my own theory that time is a fluid condition which has no existence except in the momentary avatars of individual people. There is no such thing as *was*—only *is*.[3]

In both statements what is stressed is the fluidity of time, though only in the first does Faulkner link his theory of time with Bergson's. What Bergson meant was that time as experienced by human beings is continuous—a flowing stream, carrying in it memories of past experience and foreshadowings of prospective actions. What Faulkner seems to have meant by time's fluidity was that it has "no existence" except as it is experienced in the consciousness of

2. *Lion in the Garden,* ed. Meriwether and Millgate, p. 70.
3. Ibid., p. 255.

individual human beings. In writing, "There is no such thing as *was*—only *is*," Faulkner jumps ahead to another point: we experience the pastness of the past and experience an impending future only in a *present* moment of consciousness. So what is past (Faulkner's "was") exists only in a *present state* of human consciousness. So also with Faulkner's "shall be": it too exists only in a moment of present consciousness. (Compare the earlier statement: "There isn't any time.")

A passage in *The Wild Palms* (p. 137) puts Faulkner's conception of time more clearly than he was able to state it in the interviews from which we have quoted. Faulkner has Harry Wilbourne speak "of the current of time that runs through remembering, that exists only in relation to what little of reality . . . we know, else there is no such thing as time." I take it that "what little of reality we know" means in this context the present moment—what we have immediately in our consciousness. Apart from some human being's consciousness of a felt continuity, time is a mere abstraction and so does not really exist.

The matter of continuity is of the greatest importance. As Wilbourne puts it, time is felt as a "current" that "runs through remembering. . . ." It flows out of the past through the present and toward the future. This is how Faulkner stresses Bergson's concept of time as *fluid*. A little later in the same passage Wilbourne will go on to say that before we were born, time did not exist for us. When we become aware of ourselves and of reality, "time begins" and is immediately sensed as "retroactive"; time can only be conceived of as a current flowing *from* somewhere *to* somewhere. Such is my interpretation of Wilbourne's cryptic "Then *I am,* and time begins, retroactive, is was and will be." Wilbourne goes on to say: "Then *I was* and so I am not and so time never existed" (p. 137); that is, when I am dead and no longer possess consciousness, then time does not exist for me and indeed, so far as I am concerned, might as well never have existed.

The best specific evidence for Bergson's influence on Faulkner, I am convinced, is to be found in this passage. Yet it should be noted that the idea of the "presentness" in the human consciousness of the past and of the future long antedates Bergson. For in-

stance, it was put forcefully by St. Augustine in his *Confessions,*
Book XI, Section 23:

> For if times past and to come be, I would know where they
> be. Which yet if I cannot, yet I know that, wherever they be,
> they are not there as future, they are not yet there; if there
> also they be past, they are not longer there. Wheresoever there
> is whatsoever is, *it is only as present.* [Translated by Edvard
> Bouverie Pusey. My italics.]

In citing St. Augustine, I do not mean to imply that this was
Faulkner's source. He may well have got the notion from a number
of sources, including Henri Bergson. In his 1952 interview with
Bouvard, he pointedly includes Bergson among the French writers
to whom he was indebted. He had been "influenced by Flaubert,
and by Balzac. . . . And by Bergson obviously"; and he adds: "I
feel very close to Proust." [4]

To sum up, I interpret Faulkner to be saying that time does not
exist apart from the consciousness of some human being. Apart
from that stream of living consciousness, time is merely an abstraction. Thus, *as actually experienced,* time has little to do with the
time that is measured off by the ticking of a chronometer. Such a
conception of time, however, did not impel Faulkner to destroy
his own watch as Quentin Compson did (in *The Sound and the
Fury*).[5] Though clock time, as an abstraction, might be deemed
to be in some sense unreal, Faulkner, like Bergson himself, conceded that clock-and-calendar time had its uses and that no human
life of the slightest complexity could get along without constant
reference to it.

When, in his 1952 interview with Bouvard, Faulkner declared
that "man is never time's slave," he was simply affirming that time
as man experienced it could never be adequately or accurately
measured except by the human heart. For Romeo and Juliet on

4. *Lion in the Garden,* p. 72.
5. In this context it is amusing to note that Faulkner set a high value on, and
took no little pride in, a watch that he bought from the New York firm of Black,
Starr, and Gorham. See his *Selected Letters,* ed. Blotner, pp. 209 and 210.

their wedding night, time is incredibly swift; on the next morning the sun rises all too soon. But for the lover awaiting the appointed hour to see his mistress, time seems hardly to move at all. In general, the way in which men see the world is altered both by memories of past experience and by their expectations of the future. Such a view of time is immemorially old.

Why make these points here at such length? Because I think that what Faulkner got from Bergson was essentially a confirmation, from a respected philosopher, of something that he already knew. I doubt that Faulkner read Bergson very deeply or thoroughly. I believe that the influence of Bergson on Faulkner has been generally overestimated and that its importance has been occasionally pushed to absurd lengths. In several of the articles and dissertations that argue for a strong Bergsonian influence on Faulkner, the authors manage to write as if they had forgotten that Bergson's own system was a dualism in which the philosopher found room and *need* for objectively measured time as well as for time as *duration*. Far from dismissing the spatial-temporal world as irrelevant or unreal, Bergson needed this inorganic world to set over against the organic world that was dynamic and "alive." As Thomas Hanna has put it:

> [Bergson's] contention that the inner movement of duration is the very stuff of reality becomes not only a key for an understanding of the nature of time and of memory, but, inevitably, becomes the interpretive basis for understanding the evolving character of mankind as well as of organic life in general. All of organic life is linked together in time by an enduring reality which relentlessly preserves the past, as this living past gnaws its way further into the present.[6]

(Compare Harry Wilbourne's reference to "the current of time that runs through remembering. . . .") The inner movement of duration has, to be sure, a plus value. It is more truly "real," but for Bergson, the inorganic world also had its own reality as the

6. *The Bergsonian Heritage*, ed. Thomas Hanna (New York, 1962), p. 10.

necessary foil to that "human reality" in which Bergson is primarily interested.

Faulkner's statements to the effect that time exists only in the present of some human consciousness may well account for the fact that a number of characters in his fiction assert that the past is not truly past. See for example what Gavin Stevens says in *Intruder in the Dust* (p. 194) and Mr. Compson's remark in *The Sound and the Fury* (p. 222) to the effect that "was [is] the saddest word of all[;] there is nothing else in the world[;] its not despair until time[;] its not even time until it was." Even this riddling passage begins to make some sense in view of Faulkner's special concept of time.

Because Bergson obviously attached special importance to the inner, organic, and dynamic force which, in the evolutionary process, for instance, was "gnaw[ing] its way" further into the static, inorganic world, many readers of Faulkner apparently regard as Bergsonian such remarks by Faulkner as his pronouncement that "Life is motion and motion is concerned with what makes man move—which are ambition, power, pleasure." Perhaps they are right, though I think that Faulkner did not need to be told by Bergson or anyone else that life involves motion.

Life has always been associated with motion. But for neither Faulkner nor Bergson was it enough to simply be in motion. I grant that Faulkner does not condone mere passivity in the face of adversity. He understands and may pity, but cannot approve those who retreat into the past. In a moment of bitter insight, Gail Hightower admits to himself that he has never in his whole life really lived. Moreover, though Faulkner was obviously fascinated by the Southern past, he was realistic about it too—about its faults, limitations, and sins. He often also warned about the necessity for change and man's need to adapt to new conditions. Yet merely to survive, merely to stay alive, was not at all what he meant by "endurance." Flem Snopes, for example, was able to cope with the situation in which he found himself. He did not remain passive; he did not retreat into the past. But it never occurred to Faulkner to say of Flem that he "endured," even though in a very real sense Flem not only endured but—in the language of *A Fable*—"prevailed" over other men. For Faulkner, mere financial success was a shoddy achievement.

Those who write about Faulkner, therefore, ought to be more careful about citing some of the oversimple observations that he occasionally made, particularly in interviews. For Faulkner believed that there were some things that a man must not do even as the price of his survival. There were some causes for which a man ought to be willing to give up his life.

If it was indeed Bergson who taught Faulkner to be aware of the limitations of pure ratiocination, to trust the heart, to believe in man's potentialities for growth and improvement, and to see that time as humanly experienced was an unbroken stream flowing out of the depths of his past and moving with a forward surge into a yet unexperienced future—then his debt to Bergson was indeed large. For these are the basic assumptions on which Faulkner erected his literary work. But he might easily have learned these things elsewhere, and he could have learned nothing from Bergson that made calendar time something with which man did not need to concern himself because it was "unreal." The evidence that Faulkner's characters have to contend with clock time and the intractabilities of static "things" is to be found in the fiction itself.

For instance, though Joe Christmas distrusted laws, commandments, and conventions of all kinds, and seems to have arrived at his decisions through intuitions—intuitions so spontaneous that it may be difficult for the reader to grasp their meaning—in the end, even Joe Christmas comes back to calendar time. Wandering in the woods, sought for days by the sheriff's posse, he suddenly finds that he simply has to know what the day of the week is. When a black man on a wagon tells him the day—"It's Friday. O Lawd God, it's Friday"—Joe starts immediately for his destination. His subsequent actions are those of a man who is maintaining a tight schedule in order to keep an important engagement. He needs to be present at a particular place and at a particular time.

To take another example, Harry Wilbourne spends weeks with Charlotte in a kind of Eden-like retreat. They have removed themselves from the world. But one day Harry suddenly finds that he simply has to know the calendar date, and at once begins to construct a calendar (see chapter 8, above). Wilbourne has a quarrel with the modern world, and he tries to keep its inhuman stultifications out of his intensely experienced life with Charlotte. He even speculates on the possibility that time can be "abrogated" altogether. He cites his first sexual orgasm as proof that such abrogation is possible: "for that one second or two seconds you were present in space but not in time" (*The Wild Palms*, p. 139). We have here a reference to a time that is not time, maybe a glimpse of eternity itself. Nevertheless, Wilbourne feels the necessity for mentioning clock time also: "one second or two seconds." Both kinds of time occur in Faulkner's world, and, on reflection, could it be otherwise?

To come at the problem from another direction: in spite of Faulkner's acceptance of Bergson's conception of time as fluid and continuous (time as "duration"), it is hard to think of a novelist who exceeds Faulkner in his careful attention to the details of clock time and calendar time. I am thinking here particularly of the chronology of his novels. Each conforms not only to a generally consistent time scheme; the details of the time scheme are often very precise. Indeed, it is a revelation to go through a Faulkner novel, giving special attention to its chronology, and so discover how many unobtrusive but specific time-clues Faulkner has planted. Though such clues often do not call attention to themselves, yet when noted and put together, the chronology that they plot is much too consistent to be unpurposed. Even if Faulkner did not mean for every reader to be aware of these buried chronologies, we may be sure that he was himself in command of the sequence of events.

It must be conceded that he occasionally makes mistakes. Usually these are obvious contradictions of the overall pattern. Thus, on page 322 of *Light in August* Faulkner says that Joe Christmas was captured on a Friday—a date that doesn't fit with other events in the scheme—but nine pages later the date is set right (to Saturday). Again, in *Absalom, Absalom!* (p. 99) we are told that Judith and Bon saw each other for "a total period of seventeen days," but a few lines down on the same page the number is said to be twelve. In the Texas MS the text reads "seventeen" in both instances.

Obviously, when Faulkner decided to revise the number downward to twelve, he corrected the second instance but overlooked correcting the first.

How careful Faulkner could be in organizing a consistent scheme is revealed in his first published novel (see the chronology of *Soldiers' Pay,* in my Notes to chapter 3). Other striking instances occur in *Sanctuary* (see *The Yoknapatawpha Country,* pp. 387–91); in *The Wild Palms* (see McHaney's study, pp. 195–206); in *Absalom, Absalom!* (see Appendix B, below); and even in "Miss Zilphia Gant" the chronology is carefully ordered (see below, Notes to chapter 6). In *Light in August* it is perhaps possible to assign the precise calendar date of Joe Christmas's murder of Joanna Burden (see p. 426, below). Faulkner's characters clearly lived their lives and underwent their passions in Bergson's *temps durée,* but this fact does not absolve them from living through a time that could be ticked off by the clock and measured by the calendar.

It has also been argued that Bergson's theories of time had a powerful influence on Faulkner's conception of art. Susan Resneck Parr puts the matter thus: "Life after all is dynamic, [Faulkner] believed, while art, by its very nature, is static. Life is an ever ongoing process. It is motion, change, becoming. Art, in contrast, has as its aim stillness, permanence, completeness." How then, she asks, could art "communicate the motion of life and the reality of a moment. . . ." [7] Miss Parr goes on to quote the following passage from Faulkner's interview with Jean Stein: "The aim of every artist is to arrest motion, which is life, by artificial means and hold it fixed so that 100 years later when a stranger looks at it, it moves again since it is life." [8]

Faulkner's statement is a sound way of putting the artist's age-old problem: how to salvage from the onrushing stream of time a story or episode or simply a moment of insight or revelation, and preserve it in a form impervious to time so that hundreds of years later it will exist not merely as a static entity, but, under the reader's gaze, will begin to flow once more with the movement of

7. "And by Bergson, Obviously," Ph.D. diss., University of Wisconsin, 1972 (University Microfilms, 1975), p. 8.
8. *Lion in the Garden,* p. 253.

life. Bergson had shown that reality is not fixed but mobile, continuous, and ongoing, whereas words are basically static, and, as names given to objects, manage to freeze out of the flux of reality little objective "things," which, in their definite outline and immobility, falsify the flow of reality that they propose to imitate.

Miss Parr argues that Faulkner's acquaintance with Bergson stimulated him to develop certain narrative and descriptive techniques. I do not find her argument convincing. If the problem as described by Bergson does arise from the very nature of reality and the very nature of words, the one fluid and dynamic, the other fixed and static, then such has been a problem for the literary artist from the first beginnings of language, and it existed for Homer and Sophocles, Dante and Shakespeare, as well as for Faulkner. Moreover, unless we want to argue that Homer and Sophocles, Dante and Shakespeare labored in vain, the problem of using the medium of words to convey a sense of life is not insoluble. It has been solved, more or less satisfactorily, over and over again. One of Faulkner's favorite poets, by writing what was to become perhaps Faulkner's favorite poem, the "Ode on a Grecian Urn," solved it very much to Faulkner's own special satisfaction.

So much for a common-sense view of what Faulkner did not need to learn from Bergson. If, however, we insist on applying very literally and narrowly to literary art what Bergson has to say on this subject of how the intuition grasps the nature of reality as distinguished from the way in which the intelligence is compelled to deal with it, we would have to argue that any genuine solution of the problem had to wait upon the invention of the movie camera. I have in mind the following passage from Bergson's *The Creative Mind.*

> To think intuitively is to think in duration. Intelligence starts ordinarily from the immobile, and reconstructs movement as best it can with immobilities in juxtaposition. Intuition starts from movement, posits it, or rather perceives it as reality itself, and sees in immobility only an abstract moment, a snapshot taken by our mind, of a mobility. Intelligence ordinarily concerns itself with things, meaning by that, with the

static, and makes of change an accident which is supposedly superadded. For intuition the essential is change: as for the thing, as intelligence understands it, it is a cutting which has been made out of the becoming and set up by our minds as a substitute for the whole.[9]

How is the literary artist to get from little "cuttings" or slices of reality to the movement of real life? From individual static photographs to something resembling the flow of time? If we take Bergson literally, he is saying that the problem cannot be solved by the artist whose medium is words. Since nouns are names and clot the dynamic flow of reality into little static pseudo-entities ("things"), a poem or a story necessarily denies the true nature of reality. If we insist upon a narrow interpretation of Bergson, the only arts that do not falsify reality would be such arts as music, the dance, and preeminently the art of the moving picture. In that art, the static "cuttings" from reality become a sequence of frozen moments (as seen by the camera's eye), but these are projected upon a screen so rapidly that the observer "sees" not static "things" but virtual movement.

This "cinematic" solution of the problem is, of course, not the only or even necessarily the best solution. Granted that some moving pictures do attain a very high level of art, it must be conceded that cinematic art has its own limitations. What is in fact produced in cinematic art is often mediocre if not meretricious. At all events, the cinema has certainly not pushed the other arts into an inferior category. I have cited this essentially mechanical solution of the problem of how to present the vital movement through what are essentially static items as a warning against a literalistic interpretation of Bergson. In his discussion of intuition and the artist, he surely meant something more profound. If cinematic art is truly to catch and convey the movement of dynamic life, the camera itself has to be employed by a sensitive and imaginative artist. After all, the camera is simply one more tool.

One of the best articles in which the case for Bergson's influence

9. Translated by Mabelle L. Anderson (New York: The Philosophical Library, 1946), p. 39.

on Faulkner is argued is that by Darrel Abel.[10] He points out that the "resource of the intuitive artist [for] conveying his intuitions to practical men, who must have reality represented to them in 'states' and 'things,' is symbolism," and he quotes Bergson's own assertion to that effect in *The Creative Mind:* Intuition "will have to use ideas as a conveyance. It will prefer, however, to have recourse to the more concrete ideas" and, of these, "those which still retain an outer fringe of images. Comparisons and metaphors will here suggest what cannot be expressed" (p. 48). Though "No image will replace the intuition of duration, . . . many different images . . . will be able, through the convergence of their action, to direct the consciousness to the precise point where there is a certain intuition to seize on" (p. 145).

Quite so. But with this concession that the literary artist can solve his problem by recourse to images, metaphors, and symbols, we have no proclamation of a revolutionary technique—rather, a confirmation of the age-old and thoroughly traditional means employed by the literary artist. I am not scolding Bergson for failing to produce a new technique. My purpose is rather to moderate the inflated claims of Bergsonian influence on Faulkner's technique. In this matter of narrative techniques, I believe that Faulkner learned more from Conrad and Joyce or, more largely, from Shakespeare and Keats and Eliot than he could ever have learned from Bergson.

Darrell Abel's discussion of *Light in August* is, by the way, one of the best of the earlier accounts of this fascinating novel. Abel offers excellent insights and provides a sound emphasis on what themes in this novel are truly central and important. But his insights have little to do with his argument that Faulkner has been influenced by Bergson. Actually, what Abel says would seem to imply the influence of Nietzsche rather than Bergson. For example, Abel comments on Hightower's rather detached view of the life that swirls around him as follows: "In the Dionysian dance of life there comes a serene moment of Apollonian vision." By contrast, Lena Grove "knows no reality beyond her subjective mo-

10. "Frozen Movement in *Light in August*," *Boston University Studies in English* 3 (1957) : 32–44.

ment. She represents ordinary naive mankind, inviolably innocent because it cannot enter the realm of ideas." True enough; but how does this state of affairs square with Bergson's claim that it is only by intuition that we can grasp the dynamic reality of life? Since Lena is subjective and nonintellectual, it would appear that it is she who lives in "duration" and by intuition. She swims in the very current of life and life seems to flow through her. By contrast, it is Hightower who has withdrawn from life as a "becoming," a process, and who is the creature of ratiocination and intelligence.

In Nietzsche's scheme (as described in *The Birth of Tragedy*), such a contrast makes sense: the artist is able to give Apollonian "form" to the Dionysiac dance. He has to be able to detach himself from the dance and so "see" it. The person who is wholly caught up in the dance cannot see what he is doing; he is blind to its pattern. In a famous poem Yeats asked: "How can we know the dancer from the dance?" But in the somewhat altered context presented here, the question is, how can the ecstatic dancer distinguish herself—"know" herself—from the dance. I am not here trying to convict Abel of a contradiction. Rather, I wonder whether the contradiction is not Bergson's own. If so, it would not be the first or the last time. Bergson is noted for his contradictions.[11]

The most extreme claims for Bergson's influence on Faulkner almost inevitably come to a head in discussions of *Absalom, Absalom!* Several commentators have pointed to this great novel as the special showcase for exhibiting Faulkner's way of handling the problems of truth. We are told, for example, that Quentin and Shreve begin to use what Bergson calls a "dynamic method of perceiving and responding to reality . . . as opposed to a static method." Though "dynamic" and "static" are rather slippery terms, let us grant, for the sake of the argument, that Quentin and Shreve do employ a dynamic method. Nevertheless, they first assemble all the evidence (the static facts) that they can. They use deductive methods when these apply. They make use of the law of contradiction. They eliminate some hypotheses as unlikely and others as frankly unreasonable. They do not start out by making a

11. See Hanna, *The Bergsonian Heritage,* p. 17.

set of uneducated guesses. They sort a lot of evidence before they resort to intuition.

Intuition may discover truth, but some intuitions come closer to the truth than others do. (Some intuitions amount to arrant nonsense.) In any case, intuition has to have a context. There must be a problem—not merely an empty space into which to fire off random guesses; and the context itself usually sets limits to the intuitional operation. A given context may eliminate certain possibilities and call attention to others.

One commentator on *Absalom, Absalom!*, eager to make the case for Faulkner's use of a Bergsonian method, lays great stress on the discrepancies to be found in *Absalom, Absalom!* We are urged not to try to explain them away, for these "discrepancies" have been deliberately set down by Faulkner. Furthermore, by printing at the back of the book a genealogy and chronology that differ in some details from the text, Faulkner has meant to add to the reader's uncertainty as to what is true and what is not. In short, Faulkner deliberately confuses his reader since a main theme of his novel is the "elusiveness of truth."

Several of the characters in *Absalom, Absalom!* do indeed expatiate on the difficulties of understanding history and the impossibility of ever discovering the truth about what happened to the Sutpens and why. But if the difficulties are to be made absolute or nearly so, then the quest for truth becomes pointless. To make even murkier the murkiness that envelopes the Sutpen story seems a curious way of recommending Bergson's intuition as a means of discovering truth.[12]

To sum up, though Bergson may have confirmed some of Faulkner's notions about time and about the ways in which human beings can know reality, and though Bergson may have stimulated Faulkner to experiment with the verbal presentation of motion and action, I find little in Faulkner's narrative treatment

12. For a detailed account of which character in *Absalom, Absalom!* knows what about the Sutpen story, and when he comes by his various bits of knowledge, the reader is referred to Appendix B, below, where the attempt has been made to sort out the reported facts, the deductions, the inferences, and the sheer guesses as to why Thomas Sutpen forbade the marriage of his daughter to Charles Bon and why Henry Sutpen shot Charles Bon.

that can be certainly attributed to Bergson's influence. Many of Faulkner's techniques turn out to be simply skillful and imaginative adaptations of traditional narrative methods, but if one were to specify particular influences it would not be Bergson's so much as Conrad's, the early Eliot's, and Joyce's.[13] Whatever Faulkner's indebtedness, his handling of time reached perhaps its most brilliant achievement in *Absalom, Absalom!* (see Appendix B, below).

Faulkner's concern with time is closely related to his concern with history; and it is just here, I believe, that one could most plausibly make a claim for Bergsonian influence, though the proponents of that influence seem to have overlooked this opportunity. I refer both to the sense in which the past "exists" only in the present and to a related matter: the past as a living force in the present, a force that moulds our sense of the present. These concepts have everything to do with the importance that Faulkner assigns to history. Whether or not he derived these ideas from Bergson, they do constitute his profound belief. Faulkner's own personal experience, of course, had much to do with his sense of history. Most of us who grew up, as he did, in the South of the early decades of this century had talked to Confederate veterans, who were in some instances our own grandfathers. We felt a sense of identity as "Southerners." We believed that we really constituted a kind of subnation within the United States, and were very much aware of the consequences of the South's defeat in the war. Such a defeat did make a difference in one's present life. Our loss of the war had political and economic consequences that had affected and continued to affect us.

There was of course nothing unusual about such a situation. The victors in a war quickly forget it; it is the losers who do not. In the British Isles, the Scots, the Welsh, and to a much greater extent the Irish appear to be peoples caught up in a similar cultural situation. Yet the South had not been locked into its old agrarian culture merely by custom and tradition: discriminatory freight-rate differentials, unfavorable tariff laws, and lack of capital

13. For some instances of Faulkner's borrowing from James Joyce, see below, Notes, pp. 370–72.

made it very difficult to shift to an urban-industrial culture—even for those Southerners who wanted to make the shift. There was more than its own inertia that kept the South in the role of the producer of raw materials which would be shipped abroad or into the northeastern quadrant of this country for processing and consumption. In short, the South's was a colonial economy, and the region found it almost as difficult to shake off its colonial yoke as the emerging countries (as we call them today) find it difficult to shake off theirs.

Faulkner's fiction clearly reflects this general cultural situation: there was poverty, extreme at one end of the social scale and not much better than genteel at the other. The habits and customs of an older America persisted. The South's was essentially an agricultural society, a society of small towns and farms, a hunting society where everybody had a gun and supplied the table from time to time with squirrels, rabbits, partridges, and, very occasionally, with venison.

It was family centered, both in its upper and in its lower classes. A real folk culture persisted, both in the white population and in the black. Like nearly all folk societies, there was a live tradition of story-telling, folk songs, and oratory of both the pulpit and the political varieties. For those who want to insist on time as felt *duration,* time in the South had slowed down as compared with the rest of the country. Naturally, there was a strong sense of history—local, family, and regional—but history not so much book-learned as passed down from father to son or from mother to daughter, or simply absorbed through a process of cultural osmosis. (Quentin felt that he had always known the basic outlines of Thomas Sutpen's story. Just when or from whom he had learned this or that circumstance, he would not always have found it easy to say.)

All of this has a bearing on Faulkner's sense of history. For him, the Civil War seemed a living memory in which he had not directly participated but which was *his* nevertheless. Let us grant that Faulkner sometimes gets the date of a battle wrong or is confused about this or that happening; yet there is no contradiction. He was so certain of what he knew that it apparently did not occur to him to get out a book and look up the episode. History is here passing over into myth, but I do not mean that history is thereby falsified; rather, history has become a part of lived experience, as immediate as other aspects of lived experience, and not an abstract pattern that never engages one's day-to-day life. When history as myth is reshaped by a mind of genius, it may even improve upon formal history. Certainly, in Faulkner's conception, history was more than a chronicle of events, more even than a collection of verified facts and statistics. It was a meaningful story.

Faulkner allowed some of his characters—Isaac McCaslin in "The Bear" is a notable instance—to see history as providential, something more than a sequence of causes and their effects—as a story with a purpose, even as a story that bore a high promise. Clearly he rejected the notion that history was meaningless. On the other hand, he also rejected any notion of mankind's inevitable and automatic progress. His view of history was too complex to allow him to accept either of a pair of alternatives so simple as these.

Yet before undertaking to describe Faulkner's philosophy of history—though how he would have winced at this phrase—it will be necessary to clear the ground a bit by disposing of two or three persistent misapprehensions. A sense of history does not imply an irrational reverence for the past or an antiquarian's disparagement of the present world, or some nostalgic yearning for vanished glories. To clarify my position in this matter, and to clarify what I take to be Faulkner's, will require at least a brief consideration of change, the past, the nature of history, and the nature of myth.

It has been insisted on by some critics that Faulkner regarded what is unchanging as worse than merely passive—as simply dead and inert, since he believed that change was the very principle of life and vitality. Now there is an element of truth in such observations—namely, that change is part of the process of growth in all living organisms and that change is a symptom that the organism is alive. But it is a careless, not to say a specious, logic which arrives at the conclusion that change is necessarily good. History deals out change in all shapes and sizes, all the way from the change in hairstyles to the fall of the Roman Empire. What Faulkner constantly reprehended was something very different: the failure to cope with change.

In his novels Faulkner has presented a number of characters

who are unwilling to accept change or are unable to cope with the changes that have occurred. One thinks immediately of a Quentin Compson or a Gail Hightower. As we have noted earlier, Faulkner believed that to isolate the past from the present was to falsify the very nature of time. It was a fallacy in which some of Faulkner's characters were trapped, but never Faulkner himself. The authentic human being lives in the past and future as well as in the present. Indeed, the present as such is an abstraction—an arbitrary knife-edge, over which time future constantly moves into its condition of time past. How long is the "present"? A year, a week, a day, a half-hour, a split second? Faulkner was, as we have seen, quite as clearheaded on this matter as was St. Augustine. The past does continue to live in the present, not only in the sense that it is alive in our memories, but also because we ourselves, and our very capacity to remember, have been shaped by the past. Gavin Stevens does not always express Faulkner's own opinions and beliefs, but when he says, as he does more than once, that "There's no such thing as past, . . ." he voices Faulkner's own conviction. A Quentin or a Hightower, who lives only in the past, is not fully alive. But then neither is a man like Jason Compson, who repudiates the past and lives only in future expectations.

The Sound and the Fury presents a third mode of incomplete human life, that of the third brother, Benjy. Since Benjy, the idiot, cannot distinguish between past and present and has no real prevision of the future, he lives virtually at the animal level—is barely human. Considerations of this kind lead us to a definition of history as the specifically human realm. Creatures at the animal level truly have no history. Possessing almost no memory and no sense of the future, birds and beasts live in what is to all intents and purposes a timeless present. Their basic drives and responses to their environment are largely instinctual. They are so deeply immersed in nature, they so completely lack man's self-consciousness, that they are barred out of the realm of purposes and responsibilities, which constitute the realm of history.

Though we think of history as the record of the past, human history (and there is really no other kind) tells of the deeds and misdeeds of a creature whose conscious life comprehends a continuous effort that links up his own past with the present and extends it into the future. The birds and beasts, on the other hand, live in what is a virtual present—in what amounts to a time-less dimension. Every creature, of course, will die, but it is only man who *knows* he will die—and thus conducts his whole life from babyhood onwards under the sentence of death. This is both his burden and his glory.

Since man participates in both nature and history, it is important that he should keep these realms distinct and not confuse one with the other. One such confusion involves regarding history as simply a natural process in which an empire grows like a great tree, flourishes, falls into the sere and yellow leaf, and finally crashes to the ground. When history is so regarded, there may be danger of losing the human dimension altogether. Men who really believe that the tendencies of history are simply blind natural forces may be inclined to throw up their hands and say, "What's the use of our actions?" For such a mentality, history has been eaten up by nature. On the other hand, nature may be eaten up by history. If we come to believe that man can manipulate nature to suit his own purposes, nature becomes assimilated to history—that is, we come to consider history to be simply the story of man's unlimited Promethean will as he remakes the physical universe to suit his own purposes. Such pride indeed goeth before a fall. If history teaches anything, it surely teaches that.

Most of us use the word *history* to mean the record, oral or written, of what has happened in the life of a people or a civiliza-tion. Yet, since history is possible only to a self-conscious creature like man, a creature who can remember and who can try to inter-pret the meaning of his past, the quality and complexity of re-corded history will obviously differ somewhat from culture to culture, with the extent of its knowledge of the past and the nature of its world view. It will be difficult to find a truly objective history containing no element of emotional and subjective bias.

The history of certain primitive tribes is more accurately de-scribed as being mythic rather than truly historical. If their ex-perience as a tribe has been little more than the cyclic round of "birth, copulation, and death," with no epochal events, no crises, no turning points—if their history seems to be going nowhere in particular—it will not be so very different from the "history" of unselfconscious birds and beasts; that is, it will be no history at all. It may amount to not much more than a cosmic myth, telling how the universe began and the story of a heroic eponymous ancestor whose descendants are the members of the present tribe.

Yet, though civilized man sometimes looks with a patronizing scorn on the mythic histories of primitive peoples, it is difficult to eliminate from any history the element of myth. Popular history is usually heavily tinctured with myth. We wage our wars and define our political objectives largely in terms of myths. Our professional historians are thus set a difficult task: to try to eliminate at least the more fanciful myths and to ground history, as nearly as possible, on fact; and yet to provide an interpretation of history—not just a dry chronicle of facts—something that will possess the dynamics of myth even though based on actual happenings.

With this observation one can return to the matter of Faulkner's attitude toward the Southern past and to the charge, still often made, that his fiction veered dangerously toward a celebration of what enlightened people now know was merely a myth—the account of a fabulous Old South that never really existed. Actually, Faulkner's picture of the antebellum South is no gilded dream. It is a solid world, of the earth earthy. Faulkner finds the Southerners of that time both good and bad, with the usual mixture of vices and virtues. He is essentially realistic in his account of slavery. If his novels of that older time show us some slaveholders who were fundamentally decent and honorable men, they show others who were callous and inhuman.

Moreover, in his novels he gives a great deal of attention to the whites who owned few or no slaves. Faulkner depicts a yeomanry that possesses a proper self-esteem along with the sturdier virtues. The poorer whites, including those who had been beaten down and damaged by a life of brutal toil, are usually treated with comprehending sympathy, as are the blacks, whose humanity and basic dignity have, in Faulkner's account, survived their condition of servitude.

Considering the zest with which so many of Faulkner's characters tell stories about the Civil War, it is impossible to believe that Faulkner himself did not take pride in the fight that his homeland had put up against such heavy odds. The Civil War was a bloody war and one that had grave consequences for his people and his own family. Moreover, the issues involved were too complicated to be accommodated under the rubric "a crusade to free the slaves." In *Go Down, Moses* (p. 290) Isaac McCaslin observes that the Southerners "had fought for four years and lost to preserve [slavery] . . . not because they were opposed to freedom as freedom but for the old reasons for which man (not the generals and the politicians but man) has always fought and died in wars: to preserve a status quo or to establish a better future one to endure for his children. . . ." The war was really a clash between two cultures possessed of differing manners, customs, and world views.

The antebellum South, in spite of the curse of slavery and its penchant for frontier violence, had provided a scope for courage, honor, and heroism. Faulkner even went so far as to write after the conclusion of World War II, in a letter to Lambert Davis, that there were times when he believed

> there [had] been little in this country since [1860–70] good enough to make good literature, that since then we have gradually become a nation of bragging sentimental not too courageous liars. We seem to be losing all confidence not only in our national character but in man's integrity too. The fact that we blow so hard so much about both of them is to me the symptom. [*Letters*, p. 239]

The circumstances of these comments are worth reporting. Davis had sent Faulkner a copy of Robert Penn Warren's *All the King's Men*. Faulkner had read the novel and had been much taken with the Cass Mastern episode, the principal events of which occur from about 1854–55 to 1864. In comparison with what man had had to face and had heroically faced up to nearly a century ago, the men of the mid-twentieth century did not come off well. Yet Faulkner's outburst represented more than the momentary impact on him of this fine long story. What Faulkner says here has close affinities with the speeches that he put into Ike McCaslin's mouth in *Go Down, Moses* and into Gavin Stevens's mouth in *Intruder in the Dust*.

The history of this Southern subnation was, as Faulkner depicts it, tragic in Aristotle's sense of the term. One remembers how in the *Poetics* Aristotle observed that you cannot make a tragic hero out of a base and contemptible man. The tragic hero must be literally "worth the killing." Though he has a tragic flaw, he must possess real virtues; otherwise the evocation of pity and terror that Aristotle regarded as the hallmark of genuine tragedy could not occur. For Faulkner, the tragic flaw of the South was its harboring of chattel slavery, yet the slaveholders, and in general the soldiers of the Confederacy, the majority of whom were not slaveholders at all, were essentially brave and worthy men. That was why, for Faulkner, the collapse of the Old South was authentically tragic.

There is, however, another way of approaching this matter of Faulkner's relation to the myth of the Old South. Most critics of that myth make the assumption that they themselves stand on firm historical ground. They are bringing solid truth to bear on a flimsy fairy tale. But the situation may in fact be rather different. It is entirely possible that we have here not a myth confronted by history, but one myth confronting another. For if there is a myth of the Southern past, we must recognize that there is a myth of the American future—its more respectable name is the American Dream—and with reference to the charge that the Southern myth erred in describing its past as golden, one might point out that the American myth has consistently insisted that its future was made of the same precious metal. But a golden future, never quite here, always about to be, may turn out to be quite as much a falsification. If it is dangerous to glamorize the past because one's future is dark or uncertain, the reverse process may falsify quite as much: to gild the future because the past is drab and unsatisfactory.

We are not condemned to either alternative, though the American myth has applied a constant pressure toward this either/or choice. Thus, in his day Emerson divided the American intellectuals into those who belonged to the Party of Memory and those who belonged to the Party of Hope. In doing so, he offered a false option, for there is not the slightest reason why a writer like Faulkner, who remembers, should thereby forfeit his right to be hopeful—unless, of course, one assumes that one is forced to choose between losing his memory and losing his hope. In a world of such mad choices as that, a man might as well lose his mind too and be done with it.

Faulkner may be said to have participated in both myths, that of the Old South and that of America. As an American, he felt the attraction of the American Dream, particularly as it is expressed in the opening sentences of the Declaration of Independence—the promise of freedom, equality, and the right of the individual to pursue his own notion of the good life. But Faulkner was no Emersonian; nor was he a Whitmanian, rejoicing in the promiscuous bonhomie of urban crowds. Faulkner was more realistic—some would say more pessimistic—about the general cantankerousness of human nature and the difficulties of directing the course of history, even of *predicting* its outcome. To be sure, he never quite despaired of man, but neither was he buoyantly optimistic about man's future. In 1955, some several years after his Nobel Prize speech, he observed in a letter to a friend: ". . . human beings are terrible. One must believe well in man to endure him, wait out his folly and savagery and inhumanity." Faulkner did "believe well in man," but his was no naive belief. It was a hard-won faith.

If Faulkner was willing to criticize the myth that he had inherited from his family and his local community and his region, he was also willing to criticize the myth of America, to make a realistic estimate of how far we were still from a realization of the American Dream. In 1955, he published an article entitled "On Privacy." He was always sensitive, perhaps hypersensitive, to what he regarded as invasions of his private life. What he had published was open to discussion and criticism, but his personal life was not the business of the public. He resented bitterly the fact that a magazine like *Life* should consider that everything he had ever said or done was in the public domain. But though it was a personal incident that provoked his essay, Faulkner tried to rise above the merely personal occasion. He made it plain that the issue raised was general and had reference to basic principles. It is significant that he gave his essay the subtitle: "The American Dream: What Happened to It?" He even wrote to a friend at this time that he wanted to write five or six essays on this matter of the degeneration of the American Dream. The essays might make up a small book on the subject.

The five or six additional essays were never written. But from the one that he did publish and from the novels and short stories of his later career, one can make out what his developed thesis would have amounted to. The American Revolution had been fought to free the individual citizen from all sorts of tyrannies. One's right to keep his personal life free from gossip-mongers and meddlers and censors was an essential part of his freedom. Consequently, when a soul-less corporation could invade a citizen's privacy by flaunting a banner emblazoned "Freedom of the Press" or "The Public's Right to Know," the real issues had been perverted and the individual citizen's freedom, subverted. Greed for money to be made by truckling to the curiosity of a mass audience had undone what the Declaration of Independence had proclaimed and the Constitution had been intended to confirm.

The growth of the money power represented a degeneration from the republican ideal of the Founding Fathers. The transformation of a free citizenry into a mindless mob amounted to an even worse corruption, the kind of corruption that Thomas Jefferson had foreseen as a possibility and had warned against. Harry Wilbourne (in *The Wild Palms,* p. 133) may well be speaking for Faulkner when he argues that present-day America's special vices are "fanaticism, smugness, meddling, fear, and worst of all, respectability."

I do not know that Faulkner ever consulted Alexis de Tocqueville's *Democracy in America,* but had he read Tocqueville's second volume he would have found an account of the very process by which a government set up to protect the individual's rights might end up by subverting them. Though the Founding Fathers of the United States had indeed conceived the individual to be the sole bearer of rights and responsibilities, and though democratic political institutions were devised to protect the individual's rights and privileges, Tocqueville points out that the whole tendency in a democracy is toward the standardization of culture and toward a homogenization of the mass of the citizenry. It is the needs of the average citizen that it seeks to satisfy, not those of the special person here and there whose needs are highly individual. The greatest good of the greatest number, indeed. How much could a Faulkner's rather odd desire for privacy count against the desires of the several million readers of *Life* who wanted to read all about him?

This is the sort of situation that Tocqueville foresaw; and though he thought well of democracy and hoped for the best, he was apprehensive that a democratic state might come to institute a quiet despotism, though ostensibly for the benefit of the people themselves. As Tocqueville puts it: "I have always thought that servitude of the regular, quiet, and gentle kind which I have . . . described might be combined more easily than is commonly believed with some of the outward forms of freedom, and that it might even establish itself under the wing of the sovereignty of the people." [14]

Had Faulkner gone on to write his five or six essays on what had happened to the American Dream, would he have touched upon such matters as the dissolving of community, the breakdown of the older values, and the increasing isolation and insecurity of the individual? I think it very likely, for if one examines his fiction, he will find implied a coherent ethical and moral position that is traditional and conservative. It is not mindlessly opposed to all change, nor is it unduly pessimistic about man's future, but it has little patience with utopian ideas and none with leveling tendencies.

Since I have characterized Faulkner's world view as "conservative," I should at least intimate what I mean by that term. I can do no better, I believe, than to quote two paragraphs from Robert Nisbet's *Quest for Community* (which should be read entire by those interested in Faulkner's general intellectual position). Nisbet writes:

14. *Democracy in America,* Reeve translation, Vintage edition, ed. Phillips Bradley (New York, 1945), 2 : 337.

The family, religious association, and local community—these, the conservatives insisted, cannot be regarded as the external products of man's thought and behavior; they are essentially prior to the individual and are the indispensable supports of belief and conduct. Release man from the contexts of community and you get not freedom and rights but intolerable aloneness and subjection to demonic fears and passions. Society, Burke wrote in a celebrated line, is a partnership of the dead, the living, and the unborn. Mutilate the roots of society and tradition, and the result must inevitably be the isolation of a generation from its heritage, the isolation of individuals from their fellow men, and the creation of the sprawling, faceless masses.

The conservatism of our own age of thought is new only in context and intensity. Through the writings of such intermediate figures as Comte, Tocqueville, Taine, Maine, Arnold, and Ruskin, the root ideas and values of early nineteenth-century conservatism have found their way straight to our own generation and have become the materials of a fresh and infinitely diversified veneration for community.[15]

Since he was essentially a conservative, history meant a great deal to Faulkner. He was fully aware of what the mutilation of the roots of society and tradition could mean. In portraying the life of Joe Christmas, he had actually provided a brilliant study of what a complete release from the context of community entailed, including the "isolation of individuals from their fellow men."

Faulkner believed that history might serve as a guide to mankind because he believed that fundamental human nature did not change through the ages. Man did not, even in a different epoch, become an essentially different creature. The man of the present could recognize his own lineaments in the characters described in the *Iliad* or in the Old Testament.

Though Faulkner's novels are drenched in history, they are not "historical novels" in the sense in which Hollywood costume-dramas are. Faulkner's concern is not antiquarian. His primary

15. Robert A. Nisbet, *The Quest for Community* (New York, 1953), p. 25.

intention is not the exploitation of those historical differences in order to provide colorful dress and language for the old, worn, stock characters of romance. The element of escape is never his emphasis. The past is made to reveal a connection with the present.

Faulkner's insistence on making the past impinge meaningfully on the present—on his own present, at least—shows itself in the very time scheme of his novels. The action of *Absalom, Absalom!* begins in 1833 but it does not end until 1910. *The Unvanquished* reaches back to the 1850s, but the man who narrates it does not make what is the crucial decision of his life until 1876, and, as we learn from *Flags in the Dust,* he does not die until 1919. The first episode of *Go Down, Moses* occurs in 1859, but the last episode is to be dated 1941. One might add that even *Light in August* makes use of the same basic pattern. It contains two short but very brilliant flashbacks that deal with the grandfathers of Joanna Burden and Gail Hightower, but the impact of these men on their grandchildren does not reveal its full consequence until 1932.

In sum, the past is never for Faulkner a realm of irresponsible fantasy. For his characters, the past may seem to be a doom, a judgment, a portent, a responsibility, even a providential hope. But it is never simply irrelevant—something that is finished and done with.

Faulkner, of course, was not alone in his concern for the past. The literary artists of our day have been especially concerned with it. One thinks, for instance, of Yeats, Pound, Tate, Eliot, to name only a few. Yet—and here is a sort of paradox—perhaps not for centuries has history counted for so little in the culture as a whole. The man in the street simply doesn't concern himself with it. His eyes are bedazzled by the future. Robert Penn Warren has put the matter bluntly and with somber emphasis: ours, he says, is "a world in which the contempt for the past becomes more and more marked."

The triumphs of modern technology have indeed been staggering. As a virtuoso technological exhibition, our series of moon landings, for example, is almost incredible. But less spectacular technological accomplishments had already altered the total culture. Henry Ford's humble Model T eventually put the whole nation on wheels and, by doing so, drastically altered our daily lives—where we lived, the kind of work we did, and even the makeup of the family unit. Whether or not Ford ever really said that history is bunk, his Tin Lizzie helped persuade the average citizen that history *is* bunk, and in the process also changed the average citizen's conception of nature.

The two phenomena are obviously related: Eliot's or Tate's or Yeats's interest in history is not at all like the pleasant nostalgia with which Sir Walter Scott, a century and a half ago, viewed the past in his historical novels. Nor does it reveal the spirit of detachment which forty years ago allowed millions of readers of *Gone With the Wind* to enjoy the exciting adventures of Scarlett O'Hara. Such excitement could remain a harmless diversion just because the world of Scarlett O'Hara had indeed gone with the wind.

Writers like Yeats, Eliot, and Faulkner find the past frighteningly immediate, inextricably tied up with the present, and full of portent for the future. They cannot dismiss the past as truly past. The temptation of the man in the street to dismiss mankind's earlier experience as obsolete is precisely the circumstance that portends danger. Our technology does not in itself foredoom us. What is frightening is the confidence of the man in the street that the past has been safely buried, that history holds no wisdom for him, and that he is a new, emancipated creature, a rather modest but quite authentic model of Friedrich Nietzsche's Superman.

It is just here that we encounter once more the American Dream. That Dream has always had its ingredient of millennialism,[16] for from the very beginning the American has felt that in setting sail for the New World he had rid himself of the past, and in setting foot on the shores of a virgin continent he had dismissed his old life and had become the New Adam. The New World meant another chance for man. It meant the end of the old despotic tyrannies that hampered man from realizing his proper freedom.

Faulkner, like most of the rest of us, had felt the attraction of

16. For a further discussion of this matter, see below, pp. 280–82.

the American Dream. He took its promises seriously. I judge that he never repudiated the ideals for human life that shimmered through it, but he fairly soon must have come to realize that it was unattainable or at least all but unattainable. One of his most idealistic characters, Isaac McCaslin, is made to talk to the issues directly in *Go Down, Moses*. Isaac tells his elder kinsman that he believes that Columbus's discovery of America was providential; that God did mean to give man a new chance. Out "of the old world's worthless evening," God had "discovered to [man] a new world," one in which "a nation of people could be founded in humility and pity and sufferance and pride of one to another" (p. 258). But then Isaac goes on to say that this new American land was "already accursed . . . already tainted even before any white man owned it." Yet the white men also were tainted. It was as if the sails of their ships were filled with "the old world's tainted wind."

In short, the white men from the Old World were not somehow miraculously purged of their sins through their action in crossing the Atlantic. They had within them plenty of the Old Adam, the Adam who had been expelled from Eden long ago, and so could be expected to bring into the new American Eden a propensity for evil. (I am aware that I have been quoting one of Faulkner's characters, not the author himself. Nevertheless, I see no reason to believe that Isaac McCaslin in this passage is not expresing Faulkner's own view. Such a view is implicit in the whole canon of his works.) Isaac, to be sure, is far from hopeless. He even insists that God almost miraculously brought on the Civil War because he loved the South and meant to save it from the curse of slavery; and so saw to it that the Southerners were defeated because apparently "they [could] learn nothing save through suffering, remember nothing save when underlined in blood" (p. 286).

Isaac, and maybe Faulkner himself, could hope that the South might eventually find "a happy issue out of all its afflictions," even out of a shattering defeat. Since history was not meaningless, even suffering could be redemptive. All this amounts to a kind of religious faith; but we confront here something different from the American Dream, different at least from the later modes of the

American Dream. For Isaac is here taking a realistic view of man's capacity for evil. He is also taking history seriously. Instead of dismissing history as irrelevant, he is trying to make sense of it.

The millennialist believes that man is perfectible, that he can learn the laws that govern society, and so eventually determine the course of history. A millennialist tendency is to be seen in the very beginnings of the American experience. The Puritans of New England, constituting the militant left wing of Protestantism, meant to return to God's plan as set forth in Scripture and so establish the New Jerusalem, the divine society as ordained by God, on the soil of the New World. They were of course sufficiently orthodox not to presume that man was perfectible, or that all the human miseries, including sickness, old age, and death, could be done away with. They still held firmly to the doctrine of original sin. They had no illusions that they could restore man to his immortal state, living once more in the happy garden of an unfallen nature. Yet as the doctrine of original sin faded, and as man's powers to control nature grew more and more powerful, the millennial ideal gradually became secularized. The Puritan determination to build the perfect society, far from weakening, was simply redirected from the eternal to the temporal, from the City of Heaven to an earthly city of the here-and-now.

St. Augustine, in his famous discussion of the city of God and the city of man, certainly expected the Christian to use the heavenly city as the model for his earthly enterprise, but he made it plain that it could not be built through man's efforts, but only by God's grace, and in God's own good time. In fact, whenever it was achieved, time would be at an end and the citizens of this New Jerusalem would be living in the light of eternity. The secularization of this view of history took centuries. Yet men did finally come to believe that it was possible, provided that one had a privileged insight into history and a proper social and industrial technology, to control and direct the historical process so as to achieve the perfect society on this earth.

American millennialism has never been as violent as the various revolutionary movements of Europe have been—Marxism, for example—but it has remained from the seventeenth century onward a driving and shaping force in our history. One can find it in the essays of Emerson, in the poetry of Walt Whitman, and almost nakedly in Julia Ward Howe's "The Battle Hymn of the Republic." It is still a powerful force right down to the present day, though it is now so familiar to most of us that we never refer to it by a term so formidable as millennialism, but speak of it rather fondly as simply the American Dream.

The issue of millennialism is, however, one that sets Faulkner off from a great many other American writers. He does not, of course, stand alone; yet his more old-fashioned notion of history has disquieted and confused many a twentieth-century literary critic, and it sets him off sharply from such writers as Hart Crane or, to mention one whose talents he greatly admired, Thomas Wolfe. Faulkner is far less visionary than Wolfe, less optimistic, less intoxicated with the greatness of America. By contrast, Faulkner's view is more "Southern," and though one should not claim him for Christian orthodoxy, much closer to St. Augustine's view of history.

In calling Faulkner's view more "Southern," I am thinking of what C. Vann Woodward has to say in the course of *The Burden of Southern History* (Baton Rouge, La., 1960) and particularly of such observations as the following: "An age-long experience with human bondage and its evils and later with emancipation and its shortcomings did not dispose the South very favorably toward such popular American ideas as the doctrine of human perfectibility, the belief that every evil has a cure, and the notion that every human problem has a solution" (p. 21).

Faulkner did not scorn the American Dream. Rather, he mourned the fact that it had not been fulfilled. He grieved at having to conclude in 1955 that "the American air, which was once the living breath of liberty [has] now become one vast downcrowding pressure to abolish [freedom], by destroying man's individuality. . . ." Faulkner, however, was skeptical about the full realization of *any* utopian dream, even the noblest. That is to say, he was evidently seriously concerned that his country might be undone by her sometimes overweening faith in the future, by her belief that progress was inevitable, by her confidence that man's

281

happiness would result from sociological know-how and the right set of plans, by her reliance on her technological might, by her incautious trust in her own virtues and good intentions, and, most dangerous of all, by her unprecedented record of military victories. (Faulkner died before Americans went into Vietnam.) Americans could easily get the impression that they, unlike the other nations of the earth, were immune to defeat, loss, and evil. Such innocence might in the end prove disastrous.

Appendix A

THOMAS SUTPEN: A REPRESENTATIVE SOUTHERN PLANTER?

FAULKNER SCHOLARSHIP has from the beginning been dominated by the assumption that Thomas Sutpen is typical of the Southern planter class and that Sutpen's downfall is emblematic of the downfall of the whole way of life in the antebellum South. In my earlier volume on Faulkner, I expressed my disagreement with this notion, but I daresay that I have not won many to my own view of the matter. Yet the issue still seems to me to be a very important one and to have a bearing on the very meaning of *Absalom, Absalom!* For this reason I want to address myself to the problem once more. But first, to clarify the issues, let me set forth some of the reasons I would *not* use to impugn Sutpen's status as an example of the typical Southern planter.

It is not that Sutpen came from humble beginnings.[1] Jefferson Davis, the President of the Confederacy, was born in a log cabin in Kentucky, not a hundred miles from where the future President of the United States, Abraham Lincoln, was born in another Kentucky log cabin. Mary Boykin Chesnut, who was to the manor born, regarded Davis as a gentleman, scholar, and gifted leader. Davis certainly possessed the typical virtues of the Southern ruling class.

Yet if Jefferson Davis was a Southern aristocrat,[2] why deny the same

1. In the 1830s and 1840s Mississippi was very close to the frontier, and there was a great deal of social mobility; men could go up the social ladder rapidly.

2. I wish we could substitute for Southern "aristocracy" terms more modest, such as "squirearchy" or "the planter class," but these latter phrases are clumsy, and, besides, the term "Southern aristocrat" is probably now too well established to change.

status to Thomas Sutpen? Someone will ask: Are you denying that Sutpen was an aristocrat because he lacked the social graces? Why wasn't he just as much an aristocrat as your precious Sartorises and Compsons? Simply because they had owned land and slaves a generation or so longer? The way in which they got their land won't bear scrutiny any more closely than will the manner in which Sutpen acquired his. Again, weren't all of these new people on the Mississippi frontier essentially little men on the make? Hugh Holman writes that "Sutpen and the others" in *Absalom, Absalom!* were "farmers, small business men, middle-class entrepreneurs, men whose lives shook or shaped no national structures, however much they might dream of themselves in a world of baronial splendor." [3] Someone asks: Who wants aristocratic trappings anyway? Sutpen ultimately showed Quentin Compson that "in vigour, in character, and in vision Sutpen far outstripped any of Quentin's own family, alive or dead, and that Sutpen's history . . . was only an exceptionally rapid and concentrated version of the history of virtually all Southern families, including Quentin's own." [4] Melvin Backman makes the same basic points: "the Southern aristocracy derived from the low and middle classes, and . . . the aristocracy of the Deep South was made in one generation. Scratch the veneer of the aristocrat of the Deep South and you would find a frontiersman." [5]

All three of these writers very properly appeal to history to validate their descriptions of the social and economic conditions of the time; and of course they do not appeal in vain. No one, for a very long time, has believed that even the Virginia landed gentry—much less the planters of Mississippi—were descended from the younger sons of the English nobility. But the real issue here is whether Sutpen's code of values and general outlook on life differ significantly from those of the other planters of Yoknapatawpha County. With that issue in mind, I want to appeal to the historians too, and, in what follows, I shall cite the findings of two of the most brilliant recent authorities on Southern history, Eugene Genovese and C. Vann Woodward.

What any historian may have to tell us will not, of course, be decisive for the meaning of *Absalom, Absalom!* or for the interpretation of the characters in that novel—including Thomas Sutpen. The text of

---

3. *"Absalom, Absalom!:* The Historian as Detective," *Sewanee Review* 79 (1971) : 549.

4. Michael Millgate, *The Achievement of William Faulkner* (New York, 1966), p. 157.

5. *Faulkner: The Major Years* (Bloomington and London, 1966), p. 94.

the novel must be our ultimate authority. But what some of the more recent historians of the South depose may throw needed light on the novel, and may give us more confidence that Faulkner, in writing about his Yoknapatawpha planters, was not simply indulging in myths and legends of the Old South that had no real reference to the history of the society in which he grew up.

The first of the historians that I shall invoke is Eugene Genovese. He accepts the fact that many—ultimately nearly all—of the Southern slaveholding planters were of plebeian origin, but he finds that in no way does this derogate from their status as "aristocrats." But to give proper force to his argument, it may be necessary to identify his philosophical and political position and the point of view from which he judges the culture of the Old South.

Genovese is a self-proclaimed Marxist, and he appraises the virtues of the slaveholding ruling class with considerable detachment and certainly with no concern to divert attention from its defects and limitations. In short, his position is not "Down with the damnable slavocracy," nor is it "Up with the burgeoning capitalists of the Northeast who saved the Union." As a Marxist, he has no emotional capital invested in either camp.

Having said this much, however, it is necessary to go a little further and present in at least rough outline his view of the Old South. He sees it as having, to a remarkable degree, its own character: "The uniqueness of the antebellum South continues to challenge the imagination of Americans. . . ." [6] Genovese holds that if we are to understand the Old South as a society and as a polity, we must take into account the nature and importance of paternalism. The Southern planters were paternalistic and not capitalistic. Genovese dismisses the notion that they were middle-class entrepreneurs and refuses to designate the Southern system as a "deformed capitalism." If, he says,

> we accept the designation of the . . . slave system as a form of capitalism, we are then confronted [at once with a contradiction. We are forced to entertain the notion of] a capitalist society that impeded the development of every normal feature of capitalism. The planters were not mere capitalists; they were precapitalist, quasi-aristocratic landowners [even though they] had to adjust their economy and ways of thinking to a capitalist world market.

6. *The Political Economy of Slavery* (New York: Vintage Books, 1967), p. 13.

Their society, in its spirit and fundamental direction, represented the antithesis of capitalism, however many compromises it had to make [with capitalism]. The fact of slave ownership is central to our problem. This seemingly formal question of whether the owners of the means of production command labor or purchase the labor power of free workers contains in itself the content of Southern life. The essential features of Southern particularity, as well as of Southern backwardness, can be traced to the relationship of master to slave.[7]

To sum up the gist of the argument as developed in the three books that Genovese has written on the subject: the Old South was indeed unique. In a country that generally was forward-looking, capitalistic, and expansionist, it remained "backward," pre-bourgeois, plantation-based, paternalistic, and family-centered. No wonder that it was from an early period on a collision course with the rest of the United States.

Three questions will arise at once in most readers' minds, and they ought to be dealt with here and now, though, in this essay, necessarily in brief summary. First, were the Southern slaveholders aware of their special view of the world? Genovese's answer is a considered yes.

The world view of the slaveholders contained contradictions, as every world view must, but properly understood, it demonstrated adequate coherence and integrity. Like all class ideologies, it infuriated many of those who held it. Slaveholders, like the rest of us, rarely wanted to face the implications of each notion, prejudice, or ingrained commitment. They wished their ideology to be careless, pragmatic, inarticulate, disorganized, lazy; only political fanatics, philosophers, and lunatics can live any other way. How easy, therefore, for us to judge them as cynics who rationalized a system of exploitation or as rustic windbags who talked nonsense, or as thoughtless reactionaries of no account. They were all of these, but none [of them]. No matter how guilty they may have been on each count, they did nonetheless stand for a world different from our own, [a world] that is worthy of our sympathetic attention.[8]

7. Ibid., p. 23.
8. *The World the Slaveholders Made* (New York: Vintage Books, 1971), p. 126. It is not difficult to find characters in Faulkner's novels who saw the culture of the Old South as markedly different from that of the rest of the United States.

The second question is: what about the yeoman whites and the poor whites, who together made up the larger part of the population of the antebellum South and who owned no slaves? Did they share the slave-owners' ideology? Genovese mentions the economic dependence of the poorer whites on the plantation market; but he also stresses the "distinctly Southern sense of extended family"—many of the poorer whites were bound by ties of family relationship to the planter ruling class—a fact that "provided a powerful impetus for social cohesion." [9] But Genovese rests his case upon the fact that, when the crisis came on, the slaveholders were able to carry nearly all the non-slaveholding whites along with them into the break with the Union. Only in the mountain areas, where their influence was weak, and in certain of the poorer hill counties, did they fail to do so. They even attracted strong support from the Border States.

The third question may best be put bluntly: does Genovese agree that black chattel slavery was an outrageous anachronism? Having put the question bluntly, perhaps it is best to let Genovese speak for himself, and somewhat at length—as a historian and as a contemporary citizen with strong political convictions. In *The World the Slaveholders Made,* he writes:

> If I do not dwell [in this book] on the evils of slavery . . . , it is for two reasons, the first being an assumption that all ruling-class ideologies are self-serving and that it is enough to point out the worst examples along the way, and the second being that few people any longer seem in need of sermons on the subject. . . . To insist . . . on the reality and centrality of paternalism [as it may help us to understand the mentality of the antebellum South] . . . is not to imply that paternalism was ever a good thing, much less that its current manifestations ought to be tolerated.[10]

As for the Southern antebellum slaveholders themselves, Genovese writes:

> These men were class conscious, socially responsible, and per-sonally honorable; they selflessly fulfilled their duties and did

---

An obvious example is Isaac McCaslin: see his description of the Southern slave-holding class as it existed at the outbreak of the Civil War (e.g., in *Go Down, Moses,* pp. 283–90).

9. Ibid., p. 100.

10. Ibid., p. 119.

what their class and society required of them. It is rather hard to assert that class responsibility is the highest test of morality and then to condemn as immoral those who behave responsibly toward their class instead of someone else's. There is no reason, unless we count as reason the indignation flowing from a passionate hatred for oppression, to withhold from such people full respect and even admiration. . . . If we blind ourselves to everything noble, virtuous, honorable, decent, and selfless in a ruling class, how do we account for its hegemony? The people cannot long be held down by force alone, especially since so much of this force must be recruited from the lower orders of society [e.g., in the case of the antebellum South, from the non-slaveholding whites], nor are the people so cowardly as to accept arbitrary dictation forever.[11]

The preceding summary review of Genovese's position may seem an overlong preamble to his discussion of the origins, often plebeian, of the planter class in the South. Yet I think it necessary if we are to understand Genovese's account of what the Southern ruling class believed about themselves and about the world. I think it may also be necessary if the reader is to see that a real issue is involved in refusing to regard Sutpen as typical of the Southern "aristocrat."

To return specifically to the problem of the origins of the Mississippi planters: In *The World the Slaveholder Made,* Genovese provides a detailed criticism of what W.J. Cash had to say on this subject in his *The Mind of the South,* in 1941.[12] Genovese writes:

The ruling class [of the Old South, Cash] concludes, came from among "the strong, the pushing, the ambitious, among the old coon-hunting population of the back country." In a word, the ruling class of the South consisted mostly of rough and vulgar parvenus. No one doubts it. But one question does occur: Of what aristocratic or other ruling class could not the same be said? . . . The United States, being a frontier country, produced tough, competitive, acquisitive frontier types, and all frontier parvenus look rather alike. . . . The question remains: What social vision informed these men's dreams? What kind of life did they seek for

11. *In Red and Black* (New York: Vintage Books, 1972), p. 342.
12. This book has been enormously influential and its arguments and ideas lie behind much of the Faulknerian criticism of the last three decades. It shows itself very strongly in books like those cited earlier.

their children? Parvenus are parvenus, but bourgeois parvenus are not necessarily slaveholding parvenus once one gets beneath appearances. Cash has so far begged the question.

After alleging that the Virginians who went west generally failed miserably, Cash makes a small admission, which like most of his small admissions compromises his argument: "Some of them [some of the completely realized aristocrats and a great many more of those gentleman farmers who had grown up beside them] [13] did nevertheless succeed. There were few parts of the South, indeed, in which it was not possible to find two or three— occasionally a small colony—of them." Influence, not numbers, is here in question, and Virginia influence need not have meant a recapitulation of the Virginia experience. The questions come to these: Did the rising planters of the Southwest during the 1830's have before them, as an ideal future for themselves and their children, Virginia or Massachusetts? the Cavalier or the financier? Were they, in their economy and social relations, going down a bourgeois or an aristocratic road? [14]

Where does the foregoing argument leave Thomas Sutpen? The reader may be disposed to ask whether Genovese has not here provided Sutpen his card of admission into the planter aristocracy, such as it was in Yoknapatawpha County in the 1830s. Genovese's account certainly disposes of most of the bogus reasons for denying Sutpen a place among the country gentry, but on the positive side it does no more than put him on the road to aristocracy. Whether or not we judge that he took that road will depend on the values that he cherished and the course of conduct that he pursued as revealed in the novel itself.

One may remark in passing, however, that three of Sutpen's children were indeed well on the road to aristocracy. They show the distinct traits of the planter class, the admirable as well as the less admirable. One has no difficulty in imagining Judith, had better fortune befallen her, becoming the chatelaine of a great house.[15] But

---

13. The interpolated material, in this instance, is Genovese's.

14. *The World the Slaveholders Made,* pp. 138–39.

15. Faulkner has allowed even Miss Rosa to see this point clearly. She regards Judith as a lady, a woman who has been nurtured "to pass through the soft in-sulated and unscathed cocoon stages: bud, served prolific queen, then potent and soft-handed matriarch of old age's serene and well-lived content," but not because

in dire misfortune, her credentials become all the more evident. In her dress made of flour sacks, holding the handles of a plow as she walks behind her mule, she is still a lady by the definition of her society.

Henry, for all of Faulkner's comment on his naive and gangling country awkwardness, is a quixotic devotee of honor—as much as Quentin Compson himself. Once having met Charles Bon, he lives desperately and recklessly, and finally kills the man that he looks up to and admires—not for any conceivable practical motive, but for honor—distorted and twisted though we may hold his code of honor to be.

Sutpen's eldest child, Charles Bon, is, again, the aristocrat, whatever the genes he may carry, and not either because of his grace and languor and world-weary attitudes. Rather, because he too lives for honor and is willing to die—for he clearly knows that Henry will kill him—in order to vindicate what he regards as his only honorable course of action. One remembers that Quentin tells us that nobody ever did know whether Bon knew that he was Sutpen's son; but Quentin and Shreve, in their imaginative reconstruction of events, believe that he must have known all along. Shreve even believes that as a man of honor he required of his father no more than the faintest hint of recognition. If given that, he would have removed himself from Yoknapatawpha County and, in removing himself, removed his father's problem.

Our real concern here, however, is with the status of Thomas Sutpen himself. Are his values and attitudes toward life consonant with those of the Compsons and the McCaslins, the De Spains and the other planter families, or are they different? The novel makes plain that Sutpen's plantation neighbors sense that he is a different sort of person from themselves. Were they right in their perception? Does Thomas Sutpen reflect (in his vices as well as his virtues) a conception of reality that is essentially "American" rather than its "Southern" sub-variety? [16]

---

she was born a lady. She was a lady not "by blood, not even Coldfield blood," but rather "by the tradition in which Thomas Sutpen's ruthless will had carved a niche" (*Absalom, Absalom!*, p. 156).

16. The answer to this question is important, for if we can answer that Sutpen is essentially American, the relevance of his story to our present day is sharpened. His downfall becomes, then, not primarily a story of the downfall of the Old South (though, of course, it is inextricably involved with the culture of the Old South), but may make its commentary on the character of the national culture as well.

As we have noted earlier, Genovese fixes on paternalism as the controlling element in the social structure of the Old South. He tells us that "The distinctly Southern sense of *extended family* [italics mine] cannot be understood apart from the social structure at the center of which stood the plantation, and it provided a powerful impetus for social cohesion, ruling-class hegemony, and the growth of a paternalistic spirit that far transcended master-slave and white-black relationships." [17]

He concedes that there were "powerful counterpressures, especially those associated with the egalitarian ethos," but he insists, nevertheless, on the importance of "semipaternalistic relationships" to account for "the political power of the planters and much of that oft-noted loyalty of the nonslaveholders to the regime" that the planters dominated.[18]

The other Southern historian whose work throws special light on the South as having developed its own character and ethos is C. Vann Woodward. His views are by no means identical with those of Genovese. Woodward relies on a different set of basic assumptions and considers the problems of Southern history from his own angle of vision. For these very reasons his frequent corroborations of Genovese are significant. Genovese, by the way, applauds Woodward's criticism of Cash as being unique in its discernment of the "true character" of Cash's *Mind of the South*.[19] Both men stress the paternalistic character of the Old South, and some of Woodward's remarks on this subject are particularly helpful in pointing to its specifically English ancestry and explaining why, when developed into a theory of politics, it proved so attractive to the ruling class of Virginia.[20] Some aspects of Southern

17. *The World the Slaveholders Made*, pp. 100–101.

18. Ibid., p. 101. Faulkner has in his novels provided concrete instances of this loyalty and trust. Note, for example, the relation of Old Man Falls to "Old Bayard" Sartoris in *Sartoris*, and of George Wyatt to Colonel John Sartoris in *The Unvanquished*. Faulkner also gives us instances of loyalty betrayed and trust misplaced. A signal instance occurs in *Absalom, Absalom!* where Wash Jones finds that Thomas Sutpen has not acted like a man of honor and in his outrage cuts Sutpen down with his rusty scythe.

19. Ibid., p. 140.

20. See especially *American Counterpoint* (Boston, 1971), pp. 135–37, where he gives some account of Sir Robert Filmer's *Patriarcha*, a book which takes the family as the fundamental model for the state. His opponent, John Locke, accused Filmer of making "the rules of domestic society into principles of political science." Filmer's model in life was the gentry of his native county of Kent, a community of interrelated families. Colonial Virginia soon showed an analogous pattern and

paternalism as noted by Woodward will strike the general reader as startling. For example, with reference to white-black relationship, the antebellum paternalistic relationship did not turn into a "competitive" one until the old planter regime had waned; one consequence was that not until the late nineteenth century did Jim Crow cars come in, at the insistence of the poorer whites and over the opposition of what was left of the old planter stock.

If paternalism was essentially an extension into society and politics of familial attitudes and relationships, and if Woodward (and Genovese) are correct in their insistence that the society of the Old South was paternalistic, the implications for the story of Thomas Sutpen are interesting. Sutpen's "design" ostensibly puts great emphasis on the family. He told General Compson that to accomplish his design he would "require money, a house, a plantation, slaves, a family—incidentally of course a wife." Yet everything mentioned here is "incidental" to something else, the design—which for Sutpen is an abstraction: the choosing a wife because her father was the most respectable man in town (and Sutpen realized that he was woefully short on respectability); the begetting of children, essentially to have a male heir (though some use could also be found for a daughter in cementing an alliance with another planter family). But on any concrete personal level Sutpen's family life hardly exists. This is not to argue that the Filmerian patriarch was reincarnated in the Southern planter as the genial master, the kindly husband and father. The Filmerian patriarch was not necessarily genial. Some such patriarchs must have been petty tyrants or at least blustered as if they were.

The relationship of Sutpen with the members of his family is not, however, a relationship between persons at all. Sutpen is not kindly but he doesn't even bluster. So far as we are vouchsafed glimpses of his family life, his relations are coldly formal. (Judith, to be sure, does seem to have some sort of special relationship to her father: we infer that, at least, from Mr. Compson's account: see pp. 120–21.)

Sutpen's wife, Ellen, is silly, superficial, in love with money and position, and finally too trivial to arouse much sympathy. But her despairing cry to her younger sister, "At least save Judith," speaks volumes about her relationship to her husband. As for Sutpen's sons,

---

therefore, as Woodward remarks, the wonder is "that the patriarchs of Revolutionary Virginia should have [even] temporarily embraced Locke" and not that "their sons should have returned to Filmer" (p. 137).

they seem to have no more emotional relation to Sutpen than pieces in a chess game. They are, to be sure, the most important pieces on his board, and he plays them with all the cool detachment that he can command. In his desperation, he finally asks General Compson, without ever telling him what the real situation is, for advice—whether he ought to play his trump card; or, since I prefer the chess analogy, whether he should sacrifice perhaps his most important piece rather than retain it and risk checkmate. Sutpen's relation to Henry is not a father-son relationship. Frankly, it is difficult to imagine Sutpen's ever carrying the boy Henry on his back or jogging him on his knee. The importance that Sutpen attached to the family in his attempt to establish a dynasty in north Mississippi along with his complete inability to comprehend how one lives a family life is emblematic of his whole life-style.

Psychologically, Sutpen is the convert. Like Paul on the road to Damascus, he has been struck down by a blinding revelation. His having been turned away from the front door of the mansion by a black servant in livery proved to be traumatic. It altered his whole life. Yet, if you can't beat them, you'd best join them, and the boy Sutpen immediately modified this folk maxim to read: you can beat them only by joining them. From this time on, Sutpen is held in the grasp of a cold dream. Like the convert, he outdoes in his vehement orthodoxy those generations old in the faith.

One thinks of other analogies that apply to him. The child who does not know how to spell but insists on "writing" a word, and in the process painfully draws every cusp and serif of each letter, sometimes in its trusting ignorance making, by exaggeration of certain features of the type face, the word look unexpectedly strange. Sutpen has become fixated on the planter as an abstraction—not as a role actually lived, savored, and enjoyed. He has pursued an ideal of gracious ease and leisure with an almost breathless ferocity. Mr. Compson, on p. 34, speaks of Sutpen's "furious impatience," and on p. 43 mentions that Sutpen was never to be seen "loafing, [or] idling."

In fact, though Sutpen has dedicated his life to becoming the Tidewater planter, lying in his hammock in the shade, with his shoes off, receiving drinks brought to him by a servant (p. 228), he never lolls in a hammock.[21] Rather, he lives like a puritan ascetic under the pressure

21. Late in his life, Sutpen does subside a bit. He and Wash Jones do sit in the scuppernong arbor and drink whiskey from a gourd, but by this time the game is nearly played out.

of the Protestant Ethic. His being a Puritan does not, of course, prevent his being a Southerner. There was (and is today) a great deal of Puritanism in the South. But Sutpen's adherence to the Protestant Work Ethic does tend to mark him off from the typical Southern planter (who sometimes worked hard but rarely for the sake of work).

These matters are taken up by Woodward in his extremely interesting and often amusing essay entitled "The Southern Ethic in a Puritan World." [22] The South, to the despair of a people who have wished it well but insisted that it hustle more, has always reserved a large place for leisure. Woodward, to be sure, is properly cautious in drawing hard and fast conclusions, and he concedes that a concern for leisure may appear to another's more jaundiced eye as simply "laziness."

He makes it plain that the leisureliness is not in its origin racial; the Southern people had essentially the same heritage as those of New England, that hotbed of the Puritan Ethic, and in any case the Southerners lived in close proximity to the other parts of a republic that was bursting with energy and bent on industrial development. Woodward's point is that, in view of these circumstances, the wonder is that so many Southerners somehow escaped practicing the Puritan Ethic. Many Southerners did escape it, he avers, and in his summary of the special developments that occurred in the Southern states, he quotes Genovese's analysis of the pre-bourgeois spirit of the planters who "could not accept the idea that the cash nexus offered a permissible basis for human relations."

It would be excessive for me to claim that Sutpen, in each and every detail, exemplified the Puritan Ethic as opposed to that practiced by all the other Yoknapatawpha planters who exemplified what Woodward, more or less tongue-in-cheek, calls "the Southern ethic," or that they were all imbued with what Genovese calls "an aristocratic, antibourgeois spirit." Yet some of Woodward's description of the Protestant Ethic does apply tellingly to Sutpen. Thus, Woodward quotes from Ernst Troeltsch's *Protestantism and Progress*: "For this spirit displays an untiring activity . . . it makes work and gain an end in themselves. . . . it brings the whole of life and action within the sphere of *an absolutely rationalised and systematic calculation*. . . ." [23] (italics mine). The last phrase applies to Sutpen in precise detail.

The planter's inability "to accept the idea that the cash nexus offered a permissible basis for human relations" did not hold true for

22. *American Counterpoint*, pp. 13–46.
23. Ibid., pp. 28–29.

Thomas Sutpen. He felt that his first wife had no reason to object to his breaking up their marriage since he was willing to make a just and even generous property settlement for her benefit. But General Compson is shocked when he learns about the transaction from Sutpen's own mouth.

The cash nexus, however, does accord perfectly with the values of the father of Sutpen's *second* wife. Mr. Coldfield is a "puritan," or, if we want to be more precise, we may call him an evangelical Protestant. (He was the pillar of Jefferson's Methodist church, a small store owner, and noted both for his strict probity and his "close trading.")

Coldfield, by the way, takes the concept of the cash nexus further than most of Jefferson's other shop-keepers and evangelicals. He manumits his slaves, an act for which Faulkner gives him proper credit. He provides them with a weekly wage and thus allows them to purchase freedom when they have accumulated enough credit to balance what they would bring on the slave market. Here, perhaps, especially since Coldfield is not rich, one should not be censorious. But according to Mr. Compson, Coldfield carried matters further still; on Sunday, when Coldfield and his daughter always drove to Sutpen's Hundred for noonday dinner, Coldfield would dock the wages of the two Negroes "for the noon meal which they would not have to prepare and (so the town believed) he charged [them] for the crude one of left-overs which they would have to eat." As Mr. Compson reports it, for Coldfield it is all a matter of accurate accounting and good business.

Faulkner was evidently fascinated by Mr. Coldfield's shopkeeper's mentality. He was not at all content to dismiss it with a sardonic shrug. Thus, he has Mr. Compson tell his son that Coldfield's real objection to the Civil War was not "so much to the idea of pouring out human blood and life, but at the idea of waste: of wearing out and eating up and shooting away material in any cause whatever" (p. 83); and through Mr. Compson's lips Faulkner comments on the nature of Coldfield's religious life: "Doubtless the only pleasure which [Coldfield] had ever had was not in the meager spartan hoard which he had accumulated . . . not in the money but in its representation of a balance in whatever spiritual countinghouse he believed would some day pay his sight drafts on self-denial and fortitude" (p. 84). In short, Mr. Compson surmises that Coldfield conceived of God as a just and omnipotent banker. Self-denial here on earth will prove to be an eventually excellent investment.

For our present purposes, it doesn't much matter whether Mr.

Compson is expressing the author's judgment or merely his own. For Mr. Compson himself is sufficiently typical of the old planter stock to show the difference in their attitudes and values from those of Cold-field, that true-blue representative of bourgeois values and the Protestant gospel of work.

In the years in which Faulkner was at work on *Absalom, Absalom!*, the observations that I have been quoting from Genovese and Woodward were still to be written. But Faulkner obviously did not need to read them. He had absorbed, from traditional sources, from what he saw in the world about him, and from conversations heard and stories told, all that he needed to know in order to arrive at a just conception of the "kind of world the slave-holders of the Old South had made" and the relation of that world to those dominated by quite different values. But though Faulkner obviously did not need to read the books from which I have been quoting, the contemporary reader of Faulkner's fiction may well profit from the more general and systematical account of these matters that a first-rate historian can give; such reading may well confirm the reader's confidence in the penetration of Faulkner's insight into the culture that produced him.

To sum up: the irony of Sutpen's life is (in part at least) that he was fixated on his image of the plantation which for him was an abstract idea—since he had had scant participation in it as lived experience—and that, as we have said, Sutpen pursued an ideal of gracious ease and leisure, with a breathless ferocity. Sutpen's spiritual kinship to Melville's Ahab has frequently been argued. It is justly argued, and if one asks what was the white whale that Sutpen pursued, it was, symbolically at least, the same creature that Ahab pursued: Being, itself, in its mysterious and finally incorrigible otherness. Reality must be captured and put to Sutpen's own purposes.

As I have noted elsewhere some of the more obvious traits that mark Sutpen as the typical ascetic, as the man whose appetites are in his head, not in his belly or his loins, and as the man in love with blueprints and schedules, time tables and designs, there is no need to repeat in detail here.[24] But I think that some of the traits that mark Sutpen as a rationalist, as a planner, as a man possessed of a certain megalomania, may be profitably developed somewhat further, especially as these traits are related to the American dream and are shared by other obsessed Americans who take leave of reality in order to live in a dream world.

24. See *William Faulkner: The Yoknapatawpha Country*, pp. 301–03, 306.

The best proof that Thomas Sutpen is an obsessed man, living in a private dream that has little relation to reality, is what he does and doesn't do when Charles Bon appears on the Yoknapatawpha scene. He refuses to give him any hint of recognition. Presumably, he tells Henry the truth, or part of the truth about Bon, and later on, if Quentin and Shreve are correct in their conjectures, during the war, when he has become more desperate, he tells the rest of the truth to Henry, namely, that Charles Bon is not only his son but has some Negro blood.

That action is certainly effective in preventing Bon's marriage to Judith. But by inciting Henry to murder his half-brother, Sutpen has dealt a mortal blow to his own design, for with Henry's disappearance from the scene, Sutpen is deprived of the heir that he regards as absolutely necessary to the design. Not even Henry VIII wanted a legitimate male heir more intensely. Sutpen is forced to start all over.

So powerfully has Faulkner developed our belief in Sutpen's deep commitment to his design and his inflexible will that few readers have felt his conduct to have been other than inevitable. Yet a little cool reflection will indicate that a man less obsessed than Sutpen might have saved his design at what, for many men, would have seemed a bargain price. How, for example, might his only real friend among the planters, General Compson, have handled the matter?

Whatever the General's faults, an inhumanly calculating spirit was evidently not one of them. His expression of real shock at Sutpen's assumption that intimate human problems could find an adequate solution through a cash settlement (p. 265) is obviously genuine. It is hard to believe that he would have withheld from a part-Negro son all recognition of his paternity. (Shreve believes that a gesture of recognition on Sutpen's part would have been enough, and perhaps Shreve was right.) But even if General Compson had lacked the humanity to acknowledge his son, he still would not have acted as Sutpen did. Secure in his confidence in his own dignity and standing in the world, he would never have supposed that his whole world would be smashed to pieces if it had come out that the strange young man who had appeared in the village was his son. Sutpen told General Compson that if he allowed certain things to take their course, his design would complete itself "to the public eye" with full success, "quite naturally and normally." The rub was that to Sutpen's own eye it would have been "a mockery and a betrayal" (p. 274). Though General Compson did not know what Supten regarded as the particular flaw in his first wife, he had no doubt what the real trouble was: Sutpen was "fog-bound by his own private embattlement of personal morality" (p. 271). If Sutpen had not been obsessed with the detail of his private dream, he would not have needed to repudiate his first wife and their child. General Compson believed that whatever the blemish or fault in her, Sutpen "could have closed his eyes [to it] and, if not fooled the rest of the world . . . , at least have frightened any man out of speaking the secret aloud . . ." (p. 266).

In view of what is usually written about *Absalom, Absalom!*, the basic security of Sutpen's position needs to be stressed.[25] Suppose that it had become known, either through Sutpen's action or Bon's, that Bon was his son; what, in view of the laws and customs of the time, could Bon have done? He might have created a certain amount of talk. As we have already observed, Sutpen was never truly popular in the community. But with his hundred square miles of plantation and his respectable marriage to Ellen Coldfield, Sutpen could probably have outfaced any charge of bigamy, and by letting the community know that Bon was part-Negro, could have disposed of any notion that Henry was not his legitimate heir.

Yet if Sutpen had told the truth at once, would he not have lost Henry just the same? Perhaps he would have, but if he had spoken early and with some fatherly consideration, he might have improved his chances of holding Henry's allegiance. (We should remember that Henry apparently knew all his life that the mulatto girl Clytie, who was brought up in the same household with him and Judith, was his half-sister. There is no hint in the novel that his knowledge caused any break in Henry's relations with his father.) If the reconstruction of events made by Quentin and Shreve is correct, Sutpen broke the final truth to Henry in the worst possible way.

The conditions of antebellum society in the South, as reflected in Faulkner's novel or as presented in history, did not, then, of them-selves determine Thomas Sutpen's fate. His case was more special and, as in every authentic tragedy, was finally attributable to his own char-

25. In his other novels, Faulkner gives us two other examples of Yoknapatawpha planters who sired mulatto children: Old Carothers McCaslin and Colonel John Sartoris. Their cases are not precisely parallel to Sutpen's, but it may be significant that neither came to grief because of having begotten a part-Negro child. McCaslin, who added incest to miscegenation, made a kind of acknowledgment of his son-grandson. His white sons at least knew, though it is not made plain whether or not it was public knowledge. We are not told whether anyone but Colonel Sartoris and the child's mother knew that he had a mulatto daughter.

acter. In sum, it was Sutpen's fanatical insistence that events conform to his private dream that brought about his downfall.

Though Thomas Sutpen is fixated on the details of Southern planter society, a doctrinaire fixation of this sort has a very wide general reference. In fact, it is a characteristically "American" aberration. (One is almost tempted to say an American neurosis.) Sutpen's naive confidence in his own ability to realize his dream is a function of what General Compson called Sutpen's "innocence." C. Vann Woodward speaks very precisely to the "American" quality of this innocence:

> American opulence and American success have combined to foster and encourage another legend of early origin, the legend of American innocence. According to this legend Americans achieved a sort of regeneration of sinful man by coming out of the wicked Old World and removing to an untarnished new one. . . . They were a chosen people and their land a Utopia on the make.[26]

But the South was quite another matter. Woodward goes on to say that "in the tortured conscience of the South" there was scant room for "this national self-image of innocence." An "age-long experience with human bondage and its evils and later with emancipation and its shortcomings did not dispose the South very favorably toward such popular American ideas as the doctrine of human perfectibility." [27] The "tortured conscience of the South" and the experience of tragedy are parts of the Southern heritage. One supposes that these were a part of General Compson's heritage. At any rate, they were clearly an important part of Faulkner's, but he gives no hint that they were any part of Sutpen's heritage.

Does American literature yield instances of "innocence" in the American style? Yes, many. Two rather obvious instances are to be found in Christopher Newman (in Henry James's *The American*) and Jay Gatsby (in Scott Fitzgerald's *The Great Gatsby*). In an article printed some years ago [28] I pointed out that both were self-made men (like Sutpen) and that they were dominated by a self-generated ideal.

26. "The Search for Southern Identity," *The Burden of Southern History* (Baton Rouge, La., 1960), pp. 19–20.

27. Ibid., pp. 20–21.

28. "The American 'Innocence' in James, Fitzgerald and Faulkner," *Shenandoah* 15 (1964) : 21–37; reprinted in *A Shaping Joy*, 1971.

Each pursues his private dream with almost cold-blooded pertinacity. Newman had determined to marry an aristocratic young French noble-woman and came perhaps within a hair of doing so, but he never seems to be really in love with her, though he admires her excessively and tells his confidante that he wants "a great woman . . . that is one thing I can treat myself to . . . I want to possess, in a word, the best article on the market." When his confidante reproaches him for being "so cold-blooded and calculating," he tells her that to win the most beautiful wife "a man . . . needs only to use his will, and such wits as he has, and to try." The words might almost have been spoken by Thomas Sutpen himself.

Jay Gatsby is not cold-blooded and calculating in this fashion. His passion for Daisy is consuming. But like Sutpen, he has organized his life according to a plan, he works to a schedule, and in his own kind of innocence he ignores the complications of reality. When his friend warns him that he has little chance of winning Daisy back to himself, suggesting, out of kindness, that no one can repeat the past, Gatsby cries out incredulously, "Can't repeat the past? Why, of course you can." It would be nonsense to equate the personalities of Newman, Gatsby, and Sutpen, and yet all are much too confident that by sheer will power they can adjust the world to their own dreams—make it conform to a particular "design."

It was a stroke of genius on Faulkner's part to set down in a society generally regarded as special in nearly every sense and certainly regarded as quite "un-American"—the slaveholding society of the Old South—an extreme example of "American" innocence. Sutpen, pos-sessed by an almost malignant demon of abstraction, is a shocking figure, but, we must remember, he also shocks his Yoknapatawpha neighbors. We naturally expect him to treat his slaves as things "adjunctive" to his design, but so does he treat his own children. He does not exemplify the "paternalism" that Genovese finds to be typical of the Southern planter. Paternalism, of course, can be cruel. History and literature abound in overbearing fathers. But Sutpen's treatment of other human beings, including his own flesh and blood, is some-thing else. His ruthless acts are not the occasional outbursts of a choleric father but the calculated machinations of a man completely absorbed in his cold dream of self-vindication.

Appendix B

THE NARRATIVE STRUCTURE OF
Absalom, Absalom!

EVERYONE CONCEDES that *Absalom, Absalom!* has its difficulties. The reader gets the story in bits and pieces, in a non-sequential order, with many flashbacks into the past. Moreover, the story is refracted through the minds of several different persons, each mind having its own prejudices, blindsides, and mental sets. Finally, some of the most moving and terribly poignant scenes are admittedly imaginary reconstructions —conjectures upon, and interpretations of, a sparse and disordered body of facts.

Nevertheless, *Absalom, Absalom!* has registered on most readers with astonishing impact. Except for those few who dash through the novel and then throw up their hands in disgust or despair, as if the author had played a deliberate trick on them, most readers, even those who confess their failure to comprehend every element of the story, testify to the novel's tragic grandeur. Faulkner's way of telling the story thus finally vindicates itself: the nonspecialist, wayfaring reader gets a great deal—more than God's plenty—from this powerful fiction.

Perhaps one ought to be content with such a state of affairs, and leave matters at this not unsatisfactory stage. But human nature being what it is, most of us do want to probe further. When, if ever, did Bon discover that he had Negro blood? Was he truly in love with his half-sister Judith? Would Henry have accepted the incestuous marriage between Bon and Judith had it not been for Bon's mixed blood?

There has been, therefore, a great deal of speculation about what really happens in *Absalom, Absalom!,* as the appearance of dozens of articles and discussions of the subject in books about Faulkner sufficiently attests. Some commentators argue that Faulkner has indulged in deliberate mystification: the problems of the novel are insoluble because he meant them to be.

There are, to be sure, obvious elements of the Sutpen story about which we can never arrive at certainty—matters of motivation and ultimate purpose that are involved in the mystery of the human spirit itself. About these, it is proper that we should be asked to use our imaginations and make our own interpretations. The great Shakespeare himself asks no less. But if the objection is that Faulkner has indulged in cheap mystery-mongering, planting clues that are bound to mislead the reader and playing cheap games with the reader's attempt to make sense of the story, then I must disagree. I shall claim that the basic structure of the story of Sutpen does come clear in the novel and that we never come up against a sheer blank wall.

Other commentators argue that Faulkner has been careless and forgetful. They call attention to dangling loose ends, elements of an earlier design that obtrude themselves on what represents itself as the finished fabric. Gerald Langford, for example, finds contradictory passages that go back to Faulkner's earlier conceptions of the plot, passages that remain to disturb the consistency and coherence of the novel as published.[1]

I agree that the Texas manuscript studied by Langford indicates that Faulkner radically altered (and more than once) his original conception of the plot. I admit that there are a good many minor inconsistencies that have come about through Faulkner's forgetting to alter certain dates or facts. But I shall argue that the novel is essentially coherent and its parts self-consistent. Clearly, the final draft needed better editing and proofreading than it got; nevertheless, one who reads with imagination *and* common sense will find that the novel is not embarrassed by any important self-contradiction.

I am convinced that the best strategy for refuting the notion that Faulkner has deliberately tried to baffle the reader, or that he has been careless in setting forth the Sutpen story, is to examine the stages by which it is unfolded to Quentin and the stages by which Quentin in turn unfolds it to his roommate Shreve. Though this method of examination may seem pedantic, I think that, in view of the present state of Faulkner criticism, it is necessary.

1. See the introduction to *Faulkner's Revision of "Absalom, Absalom!"* (Austin, Texas, 1971).

Besides, an examination of how Quentin acquired his knowledge and how he chose to divulge it to Shreve has an important positive side. It can tell us a good deal about Quentin's character and perhaps explain his diffidence in talking to Shreve about the Sutpen story. (One notices that it is the *outsider*, Shreve, who does most of the talking about Sutpen in that cold Harvard dormitory room.) More important still, an examination of the way in which the story of Sutpen is revealed to Quentin and by him to Shreve—and so through both modes, to the reader—can illuminate the most brilliant and audacious technique for fictional presentation to be found anywhere in Faulkner.

In order to be concise and yet clear, I shall try to distinguish the various strata of Quentin's knowledge.

STRATUM A

TIME: *From Quentin's boyhood until the time of the quail-hunt, which is probably to be dated in the fall of 1907 or 1908.*

CONTENT: *During this period Quentin apparently knew the Sutpen story in general detail: Sutpen's arrival in Jefferson as a stranger, the great mansion that he built, his service in the Civil War, Henry's murder of Judith's fiancé, and Sutpen's own violent death.*

When Quentin was listening to Miss Rosa on the subject in September of 1909, her talk seemed "mostly about that which he already knew" (p. 31). Quentin as a boy had seen the Sutpen mansion. With four other boys, he had had a glimpse of Clytie and Jim Bond in the cabin behind the mansion (pp. 213–14).

One is tempted to date this event in 1904 or 1905 (when Quentin was thirteen or fourteen). At this time, Clytie and Bond were apparently not living in the big house, to which Henry returned in 1905 (p. 373). We can't be sure, of course, that Clytie ever moved back into the big house, but she and Bond were in it when Quentin and Miss Rosa appeared on their night visit in 1909 (p. 369). Incidentally, did the travelers who tried "to stop and spend the night" (p. 213) in the Sutpen mansion hear noises emanating from Henry's room upstairs? Was Henry the ghost that sent them away in panic "until they reached Jefferson?" The people of Jefferson evidently heard about their scare. Was it this story that gave Miss Rosa the notion that Henry might possibly have returned? Did it enable her to be so precise as to date? She tells Quentin (p. 172), "It has been out there for four years," i.e., since 1905.

STRATUM B

TIME: *The quail hunt in the autumn of 1907 or 1908.*

CONTENT: *What Mr. Compson told Quentin in the talk that was set off by their visit to the Sutpen graves (pp. 187–214).*

The quail hunt must have taken place some years after the period when Quentin still considered himself a boy. The character of his own thoughts about the Sutpen graves and the language in which his father speaks to him about the Sutpens (on pp. 187–215) imply that he was now a youth nearing college age. The year would have to be earlier than 1909 because of the following circumstances. The season for hunting game birds is autumn, but the autumn of 1909, in which Quentin left to enter Harvard, is impossible, for on the day of the hunt that took Quentin and his father to the vicinity of the Sutpen graves, the whole countryside was sodden with rain (p. 187). Yet when Quentin and Miss Rosa paid their visit to Sutpen's Hundred early in September (p. 10) no rain had fallen for some sixty days (p. 175).

Would it not have been possible, however, for the quail hunt to have taken place *after* Quentin's visit to Sutpen's Hundred but before he left for Harvard, later in September? The answer has to be no. For after Quentin had discovered that Sutpen was living in the house and had reported the fact to his father (see pp. 309–10, below), it is unthinkable that they could have teased Luster about the house's being haunted, making jesting remarks such as "Come on in out of the rain. I won't let the old Colonel hurt you" (pp. 213–14).

It is difficult to say how much was new to Quentin in Mr. Compson's additions to the Sutpen story on the occasion of the quail hunt. I am inclined to think that some of the items were new: the visit of the octoroon woman to Bon's grave; Judith's bringing Bon's child to live at Sutpen's Hundred; the town's belief that Judith was the mother of the child; the subsequent life of Charles Etienne and his death and the circumstances of Judith's death. Against this supposition must be balanced Quentin's reflections that he has had to listen to "too much, too long," or that he "didn't need to listen" (p. 211), or that he was not listening "because [he] knew it all already, had learned, absorbed it already without the medium of speech" (p. 212). It may be that my stipulated Stratum B cannot in fact be separated from Stratum A. If so, that fact doesn't matter so far as my general argument is concerned, though I have the feeling that on the occasion of the quail hunt Mr. Compson brought at least a wealth of circumstantial detail to whatever Quentin already knew. Moreover, one has the sense that Quentin is now no longer the mere boy who with Luster and three other boys of their age had found himself on the grounds of the ruinous Sutpen mansion, an obvious "haunted" house.

STRATUM C

TIME: *An afternoon in early September, 1909 (p. 10).*

CONTENT: *What Miss Rosa told Quentin before they drove out that evening to Sutpen's Hundred (pp. 9–30, 134–72).*

We have earlier remarked that in 1909 Quentin was listening "mostly [to] that which he already knew" (p. 31) and presumably the statement would also apply to what Quentin heard through the September afternoon from Miss Rosa. But hearing the story from Miss Rosa's lips was in itself new (p. 10), and whether or not Quentin learned many new facts, he was given Miss Rosa's perspective on the story. She speaks out of her hatred and outrage—and ignorance. For she presumably knows nothing about Sutpen's boyhood and his traumatic experience at the door of a great house in the Virginia Tidewater.[2] It is small wonder that, to her, his conduct could have sprung from a motiveless malignancy and that he had to be seen not as a man but a demon.

Quentin learned from Miss Rosa (or might have learned if he had been listening) about the racing to church (p. 23), Ellen's begging her sister to protect the children from themselves (p. 27), Sutpen's having married for the sake of respectability (p. 16 and p. 28 and confirmed by Mr. Compson on p. 37), Sutpen's fighting with his slaves and the

2. On page 8 we are told that while Quentin sat in the room and listened to Miss Rosa's voice, Sutpen would "abrupt" with "his band of wild niggers" and among them "the French architect" (see also p. 16). But whether Miss Rosa knew that Sutpen had brought his Negroes from the West Indies is not clear. Miss Rosa makes no reference to Haiti or to the first wife.

two children's different responses to witnessing the fighting (pp. 29–30 and 136). Since Miss Rosa didn't see the fight, she probably learned about it from her sister Ellen. But the fighting itself was generally known in the town: Mr. Compson alludes to it on page 259.

Pages 134–72 of chapter v are printed in italics except for a part of the very last page. This long italicized passage represents an unbroken monologue from the lips of Miss Rosa—presumably while Quentin sat in the room (p. 172). Miss Rosa's long harangue begins in mid-career. It does not follow on directly from page 30, where Miss Rosa's talks about the Sutpens breaks off.[3] Moreover, on page 134 her telling abruptly resumes, without any preliminaries. She is talking about her ride out to Sutpen's Hundred with Wash, who had come into Jefferson to tell her—according to Mr. Compson's account on page 133—that Henry had "Kilt [Bon] dead as a beef." In chapter I (p. 18), she had dealt with this matter in a most summary fashion. There she had said only that "I saw Henry repudiate his home and birthright and then return and practically fling the bloody corpse of his sister's sweetheart at the hem of her wedding gown. . . ." In the course of chapter v, Miss Rosa treats not only her ride with Wash out to Sutpen's Hundred, but subsequent events—and many earlier events—in great detail. Presumably through the whole time Quentin is sitting in the room with her; yet the author tells us on page 172 that "Quentin was not listening. . . ."

He was not listening, we are told, "because there was also something which he too could not pass—that door, the running feet on the stairs . . . , the two women, the negress and the white girl in her underthings. . . ." In sum, Quentin was not listening to Miss Rosa's account because his imagination remained gripped by the confrontation between Henry and Judith when Henry bursts into her room to tell her he has killed her fiancé.

This is a scene which Miss Rosa could not have personally witnessed; and though she may, nevertheless, have been capable of giving a detailed account of it, the reader does not hear her do so anywhere in chapter v. We have already remarked that her monologue begins on page 134 abruptly, without such preliminaries as her first sentence

3. It has been suggested that chapter v has to do with what Miss Rosa told Quentin as they rode out to Sutpen's Hundred, but Miss Rosa's question ("Do you mark how the wistaria, sun-impacted on the wall here, distills and penetrates this room . . . ?", p. 143) makes it clear that she is speaking not in the buggy but in her own house.

("So they will have told you doubtless . . .") would suggest. Perhaps she had given Quentin an account of the murder and Henry's bursting into Judith's room at some time before her monologue suddenly resumes on page 134; but one should note the consequences of this reasonable deduction. If it was the scene of Henry's confrontation with Judith which so arrested Quentin's attention that he couldn't "listen" to Miss Rosa, then, if we take the author's statement literally, Quentin didn't listen to *anything* that was said in chapter v.

We are probably not to take the statement literally. Throughout the novel, Quentin manifests an irritated fatigue at having to hear over and over a story that was evidently peculiarly painful to him, and yet to which he felt forced to listen. Perhaps the author means that in chapter v Quentin was listening to Miss Rosa with only half his mind.

To at least one incident in Miss Rosa's account Quentin obviously did listen: Sutpen's greeting of Judith when he returned, and her brief tears. Compare page 159 with page 277. Even if we assign the speech on page 277 to Shreve rather than Quentin—there seems to be some textual confusion here—the result is the same: Shreve must have heard it from Quentin, and it is more likely that Quentin heard it from Miss Rosa than from his father.

Whether or not Quentin was listening or merely sitting there bemused, the reader, of course, has the benefit of Miss Rosa's account. The reader at least learns about the burial of Bon and of Judith's stoical calm. He also learns a great deal about Miss Rosa—of her childhood, her vicarious participation in Judith's love for Bon, of her life at Sutpen's Hundred after Bon's death, of Sutpen's return from the war, of his proposal of marriage, and his later proposal that they mate without benefit of clergy to see whether they can produce a son.

Whether or not Quentin needed, in order to come to an understanding of the Sutpen story, the information provided by Miss Rosa in chapter v, the reader of *Absalom, Absalom!* does indeed need it and is grateful to get it. For one thing, the reader needs to know more about Miss Rosa's mind and personality if he is to understand her outrage and to gain a knowledge of certain aspects of Sutpen's personality.

One further question obtrudes itself, however—why has Faulkner sandwiched *between* chapters i and v (in both of which we hear Miss Rosa talking to Quentin) Mr. Compson's conversation with Quentin (chapters ii–iv), a conversation that took place later on in the day? Presumably because Faulkner wanted to refocus our attention on Miss Rosa just before she and Quentin started their journey out to

Sutpen's Hundred. That journey presumably began very soon after Mr. Compson's concluding words on page 133, at the very end of chapter IV.

Did Faulkner, however, have any right to revert so arbitrarily to a speech—one can hardly call Miss Rosa's monologue a conversation—that took place somewhat *earlier* in the afternoon? One has to answer: every right. We must remind ourselves that in spite of the many conversations between characters and the long reveries and monologues of a single character, *Absalom, Absalom!* is finally a novel written in the third person by an omniscient author. Faulkner is noted for his use of flashbacks and time-shifts. In any case, the proof of an aesthetic pudding, like that of any other kind of pudding, lies in the eating; and readers who have sometimes been troubled by other matters in the novel have never expressed—so far as I know—any complaints about Faulkner's placing the material of chapter V *after* that of chapters II, III, and IV.

STRATUM D

TIME: *Sometime after five o'clock of the same afternoon as Quentin's call on Miss Rosa.*

CONTENT: *What Mr. Compson told Quentin on pages 31–133.*

Though we are told on page 31 that Quentin heard "mostly about that which he already knew," Mr. Compson does give him a rather consecutive account of Sutpen's arrival in Jefferson, his "dreams of grim and castlelike magnificence," his building his great mansion, and, after two years, completing and furnishing it; of his courtship and marriage to Ellen Coldfield; of the shady deal in which he involved his father-in-law; of Charles Bon's coming home with Henry for a Christmas visit; of the understanding between Judith and Bon; of the rupture between Henry and his father at Christmas in 1860; of the outbreak of the War; of the letter written to Judith by Bon in 1865 (which Mr. Compson actually shows to Quentin); and of Henry's shooting Bon in 1865 at the very gates of Sutpen's Hundred.

It is noteworthy that Mr. Compson provides in passing a few hints about Sutpen's life prior to his coming to Jefferson. There are references to Sutpen's possessing Spanish coins (p. 34); to the fact that the slaves Sutpen brought with him could not speak English (p. 36); and to the fact that Sutpen at the age of fourteen had "set out into a world which even in theory he knew nothing about, and with a fixed goal in his mind (p. 53). Mr. Compson also refers to a child born to Sutpen before Sutpen had come to Jefferson (p. 62); and Mr. Compson even makes reference to "Sutpen's fierce and overweening vanity or desire for magnificence or for vindication or whatever it was . . ." (p. 38).

In view of later revelations about Sutpen's life, items of this sort become very important. But Mr. Compson in this early chapter seems to attach no great importance to them, and Quentin, though he asks occasional questions of his father, never shows an interest in following up any of these matters. He does not, for example, ask his father into what world Sutpen "set out," though knowing nothing about it.

STRATUM E

TIME: *On toward midnight of the same day on which he had listened to Miss Rosa and his father.*

CONTENT: *Quentin discovered that Henry was (as Miss Rosa had guessed) in hiding at Sutpen's Hundred; and he learned that Charles Bon was Sutpen's son by his first marriage.*

We learn that Quentin saw Henry (p. 373) and that he did discover the secret of Bon's parentage on the occasion described (p. 266 and 274), but we are not told precisely how the secret was divulged or by whom. These matters will be discussed later.

STRATUM F

TIME: *Probably the next day after Quentin's visit to Sutpen's Hundred.*

CONTENT: *Presumably that Bon and his mother had been repudiated by Sutpen because she was of mixed blood, that Sutpen told Henry that Bon was his brother when Henry brought Bon home as his guest for Christmas of 1860, and that Henry shot his friend to prevent Bon's marrying his half-sister or because Bon had a trace of Negro blood.*

309

With the last item of the statement of contents just given above, we get into the realm of conjecture, and, as every reader knows, the later chapters of *Absalom, Absalom!* are filled with conjectures, most of them proposed by Shreve, though many of them, it would seem, are silently endorsed by Quentin. In this essay, however, I shall be concerned only incidentally, if at all, with the conjectures—important as they are for the novel and plausible as many of them will seem to most readers. The purpose of this study is to establish the facts—provable or highly probable.

It is no mere conjecture, however, that Quentin told his father, and almost at once, what he had discovered at Sutpen's Hundred. (See page 266 and page 181—*"if father had known as much about it the night before I went out there as he did the day after I came back. . . ."*) With this key piece in the puzzle retrieved, Quentin and his father must have been able very quickly to make out the basic facts—including the probability that the "defect" in Sutpen's first wife which caused him to repudiate her and their child was her possession of Negro blood. Many other important matters would be subjects of speculation —for instance, how much of the facts Bon actually knew, or the precise motivation of Henry in shooting his best friend. But Sutpen's opposition to the marriage of Bon and Judith would become obvious, and Henry's killing his best friend (though waiting to the last minute to fire the shot) would no longer be a mystery and a puzzle.

It is important to realize how much Quentin knew when he came to Harvard. He clearly grasped the essential story. He had actually spoken with two of the chief actors in the tragedy. He had been affected by it powerfully and for personal reasons. If we wish to take into account what we know of Quentin from *The Sound and the Fury,* Quentin could share Henry's fascination with, and yet dread of, incest, through his feelings for his own sister. But Quentin could not uphold the family honor or protect his sister from a sexual interloper whom he despised. Henry had loved Bon like a brother, yet even so had been able to make the horrifying choice and had been able to act. But Quentin has seen with his own eyes the price that Henry paid. Though he cannot abide the emptied unheroic world in which he feels he is condemned to live, the heroic world is a terrible world—it demands so much. Even if it were available to him, Quentin knows he could not live up to its standards. What is there left for him but suicide? Here Quentin is the true samurai. Disgraced in his own eyes, he will later carry out his own version of a bloodless hara-kiri.

Moreover, if we are fully aware of how much Quentin already knows, we may be the less surprised at his reluctance to enter into Shreve's game of speculation—even though his speculations amount to shrewd and probably true guesses as to what Henry thought or why Bon acted as he did. Shreve, the outsider, to whom the imaginative reconstruction of events is a game at which he wants to "play," leads the way in the later chapters.

Again, if we are aware of how much Quentin felt involved in, and how much he was shaken by, his encounter with Henry, we can better understand why he shrank from having to repeat certain experiences, even in memory—though he sometimes did repeat them compulsively. These latter considerations will be seen to apply to certain incidents that apparently he withheld from Shreve until very late in the day—notably the precise way in which he learned of Bon's parentage.

It is more difficult—and perhaps less profitable—to try to set forth the various layers of Shreve's knowledge of the Sutpen story. Presumably, long before 13 or 14 January 1910, when he probably delivered to Quentin Mr. Compson's letter of 10 January 1910, he had learned the Sutpen story in its general outlines.

When Shreve comes in with the letter telling of Miss Rosa's death, Shreve affects not to believe that she was not Quentin's aunt, or at least a cousin: "You mean . . . that there was actually one Southern Bayard or Guinevere who was no kin to you?" (p. 174). We are told that this was not Shreve's first time—was indeed "nobody's first time in Cambridge since September"—to demand: "Tell about the South" (p. 174). Thus, one has a right to assume that very early in their acquaintance at Harvard, Shreve learned from Quentin about Miss Rosa and the Sutpens. When Mr. Compson's letter arrives, Shreve shows that he already possesses a good deal of information about Miss Rosa and Thomas Sutpen. He is able to rattle off at once the account of their relations (which he must have got from Quentin, perhaps weeks before) that occupies pages 176–81. His recapitulation of the story, however, makes it plain that at this point he does not at all understand the driving force behind Sutpen. For him, Sutpen is a kind of restless freak who gets into marriage and then extricates himself from it and then gets back into it for no accountable reason (pp. 180–81). But even by this time, Shreve evidently knows that Charles Bon was Sutpen's son, for he knows as much as Mr. Compson knew *"the day after [Quentin] came back* [from Sutpen's Hundred]" (p. 181), and

Quentin at that time must have told his father that he had discovered that Henry and Charles were half-brothers. But there is ample evidence that Quentin had not informed Shreve of *how* he had come by this information (see pp. 266 and 274).

At some time or other during his first months at Harvard (the autumn of 1909), Quentin must also have told Shreve about Mr. Compson's conjecture as to why Sutpen forbade the marriage of Judith to Charles—namely, that Sutpen was certain that Bon already had an octoroon mistress in New Orleans. But when Quentin told Shreve about his father's notion, he (and presumably Shreve also) must have been aware that it had no validity: there was a far more formidable impediment to the marriage. Why, then, does Shreve refer to the hypothesis at this point (p. 266)? Because Quentin has for the last few minutes been talking (on pp. 265–66) as if Mr. Compson *did* know that Henry and Charles were half-brothers. No wonder that Shreve interrupts Quentin to ask "If [your father] knew all this, what was his reason for telling you that the trouble between Henry and Bon was the octoroon woman?" The query prompts Quentin to explain that it was only later on that Mr. Compson learned the truth and that he learned it from Quentin himself.

In sum, Quentin must have told Shreve much of the Sutpen story at one time or another, but he had not told the story coherently. He had neglected to fill in certain gaps. Some matters, Quentin seems almost pointedly to have sheered away from. Later on in the novel we shall come to see why. Quentin's mode of telling the Sutpen story with gaps and omissions makes dramatic sense. He is not writing a short story: he is talking with a college roommate and he is in large part responding to the degree of interest that his friend manifests.

On this evening in mid-January, Shreve's interest has revived and has risen to a new height as a result of the letter that Quentin has received from his father a few hours earlier (p. 173). The letter is important: it is referred to again and again throughout the evening, on pages 207, 217, and 377, where the reading of it is completed.

Because Shreve, by the time he enters the novel (at the beginning of chapter vi, page 173), already knows the basic facts about the Sutpen story, it will be expedient to indicate from this point on only what he evidently did not know when Mr. Compson's letter arrived. In the first place, Quentin had presumably not told him about the fire that had destroyed Sutpen's Hundred in which Clytie and Henry had died, for later on that same evening (p. 215), Shreve refers to Clytie as "the old woman who must be more than seventy now. . . ." (It may seem rather strange that Quentin had failed to do so. But, as we shall see, he seems reluctant to call to mind anything connected with Henry Sutpen. Besides, if Quentin went home for the Christmas holidays, as we would expect him to do and as *The Sound and the Fury* has him do, he has now been back in Cambridge for only a few days.) But it is clearly implied that at some point—presumably later on during this same evening—he does tell Shreve about it (pp. 376–78).

Nor does Quentin seem to have ever told Shreve about Sutpen's boyhood or about the traumatic experience in tidewater Virginia that commits him to his "design" or about his life in the West Indies. At any rate, when Quentin begins on this January evening to tell this story, Shreve listens with apparent interest and no interruptions—from page 218 to page 254—quite a record for Shreve. Usually, when Quentin mentions some series of events the substance of which Shreve knows, he proceeds to rattle them off in swift recapitulation (for example, pp. 176–81 or pp. 350–51); but there are no recapitulations here. Shreve seems to find the story fresh—at the least in its circumstantiality and its detail.

Finally, though Shreve has learned at some point that Miss Rosa had persuaded Quentin to drive her out to Sutpen's Hundred one night to test the correctness of her surmise that somebody was hidden out there (p. 176), he obviously does not yet know the outcome, for somewhat later he asks incredulously, "and there was [someone besides Clytie and Bond living at Sutpen's Hundred]?" (p. 216). When Quentin replies affirmatively, Shreve cries out, "Wait," and will not let Quentin go on to name the person. Shreve evidently wants to savor the denouement of the story—to roll it over his tongue, not to have to gulp it down.

Quentin, on the other hand, reacts to the telling of the story with something like fatigue and somber irritation. It is too close to his own life: it is all too painfully real. But Shreve's postponements spring from a diametrically opposite reason. The South is horrifyingly (but delightfully) unreal. As he has remarked to Quentin, the South "is better than the theatre . . ." (p. 217), better than that exciting melodrama *Ben Hur*. With all the detachment of the mere spectator, Shreve would postpone the denouement in the interest of a longer and deeper relishing of the story.

Some time and some pages later (p. 274), his reference to Clytie suggests that he is still in the dark about Henry's presence in the Sutpen mansion. Yet at some time during the long January evening, Quentin must have told Shreve a good deal about his night visit to Sutpen's Hundred—perhaps all of it, including his confrontation with Henry. For on page 350, Shreve launches forth on one of his recapitulations: "And so you and the old dame, the Aunt Rosa, went out there that night," etc. (Compare the recapitulation found on pages 176–81 which begins, "That this old dame," etc.) Like the earlier, the later provides a résumé, in Shreve's cheerfully mock-heroic style, of events evidently narrated to him earlier by Quentin, yet there is no place *in the text of the novel* where we are allowed to read the details of such a conversation between Quentin and Shreve. But the two evident breaks in the continuity of the boys' conversation—the one between chapters VI and VII and the one between VII and VIII—make it clear that Faulkner does not pretend to recount in the *text* all that passed between Quentin and Shreve on this January evening.

Shreve's second recapitulation of events breaks off at the point where Miss Rosa knocks Clytie to the floor and goes on upstairs. We know from the account on pages 362–72 how Quentin and Miss Rosa effected an entrance into the decaying mansion and that Clytie tried to prevent Rosa's going upstairs, but failed to do so. We know also that Miss Rosa eventually came down the stairs, and that Quentin himself mounted the stairs and in his turn came down, eventually caught up with Miss Rosa and drove her home, for we are allowed to watch all these events run through Quentin's memory as he vividly relives them.

Thus we can check on the accuracy of some parts of Shreve's fragmentary résumé, and we can assume, I believe, that though the novelist causes Shreve suddenly to break off the résumé, there is no reason to believe that Quentin hadn't earlier provided him with the rest of the story. (It's hard to imagine Shreve giving over until he had heard it all.) But whether Faulkner lets his *reader* learn all that Quentin experienced on this evening is quite another matter. The cinema reel of Quentin's memory as it runs before our eyes on pages 362–72 presents a series of pictures and events that are remarkably detailed, but it clearly does not include everything, and it strangely omits Quentin's discovery of Henry, an event that is the climax of Miss Rosa's quest and the corroboration of her "feeling" that something is "living hidden in that house" (p. 172).

One of the most interesting aspects of Faulkner's fictional technique is the position in the novel to which he assigns Shreve's recapitulation of the story of Quentin's night-visit to Sutpen's Hundred. It is sandwiched in between two "visualizations" of Bon and Henry in the

Carolinas in 1864. But to see the significance of this positioning, we must go back a bit, say to page 340. Shreve is here setting forth his conjectures about the agonized relations between Henry and Bon. He imagines their conversations at the beginning of the War and, later on, at the Battle of Shiloh, where Henry (or was it Bon?) was wounded. Suddenly (p. 345) Shreve breaks off—the break is indicated by an em dash—and the author's voice takes over as he describes Henry and Bon among the others in "the starved and ragged remnant" of an army retreating before Sherman, across Alabama, into Georgia, and finally into the Carolinas. But since the author is speaking here in his own voice, he can move directly from an account of Bon and Henry to a description of Quentin and Shreve as they sit in the cold dormitory room imagining what went on between the two young Confederate soldiers. The author tells us that Quentin and Shreve "bore [the cold] as though in deliberate flagellant exaltation of physical misery trans- mogrified into the spirits' travail of the two young men [Bon and Henry] during that time fifty years ago . . ." (p. 345); and the author goes on in his own voice to sketch the retreats, lost battles, and general physical and spiritual miseries experienced by Bon and Henry into whose minds Quentin and Shreve now project themselves. The author insists upon a varying pattern of interchange between the two young men and the two others about whom they have been talking: "two of them, then four; now two again." (This formula, or a variant of it, is used on page 345 and also twice more, on page 346.) In short, Quentin and Shreve keep identifying themselves so thoroughly with Henry and Bon that the four individuals from time to time compress themselves into just two, Quentin and Shreve *becoming* the young Confederate soldiers.

This meeting of minds has been carefully prepared for on earlier pages in a related phenomenon in which Quentin and Shreve find their thoughts so thoroughly attuned that neither needs to hear the other's words in order to know what the other is thinking. For example, see pages 303, 311, 314, and 321. On page 314 the author tells us that "it was not Bon [that] Shreve meant now, yet again Quentin seemed to comprehend without difficulty [whom he meant]," or note page 316: "That was why it did not matter to either of them which one did the talking, since it was not the talking alone which . . . performed and accomplished the overpassing, but some happy marriage of speaking and hearing. . . ." (For an earlier foreshadowing of such wordless communications between Quentin and Shreve, see page 215.)

There follows (on p. 346) a long passage in italics and enclosed in parentheses. It begins abruptly, with an em dash and as a sentence fragment, thus: "(—*the winter of '64 now* . . ." Yet the careful placing of the passage indicates that the author is here reproducing the thoughts of Quentin and Shreve, thoughts about Henry and Bon—in fact, this third-person account is a kind of joint re-creation of what Quentin and Shreve evidently believed must have been experienced by the young Confederate soldiers.

The rationale of the colon that ends the passage decribing Shreve and Quentin facing each other "in the tomblike room" becomes clear. It is an "introductory" colon, meant to alert the reader with reference to something to follow, something connected with, or a consequence of, what has preceded it. In this instance, the long italicized parenthetical passage that follows is a "consequence"—it proceeds from the four minds having become "two" (p. 346). Such an interpretation is reinforced by the fact that at the end of the italicized passage we are presented with a rhetorical question voiced by Shreve. That is, Shreve now withdraws himself from the visualization by the Quentin-Shreve joint entity and speaks out in his own person: "And so you and the old dame . . ." (p. 350), and begins to recapitulate Quentin's night visit to Sutpen's Hundred.

Why? Because it was on that visit that Quentin learned that Bon and Henry were brothers, and, inferentially, that Bon possessed Negro blood. These are the matters that dominate (as Quentin and Shreve think) the final showdown between Henry and his father and that between Henry and Bon. The very last sentence of the long italicized passage signals the imminent showdown between Henry and his father, for it reads: ". . . *and an orderly came along the bivouac line and found Henry at last and said, 'Sutpen, the colonel wants you in his tent'* " (p. 350). Sutpen has now decided to play his trump card—to tell Henry, so Quentin and Shreve conjecture, that Bon is not only his half-brother but is also part-Negro. Thus, Shreve, in his rising excitement, suddenly recurs to the events that led up to Quentin's discovery of the secret.

But, as we have remarked earlier, Shreve quickly breaks off his recapitulation of what went on that night at Sutpen's Hundred and returns to the drama of the impending scene in the Carolinas, which still holds him in its grip, and holds Quentin, too—"Because now [the voice of the author tells us] neither of them were there [in the room]. They were both in Carolina." So the joint visualization is quickly resumed (p. 351), and italics once more mark it as a joint visualization.

Earlier I observed that the thoughts of Quentin and Shreve were so attuned that it "did not matter to either . . . which one did the talking," and now, we are told, they did not need to talk at all. We have a specific illustration in the passage which follows (p. 351). The author tells us that Shreve ceased, because "he had no listener" and because suddenly "he had no talker either. . . ." The author here takes the four-into-two comparison (p. 346) up another notch: "it was not even four now but compounded still further, since now both of them were Henry Sutpen and both of them were Bon, compounded each of both yet either neither . . ." (p. 351). The imagined events (pp. 351–58) are given something like the authority of objective events. It is no longer *I think this* or *I believe that,* but the events take place before the waking eyes of Quentin and Shreve.

The technique used here, and in pages 346-50 (and perhaps elsewhere in this novel) may, for want of a better term, be called "cinematic." I am not insisting that this fictional device was inspired by Faulkner's work in Hollywood, though he had been working on screen plays for some years before he completed *Absalom, Absalom!* What I mean to indicate by this term is something that a writer of genius who also possessed experimental audacity could have learned from going to the movies at the local Oxford moving picture theater. Thus, instead of having the character tell of a certain experience, we move through a fade-out-dissolve into a sequence that *presents* the experience. It is true enough that Faulkner cannot, with his verbal medium, quite manage a fade-out-dissolve; so we get juxtapositions instead, with transitions of the sort mentioned above. But on page 190 Faulkner comes close to the precise fade-out-dissolve effect. Quentin, reacting to his father's account of how Sutpen had got the tombstones (intended for himself and his wife) from Europe, through the Union blockade to a Southern port, imagines how they might have made their progress inland to Mississippi. He goes on to imagine how Sutpen might have set the one reversed for himself "upright in the hall of the house, where Miss [Rosa] Coldfield possibly . . . looked at it every day as though it were his portrait, possibly . . . reading among the lettering more of maiden hope and virgin expectation than she ever"—and here comes the dissolve: the text does not read "told him about" but "told Quentin about." We have shifted from Quentin's musing to the author's narration in the third person. (Even if we regard the substitution of the word "Quentin" for the word "him" as a slip, occasioned by Faulkner's forgetfulness, the instance will suggest the spirit of these shifts, the more important of which, however, must be deemed calculated and purposeful.)

The supposition that the long italicized narrative (pp. 351–58) is a *joint visualization* in which Quentin and Shreve "see" in narrative progression the anguished and passionate events involving Sutpen, Henry, and Bon in 1865 is given further support by the nature of Shreve's comment when the visualization breaks off. Shreve's speech has precise relevance to the last item of the silent reverie, which is Bon's voicing his decision to go back and marry Judith. Bon's statement ends: "—*You will have to stop me, Henry*," with reference to which, Shreve, coming out of the silent reverie, audibly comments: "And [Bon] never slipped away. He could have, but he never even tried. Jesus, maybe he even went to Henry and said 'I'm going, Henry,' and maybe they left together . . ." (p. 358).

Such brilliant though unsequential presentations of events also occur in the last chapter. Though I have earlier remarked on the arrangement of the scenes that make up this last chapter, it may be useful at this point to offer a summary. The young men have finally got into bed, but they continue to talk about the story that has so thoroughly gripped their imaginations. Shreve, though he had become almost as fully engrossed as Quentin, is already beginning to work back toward disengagement. After all, Mississippi was for him another country and besides the wench—along with her whole family—is dead. Shreve continues to ask a few questions, some of which are serious and even show a half-sincere envy of the historical burden that, as a Southerner, Quentin bears; but others are cynical and flippant. In short, Shreve has been impressed, even deeply moved, but he is rapidly disentangling himself from sympathetic emotions.

Quentin, however, cannot disentangle himself. He has genuinely dreaded the mental and emotional reenactment of the story. He has, except possibly in the instance of the story of Wash, spoken as little as he could. He does not want to relive what for him is a painful experience. But he has been forced to do so; as a consequence he begins "to jerk all over, violently and uncontrollably" (p. 360), though not with the cold. He manages to provide brief answers to Shreve's questions, but his mind is engaged elsewhere, for he is compulsively reliving the ride in the buggy with Miss Rosa toward Sutpen's Hundred on that past September evening (pp. 362–72). He runs through the events from the beginning of the drive to his return to his father's house, yet somehow he manages to block out of his memory his sight of Henry, the thing he had told himself that night "I shall be sorry tomorrow [to have seen], but I must see."

But Quentin's horrible vision of Henry Sutpen eventually cannot be repressed. As he tries to compose himself for sleep, he is suddenly back in a similar attempt to compose himself for sleep, not on a cold January night in Massachusetts, but on a hot September night in Mississippi, after he had hurried into bed upon his return from Sutpen's Hundred. Now, as on that occasion, he suddenly finds that he cannot close his eyes against the sight of "the wasted yellow face with closed, almost transparent eyelids . . ." and hears himself again addressing the figure lying on the bed.

This, of course, is the climactic point of the novel. The heroic and tragic past, "the deep South, dead since 1865," turns out to be not dead but alive—not a shadowy memory but a wasted body, breathing contemporary air. Quentin's mind, we have been told earlier, is a "barracks filled with stubborn back-looking ghosts" (p. 12). Suddenly, a door opens and one of those ghosts has become a flesh-and-blood man.

The reader experiences this scene with maximum intensity, not only because it has been delayed and delayed and most cunningly led up to, but also because he feels the power of its impact through its impact on Quentin. The reader has not heard Quentin describe it to Shreve, though Quentin must almost certainly have done so earlier. Instead, the reader is allowed to realize how painfully immediate it still is for Quentin.

Then Shreve's voice breaks in. He has another inquiry. Quentin must have told him earlier about Miss Rosa's trip out to Sutpen's Hundred to bring Henry in an ambulance back into town. Shreve now wants to know why she waited for three months to do so. Quentin might have answered that perhaps the Christmas season had softened her heart.[4] Quentin doesn't answer, perhaps, because he is tired of speculation. Besides, he is still caught up in his vision of the emaciated Henry, and as Shreve continues to talk about Miss Rosa's arrival with the ambulance at Sutpen's Hundred there rises up in Quentin's mind the scene of the fiery destruction of Sutpen's Hundred though "he had

4. Mr. Compson, in his letter (p. 173) dated 10 January, indicates that Miss Rosa had died on 8 January, having remained in a "coma for almost two weeks" If she lost consciousness (suffered a stroke?) on the day that she drove out in the ambulance to get Henry—we learn that she went wild and fought to get into the burning mansion (p. 375)—then "almost two weeks before" 8 January is 26 or 27 December.

not been there" (p. 374). Quentin (at home for the Christmas holidays) must have got all the gory details when the ambulance crew came back to Jefferson. One assumes that the town scarcely talked of anything else for several days.

Yet Faulkner knows that the imagined scene may be more vivid than any scene actually viewed by the human eye. It is Quentin's imagined vision that is presented to the reader. We are told four times that "Quentin could see"—the ambulance arriving (p. 374), the deputy and ambulance driver having to hold Miss Rosa (p. 375), the vanishing of the whole hall of the house in the flames (p. 375), and Miss Rosa struggling "like a doll in a nightmare" (p. 376). Clearly, Quentin does *see,* though his vision has to do with a mental, not a literal, image. The invitation to the reader to see with his mind's eye is irresistible. He also "sees" the scene.

A sensitive but skeptical reader may wish at this point to make an observation to this effect: yes, the presentation of events has been very brilliant, but there is one question that will not down. Just how did Quentin learn the secret of Bon's parentage? There is no scene in the text where the reader can actually observe Henry or Clytie or Miss Rosa or anyone else revealing to Quentin that secret. How satisfactory, then, is Faulkner's brilliant presentation of events if the key piece in the puzzle is permanently withheld?

With this question, we are back into Stratum E. For in order to validate the fact that Quentin learned the secret of Bon's parentage on that particular night at Sutpen's Hundred we have to inquire whether it was possible that he could have learned it there—indeed, to assure ourselves that Faulkner in his account of the events of that night has not closed off the very possibility.

If we assume that the thirty-six words printed on page 373 were all that were spoken by Quentin and Henry, then Quentin could not have learned the secret from Henry's lips. Henry does not there divulge the secret. But have we the right to assume that the words printed on page 373 constitute the whole exchange between the two men? In order to answer this question, it will be necessary to go back a bit and reinspect the other elements in the narrative.

We have indeed been offered a collection of fragments: there is no full sequential account. (1) Shreve's recapitulation (pp. 350–51) of what Quentin must have told him at some earlier time breaks off with Clytie's lying on the floor, having been knocked down by Miss Rosa in her rush to mount the stairs. (2) The first of Quentin's compulsive relivings of his visit (pp. 174–76) begins with his calling for Miss Rosa at her house and their setting out on the dusty road. (3) The second, pages later (pp. 362–72), picks up about where the first one left off and takes us through a whole series of events, including taking Miss Rosa home and coming home himself and trying to get to sleep. But this longest and most circumstantial of the accounts pointedly leaves out what Quentin found in the upstairs room. We are told of his compulsion to see what Miss Rosa had evidently seen, and he remembers that when he came down the stairs he had thought, "Maybe my face looks like . . . [Miss Rosa's] did, but it's not triumph" (p. 371). (4) Last of all, in proper climactic, but not sequential, position, we get the brief passage (pp. 372–73) which tells us of Quentin's entry into the room and what he saw and what he and Henry said. Is it a fragment too?

When Quentin comes down the stairs, Miss Rosa has already gone out of the house on her way back to the buggy that they had left at the gate, "a half a mile" (p. 365) from the house. We are told that Quentin did not "overtake Miss Coldfield and the negro [Bond, who had gone along with her to escort her to the gate]. It was too dark to go fast, though he could presently hear them ahead of him. She was not using the flashlight now. . . ." When Quentin comes up with her she has stopped, having "stumbled and fallen."

Now we don't know how much of the half mile back to the buggy Miss Rosa had got over before Quentin caught up with her, though she was evidently out of earshot when he got outside the house. Yet, if the words printed on page 373 were all that passed between Quentin and Henry, and if after that, shocked and awed, he left the room—we know he did not linger with Clytie (p. 371)—he should have overtaken Miss Rosa almost before she got off the porch. For one can speak the thirty-six words on page 373, slowly and making all the proper pauses, in twenty seconds. This does not prove, of course, that more words were spoken; only that more could have been.

There is a further question, however. Would Quentin, as a stranger entering the room uninvited, have broached intimate matters to Henry? It's a fair question. But one may observe that if the thirty-six words do constitute the whole of the conversation, Henry is certainly forthcoming in his answers. It is Quentin who is rather tentative and hesitant with his questions. Henry is far more circumstantial than he need have been ("Four years") and more personal ("To die"). It is as if he were actually eager to talk. If Quentin had merely formed the words "Charles Bon was your friend—?", it is easy to imagine Henry's replying: "More than my friend. My brother." Faulkner has preferred to leave it to his reader to imagine this or something like it.

The phrase "My brother" would have been all that was needed to clear up the mystery that hung over the story of the Sutpens. With this new bit of information to be added to what Mr. Compson already knows, he and Quentin could have put all the pieces together the next morning.

Faulkner has also left to our imaginations what, if anything, Miss Rosa said to Henry or Henry to her. But they must have immediately recognized each other, and even if Miss Rosa had simply stood there for a time in stunned silence, her appearance must have given a rationale to Quentin's subsequent appearance in the room. Quentin would not have come in like a chance stranger out of the night. If Miss Rosa did speak and mentioned the name of her escort, Henry would have recognized it as the name of the only friend in Yoknapatawpha County that his father ever had. Faulkner evidently again wanted to leave to the reader's imagination the precise way in which Quentin learned the truth about the Sutpens. Or, we may put it in another way, perhaps more accurately: since Faulkner wanted to engage his reader's imagination fully, he believed that the price he would have to pay would be a certain ambiguity. In short, he would have to allow some latitude to the reader in piecing the fragments together and in completing the pattern implied by the fragments presented to him. But an author can allow such latitude without indulging in pointless mystification. I find no such deliberate mystification. The author has made it thoroughly plain that it was Quentin who discovered the secret and on what occasion he made the discovery. I believe that he learned the secret from Henry's own lips, but it will be proper to canvass other possibilities.

What about the possibility that Quentin might have learned the secret from Miss Rosa, who learned it from Henry and later, on the long drive back to Jefferson, passed it on to Quentin? Perhaps, but if Quentin's memory of the ride can be trusted (pp. 371–72) she remained in an almost catatonic state and so was unwilling—perhaps unable—to talk.

Could Quentin have learned the secret from Clytie? To begin with, we have no evidence that Clytie ever knew it. But assuming that after his return to Sutpen's Hundred, Henry did tell her that Bon was his half-brother, was there any opportunity for her to have passed this information on to Quentin? She could not have done so before the night on which Quentin and Miss Rosa drove out to Sutpen's Hundred. Apparently Quentin had not set eyes on her again since the day he saw her on one of his boyhood rambles that took him to the Sutpen mansion.

The two accounts that we have about what happened on Quentin's night visit to the Sutpen mansion would seem to provide no opportunity for Clytie to have said anything of consequence to Quentin. In Shreve's recapitulation (pp. 350–51) we are told of Clytie's trying to prevent Rosa's going upstairs and having been struck down by Rosa, and of Quentin's helping her to her feet. But there is no allusion to any conversation. There are, to be sure, in this account two allusions to something Clytie wordlessly communicated to Quentin: the first reads "she didn't tell you in so many words because she was still keeping that secret for the sake of the man who had been her father too as well as for the sake of the family which no longer existed" (pp. 350). These words seem promising—though it's hard to conceive how Clytie could have told the secret of Bon's relation to Henry apart from telling it in so many words. In any case, why should her look be one "of terror"? In his recapitulation, Shreve makes a second reference to Clytie's terror, and this time it becomes clear what occasioned the terror: "because [the terror] was not about herself but about whatever it was that was upstairs, that she had kept hidden up there for almost four years; and she didn't tell you in the actual words because even in the terror she kept the secret; nevertheless she told you, or at least all of a sudden you knew—" (p. 351). Clytie's secret, then, would seem to be that Henry lay hidden upstairs. Her terror was that if Rosa discovered Henry's presence she would report him to the sheriff. The proof that this was what Clytie feared becomes clear when Miss Rosa, three months later, does return with the ambulance, and Clytie, having prepared for just this eventuality, fires the house.

If it is difficult to believe that Clytie imparted the secret of Bon's parentage to Quentin before he went upstairs, what about on his return? Quentin remembers that when he had had his look and came back down the stairs, Clytie was "sitting still on the bottom step. . . . She did not even look at him when he passed her" (p. 371). There would seem, then, to have been no opportunity for Clytie to tell the secret of Bon's parentage to Quentin, and surely she has no possible motive for doing so.

On page 350 Shreve says something that is puzzling. After remarking that Clytie was "still keeping that secret for the sake of the man who had been her father . . . whose . . . rotten mausoleum she still guarded," Shreve goes on to say, "[she] didn't tell you in so many words anymore than she told you in so many words how she had been in the room that day when they brought Bon's body in and Judith took from his pocket the metal case she had given him with her picture in it . . ." (p. 350). But when could Clytie have ever been in a position to give this information? And anyway, wouldn't one have *expected* her to be in the room with Judith? Unless this passage is an oversight made by the author—which is what I am inclined to take it to be—then it is one more indication that conversations not directly described to the reader must have occurred on the occasion of Quentin's night-visit; if so, another matter that Clytie told Quentin, though not "in so many words," must have later been related to Shreve by Quentin.

Hershel Parker has offered an interesting theory as to how Quentin learned the secret.[5] Parker suggests that no one out at Sutpen's Hundred "told" Quentin the secret, but that on that evening Quentin, looking at Jim Bond, "saw" that he bore "the Sutpen face" and suddenly realized that he could bear such a resemblance to the Sutpens only if Charles Bon, his grandfather, had been Sutpen's son. In view of the fact that *Absalom, Absalom!* contains no scene in which someone *tells* Quentin the secret, the "seeing" theory apparently offers real advantages.

Parker points out that Quentin remembers that when he saw Jim Bond "he thought, 'The scion, the heir, the apparent (though not obvious)' " and argues that this phrasing means that Quentin realizes that Jim is Sutpen's descendant, even before he goes upstairs and discovers the presence of Henry. That is, Quentin has noticed that "the saddle-colored and slack-mouthed idiot face" is nevertheless the "Sutpen" face and that his choice of the word "scion," meaning descendant (of Sutpen) acknowledges that fact. But "scion" can mean merely "inheritor"—it is here paired with "heir"—and the whole phrasing has to be highly ironical. Clytie and Jim Bond are neither of them true heirs. They are only squatters on a property that no one wants to live on: *"the domain . . . had reverted to the state and had been bought and sold . . . again and again"* (p. 213). Bond could not be literally heir to anything. The irony of his "heirship" is further emphasized by the rhetorical play: "apparent" and "obvious" mean in this context very

5. See "What Quentin Saw 'Out There,' " *Mississippi Quarterly* 27 (1974) : 323–26.

nearly the same thing. So that the "scion and heir, the apparent (though not obvious)" would seem to mean: Jim Bond, in spite of appearances, is clearly the heir-apparent of this great decaying mansion. This is what Sutpen's great dream has come to. But in any case, there are difficulties in believing that Quentin could have recognized the lineaments of Sutpen, the cast-iron man, in the "slack-mouthed idiot face."

For one thing, the light is not of the best; one coal-oil lamp has been lit. More importantly, Quentin's only notion of what the Sutpen face is like rests on Miss Rosa's testimony that Clytie also wears the Sutpen face. (Quentin has never seen Thomas Sutpen or Judith, nor, so far as we know, any pictures of them, and will not have seen Henry until he has gone upstairs.) But Miss Rosa, Quentin's sole authority for what the Sutpen face looks like, apparently doesn't herself recognize it in the features of Jim Bond, though she passes by Bond when she comes down the stairs and is accompanied by him out of the house. She clearly has not recognized the Sutpen in him, for later she says to him, "Help me up. You ain't any Sutpen." Yet Quentin is supposed to have recognized the Sutpen resemblance in Bond and made the almost instantaneous deduction that Charles Bon was therefore Thomas Sutpen's son.

I suppose that it is just possible that Parker's hypothesis is true, but this kind of revelation seems to me to go against the grain of the book. If accepted, the solution of the riddle is dissociated from what is the prime dramatic confrontation, that of Quentin and Henry. Moreover, Faulkner seems to have done nothing to prepare for Quentin's instant realization of the true facts when he looks at Jim Bond.

There are other problems, of which Parker himself takes cognizance. In spite of the interest created by Henry's shooting of his best friend, nobody seems to have noticed any physical similarity between Bon and Henry or between Bon and Thomas Sutpen. If the secret was learned from something that Quentin saw rather than something that he heard, then some hint that Bon himself had a teasing resemblance to Thomas or Henry or even Judith would have given the reader a most helpful clue. I myself continue to believe that on page 373 we have been given only a fragment of the conversation and that Quentin found a solution to the riddle in something that he *heard*.

This has been a patient and perhaps tedious attempt to isolate the stages of intelligence through which Quentin came to know the basic events in Sutpen's life, along with an attempt to indicate the stages by which the story was revealed to Shreve. But at this point the reader may want to question whether the game has been worth the candle. What, aside from a display of pedantry, has been accomplished?

I would answer: first, a general clearing up of the facts and a clearing away of false inferences, though only one or two examples must suffice to illustrate this latter point. For my first example, let me cite the passage in chapter III (p. 62) where Mr. Compson tells Quentin that Sutpen "named Clytie as he named them all [i.e., all of his children], the one before Clytie and Henry and Judith even. . . ." To some scholars this passage proves that Faulkner originally meant for Mr. Compson to be aware even at this early point in the novel that Charles Bon was Sutpen's son and that only later did Faulkner postpone Mr. Compson's knowledge of this fact until told by Quentin after his return from Sutpen's Hundred (p. 266). Thus, the retention of the passage indicating that Mr. Compson knew the truth all along is a blemish: Faulkner should have remembered to excise it when he changed his conception of the plot. However, John C. Hodgson [6] argues that the passage is not the result of Faulkner's forgetfulness but is meant to signal to the alert reader that the conversation between Quentin and his father recorded in chapter III occurred *after* Quentin had returned from Sutpen's Hundred; that is, that chapter III represents a period of time *later* than that of the two chapters that flank it. But if we know our facts, we are not forced to accept so arbitrary an arrangement of the time sequences on the one hand nor, on the other, to conclude that Faulkner simply forgot. If Mr. Compson, as early as page 62, had known that Charles Bon was Sutpen's son, he surely would have said: ". . . named Clytie as he named them all, Charles Bon, Clytie, Henry and Judith. . . ."

A second example has to do with General Compson's not having surmised almost at once that the defect in Sutpen's first wife had to be her possession of Negro blood, particularly in view of the fact that Sutpen said to General Compson: "I found that [my first wife] was not and could never be, through no fault of her own adjunctive . . . to the design which I had in mind" (p. 240).[7] But the phrase

---

6. "Logical Sequence and Continuity: Some Observations on the Typographical and Structural Consistency of *Absalom, Absalom!" American Literature* 43 (1971): 97–107.

7. Gerald Langford wonders why General Compson, having heard Sutpen say this, should not have guessed the defect at once. See the introduction to Langford's *Faulkner's Revision of "Absalom, Absalom!"*, p. 7.

"through no fault of her own" need not imply her being part-Negro. Other possible disabilities could conceivably have been an organic disability or chronic disease or some neurosis. But we can best protect General Compson's reputation for being a reasonably astute man by appealing to a fact that should by now be right in front of the reader's eyes. What Sutpen told General Compson about his early life and his first marriage is not to be read as if it were a sworn affidavit. What we read on pages 240 and 263–64 are General Compson's impressions as passed on by word of mouth to his son, Mr. Compson, and then passed on by him to *his* son, Quentin, again by word of mouth. The mode of transmission does not change even here, for the reader of *Absalom, Absalom!* hears this account (and interpretation) of Sutpen's actions as they are being passed on, once more by word of mouth, to Quentin's roommate. Thus, we would be foolish to treat the relevant pages in *Absalom, Absalom!* as providing a verbatim report of what Sutpen told General Compson. The basic facts are presumably correct, and Faulkner would be a faulty novelist indeed if they were deliberately misleading. But when it comes to the niceties of Sutpen's motives and judgments, we must remember that we are getting a reinterpretation (all the more deceptive if it is a quite unconscious reinterpretation) of a reinterpretation of an interpretation of Sutpen's attitudes and even his words. Did Sutpen actually say to General Compson, in "the bombastic phrases" with which "he even asked you for a match for his cigar" (p. 240), something like "Mind you, I don't impute any special guilt to my first wife. My blame falls rather upon her parents"? Or "My first wife was, as one would expect, a dutiful and submissive daughter. She undoubtedly said and did—and perhaps even 'knew'—only what her parents told her to say and know." It is possible that some such statement, made by Sutpen in 1864, has become, by the time it reaches Shreve (and the reader), the statement of the case that we find on page 240: "she was not and could never be, through no fault of her own, adjunctive . . . to the design which I had in mind. . . ."

So far, of course, I have tried to indicate the negative value of the exegesis here attempted. Attention to what Quentin and Shreve knew about the Sutpen story and to the various stages of that deepening knowledge does serve to clear up problems of the sort cited in the pages immediately preceding. But there is a positive value too.

If the reader is fully to appreciate the quality of narrative art in this novel, he will have to become aware of the various modes of Faulkner's presentation of the story and of the brilliance with which he has used them. By withholding elements of the story until he is ready to divulge them; by whetting the reader's appetite through such postponements; by using devices that either mitigate or prevent repetition—devices such as having Shreve make half-mocking or quite serious brief recapitulations of what Quentin has previously told him; by arranging to have the reader hear for the first time through Quentin's narration to Shreve what Mr. Compson had told Quentin months and even years before; by sometimes avoiding any "telling" at all and allowing us to experience the action immediately, as when we relive Quentin's memory of certain episodes or follow the play of events as Shreve or Quentin imagine they must have happened; or, most daring of all, by letting the speculations or meditations of Shreve-Quentin become a cinema reel that projects upon the screen of our minds the events that Shreve-Quentin passionately believe must have occurred—by using such techniques of presentation, Faulkner has completely involved his reader in what is perhaps his supreme story of the human heart in conflict with itself.

Appendix C

FAULKNER AND W. B. YEATS

In Faulkner's "The Old People," Isaac McCaslin undergoes his initiation into the code of the wilderness. He ceases "to be a child and [becomes] a hunter and a man" (*Go Down Moses,* p. 178). After he has killed his first buck and has been anointed on the forehead with its "hot smoking blood" (p. 164) by Sam Fathers, the officiating priest of the rite, something else happens to Isaac: later on that afternoon he has a vision of a great antlered buck that must have been, as later events indicate, a ghost, not a flesh-and-blood animal.

Isaac is troubled by the phenomenon and refuses to believe that the buck was merely a figment of his imagination. That night he describes his experience to his elder cousin, McCaslin Edmonds, and though McCaslin listens to him quietly Isaac suddenly bursts out: "You don't believe it. I know you don't—." But McCaslin reassures the boy. Why shouldn't the slain animals who have never had "enough time about the earth" haunt the "places still unchanged from what they were when the blood used and pleasured in them . . . ?" (pp. 186–87). And when the boy, still not quite satisfied, cries out: "But I saw it," his kinsman says: "I know you did! So did I. Sam took me in there once after I killed my first deer" (p. 187).

William Butler Yeats too has something to report about a phantom deer. In his "General Introduction for My Work," Yeats tells of a gamekeeper on Lady Augusta Gregory's estate at Coole who "heard the footsteps of a deer on the edge of the lake where no deer had passed for a hundred years. . . ." [1] A trivial and inconsequential coincidence? Perhaps so, but note what Yeats goes on to say by way of accounting for the century-dead buck's walking by the lake. A certain cracked old priest, he tells us, gave out that "nobody had been to hell or heaven in his time. . . . that the dead stayed where they had lived, or near it, sought no abstract region of blessing or punishment but retreated, as it were, into the hidden character of their neighbourhood" (p 518).

The old priest's explanation of why the dead preferred to stay where they had lived is not remarkably different from McCaslin Edmonds's way of accounting for the phantom deer's haunting the earth:

> . . . you can't be alive forever, and you always wear out life long before you have exhausted the possibilities of living. And all that must be somewhere; all that could not have been invented and created just to be thrown away. . . . Besides, what would it want . . . knocking around out there [under the icy stars], when it never had enough time about the earth as it was. . . . [pp. 186–87]

True, McCaslin is talking about the animals' not wanting to leave the earth that they had loved, whereas the old cracked priest—even though Yeats refers to him in the immediate context of his remarks about the ghostly deer—is surely talking principally about human beings. But in the world imagined by Faulkner, McCaslin's reasoning about the animals' yearning to stay close to the earth on which they had lived also applies to human beings. Think of Faulkner's beautiful and moving story "Pantaloon in Black." The wife of a young black man named Rider has suffered an untimely death. After her body has been put in the grave, the bereaved husband starts to walk back to the cabin in which they had spent their few months of happiness. But his friends and kinsfolk try to dissuade him. One of them says, awkwardly enough,

> what he had not intended to say, what he had never conceived of himself saying in circumstances like these, even though everybody knew it—the dead . . . either will not or cannot quit the earth yet although the flesh they once lived in has been returned to it,

1. W. B. Yeats, *Essays and Introductions* (London, 1961), p. 518.

let the preachers tell and reiterate and affirm how [the dead] left [the earth] not only without regret but with joy, mounting toward glory. . . . [*Go Down, Moses,* p. 136]

and so Rider's friend, almost in spite of himself, does blurt it out: "You dont wants ter go back dar. She be wawkin yit."

Mannie, Rider's dead wife, *is* walking. Rider sees her for a moment quite plainly when he enters their cabin, but she quickly fades, as heartbreakingly as Eurydice faded before the anguished eyes of Orpheus.

A courteous devil's advocate might have some questions to put. I can imagine him asking: Well, if one grants the parallels cited between Yeats and Faulkner, one must still ask: what is the point? We all know that Yeats was notoriously given to esoteric studies, was a member of the Order of the Golden Dawn, and belonged to Madame Blavatsky's inner circle of devotees. That Yeats should have seriously reported spiritualistic nonsense is hardly surprising. But isn't Faulkner's case quite different? Oxford, Mississippi, at most could scarcely have yielded anything more sinister than a half-dozen ouija boards, or have boasted the presence of even one lonely member of the Rosicrucian Order who, if he existed, probably was no more than a mail-order member, having answered in hopefulness or hopelessness the modest advertisement he had seen on a back page of a copy of *Argosy* magazine or *Western Stories* picked up at Chisholm's drugstore on the square. Is there any genuine relation between Yeats's concern for ghostly happenings and the fact that Faulkner endowed some of his characters with a nature mystique?

Such a set of questions would be fairly put, and I shall try to be equally honest in my answers. My point in calling attention to parallels between Yeats and Faulkner has little to do with whether Yeats seriously believed in spiritual phenomena. W. H. Auden once told me that although T. S. Eliot had had real visions about which he very rarely talked, Yeats talked about his all the time, though Auden doubted that Yeats had ever experienced one in his entire life. Be that as it may, such is not the matter of my concern here. Nor am I concerned with whether Faulkner really believed in revenants and hauntings. What interests me in both men is their warm and sympathetic appreciation of men who did literally believe in supernatural happenings. Though Yeats extended his interests far afield—to the writers of Hermes Trismegistus, the medieval alchemists, and the

Cabalists, his direct hold on the esoteric traditions was through the legendary past of Ireland, and through his first-hand acquaintance with the Irish peasantry. Faulkner had a comparable resource in the genuine folk culture that existed in the rural South. A fruitful comparison of Yeats and Faulkner must proceed from a recognition of the general parallels between the provincial cultures that nourished the genius of both men.

I would stress the importance of their provincial cultures by insisting on the differences between their personalities. Otherwise, a hasty glance might in fact prompt the question: what do these two distinguished writers have in common except their Nobel Prizes? Yeats, with his flowing tie and carefully disarranged hair, Yeats, the friend of such decadent poets as Ernest Dowson and Lionel Johnson, Yeats of *The Yellow Book* and the Cheshire Cheese—what possible affinities could there be between this late Romantic, son of a distinguished pre-Raphaelite painter, and William Faulkner, who was long content to be the ne'er-do-well Count No-Count, Faulkner who was sometimes seen wearing "mismatched shoes" and with "the elbows out of his coat," Faulkner, the dreamy young man, the jest of his friends and sometimes the despair of his family, who lacked a respectable job? I cheerfully admit the real and great differences between the two men. Indeed, I shall go further: I shall dismiss as of no special consequence for my argument that Yeats very early became Faulkner's favorite poet. My basic thesis has little to do with Faulkner's reading of Yeats or any attempt on his part to imitate his poetry. What I shall stress will be the parallels between the cultures out of which Yeats and Faulkner came.

To return to the folk cultures of Ireland and the South: A vigorous folk culture itself implies a number of other parallel features—conservatism, old-fashioned customs and ideas, a paternalistic system centered in an aristocracy or at least a landowning squirearchy. In short, a folk society based on the land implies the Big House with landed proprietors and the ethos that goes with such a governing class as part of the larger cultural continuum in which the folk subsists.

The particular details of the cultural situation as between Ireland and the Old South were, as we would expect, vastly different. In the American South there were both whites and blacks, and though at points they shared a common culture, they were separated by a caste barrier. One effect of the caste barrier was to mitigate somewhat the rigors of a class system. In one sense, all the whites stood together despite the class barriers that existed within the white society. That fact, and the persistence of the frontier virtues in the Old Southwest, operated to unite the whites. At all events, in Faulkner's novels people of yeoman stock such as V. K. Ratliff have a truly friendly relation with the likes of Harvard-educated Gavin Stevens; young Bayard Sartoris is on easy terms with the admirable MacCallum family, and even the "gaunt, malaria-ridden" swampers, when they meet up with Major de Spain on the annual bear hunt, are greeted in friendly fashion. Their spokesman speaks with some diffidence, explaining that "We figgered we'd come up and watch, if you don't mind." The Major replies at once: "You are welcome. You are welcome to shoot. He's more your bear than ours" (*Go Down Moses*, p. 223).

The black folk constituted, to be sure, a special case, but out in the country, at least, the old patriarchal system had enough slack in it to allow the development of human relations between plantation owner and black tenant: witness Lucas Beauchamp and Roth Edmonds, or Bayard Sartoris and the black family with whom he finds shelter on Christmas Eve. Much more to the point, of course, is Faulkner's own attitude as man and as artist. He writes without condescension or disparagement about the yeoman whites, about the landless whites, and about the almost always landless blacks. I don't mean to say that he sentimentalizes men because they were deprived. He knows a Snopes when he sees one. But he rarely falls into cuteness or folksiness, or the other vices of local colorism.

The gap between both Yeats and Faulkner and their respective folk cultures clearly existed—and however important it is that the writers' human sympathies did bridge the gap, the fact of the gap is important. Though Yeats as a writer needed the world of the Irish folk, he also needed a certain detachment from it in order to be able to articulate what he saw and felt. He needed to have a knowledge of history, literature, and philosophy—to be able to stand at a window opening on the great outside world. To be totally immersed in the world of the folk is to become only partially articulate—to become an instance of the folk culture rather than a voice for its aspirations or an interpreter of its meaning. However important Ireland was for Yeats, the artist, the great outside world was essential for him too.

I speak of Yeats, but all that I have said applies fully to Faulkner. What was crucial for both men was the fact that, in spite of their necessary detachment from County Sligo, Ireland, or Lafayette County, Mississippi, neither was insulated from his local culture; thus, it could become for him an enormously valuable resource.

In developing one aspect of the cultural situation common to Yeats and Faulkner, I have already implied a number of others. Perhaps a sensible strategy at this point would be to make some of them explicit, thus developing and clarifying the cultural context out of which they came and upon which they drew. In the first place, that context contained the large landholder as distinguished from the small holder and, of course, the landless. As for the middle class, in the west of Ireland it was small; in late nineteenth-century north Mississippi, it was considerably larger. In this connection, one must be cautious in using the term "aristocracy," for it can be misleading, particularly as applied to Faulkner's country. In Ireland, of course, many of the large landholders were titled, like Yeats's friend Lady Augusta Gregory. But even with Ireland, I believe it would be safer to refer, not to aristocratic tradition, but to the tradition of the Big House. In north Mississippi, the big house was, of course, the plantation house, not nearly so large, however, as the manor houses of Ireland or even some of those to the south in the Natchez country or the great sugarcane plantations in Louisiana. In any case, the members of plantation stock in north Mississippi were relative newcomers to the land, a sort of country gentry or squirearchy, who may have achieved substantial property in one or two generations, in much shorter time than the country families of the Virginia Tidewater or the Low Country around Charleston, and of course much more recently than those families that occupied the Big Houses of Ireland.

Yeats, by the way, though proud of his connection with the Butler family, and sharp in his condemnation of the tradesmen and the hucksters, admitted that "the family of Yeats" were "never more than small gentry." [2] His father was a painter; his father's father a country parson. Nor were Faulkner's more immediate forebears great plantation owners. His great-grandfather, the Old Colonel, walked into the state from Tennessee as a penniless boy. In the almost frontier world of north Mississippi of the 1830s and 1840s, he rapidly became a pillar of the community, in due time built and owned a short-line railroad, made the grand tour of Europe, and had some success as a novelist. He had become a leader in the community; his great-grandson was proud of the fact that the Old Colonel was "part of Stonewall Jackson's left at 1st Manassas." [3]

Donald Torchiana remarks that what attracted Yeats to the tradi-

2. Donald T. Torchiana, *Yeats and Georgian Ireland* (Evanston, Ill., 1966), pp. 89–90.

3. *The Faulkner-Cowley File,* ed. Malcolm Cowley (New York, 1966), p. 66.

tion of the Anglo-Irish landholders of eighteenth-century Protestant Ireland was more a "quality of intellect than any necessary class distinction." Certainly what Yeats valued in Lady Gregory was not her title nor her wealth—which, in fact, was not great. It was rather her courage, self-discipline, magnanimity, courtesy, graciousness—in short, the aristocratic virtues. This was what he had in mind in his celebrated speech to the Irish Senate, when he said of his own forebears, the Anglo-Irish: we "are no petty people. We are one of the greatest stocks of Europe." [4] The individuals whom he cited—Burke, Grattan, Swift, Parnell—were not men of weath but of selfless devotion to the state; and what Yeats went on to praise as the special contributions of his people to Ireland were "literature" and "political intelligence."

Such too, were the qualities and virtues that Faulkner admired in the Old South. There are no plaster saints in Faulkner's pantheon, nor are there fake aristocrats. The virtues displayed by "Old Bayard" Sartoris, by his Aunt Jenny Du Pre, by Mrs. Rosa Millard, and by Uncle Buck and Uncle Buddy, are essentially the virtues of V. K. Ratliff and of Lucas Beauchamp, for in Faulkner's world the yeoman white and the black man can, in their own terms, qualify as "aristocrats."

Faulkner's "aristocrats" have, it is true, the defects of their virtues. Col. Sartoris is irascible, given to violence, proud, ambitious, and vindictive—though he is never mean or petty and he is absolutely fearless. (One could use very nearly these same words to describe the black man Lucas Beauchamp.) Drusilla Hawk's aristocratic virtues become perverted: she is dauntless, but in her worship of honor and courage, she has forgotten pity, compassion, and even her womanhood. She is willing to send her stepson to his probable death, not because of grief for her slain husband, but because she is utterly fascinated by the notion of death (or risk of death) in defense of some abstract conception of masculine honor.

Horace Benbow, too, exhibits the aristocratic virtues only partially and in defect. That is to say, Horace is a man of honor; he is magnanimous, public-spirited, eager to promote justice. He sincerely wants to secure the acquittal of Lee Goodwin; he is genuinely shocked when Lee's wife offers her body to him in payment of the fee that she is confident any lawyer would ask. But Horace is naive; he underestimates the power of evil. When it comes to women, he is weak and pliable—with his wife Belle and with his sister Narcissa. He cannot be

4. Torchiana, p. 89.

brought to realize that few people in the modern world possess either honor or decency and that many lack respect for such virtues in others.

Narcissa is no aristocrat at all, having lost the virtues that should have come to her from her forebears. She is a selfish, calculating woman, completely in thrall to bourgeois respectability—and Faulkner almost rivals Yeats in his detestation of the bourgeois concern to keep up appearances. Narcissa doesn't care whether Lee Goodwin hangs or not. She simply objects to her brother's having taken the case of a common bootlegger accused of murder. So she sells out her brother to the district attorney and thus insures Lee Goodwin's death, just as later (in "There Was a Queen") she offers her body to the Federal agent in return for letters that he holds—anonymous, obscene letters written to her years before. Nobody will ever know that she slept with the agent; thus she chooses fornication in fact rather than risk the possibility that strangers might read letters to her proposing a fornication that never took place. Such is respectability. As an "aristocrat," Narcissa Benbow Sartoris is a whited sepulchre. But it is I who borrow the biblical phrase. What Faulkner actually wrote of her was this: she "looked full at [Horace] . . . with that serene and stupid impregnability of heroic statuary; she was in white" (*Sanctuary*, p. 102).

The district attorney to whom Narcissa sells out Horace has no claim to the aristocratic virtues by background or nurture, and even if he had, he would have long ago repudiated them. Faulkner describes him as a "young man with a word for everyone and a certain alert rapacity about the eyes" (p. 254). In his college days, he had gained a reputation for cheating at poker, but when he talks with Narcissa about the sell-out, he is a straight law-and-order man. We must not, however, linger over Eustace Graham. He is a common enough shyster lawyer with political ambitions. A more nearly final case is Faulkner's Flem Snopes. He is utterly without honor, completely avaricious, and scarcely human in his absolute devotion to making money. Faulkner apparently regards it as natural and appropriate that Flem should show a great concern for respectability. (Today we would say that Flem is acutely aware of his "public image.") Flem is the mercantile spirit walking around on two legs as he remorselessly chews his worthless quid of gum.

Yeats, too, carried on a lifelong quarrel with the bourgeoisie. The objects of his affection were the country gentleman and the peasant, the artist, and the saint. His valedictory poem urges the Irish poets of the future to

> Sing the peasantry, and then
> Hard-riding country gentlemen.
> The holiness of monks, and after
> Porter-drinkers' randy laughter.[5]

In one of his poems he urges Lady Gregory to accept the inevitability of defeat in any competition with men who are honorless:

> Be secret and take defeat
> From any brazen throat,
> For how can you compete,
> Being honour bred, with one
> Who, were it proved he lies,
> Were neither shamed in his own
> Nor in his neighbours' eyes? [6]

Yeats's harshest lines are reserved for those mean and narrowminded people who ". . . fumble in a greasy till / And add the halfpence to the pence" until they have ". . . dried the marrow from the bone." It was in consideration of the number of such petty hucksters that Yeats uttered his famous lines, "Romantic Ireland's dead and gone / It's with O'Leary in the grave." [7]

Later on, Yeats was moved, principally by the events of the Easter Rebellion of 1916, to revise his despairing verdict, though he never ceased to resent the bourgeois ethic, which he believed was inimical to all that was high-hearted, passionate, and heroic. A close look at his career reveals a continuing alteration of love and loathing for his native land, a conflict that closely parallels Faulkner's love-hate relation with his native region.

Faulkner never said so in so many words—not, at least, any that I have found—that the romantic South was dead and gone. But some of the older characters in his fiction occasionally express this view, and in general the ethos of Faulkner's stories and novels reflects that of an older, more heroic society. Moreover, the clear import of Faulkner's observation that the prime question now was whether the Snopeses were going to take over the country is that the older aristocratic code was under attack and might not survive. Yet the strength

5. W. B. Yeats, *Collected Poems* (New York, 1955), p. 343.
6. Ibid., p. 107.
7. Ibid., p. 106.

of Faulkner's work is that even less than Yeats did he risk sentimentalizing the life of the gentry or of declaiming their virtues in his own voice. Rather, the code is implicit, both positively and negatively, in the speeches and actions of Faulkner's characters.

At this point it may be useful to pause for a kind of summation of what has been said and to spell out some of the further implications. The kind of culture that I have thus far described is obviously old-fashioned and provincial—quite out of the mainstream of life in our advanced civilization of the West. The ethos of an aristocratic governing class exists, in memory at least, along with a vigorous folk culture, a culture of farms and small towns, where personal relationships will be concrete and morally uncomplicated, with very little buffering by abstract entities such as corporate bureaucracies, trade unions, and such. In this society one will have a good idea of who has done him a service and who has done him a hurt. The consequence of this will be a certain level of violence and a definite stress on manners. That is, everyone will take care not to offend unless the offense is deliberate.

Add to these elements certain historical conditions true for both Ireland and the South—defeat in war, economic stagnation, and a colonial economy—and one finds as a consequence that history is very much alive in the minds of the people, for the dead lost causes are precisely those that live in memory. Yeats saw the Irish as good haters. In one of his late poems he was still writing about "The Curse of Cromwell," and in another he says:

> Out of Ireland have we come.
> Great hatred, little room,
> Maimed us at the start.
> I carry from my mother's womb
> A fanatic heart.[8]

Southerners have also proved to be good rememberers—and sometimes good haters. But if there are risks, there are also values in being unable to forget one's past history. Faulkner wrote to Malcolm Cowley that the only "clean thing about War is losing it," [9] and the context in which he makes this rather cryptic statement suggests that he meant that a lost war continues to feed the imagination. C. Vann Woodward makes the point with a different inflection. In his *Burden of*

8. Ibid., p. 249.
9. *Faulkner-Cowley File*, p. 79.

Southern History, he observes that past defeat begets realism.[10] It tends to inoculate a culture against the perils of futurism, the pursuit of an ever-receding Utopia. Wisdom itself may be said to reside in a lively sense of history. But it is not my aim to argue that it is better for a country to be poor and proud, provincial and old-fashioned. Ireland and the American South have both paid dearly for such not unmixed blessings.

What I am concerned to say is that the kind of cultural situation into which Yeats and Faulkner were born yielded material which, when seized upon by genius, could be shaped into very great poetry and fiction.

There are a multitude of ways in which the resources of a traditional culture could be drawn upon by these two writers. I must therefore select only a few examples. Here is a simple but very important example with reference to style. To both men there was available an oral tradition—a fountain of living speech. The Irish like to talk: story-telling and political oratory are their special delight. Joyce's *Ulysses* is made of such talk, ranging from an admiring recital of John F. Taylor's famous oration on the Irish language to the witty give and take of two raconteurs in a pub. Southerners also like to talk. Southern oratory is now considerably frayed, but Senator Ervin, as people who heard him in the Watergate hearings can testify, could still produce the authentic ring, and the art of telling a tale is still very much alive. Andrew Lytle, for example, is a living master of this style that comes down from hunters around a campfire or a group chatting on the porch of a country store.

In 1937 Yeats, in one of his latest pieces of prose, talked about the importance to him of this oral tradition. He says: "I have spent my life in clearing out of poetry every phrase written for the eye, and bringing all back to syntax that is for ear alone." This is surely part of the secret of the great sinewy style of his later poetry—the poetry that by 1914 was beginning to replace the languid, dreamy verse of his earliest period and the mannered prose of "The Tables of the Law." Let me repeat Yeats's wonderful phrase: "bringing all back to syntax that is for ear alone." [11] Could there be a better description of Faulkner's prose? One need only to recall such passages as Jason's furious monologue in *The Sound and the Fury,* or Miss Rosa's frenetic tirade in *Absalom, Absalom!* or the wonderful "Spotted Horses" portion of

10. Baton Rouge, La., 1960, p. 21.
11. *Essays and Introductions,* p. 529.

339

The Hamlet. The ear does indeed rejoice in these passages. Moreover, even Faulkner's long, involved sentences, the syntax of which sometimes seems impossibly tangled, straighten themselves out when read aloud—perhaps *only* when read aloud.

I have alluded to Yeats's celebrated change in style. But Faulkner changed his style too, in moving from poetry to prose and, in doing so, effected a radical shift of the same order. For Faulkner's formal verse is dreamy and romantic in much the same way as is Yeats's early poetry and indeed consciously imitates it and the poetry of Yeats's friends and companions of the period. Faulkner always spoke of himself as a failed poet: he could not write the poetry he wanted to write, he tells us, and so turned to prose. But what a fortunate failure. Moreover, how quickly, as compared with Yeats, did Faulkner sense the need for a new direction and take it. Indeed, if we date Yeats's great alteration of style to about 1914, it is worth noting that Faulkner, though thirty-four years younger, had set his feet on his proper course only a dozen years later than had Yeats himself.

The change was of crucial significance for both writers as they emerged from their more limited provincial cultures to confront modernity. Perhaps Pound deserves most credit for bringing Yeats to the confrontation; one might argue that it was principally Eliot and Joyce who, not personally, but in their writings, performed a like service for Faulkner. It was not enough that Yeats should continue a minor Irish poet. His local resources became important only as he brought them to bear upon the crucial issues of the twentieth century and so joined the mainstream of international literature. The same should be said of Faulkner. It would have been stupid to praise him as a superb local colorist, just as it was stupid to praise him for conducting an alleged exposé of Southern degeneracy. His fiction was not designed either to congratulate or to scold his fellow Southerners. What he succeeded in doing was to use the experience that he knew best in order to interpret universal issues. His cultural heritage proved to be ultimately important in providing him with a special and most valuable perspective on Western civilization as a whole.

One of the universal issues to which his fiction addresses itself is man's relation to nature and to history. Man is clearly a part of nature. When does his departure from nature become a perversion and when a fruitful transcendence? The question arises, for, unlike the other natural creatures, man is able to suspend his natural instinctive drives and break through into the realm of history. Even the wisest of the beasts do not have a proper history. Man does.

Now that we live in a culture that has become more and more ruthless in exploiting nature and more and more contemptuous of the past—and therefore contemptuous of history—it becomes even more important to consider man's relation to nature and to history. In a Promethean age, oriented to the future, the past seems dead because nonsignificant. Modern man simply finds it irrelevant.

Yeats and Faulkner found the past alive and meaningful. It was still a living force in Ireland and in the South. The greatest work of both men is suffused with history—not as barren antiquarianism, but as a record of the striving of man—ultimately unchanging Man—to realize his true self by rising above his habitual self.

There are, however, some significant differences in the role that the two men assign to nature and history. Faulkner addresses himself to nature far more fully than Yeats. Yeats knew the Irish landscape well and he can describe it in loving detail, but his nature is never as immediately impressive as Faulkner's. Faulkner has the more innocent eye for nature and gives himself to it more directly, sometimes veering close to nature worship. One remembers the great hymns to nature in "The Bear" and in *The Hamlet*. In the character of the almost subhuman Ike Snopes, Faulkner describes someone almost as deeply immersed in nature as any animal but not quite. The vital human difference is safeguarded. There is a margin for aesthetic appreciation and even ethical choice. Ike is not just a creature like his beloved cow. He is still recognizably human. In contrast to Faulkner, Yeats never sinks his characters so deep into nature, not even his Crazy Jane or his Tom the Lunatic.

Yet there is one important sense in which Yeats makes history, that specifically human realm, actually subservient to nature. For Yeats, history has no goal; like nature itself, history is not going anywhere. It simply moves through predetermined cycles, of birth, growth, maturity, and decay. Civilizations are like plants that come to flower and fruit in their season, and then suffer their winter of denudation and death. Yeats's favorite metaphor for this process is the waxing and waning of the moon. Our own civilization, he says, lies now under a rapidly darkening moon.

Naturally, Yeats did not believe in progress, calling it "the sole religious myth of modern man." After all, it was "only two hundred years old." [12] Faulkner evidently did not believe in progress, either, for his Nobel Prize speech does not predict greater triumphs for man in the future but rather insists upon the indestructibility of the

12. *Wheels and Butterflies* (London, 1934), p. 20.

341

human spirit, no matter what the historical vicissitudes that may lie ahead for mankind. Moreover, if I read his fiction aright, there is no more worship of the future than there is of the past.

But to return to this matter of nature and history: in spite of Faulkner's love for nature, he saw that the human being has to transcend nature. Thus, Ike McCaslin learns something very important from his experience of the wilderness: his teacher, Sam Fathers, is a hunter, and he anoints Ike, not with the water from some clear stream or the juice of some wild fruit, but with the hot blood of the slain deer. The choice of blood is significant. Man cannot simply live on nature's freely offered bounty, gathering food from bushes and trees like the unfallen Adam in the Garden of Eden. Man's rupture with nature occurred long ago, and it is irreparable. Man cannot be innocent as an animal is, relying on its own instincts, capable of no "unnatural" action, incapable of moral choice, and thus barred out from the realm of moral good and evil, which is the realm of history and the peculiarly human dimension. Man is compelled to be either better or worse than the beast. He does not live like a bird or a bear in a virtual present, but in the dimension of the past and of the future.

Man must achieve his goodness—even his basic humanity—by discipline and effort. True, he must respect his creaturehood. He must respect nature and the other natural creatures. If he kills deer and bear, he must try to be worthy of the blood that he spills. He must, if this does not sound too much of a contradiction, actually do his killing not wantonly, but out of respect and love. More is expected of man than of any other creature. He must do much better than nature, lest he do worse. He must therefore live by a discipline and self-imposed code of honor. The history of man is the history of the creation of such codes and man's struggle to live up to them or his failure to do so. Faulkner's heroes struggle mightily to do so. His villains like Flem Snopes or Jason Compson are men who deliberately disavow not only the aristocratic code of the Old South but any fully human code. Flem Snopes is no aristocrat; he is a successful plutocrat; Jason Compson is a failed plutocrat.

Yeats's view of man in relation to nature and history is rather surprisingly like Faulkner's. In his magnificent "Prayer for My Daughter," written in 1919, the poet views with foreboding the stormy future that faces his infant daughter. Yeats proved to be a true prophet: the worldwide Depression, Hitler and the Second World

War, the Cold War, and all the other ills of the midcentury lay ahead.

The poet prays that his daughter will be beautiful, but not so beautiful as to have a proud and disdainful heart; that she may be chiefly learned in courtesy; that she may never be filled with intellectual hatred; and that she may recover a radical innocence by coming to know her deepest self. The concluding stanza reads as follows:

> And may her bridegroom bring her to a house
> Where all's accustomed, ceremonious;
> For arrogance and hatred are the wares
> Peddled in the thoroughfares.
> How but in custom and in ceremony
> Are innocence and beauty born?
> Ceremony's a name for the rich horn,
> And custom for the spreading laurel tree.[13]

We ordinarily think of innocence and beauty as the free gift of nature, and we commonly oppose them to custom and ceremony, which we too often dismiss as at best empty formalisms and at worst as corrupting sophistications; but Yeats has boldly inverted these relationships. True innocence and beauty, he declares, are not the produce of nature, but the fruits of a disciplined life. Far from being capriciously given to us, we must achieve them for ourselves. They are not from nature but from nurture. To all of which, Faulkner's Miss Jenny Du Pre, I have no doubt, would have uttered a fervent Amen.

I have suggested that the view of man held by both Yeats and Faulkner is on its positive side aristocratic and heroic. Clearly, if I am right, it also has close affinities to the orthodox Classical-Christian view of man, though both writers had some very severe things to say about the institutional Christianity of their times. Perhaps I can best approach their basic conception of man by looking at it from the negative side. Faulkner very often implied his positive view by a scarifying depiction of what was *not* good, beautiful, or true. *Sanctuary* constitutes an extreme instance. Horace Benbow learns (and the reader with him perhaps) that girlish innocence as incarnate in Temple Drake and Little Belle is not innocent in the least.

Yeats opposed to his heroic idea what he called "Whiggery." In a poem called "The Seven Sages," seven old Irish grayheads discuss the Irish past and its eighteenth-century heroes and the state of the

13. *Collected Poems*, p. 187.

modern world. One of them observes that their heroes were united in their hatred of Whiggery, and proceeds to define the hated thing:

> . . . what is Whiggery?
> A levelling, rancorous, rational sort of mind
> That never looked out of the eye of a saint
> Or out of a drunkard's eye.[14]

Faulkner never used the term "Whiggery." For him, it would probably have denoted no more than a quite defunct, pre–Civil War American political party. But Faulkner knew the thing even though he did not know Yeats's and T. S. Eliot's, name for it. Who would be some of his "Whigs"? For an excellent example of the "rancorous, rational sort of mind," what about Jason Compson? He is quite sure that he is practical and reasonable. Let others be sentimental, or enthusiastic, or silly in their emotional excesses. He will be eminently rational. In the Appendix of *The Sound and the Fury*, Faulkner sarcastically calls him "the first sane Compson since Culloden" (p. 420).

As for the kind of eye through which the mind of Whiggery looks out upon the world, what about Flem Snopes's? Faulkner describes Flem's eye as the color of stagnant water, and the description is telling. Flem lacks the other-worldly rapture of the saint or the drunkard. Ecstasy—being able to stand outside one's self and one's narrow range of interests—that is what is quite impossible for Flem, who is impotent and without appetites of any kind. It is just as hard to imagine him jovially tipsy as it is to imagine him on his knees in prayer.

14. Ibid., p. 236.

Notes

1. FAULKNER'S POETRY

Faulkner's Translations of Verlaine

Faulkner's translations of four poems by Paul Verlaine were published in *The Mississippian* in the early months of 1920. Martin Kreiswirth has recently pointed out that all four had been previously translated by Arthur Symons and appear in an appendix to his *Symbolist Movement in Literature*. This work, dedicated to William Butler Yeats, was first published in 1899. It was somewhat revised and expanded in 1908 and would have been readily available to Faulkner in a New York reprint dated 1919.

Kreiswirth thinks it likely that Faulkner's friend, Phil Stone, in view of his interest in French literature, would have possessed a copy of this well-known work. At all events, on the basis of the correspondences between Symons's translations and Faulkner's, Kreiswirth judges that the young translator was thoroughly familiar with Symons's texts and was influenced by them in making his own translations. See "Faulkner as Translator: His Versions of Verlaine," *Mississippi Quarterly* 30 (1977) : 429–32.

Literary Borrowings and Echoes in Faulkner

The lists that follow make no pretense to being exhaustive. I have added to my own findings items discovered by others, and am particu-

345

larly indebted to the late Richard P. Adams, "The Apprenticeship of William Faulkner," *Tulane Studies in English* 12 (1962) : 113–56.

A. E. HOUSMAN
(See also in this volume, pp. 61–63.)

New Orleans Sketches

Page 7	Last Poems, X

A sound footing is good, and wine and women and fighting; but soon the fighting's done. . . .	Could man be drunk for ever
	   With liquor, love, or fights,
	Lief should I rouse at morning
	   And lief lie down of nights.

Page 28	A Shropshire Lad, XLIX
Thinking, indeed, lays lads underground.	Think no more; 'tis only thinking Lays lads underground.

Page 48	Ibid., XL
"Into my heart an air that kills"—	Into my heart an air that kills

A Green Bough

XIII	Last Poems, XXXIX
When I was young and proud and gay	When I was young and proud

XVI	Ibid., XLII
Behold me, in my feathered cap and doublet	Behold a youth that trod, With feathered cap on forehead.

XXI	A Shropshire Lad, XLIX
will prop the shaken sky	And the feather pate of folly Bears the falling sky.

XXV	Last Poems, IX
unprop the ultimate skies	Shoulder the sky, my lad, and drink your ale.

XLII	A Shropshire Lad, XXXI
Nazarene and Roman and Virginian	Then 'twas the Roman, now 'tis I.

Soldiers' Pay

Page 64	Ibid., XLIII
gets his sullen bones up and hales them along	Shall hale the sullen slaves [his bones] along

Page 291	Ibid., IV
evening, like a ship with twilight-colored sails, dreamed on down the world	And the ship of sunrise burning Strands upon the eastern rims.

Mosquitoes
Page *346*
and hearing his grumbling skeleton—that smug and dour and unshakable comrade who loves so well to say I told you so—

Ibid., XLIII
When I meet the morning beam
Or lay me down at night to dream,
I hear my bones within me say,
"Another night, another day.

"When shall this slough of sense be cast"

Flags in the Dust
Page *288*
it's all sort of messy: living and seething corruption glossed over for a while by smoothly colored flesh; all foul, until the clean and naked bone. . . .

Ibid., XLIII
And leave with ancient night alone
The stedfast and enduring bone.

Page *307*
letting his skeleton rest at last

[*as above*]

The Sound and the Fury
Page *219*
we must just stay awake and see evil done for a little while its not always
[See also Blotner, p. 544, who quotes part of a poem dated 14 March 1927, beginning: "Once there was a lightless time: I had not birth / —Be still, my heart, be still: you break in vain"]

Ibid., XLVIII
Be still, be still, my soul; it is but for a season;
Let us endure an hour and see injustice done.

The Wild Palms
Page *59*
If thine eye offend thee, pluck it out, lad, and be whole.

Ibid., XLV
If it chance your eye offend you,
Pluck it out, lad, and be sound:

Page *254*
leaving only the old permanent enduring bone, free and tramelless

Ibid., XLIII
And leave with ancient night alone
The stedfast and enduring bone.

See also Blotner (pp. 185–86 and p. *40*) for further examples of poems imitative of Housman.

T. S. Eliot
(See also in this volume, pp. 65–66.)

"Portrait of Elmer"
a sky like a patient etherized and dying after an operation

"The Love Song of J. Alfred Prufrock"
When the evening is spread out
    against the sky
Like a patient etherised upon a table;

The Marionettes	
Page 38	"Preludes"
the earth is like an aged woman gathering fagots in a barren field.	The worlds revolve like ancient women Gathering fuel in vacant lots.

"Nympholepsy"	
Pages 403 and 409	"Burbank with a Baedeker"
a girl like defunctive music	Defunctive music under sea

A Green Bough	
IV	*The Waste Land*
o spring	April is the cruellest month
above unsapped convolvulae of hills april a bee sipping perplexed with pleasure o spring o wanton or cruel	

VII	"Rhapsody on a Windy Night"
They [human beings] pass and pass, she [the moon] cares not whither;	La lune ne garde aucune rancune. . . . She is alone With all the old nocturnal smells That cross and cross across her brain.

XIX	"The Love Song of J. Alfred Prufrock"
He joins in green caressing wars With seamaids red and brown. . . .	We have lingered in the chambers of the sea By sea-girls wreathed with seaweed red and brown

XXVII	"Sweeney among the Nightingales"
The Raven black and Philomel Amid the bleeding trees were fixed. His hoarse cry and hers were mixed And through the dark their droppings fell. [This and two further stanzas of this seven-stanza poem are quoted on p. 247 of *Mosquitoes*.]	The nightingales are singing near The Convent of the Sacred Heart. And sang within the bloody wood When Agamemnon cried aloud, And let their liquid sifting fall To stain the stiff dishonored shroud.

Soldiers' Pay	
Page 134	"Rhapsody on a Windy Night"
La lune en grade [*sic*] aucune rancune	La lune ne garde aucune rancune

Pylon	
Page [236]	
"Lovesong of J. A. Prufrock" [title of chapter 6]	"The Love Song of J. Alfred Prufrock" [title of the poem]

Page 244	*Ibid.*
Jesus, if I was to go in there [where human beings are talking] I would drown.	Till human voices wake us, and we drown.

The Wild Palms

Page 19	"Preludes"
ghosts of a thousand rented days and nights	One thinks of all the hands That are raising dingy shades In a thousand furnished rooms.

A Fable

Page 223	"The Hippopotamus"
above earth's old miasmic mists	Wrapt in the old miasmal mist

Richard P. Adams discusses a half-dozen further borrowings from Eliot in his article cited above on "The Apprenticeship of William Faulkner." I think he may well be right in regarding them as such. The reader who is interested in the subject will want to consult Adams's essay. I believe, however, that the case is less clear than the instances I have noted.

MISCELLANEOUS BORROWINGS

The items mentioned in this list do not extend beyond such works as are discussed in the first six chapters of this volume. Omitted here also are borrowings from Housman, Eliot, Cabell, and Joyce, and items already treated in the foregoing chapters. For the borrowings from Cabell and Joyce, see pp. 364–66 and 370–72.

Man Collecting

	Kipling, chapter heading for "Lispeth"
Page 125	(from *Plain Tales from the Hills*)
"Aubade: Provence Sixth Century"	To my own gods I go.
With tangled trinities	It may be they shall give me greater ease Than your cold Christ and tangled Trinities.

The Marionettes

Page 33	*Romeo and Juliet* III.v.2
Never the nightingale 　Oh my dear, Never again the lark 　Wilt thou hear. . . .	It was the nightingale, and not the lark.

Page 40	Keats's "La Belle Dame Sans Merci"
no birds here call	And no birds sing.

Page 49	Amy Lowell's "Patterns"
and I shall wear a jade gown, and walk on the gravel paths in my garden	and I shall walk Up and down The patterned garden paths In my stiff, brocaded gown. . . .

Page 49	Oscar Wilde, *Salomé*
the jade on my fingernails	the silent, subtle Egyptians, with long nails of jade

The Marble Faun
> Page 28

The horns of sunset slowly sound

Tennyson's "Bugle Song"
The splendor falls on castle walls
And snowy summits old in story:
The long light shakes across the lakes,
And the wild cataract leaps in glory. . . .

O hark, O hear! how thin and clear, . . .
The horns of Elfland faintly blowing!

New Orleans Sketches
> Page 5

Ah God, ah God, that night should come so soon

Swinburne's "In the Orchard"
Hold my hair fast, and kiss me
    through it so.
Ah, God, ah God, that day should
    be so soon.

hold my hair fast, and kiss me through it—so: Ah, God, ah God, that day should be so soon.
See also *Soldiers' Pay*
> Page 181

Kiss me, kiss me through my hair. Dick, Dick.

[*as above*]

> Page 182

Kiss me through my hair, Dick, with all your ugly body.

[*as above*]

A Green Bough
> IV

        decay
makes death a cuckold yes lady
8 rue diena we take care of that yes

E. E. Cummings
[Compare the typography and format of almost any of the poems in Cummings's *XLI Poems*.]

> IX

The plowman slowly homeward wends

Gray's "Elegy in a Country Churchyard"
Slowly the ploughman wends his weary way

> X

—A terrific figure on an urn—

Keats's "Ode on a Grecian Urn"
[*generally*]

> XVI

strutting across this stage that men call living

Macbeth V.vi.24
That struts and frets his hour upon the stage

> XX

two walls of gray and topless stone

Marlowe's *Doctor Faustus*, line 1329
. . . the toplesse Towres of *Ilium*

A Green Bough [cont.]

XXIII Somewhere a moon will bloom and find me not	Fitzgerald's *Rubaiyat* (first edition), C How oft hereafter [the moon] rising shall she look Through this same Garden after me—in vain!
XXIV Wherein thy name like muted silver bells	Rostand's *Cyrano de Bergerac* [See pp. 55–57, above]
XXV And with the curving image of his fall Locked beak to beak	Whitman's "The Dalliance of Eagles" The clenching interlocking claws [Possibly also influenced by John Gould Fletcher's "Midwinter Love": "Straining to each other, grappling claw to claw"]
XXX Naught is bowled Save winter, in the sky	Fitzgerald's *Rubáiyát* (first edition), I . . . in the Bowl of Night. . . . *Ibid.,* LII And that inverted Bowl we call The Sky.
And Grief and Time are tideless golden seas	Swinburne's *Atalanta in Calydon* Time, with a gift of tears; Grief, with a glass that ran. Swinburne's *The Triumph of Time* By the tideless, dolorous midland sea, In a land of sand and ruin and gold.
XXXVIII [The poem is quoted entire on p. 252 of *Mosquitoes,* where it is given the title "Hermaphroditus."]	Swinburne "Dolores" and "The Garden of Proserpine" (passim). "Hermaphroditus" (source of the title of Faulkner's poem)
XLIII I would break so soft I'd break that hushed virginity of sleep that in her narrow house would she find me drowsing when she came awake—	Keats's "The Eve of St. Agnes" Stanzas XXXVI and XXXVII

Soldiers' Pay

Page 9 Alas, poor Jerks or something (I seen that in a play, see? Good line)	*Hamlet* V.i.202–03 Alas, poor Yorick! I knew him

Soldiers' Pay [cont.]

Page 10

Hark! the sound of battle and the laughing horses draws near. . . . But I would like to of seen one of them laughing horses.

The Book of Job 39 : 25

[the horse] saith among the trumpets, Ha, ha; and he smelleth the battle afar off, the thunder of the captains, and the shouting.

Page 37

. . . April come again into the world. Like a heedless idiot into a world that had forgotten Spring.

Edna St. Vincent Millay's "Spring"

April

Comes like an idiot, babbling and
    strewing flowers.

Page 44

high above a world of joy and sorrow and lust for living

Swinburne's "A Forsaken Garden"

In a coign of the cliff between lowland
    and highland

"The Garden of Proserpine"

From too much love of living,
From hope and fear set free. . . .

Page 49

. . . asked Cadet Lowe, swept and garnished and belligerent.

Matthew 12 : 44

I will return unto my house from whence I came out; and when he is come, he findeth it empty, swept, and garnished.

Page 57

Integer vitae scelerisque purus

Horace

Book 1, Song 22

Page 107

But here comes Othello. . . .

Shakespeare's *Othello*

Page 227

Do you know how falcons make love?

Whitman's "The Dalliance of Eagles"

Page 290

rigid as coral in a mellow tideless sea

Swinburne's "The Triumph of Time"

By the tideless dolorous midland sea

Page 315

Ah, Moon of my Delight, that know'st no wane [etc.]

[The stanza beginning "As autumn and the moon" is apparently of Faulkner's own composition.]

Fitzgerald's *Rubáiyát* (first edition)

Stanza LXXIV quoted

Page 318

Men have died and worms have eaten them, but not for love

As You Like It IV.i.81–82

But these are all lies: men have died from time to time and worms have eaten them, but not for love.

Mosquitoes

Page 49

coral in a tideless sea

Swinburne's "The Triumph of Time"

By the tideless dolorous midland sea

Mosquitoes [cont.]

Page 72	Fielding's *Tom Jones*
like Squire Western's hollo	

Page 169	Conrad's "The Heart of Darkness,"
(Section entitled "Six O'Clock")	Chapter 2, paragraph 4
Trees heavy and ancient with moss loomed out of it hugely and grayly: the mist might have been a sluggish growth between and among them. No, the mist might have been the first prehistoric morning of time itself. . . . [etc.]	Going up that river was like traveling back to the earliest beginnings of the world, when vegetation rioted on the earth and the big trees were kings. . . . [etc.]

Page 187	Poe's "Israfel"
ay ay strangle your heart o israfel winged with loneliness	In Heaven a spirit doth dwell "Whose heart-strings are a lute"

Page 339	Keats's "Ode to a Nightingale"
Genius . . . that instant of timeless beatitude . . . that passive state of the heart with which the mind, the brain, has nothing to do at all.	. . . I will fly to thee, Not charioted by Bacchus and his pards But on the viewless wings of Poesy, Though the dull brain perplexes and retards.

Flags in the Dust

Page 53	Kipling's "Recessional"
at last the tumult died and the captains departed	The tumult and the shouting dies— The captains and the kings depart—

Page 56	Kipling's "Tommy"
but when de trouble bust loose, hit's "Please, suh, Mr Colored Man, right dis way whar de bugle blowin', Mr Colored Man; you is de savior of de country	While it's Tommy this, an' Tommy that, an' Tommy fall be'ind," But it's "Please to walk in front, sir," when there's trouble on the wind— . . . . For it's Tommy this, an' Tommy that an' "Chuck him out, the brute!" But it's "Savior of 'is country" when the guns begin to shoot.

Pages 162 and 340	Keats's "Ode on a Grecian Urn"
Thou still unravished bride of quietude	Thou still unravish'd bride of quietness

Page 167	Milton's *Areopagitica*
removed from the dust and the heat	where that immortal garland is to be run for, not without dust and heat

Page 173	Swinburne's *Atalanta in Calydon*
Oaten reed above the lyre	And the oat is heard above the lyre

Flags in the Dust [cont.]

Page 205	The Tempest IV.i.47
while Simon bobbed and mowed in the corner	Each one, tripping on his toe, Will be here with mop and mow.

Page 241	Keats's "Ode on a Grecian Urn"
twilight, foster-dam of quietude and peace	Thou foster-child of silence and slow time

Page 339	Byron's *Don Juan*, VI.xxvii
I'd be sad that I couldn't be everywhere at once, or that all the spring couldn't be concentrated in one place like, Byron's ladies' mouths.	My wish is quite as wide . . . It being (not *now*, but only while a lad) That womankind had but one rosy mouth, To kiss them all at once from North to South.

Page 347	Shakespeare's "The Phoenix and the Turtle"
Reason in itself confounded. If what parts can so remain.	Reason, in itself confounded, Saw division grow together. . . .
	That it cried, "How true a twain Seemeth this concordant one! Love hath reason, reason none If what parts can so remain."

For borrowings from Siegfried Sassoon in Faulkner's "Literature and War" and in *Mosquitoes,* see Michael Millgate, "Faulkner and the Literature of the First World War," *Mississippi Quarterly* 26 (1973) : 389; and Martin Kreiswirth, "William Faulkner and Siegfried Sassoon," *Mississippi Quarterly* 29 (1976) : 433–34.

Miss Rosa Coldfield's Poetry

Though Miss Rosa Coldfield's creator has, perhaps wisely, refrained from providing the reader of *Absalom, Absalom!* with any examples of her verse, she had her pretensions, nevertheless. She was the self-appointed Poet Laureate of Yoknapatawpha County, and her principal theme, Faulkner has told us, was the gallantry and heroism of the Confederate soldier. Although Faulkner himself is on record with testimony to that gallantry and heroism, it is all too easy to imagine the banal and hackneyed quality of Miss Rosa's verse tributes. But Miss Rosa's real poetry—her long tirade against Thomas Sutpen which comprises nearly all of Chapter V—is a very different matter. It is a limited and contorted poetry, to be sure, much of it a dithyramb of hate—obsessed, bardic, self-intoxicated—but it is a kind of poetry nevertheless and possesses its own inner logic. Her shrill tense voice is not to be confused with Faulkner's, but her "poetry" can throw a good deal of light on Faulkner's own, for he undoubtedly put a great deal of himself into Miss Rosa; and though he always stands outside and above her Norn-like frenzy, she provided him with an outlet for an elevated, involved, highly mannered strain of rhetoric which was very dear to his own heart.

Miss Rosa, who, some forty-three years earlier, had been shocked by Thomas Sutpen's bald proposal that they should breed a child, with the promise that if the child should prove to be a male he would marry her, has lived ever since in, as Mr. Compson puts it, a state of permanent outrage. Now as she sits in her parlor with Quentin Compson through the long September afternoon, she pours out her indignation against Sutpen, the "demon." Thrice she refers to herself as a "self-mesmered fool." The adjective is obviously a clipped form of "self-mesmerized." Perhaps Faulkner saw nothing odd in the phrase, though he may have consciously tailored it to fit Miss Rosa's rather eccentric use of the language. We know that this is the way in which she would have put it and the phrase is beautifully accurate. What pours out through Miss Rosa's lips is a self-mesmered fool's furious, exuberant rhetoric. Nevertheless, the more passionate parts of it are telling and effective.

Like all passionate speech, Miss Rosa's is highly rhythmic and some of it comes close to a formalized accentual structure. One can clearly hear the beat and cadences in the following passage in which Miss Rosa tells how as a young girl she observed the garden paths through which the lovers, Judith and Bon, walked:

> I was not spying, who would walk those raked and sanded garden paths and think "This print was his save for this obliterating rake, that even despite the rake it is still there and hers beside it in that slow and mutual rhythm wherein the heart, the mind, does not need to watch the docile (ay, the willing) feet"; would think "What suspiration of the twinning souls have the murmurous myriad ears of this secluded vine or shrub listened to? what vow, what promise, what rapt biding fire has the lilac rain of this wistaria, this heavy rose's dissolution, crowned?" [p. 148]

One can hardly avoid scanning the last clause, so regular is the beat of its measure. (See p. 356.)

What vow, | what pro|mise what | rapt bi|ding fire
has the li|lac rain | of this | wistar|ia
this hea|vy rose|'s dis|solu|tion crowned

Much of her speech is taken up with trying to convey to Quentin the experience of a lonely, shy, fourteen-year-old girl, so yearning for love that she comes to participate vicariously in Bon's courtship of Judith. Her motive was not envy, she assures Quentin, nor was she spying on the young couple. She is certain that she herself was not in love with Bon. She tells Quentin:

> (I did not love him; how could I? I had never even heard his voice, had only Ellen's word for it that there was such a person) and quick not for the spying which you will doubtless call it, which during the past six months between that New Year's and that June gave substance to that shadow with a name emerging from Ellen's vain and garrulous folly, that shape without even a face yet because I had not even seen the photograph then, reflected in the secret and bemused gaze of a young girl: because I who had learned nothing of love, not even parents' love—that fond dear constant violation of privacy, that stultification of the burgeoning and incorrigible I which is the meed and due of all mammalian meat, became not mistress, not beloved, but more than even love; I became all polymath love's androgynous advocate. [p. 146]

"All polymath love's androgynous advocate" has, of course, been pounced upon as absurd: on reflection one realizes that it is a perfectly accurate description of Miss Rosa's state of mind in that faraway summer. Moreover, by this time we have been convinced that Miss Rosa is quite capable of this phraseology: this is just what she would have said. If the adjective "androgynous" sticks in the reader's craw, he might turn back to page 144. There one finds the preparation for "androgynous" in Miss Rosa's confession that during this "miscast summer of my barren youth which (for that short time, that short brief unreturning springtime of the female heart) I lived out not as a woman, a girl, but rather as the *man* which I perhaps should have been" (italics mine). Indeed, the special pathos of her situation, as Miss Rosa now sees it, was that Judith's love affair summoned her own stunted womanhood to birth.

The metaphor of a reluctant and difficult birth haunts Miss Rosa's account of her early life. In describing her childhood (p. 144) she suggests that it was not the experience of a person living in the world but more nearly that of a babe unborn. She was then not truly alive but "some projection of the lightless womb itself; I [,] gestate and complete, not aged, just overdue because of some caesarean lack, some cold head-nuzzling forceps of the savage time which should have torn me free. . . ."

"Caesarean lack" represents a fierce compression which in any freshman theme would doubtless earn the blue pencil. But again, it is a phrase that one would rather expect Miss Rosa to invent and perhaps it makes the notion more compact by its ungrammatical compression: her difficult birth struggle required a caesarean section or—if not that, at least a "cold head-nuzzling forceps" to pull her into the light.

The birth imagery continues: she tells Quentin that "instead of accomplishing the processional and measured milestones of the childhood's time I lurked, unapprehended as though, shod with the very damp and velvet silence of the womb, I displaced no air, gave off no betraying sound, from one closed forbidden door to the next [the womb image merging into that of a long corridor of closed doors] and so acquired all I knew of that light and space in which people moved and breathed as I (that same child) might have gained conception of the sun from seeing it through a piece of smoky glass—fourteen, four years younger than Judith, four years later than Judith's moment which only virgins know: when the entire delicate spirit's bent is one anonymous climaxless epicene and unravished nuptial . . ." (p. 145).

Absurd or not, Miss Rosa can rise to the occasion with the proper metaphor. She does so when she describes her coming into the house in response to the news that Henry has killed Charles Bon. Miss Rosa possesses something of Cassandra's prophetic vision. As she faces the house she sees in it "some desolation more profound than ruin, as if it had stood in iron juxtaposition to iron flame, to a holocaust which had found itself less fierce and less implacable, not hurled but rather fallen back before the impervious and indomitable skeleton which the flames durst not, at the instant's final crisis, assail . . ." (p. 136).

The essential metaphor is that which identifies a man with his house. But how powerfully it is used here! Sutpen's mansion, which he has wrested from the swamp almost as if by supernatural power, has a special relation to him, seems to be an extension of him, and since, in Miss Rosa's eyes, he is a demon, it reveals itself as the fit abode for a demon, a kind of metallic inferno, impervious to fire.

Miss Rosa goes on to say: "there was even one step, one plank rotted free and tilting beneath the foot (or would have if I had not touched it light and fast) as I ran up and into the hallway whose carpet had long since gone with the bed- and table-linen for lint, and saw the Sutpen face. . . ."

The Sutpen face belongs to Clytie, the mulatto woman who is Sutpen's natural daughter and Judith's half-sister. Miss Rosa has always despised and feared Clytie and now Clytie is "there in the dim light, barring the stairs: and I running out of the bright afternoon, into the thunderous silence of that brooding house where I could see nothing at first: then gradually the face, the Sutpen face not approaching, not swimming up out of the gloom, but already there, rocklike and firm and antedating time and house and doom and all, waiting there (oh yes, he chose well; he bettered choosing, who created in his own image the cold Cerberus of his private hell)—the face without sex or age because it had never possessed either: the same sphinx face which she had been born with . . ." (p. 136).

One assumes that Miss Rosa had read Byron and Scott; but evidently she knows her Shakespeare too. When she bursts into the house, aghast at what she has heard, eager to find out just what had happened, she is met by more than Clytie's sphinx face: she is arrested by Judith's quiet and apparently unperturbed voice, and Rosa sees herself as a Hamlet, standing before the arras behind which is concealed some secret terror. She is afraid to slash through it to reveal the truth. She tells Quentin that "even at nineteen [I] must have known that living is one constant and perpetual instant when the arras-veil before what-is-to-be hangs docile and even glad to the lightest naked thrust if we had dared, were brave enough (not wise enough: no wisdom needed here) to make the rending gash" (pp. 142–43).

Miss Rosa's mind is evidently saturated with Macbeth's great final soliloquy: "Life's but a walking shadow, a poor player" etc. The shadow image comes into her speech as she tries to convey to Quentin the demonic quality of Thomas Sutpen. To Quentin she insists that Sutpen "was not articulated in this world. He was a walking shadow. He was the light-blinded bat-like image of his own torment cast by the fierce demoniac lantern up from beneath the earth's crust and hence in retrograde, reverse; from abysmal and chaotic dark to eternal and abysmal dark completing his descending (do you mark the gradation?)

ellipsis, clinging, trying to cling with vain unsubstantial hands to what he hoped would hold him, save him . . ." (p. 171).

I don't contend that all the rhetoric that Faulkner puts into Miss Rosa's mouth can be defended—nor that all the author's own rhetoric in this novel and in others is defensible. But Faulkner is much more often the master of it than his early critics have given him credit for being. In any case, by making Miss Rosa responsible for the most overblown rhetoric of *Absalom, Absalom!* Faulkner has gone far toward providing it with a dramatic justification.

Since Miss Rosa does not know why Henry killed Charles Bon, she cannot possibly make sense of the events that brought about the fall of the house of Sutpen and destroyed her own family. She is necessarily forced into a "devil theory" in order to account for them and she expresses her sense of the demonic brilliantly. But Miss Rosa is not without insight, nor, in spite of her inflamed rhetoric, does she lack literary flair. She is utterly sincere; she is carried away with her rhapsodic convictions; yet at the same time she manages to maintain something of an artist's detachment. She has, for example, a good sense of the histrionic. She is conscious of the fact that she is acting a part, and from page 169 to 171 she actually refers to herself in the third person as if she were a character in a play.

To listen to her, as Quentin is compelled to listen to her through that September afternoon, is to witness the eruption of a small volcano, pouring forth its long pent-up subterranean fires. The perfervid emotion is there, and her torrent of words is impelled by an inner necessity. But it is not mere raving. On the contrary, she is able to dramatize her convictions, to make credible a demonic force, and to set before our imaginations a scene in which this force resides as an immanent power.

Miss Rosa, it should be pointed out, is largely responsible for the celebrated "Gothic" quality of this novel. Mr. Compson's stoicism and his weary cynicism hardly point in this direction. It is Miss Rosa who invests Sutpen's Hundred with nameless horrors and infernal presences. Again and again, in her long tirade, she speaks of hearing something different from Clytie's voice or Judith's. It is an inhuman voice, that of the house speaking, and (p. 160) she creates for the reader, if he will attend to her, what the house means to her. The house is the physical shell of the master who has created it for his own purposes. Thus she describes her life with Clytie and Judith at Sutpen's Hundred while Sutpen was away at the War:

> Something ate with us; we talked to it and it answered questions; it sat with us before the fire at night and, rousing without any warning from some profound and bemused complete inertia, talked, not to us, the six ears, the three minds capable of listening, but to the air, the waiting grim decaying presence, spirit, of the house itself, talking that which sounded like the bombast of a madman who creates within his very coffin walls his fabulous immeasurable Camelots and Carcassonnes. [p. 160]

This is a brilliant rendition of Sutpen's megalomania, and though Miss Rosa, in her excited reverie, gives it the quality of a myth, the description has such truth as myth is capable of. Sutpen may or may not have ever heard of Camelot, but Miss Rosa has apprehended the nature of his obsessive dream.

For Miss Rosa, Sutpen speaks "the bombast of a madman," and she takes her cue from him, replying with a bombast of her own, that of a woman warped by loneliness and outrage. But even bombast, as directed by a master rhetorician, can on occasion touch poetry, can become the inevitable means of revealing something about Miss Rosa and, in its own perverse way, something about Sutpen also.

As I have remarked on an earlier page, Miss Rosa's "poetry" is a special and limited kind of Faulkner's prose-poetry. It lacks, for example, the quality of passionate nature-worship that invests the account of Ike McCaslin's visit to the graves of Lion and Sam Fathers in "The Bear," and it has little in common with the deeply moving pastoralism of those passages in *The Hamlet* where Faulkner describes the wanderings of Ike Snopes and the goddess whom he worships, the cow. In chapter 1 of Book 3 of *The Hamlet*, a rainstorm overtakes them. We are told that the rain descended "without warning" but that, nevertheless, Ike watched it "for some time and without alarm." The gathering rainstorm was at first

> wanton and random and indecisive before it finally developed, concentrated, drooping in narrow unperpendicular bands in two or three different places at one time, about the horizon, like gauzy umbilical loops from the bellied cumulae, the sun-belled ewes of summer grazing up the wind from the southwest. It was as if the rain were actually seeking the two of them [cow and boy], hunting them out and where they stood amid the shade, finding them finally in a bright intransigent fury. . . . striking in thin brittle strokes through [Ike's] hair and shirt and against his lifted

face, each brief lance already filled with the glittering promise of its imminent cessation like the brief saltless tears of a young girl over a lost flower. [pp. 184–85]

This is vigorous—even exuberant writing. The writer has let himself go. He is not even pretending in his description to be following the movement of the idiot's mind, but how vividly he makes us participate in the scene!

But Faulkner has also let himself go—albeit in another spirit and in an attempt to secure another effect—in penning Miss Rosa's tirade against her demon brother-in-law. In her impassioned narrative to Quentin Compson, as she warms to her subject, she reveals a strain of genius which one is certain never showed itself in her banal celebrations of Confederate heroes. (Those poems were surely feeble conventional imitations of Father Ryan's "Furl that banner, for 'tis weary" or "The Sword of Robert Lee.") The Poetess Laureate of Yoknapatawpha County, one is certain, was not able to succeed in her formal verse any more than her creator was able to succeed in his. Yet if Miss Rosa shared this weakness of her great creator, she also inherited some portion of his strength. It will be an insensitive reader indeed who cannot find flecks of genuine poetry in her prose narrative. One may be sure that Faulkner wrote it *con amore*.

Like Miss Rosa, Faulkner also had a hankering for the highfalutin and the grandiloquent, for a sonorous and bardic rhetoric. He never quite put this hankering aside. His creation of Miss Rosa gave him a privileged means for indulging it and, in indulging it, he proved that it could be turned into a kind of poetry. Baroque pearls are misshapen but they have the substance of genuine pearls.

2. EARLY ROMANTIC PROSE

PRUNELLA

In an article entitled "William Faulkner's *The Marionettes*" (*Mississippi Quarterly* 26 [1973] : 247–80), Noel Polk suggests *Prunella* as a possible source for *The Marionettes*. This play by Laurence Housman and H. Granville-Barker was first produced at the Royal Court Theatre in London on 23 December 1904 and was first published by A. H. Bullen in London in 1906.

Polk concedes that there is no evidence that Faulkner ever knew of the play or read it; nevertheless, the number of parallels between *The Marionettes* and *Prunella* is remarkably large. In both plays, as Polk points out, the action takes place in a formal garden enclosed within a thick hedge or wall, and containing a fountain and pool. In both plays, the heroine is the daughter of a young woman who has been enticed away from her garden by a man who declares his undying love for her but who later on abandons her. Pregnant with his child, she makes her way back to her home to die. The child (named Marietta in *The Marionettes*, Prunella in the Housman-Barker play) survives and is reared by her three maiden aunts, who bring her up strictly and carefully shield her from all traffic with the outside world.

The girl is, however, in her turn, seduced by a character who calls himself Pierrot. He persuades her to accept his love and to follow him out into the world. (In *The Marionettes*, Pierrot calls the moon "his foster mother"; in *Prunella*, he tells the girl that he is the man in the moon.) In both plays Pierrot subsequently abandons the girl and she returns to her home alone. Polk is surely right in claiming that these make up quite a bundle of resemblances, if they are no more than that.

I can add one more item to the list. In *The Marionettes* there is a rather mysterious figure called the Spirit of Autumn, who accompanies himself on the violin as he descants at length on the desolation of the autumnal garden and the loss of love. In *Prunella*, the marble fountain statue, said to represent Love, holds a "viol and bow" as if ready to play a melody. In two crucial scenes in *Prunella* the statue comes to life and actually plays on his viol.

In their general atmosphere, however, the plays differ radically. *The Marionettes* concludes as a very ornate mood piece, with Marietta admiring her own beauty and looking forward, with what amounts to somber relish, to her eventual death in her formal garden. The authors of *Prunella*, however, manage to contrive a happy ending, with a contrite Pierrot returning to the garden to find that Prunella herself has also just returned. The curtain falls with the statue of Love now madly playing on his viol as the ecstatic lovers fondly embrace.

Prunella is as silly and sentimental as *The Marionettes* is perversely and almost lushly "decadent." Yet the resemblances between them are striking, and one is tempted to believe that Faulkner may have been influenced by the earlier play. Polk points out that through his friendship with Phil Stone or "with drama critic and novelist Stark Young,"

Faulkner might have had *Prunella* called to his attention. He dated at least three copies of *The Marionettes* "1920" (Polk, p. 252); by September 1920, there had been twelve printings of *Prunella*. Evidently, one need not have been a collector of rare books to have come by a copy.

In his article, Polk pretty effectually disposes of another proposed source for *The Marionettes*—Edna St. Vincent Millay's *Aria da Capo*, another play about Pierrot. We know that Faulkner reviewed it for *The Mississippian*. But as Polk points out, there are few close parallels between the Faulkner and the Millay plays. Furthemore, *Aria da Capo* was not published until 1920, and if Faulkner is correct in the date he assigns to his composition of *The Marionettes*, the chances of his having had a chance to read it before starting work on his own play are slim.

Modern Literary Sources for Faulkner's Use of Nympholepsy

Phyllis Wheatly has discovered the probable source of Faulkner's reference to Pico della Mirandola (in *Soldiers' Pay*, p. 225) and the Platonic Academy at Florence in Joseph Hergesheimer's novel, *Linda Condon* (1919), a book which Faulkner reviewed (see *Mississippi Quarterly* 22 [1969]: 207–13). Faulkner's association of "nympholepsy" with Platonism and Mirandola would confirm the view, expressed earlier in chapter 2, that Faulkner regarded the nympholeptic experience as one in which the divine idea or form shone through the sensual experience.

Ellen Graham has called to my attention another possible modern source for Faulkner's concern with nympholepsy and the nympholeptic experience, Conrad Aiken's *The Charnel Rose*. In a letter of 8 June 1928 Aiken tells Houston Peterson that in 1915 he "began the first out-and-out symphony, on the theme of nympholepsy: The Charnel Rose." [1] The term *nympholepsy* is, to be sure, never mentioned in the poem itself, but the elusive maiden does appear again and again. For example, the speaker at one point says to the wind, "was it you I followed after / And your cool hand I felt against my face?" But he only hears "in the dark, a stifled laughter." Later, he "dreamed of the dream he saw among the shadows, / And followed her through

1. See *Selected Letters of Conrad Aiken*, ed. Joseph Killorin (New Haven, 1978).

his dreams, despairingly." His pursuit of this dream maiden, like that of the young man in Faulkner's "Nympholepsy," is unavailing. Yet she haunts his consciousness and he cannot give up his search for her.

The young Faulkner was familiar with the poetry of Aiken and was high in his praise of it. In his "Verse Old and Nascent" (*The Double Dealer* for April 1925) Faulkner tells his reader that "Conrad Aiken's minor music still echoes in my heart," and in *The Mississippian* (for 16 February 1921) he reviews, and most favorably, Aiken's *Turns and Movies*. In that review he does not refer specifically to *The Charnel Rose*, but he does refer to *The Jig of Forslin* and *The House of Dust*. He concludes his review with a prophecy: that in fifteen years, say, "when the tide of aesthetic sterility which is slowly engulfing us has withdrawn," perhaps Aiken will emerge as "our first great poet."

The Influence of JURGEN

The basic theme of *Mayday* may be said to derive from Housman, though its more playful and cynical tone, especially in the treatment of sex, comes straight out of James Branch Cabell's *Jurgen*. Faulkner's debt to this book in his early period is immense. It would be tedious to try to record all the passages in *Mayday* that echo descriptions and episodes in *Jurgen*, but the following citations should establish the fact that the number is very large.

Early in the narrative of *Mayday* Galwyn sees his future life exhibited in pictures of people and events within the stream on the banks of which he stands. Compare "persons . . . were seen by him in quick bright flashes, like pictures suddenly transmuted into other pictures" (*Jurgen*, New York, 1919, p. 17).

A little later Galwyn comes through a forest up to the door of a large house that seems at first quite empty. Compare: "Then Jurgen came through a forest, wherein he saw many things not salutary to notice, to a great stone house like a prison. . . . But he could find nobody about the place . . ." (p. 39).

Jurgen discovers that "Guenevere was behaving with not quite the decorum which might fairly be expected of a princess" (p. 108). It is the discovery that Galwyn makes over and over in the course of his adventures.

Galwyn decides to quit life because life is meaningless. Jurgen, to be sure, does not, but the same lesson about life is read to Jurgen over and over: The brown man, Jurgen protests, would have it "that even I am of no importance" (p. 138). That "queer Horvendile would have me think," Jurgen reflects, that life "was a dream that had no sense to it" (pp. 222–23). Jurgen observes: "Many lands we have visited and many sights we have seen: and at the end all that we have done is a tale that is told; and it is a tale that does not matter" (p. 314).

The influence of *Jurgen* extends far beyond *Mayday*. There are plenty of borrowings and echoes to be found in Faulkner's other early writings. In *Soldiers' Pay* (p. 67) Januarius Jones, "like Jurgen," says, "I will try any drink once." Galwyn, too, borrows these words from Jurgen. Also in *Soldiers' Pay* (p. 44), Margaret Powers thinks of the body of her dead husband as having "become now a seething of worms, like new milk." Margaret may not have read *Jurgen*, but Faulkner had. Witness: "Worm's meat! this is the destined food, do what you will, of small white worms. This [hand] by and by will be a struggling pale corruption, like seething milk" (p. 35). Faulkner uses the figure again in "Carcassonne": "Of a man the worm should be lusty, lean, hairedover. Of women, of delicate girls . . . it should be suavely shaped, feeding into prettiness, feeding. *what though to Me but as a seething of new milk. Who am the Resurrection and the Life*" (*Collected Stories*, p. 897).

Even in Faulkner's later work one finds echoes of *Jurgen*. The "seething worms" image turns up in *The Wild Palms* (p. 138). The Library of Cocaigne (*Jurgen*, p. 176) provided the "Gratifications" which were one of the temptations vainly dangled before the eyes of Flem Snopes by the Prince of Hell in *The Hamlet* (p. 152). Faulkner's reading of *Jurgen* also accounts, I should think, for the name "Spintrius," given to a slave by Uncle Buddy in *Go Down, Moses*. In the Library of Cocaigne, Jurgen read "the Spintrian Treatises and the Thirty-two Gratifications" (p. 176). Faulkner read the titles of these mythical books and, I suppose, looked up "Spintrian" and found that it led him to *spintrius*, which some commentator has assumed to be the Latin noun meaning brothel-keeper, a post that the man who claimed to be a preacher and proved to be worthless for anything else about the plantation finally achieved.

An interesting question is how Uncle Buddy became acquainted with the word *spintrius* or how he knew any Latin at all. But though his spelling of English words was often shaky, perhaps he had had some bits of a classical education. If so, his knowledge of Latin was very shaky too. The proper noun is not *spintrius* but *spintria*, masculine in gender though belonging to the first declension (cf. *nauta, poeta, agricola,* etc.); and it signifies a male prostitute, not a brothel-keeper.

The most astonishing echo of *Jurgen* is heard in *A Fable,* in the crucial scene in which the Corporal confronts the Old Marshal. This scene and its ultimate derivation from *Jurgen* is discussed on pp. 245–46, above.

3. *SOLDIERS' PAY*

A Chronology for SOLDIERS' PAY

In this chronology I have tried to see just how precisely one might date the various events, not because such fine precision is important to the meaning of the novel, but because I wanted to test Faulkner's own care in controlling his time scheme. The answer that I get is: almost unbelievably precise, a matter all the more surprising in view of the fact that *Soldiers' Pay* is a first novel.

Precision of this order has to be intentional. There are plenty of hints to confirm this supposition. Why the careful dating of Lowe's letters except to supply a sort of calendar? Why else the mention of a half moon on page 286 (the day of Donald's death) and of a full moon on page 312 (the night of Margaret's departure)? Why else several indications of a Saturday by the mule-drawn wagons ranged around the courthouse square or the statement that the Rector was busy writing his sermon?

I had worked out a rough chronology before I discovered that Margaret Yonce had already constructed one as an appendix to her dissertation entitled *"Soldiers' Pay:* A Critical Study of William Faulkner's First Novel" (University of South Carolina, 1970). Our chronologies differed in only minor ways. But, by taking into account the days of the week (which one is able to do since we know that the year was 1919) I have been able to add some refinements and usually to name a specific day rather than to suggest two or three possible days. In what follows, I acknowledge my debt to Margaret Yonce and to two of my graduate students at the University of North Carolina at Chapel Hill, Patricia Johnson and Marlene Youmans, who have turned up other specific hints and clues.

The year is 1919 (see p. 188).

30 March *Sunday*	Gilligan and Lowe get drunk on a train headed for Buffalo (pp. 19, 22).
31 March *Monday*	This must be the day following 30 March (see p. 24). Gilligan and Lowe board a train on which they meet Donald Mahon and also Margaret Powers. All four stop at Cincinnati and spend the night in a hotel (p. 34). That night there is a "prophecy of April come again into the world" (p. 37).
1 April *Tuesday*	Margaret persuades Lowe to board a train for San Francisco, his home. Margaret and Joe Gilligan decide to see Donald safely home (in Charlestown, Ga.).
2 April *Wednesday*	Lowe writes a letter to Margaret from some point west of St. Louis (p. 103). If the letter must have taken at least two days to reach Charlestown, Ga., the events related on pp. 103–40 must have occurred on 4 April.
3 April *Thursday*	Margaret, Joe, and Donald arrive in Charlestown in the early afternoon (pp. 75–94).
4 April *Friday*	The events recorded on pp. 103–40 occur on this day: see entry of 2 April.
5 April *Saturday*	Cecily Saunders declares that she will have nothing to do with Donald. Her father then forbids her to see George Farr; nevertheless, she slips out to see him and later sends him a note arranging to meet him that night (pp. 140–46). That it is a Saturday is confirmed by the concourse of mules and horses in the town square (pp. 144, 146).
5–6 April (*night of*)	Cecily loses her virginity to George (p. 147).
6 April *Sunday*	George encounters Cecily on the street but she astonishes him by hurrying away after only the briefest of greetings (p. 148).
12 April *Saturday*	On this day Donald's "homecoming was hardly a nine days' wonder even" (p. 149). (Donald had arrived on 3 April.) The day is a Saturday, for the town square is thronged with wagons in from the country (p. 151), and the Rector is writing out "to-morrow's sermon" (p. 151).

Margaret receives a letter from Lowe (writing from San Francisco) dated 5 April (p. 153).

14 April *Monday*	The specialist from Atlanta arrives and examines Donald. He tells Margaret that Donald's sight "is practically gone now" and that he will soon die (p. 154). Margaret tells the doctor that Joe had already "two weeks ago" prophesied Donald's death. (Joe made his comment on 31 March; p. 40.) After the Atlanta specialist leaves, Margaret and Joe go for a walk and pass a lumber mill where Negroes are at work (p. 157); thus, it is presumably a Monday, not a Sunday and probably not a Saturday afternoon.
19 April *Saturday*	Dr. Gary, a local physician, calls, and reports that Donald is blind—has been for "three or four days" (p. 167). Compare this information with the entry for 14 April above. The Rector is writing a sermon (pp. 167–68), a circumstance that suggests a Saturday: compare with the entry for 12 April. A letter dated 14 April arrives from Lowe (p. 186). Mrs. Wardle gives a dance, at which Margaret, Joe, and Donald are present (pp. 187–211).
28 April *Monday*	Cecily meets George at the drugstore (p. 214), but later is startled to see Jones, who she fears may have overheard her conversation with George. She dismisses George and takes Jones home with her for lunch. Yonce dates this meeting 26 or 27 April, but since Cecily's mother mentions that this is a school day for Cecily's young brother (p. 230), the date is probably Monday, 28 April.
28–29 April (*night of*)	George tries to keep his tryst with Cecily, but Jones appears too. They scuffle, but neither is able to drive the other off. The darkness of the night is stressed (pp. 236, 239), but since the stars can be seen (p. 236), the time would seem to be the dark of the moon. (See 6 May below.)
29 April *Tuesday*	Cecily comes to the rectory to tell Donald that she will marry him after all (pp. 244–45).

29–30 April (*night of*)	It rains (p. 247).
30 April *Wednesday*	A letter from Lowe dated 24 April reaches Margaret (p. 246). On this day occur the events described on pp. 247–79, including Cecily's elopement with George.
1 May *Thursday*	Cecily Saunders was married to George "the next day" after she and George "drove out of town" (p. 281) and Margaret was married to Donald, having "at last married someone, putting an end to [an] equivocal situation" (p. 281). "And so April became May" (p. 281).
? 6 May *Monday*	Donald Mahon dies (p. 294). On that evening there was a half moon in the sky (pp. 286–91). If 28 April was the dark of the moon and if this half moon is the first quarter of its monthly cycle, the date should be about 6 May.
7 May *Tuesday*	Donald Mahon's funeral (p. 295). Presumably the funeral took place the day after he died. On the evening after the funeral, Emmy remembered that "Tomorrow was washday" (p. 301). But her regular washday, if she has one, must be Wednesday; see the entry for 30 April and p. 250. After the funeral, Margaret tells the Rector that she will soon be leaving (p. 300).
14 May *Tuesday*	Margaret takes the train from Charlestown. The moon is full (p. 312).

It must be conceded, however, that "Section 7" on page 315 cannot be reconciled with the chronology given above. But then I believe that this section cannot be reconciled with any reading of the text printed in *Soldiers' Pay*. For in Section 7 we are told that, on the day that Margaret departed, there lay on the Rector's desk a letter from Margaret to Julian Lowe in which she had told him of her marriage to Donald and of Donald's death. The letter has been returned with the notation, "Removed. Present address unknown." But for a letter to be sent to San Francisco and returned, even if the return was immediate, would require a period longer than eight days. If we try to remedy this matter by ignoring the apparent reference to the new moon (28–29 April) and consider the half moon referred to on page 286 as the moon of the *last* quarter, then the time until the next full moon would extend to three weeks, much too long for Margaret to have tarried in Charlestown. Note that she tells the Rector right after Donald's funeral that she will be leaving (p. 300). It is hard to believe that she would have then stayed three weeks longer. Moreover, such a time scheme ignores other events in the novel. For example, George and Cecily return from their honeymoon on the very day of Margaret's departure, and the interval between 1 May and 14 May provides a more probable length for the honeymoon than from 1 May to, say, 28 May, the next full moon which was shining when Margaret departed and George and Cecily returned.

In the chronology I have proposed, the length of time between Donald's marriage (1 May) and his death (6 May) may seem somewhat short in view of the fact that the Atlanta specialist calls twice during this period; but two calls are not impossible. Granted a few days' leeway, the chronology proposed is thoroughly credible (Section 7 on p. 315 excepted), and the dates, especially those from 30 March to 1 May, fit together with unexpected precision and coherence.

The Influence of James Joyce

Clearly Faulkner knew Joyce's "Portrait of the Artist as a Young Man" by the time that he was writing *Mosquitoes* (published in 1927). (See p. 132, above.) I think that he probably also knew *Ulysses* at this time. Compare the following passages from *Mosquitoes* (p. 206) and *Ulysses*. In the first, David, the cabin boy, tired and thirsty, is walking along a Louisiana road on an August afternoon.

> Getting to be afternoon, getting to be later than it was once. Three steps, then. All right. Man walks on his hind legs; a man can take three steps, a monkey can take three steps, but there is water in a monkey's cage, in a pan. Three steps. All right. One. Two. Three. Gone. Gone. Gone. It's a red sound. Not behind your eyes. Sea, See. Sea, See. You're in a cave, You're in a cave of dark sound, the sound of the sea is outside the cave. Sea. See. Sea. See. Not when they keep stepping in front of the door.

The following passage is from the opening paragraphs of the third chapter of *Ulysses*. Stephen Dedalus is walking along Sandymount strand.

Stephen closed his eyes to hear his boots crush crackling wrack and shells. You are walking through it howsomever. I am, a stride at a time. A very short space of time through very short times of space. Five, six: the *nacheinander*. Exactly: and that is the ineluctable modality of the audible. . . . Open your eyes now. I will. One moment. Has all vanished since? If I open and am for ever in the black adiaphane. *Basta!* I will see if I can see.

There are hints that Faulkner knew Joyce before he published *Mosquitoes*. The clearest that I have found occur in *Soldiers' Pay*, where page 152 is broken into sections with such captions as "The Town," "Young Robert Saunders," "George Farr," etc.; page 261 has similar captions. Compare the similar pattern in the Circe chapter of *Ulysses*. Pages 492–93, for example, contain captions that read "Alexander J. Dowie," "The Mob," "Bloom," "Dr. Mulligan," etc.[1]

In *Flags in the Dust* there seems to be another fairly clear echo of *Ulysses*. On page 173 the author reveals Horace Benbow's thoughts as he regards the figure of his young tennis partner, a girl in her early teens. He watches "the taut revelations of her speeding body in a sort of ecstasy. Girlwhite and all thy little Oh. Not pink, no. For a moment I thought she'd no. Disgraceful, her mamma would call it. Or any older woman." Compare Leopold Bloom's musings on the exhibition put on by Gerty MacDowell as she sits on the beach some distance away: "O sweety all your little girlwhite up I saw dirty bracegirdle made me do love . . ." (*Ulysses*, Modern Library, 1961 printing, p. 382).

The most interesting examples of the influence of Joyce on Faulkner, however, occur in *Absalom, Absalom!* They represent important adaptations of Joyce's more audacious strategies to the problems of presentation that Faulkner encountered in this highly complicated novel. On page 187 Shreve asks Quentin to tell him again about his visit to Sutpen's Hundred when he and Mr. Compson found themselves on the grounds of the plantation one autumn afternoon. (They had been hunting quail.) Shreve's speech ends thus: ". . . what was his name? the nigger on the mule? Luster—Luster to lead them around the ditch. . . ." Quentin answers, "Yes," but he does not utter the word "Yes" until the reader has been forced to read some twenty-seven pages further into the book—pages filled with Quentin's memories of the sodden day, his conversations with his father, a long account (by

1. Another possible borrowing from *Ulysses* to be found in *Soldiers' Pay* has been discussed above, on p. 75.

his father) of the quadroon woman's visit to Bon's grave, and the story of the life and death of Charles Etienne Bon at Sutpen's Hundred. Moreover, the reverie goes on to provide the reader with Quentin's conjectures about Judith's life and death and Quentin's memories of a much earlier visit to Sutpen's Hundred, the one on which, as a boy, he had had his first glimpse of Clytie and Jim Bond.

When Quentin does answer "Yes" to Shreve's question, Shreve then makes this comment: "And that was the one Luster was talking about now" (p. 215). The context makes it plain that "the one" has to be Jim Bond, though Quentin *has not called his name*. In fact, Shreve has in effect pulled out of Quentin's *unvoiced* reverie his reference to "Jim Bond, the hulking . . . boy a few years older and bigger than you were . . ." (p. 214).

Shreve and Quentin evidently enjoy an intimate mental rapport on this night in which they are trying to discover the truth about Thomas Sutpen's life and death. Later in the novel (on p. 358) there is an even more astonishing instance of such rapport. At the end of a seven-page reverie in Quentin's mind (or perhaps it is a joint reverie—his mind and Shreve's visualizing together) Shreve picks up the last item in the reverie, as if it had been spoken aloud, and makes a pointed and relevant comment upon it. In his mind he has evidently followed every thought in the sequence that has run through Quentin's mind. (For further discussion of these matters, see pp. 314–18, above.)

Compare with such narrative strategies the following passage from the Circe chapter of *Ulysses*. On page 478 Leopold Bloom is talking with the young whore Zoe. Zoe jollies him for his volubility, saying: "Go on. Make a stump speech of it. Talk away till you're black in the face." But this third and last sentence in her speech does not appear in the text until page 499, for Joyce has sandwiched in some twenty pages of Bloom's hallucinatory experiences in which he makes all kinds of speeches, some of which bring him plaudits, but others of which finally cause him to be burned at the stake for heresy. All of these fictional adventures are, of course, quite inaudible to Zoe, but her jeering "Talk away till you're black in the face" uncannily caps the last item in the reverie where Bloom, having suffered death at the stake, is described as "mute, shrunken, carbonized."

In such audacious strategies as Faulkner uses in the passages cited above (on p. 187 and on p. 358) he had the authority of James Joyce solidly behind him.

Faulkner's Use of "Atthis"

On page 227 of *Soldiers' Pay*, Januarius Jones addresses Cecily Saunders as "Atthis" and, after repeating the word, proceeds to quote lines 2 and 3 from Poem XVII of *A Green Bough*. Jones teaches the classics, and it is dramatically proper that he should know who Atthis was. But her name is an unusual one, and it may be interesting to speculate on how Faulkner came upon it.

We can dismiss from consideration the Atthis cited by the grammarian and mythologist Apollodorus as the woman for whom the land of Attica was named; we obviously have here merely an instance of eponymy. The only other occurrences of Atthis that have survived are connected with fragments of Sappho's poetry, where a girl by this name is mentioned several times.

In Faulkner's poem the occurrence of "Atthis" and "Lesbos" would seem to clinch the ultimate derivation of his poem from Sappho; but it is most unlikely that Faulkner drew directly from a collection of Sappho's poetry. The intermediary could have been a poem by Faulkner's old favorite, Swinburne: his "On the Cliffs" incorporates and greatly expands a line by Sappho which may be literally translated: "I loved you once, Atthis, long ago." But Faulkner's poem is not at all in the Swinburnian mode, a style with which Faulkner was entirely familiar and which he was able to imitate rather faithfully (see p. 3, above). Instead, it is elliptical, uncommitted to syntax, a heap of juxtaposed images, much in the manner of Pound's "Ἱμέρρω," which reads as follows:

> Thy soul
> Grown delicate with satieties,
> Atthis.
> O Atthis,
> I long for thy lips.
> I long for thy narrow breasts,
> Though restless, ungathered.

Faulkner's third line, "above the narrow precipice of thy breast," may just possibly have been influenced by Pound's line, "I long for thy narrow breasts." "ἱμέρρω" (literally, "I long for") occurs in a line from another poem by Sappho in which the name of Atthis also occurs.

Pound's poem was first published in 1916 in the September number of *Poetry: A Magazine of Verse* and in London in a volume entitled *Lustra* (1916; New York, 1917). Even if Faulkner did not come upon Pound's poem in either of these places, he might have read it when *Personae: The Collected Poems of Ezra Pound* was published in 1926 by the same New York firm that published Faulkner's first two novels. In that case, however, he must have seen an advance copy or the poet's MS at the publishers, for *Soldiers' Pay* was published early in 1926: viz., on 25 February.

The Sappho text which yielded the germ of Pound's poem was a rather late addition to the Sappho canon. The parchment on which the poem was written came to Berlin from Egypt as late as 1896. Richard Aldington in 1912 produced a poem entitled "To Atthis (*After the Manuscript of Sappho now in Berlin*)." Pound read Aldington's very free translation—actually an imaginative reconstruction of several fragments—and tried to get Harriet Monroe to accept it for *Poetry;* having failed, he published it himself in *Des Imagistes* (1914). There is nothing to indicate that Faulkner ever saw the Aldington poem, and except for the reference to Atthis, Faulkner's poem has nothing in common with Aldington's.

I have borrowed the foregoing account of the development of Pound's poem from Hugh Kenner's *The Pound Era* (Berkeley, California, 1971). The whole chapter, "The Muse in Tatters," on which I have levied, is fascinating, and the story is worth reading in the detail in which Kenner has related it.

Not the least puzzling aspect of Faulkner's poem is its title. In spite of its associations with Sappho of Lesbos, he called it originally "On Seeing the Winged Victory for the First Time." [1] The reference is, of course, to the famous Winged Victory of Samothrace, which Faulkner had seen in the Louvre when he was in Paris in 1925. The mood of Faulkner's poem is indeed neither elegiac nor lovesick, but dynamic, and a fresh wind like the one that flutters the garments of the goddess of victory is made to blow throughout the poem.

1. See Keen Butterworth, "A Census . . ." in *Mississippi Quarterly* 26 : 346.

4. SKETCHES, EARLY STORIES, AND AN ABORTIVE NOVEL

The Influence on Faulkner of Irvin S. Cobb

Irvin S. Cobb (1876–1944) was a very popular short-story writer of the first decades of the twentieth century. He was almost as gimmicky as O. Henry—whose general influence suffuses the *New Orleans Sketches*—and quite as light-weight in his presentation of character and theme. But he was immensely popular: Faulkner as a young man must have read his *Cosmopolitan* and *Saturday Evening Post* stories, and Cobb's example may have helped confirm Faulkner in using what was to become his characteristic material. Though Cobb was born in Paducah, Kentucky, the culture reflected in his stories, that of western Kentucky, is continuous with that of west Tennessee and north Mississippi. The special heroes of many of Cobb's stories are Confederate veterans, most of whom had served with General Nathan Bedford Forrest. Forrest is, of course, the special Confederate hero of north Mississippi and of a number of Faulkner's own Civil War stories.

The character who dominates a number of Cobb's early stories is old Judge Priest. The judge, a Civil War veteran, like Faulkner's Judge Dukinfield in "Smoke," has a faithful Negro servant on whom he depends utterly and who is his veritable shadow. Faulkner's Judge Dukinfield and his servant Job owe, I suspect, a good deal to Cobb's Judge Priest and his servant Jeff Poindexter.

One of the mysteries of Judge Dukinfield's death is how the murderer could have got unobserved past Uncle Job dozing in his "wire-mended splint chair" in the passageway to the Judge's office. Judge Priest's Jeff also is known to doze while he waits for the old judge to gather up his papers toward quitting time. He can doze even while leaning "against a bookrack" in the Judge's office.

Judge Priest has also probably left his impress on the man who manages to discover Dukinfield's murder: Gavin Stevens. Gavin is a much younger man than Priest and he boasts degrees from Harvard and Heidelberg. But though lacking in impressive degrees, Judge Priest is something of a scholar. At all events he is a sound student of human nature, a wise counselor, and as such he is accorded great respect by the community in which he lives. Like Gavin Stevens, Judge Priest is also an amateur detective, and one of Cobb's books about Priest is actually entitled *Judge Priest Turns Detective*.

There are some fairly specific parallels that may indicate Faulkner's—perhaps unconscious—borrowings from Cobb. One of Cobb's stories tells how a Confederate veteran, on his way home from Virginia, was killed by bushwhackers in the mountains of east Tennessee, just as in Faulkner's "Mountain Victory" Major Saucier Weddell, returning from the Virginia campaigns to his home in Mississippi, is killed by a Unionist mountaineer as he makes his way through east Tennessee. Judge Priest has a cook who, like that admirable woman who looks after the Compson family in *The Sound and the Fury,* is named Dilsey. In *Soldiers' Pay* Faulkner tells us that Cadet Lowe's eyes were "like two oysters." I had always supposed that he was remembering Joyce's description of John Henry Menton's "oyster eyes" and perhaps he was. But a character in Cobb's "The Life of an Ant" has an eye "the color of a boiled oyster," and Cobb could not have borrowed from Joyce. His story antedates *Ulysses* by seven years.

Parallels of the sort I have mentioned are in themselves trivial, and are cited here merely to point the connection. But one device that Faulkner possibly borrowed from Cobb has real importance. Almost all of Cobb's Judge Priest stories are told in the first person by a well-informed member of the community. The teller himself is not involved in the plot and his fortunes are not at stake, but he is a good observer and something of a raconteur. Such a mode of narration is the staple device, not only in the stories printed in *Knight's Gambit,* where it is Gavin Stevens who plays detective, but in many other Faulkner stories, including such early ones as "Idyll in the Desert" and "A Rose for Emily." Whereas Cobb uses the device perfunctorily and sometimes almost absent-mindedly, Faulkner employs it intelligently and responsibly. In Faulkner's skillful hands, such a narrator of the story—often a mere nameless observer—takes on something of the quality of the Sophoclean chorus, voicing the expectations and anxieties of the community and reflecting—often to the great benefit of the reader's comprehension—the community's values and basic assumptions.

Faulkner's Knowledge of Freud

In Freudian fashion, Thomas L. McHaney [1] interprets Elmer's making drawings of tubular objects and his interest in phallic shapes of all

1. "The Elmer Papers: Faulkner's Comic Portrait of the Artist," *Mississippi Quarterly* 26 (1973) : 281–311.

kinds from screwdrivers to cigars as showing the boy's growing interest in the male and female genitals. But McHaney is careful to note that "Faulkner's knowledge of Freud is still in dispute." He points out, however, that Freud's "ideas about dream interpretation, symbolism, and sex were widely known, and disputed, in both medical and popular literature during the second and third decades of the twentieth century" (pp. 284–85). That is true: the ideas were in the air and Faulkner may well have heard them discussed. But he might well have picked up the use of phallic imagery from reading *Jurgen* (as Michael Millgate [2] has suggested), and if we take into account his reading of *Mlle. de Maupin* as well, the two books between them might have supplied much of his interpretation of the sexual material found in his early works. Not much talk about Freud's theories would be required to account for it.

On at least one occasion Faulkner remarked that he had learned what little of psychology he knew "from listening to people that do know. . . . Freud I'm not familiar with." This ought to be decisive, but it is not: Faulkner's memory is not always to be trusted, nor his full truthfulness when people put questions to him about what he had read. Nevertheless, the burden of proof remains on those who insist that he had read a great deal of Freud.

With reference to the talk about Freud that Faulkner might have heard in New Orleans around 1925–26, it is worth quoting the testimony of one of the editors of *The Double Dealer,* Julius Friend. In the passage I shall quote, he is speaking specifically about Sherwood Anderson, not Faulkner: Anderson "talked a great deal about Freud when he was here [in New Orleans] in 1922. I am sure he never read the books and that he got Freud second hand from Rosenfeld and the New York intellectuals who appear to have persuaded him that his own ideas were borne out by Freudian theory." Though the remark is about Anderson in 1922 and not Faulkner in 1925, the implication is clear that among the New Orleans literati of the time there were more people who talked about Freud than seriously read him.

The late Julius Friend's papers, including an unpublished history of *The Double Dealer,* are preserved in the Tulane Library. Mrs. Julius Friend has kindly allowed me to go through these papers, and I am grateful to her for permission to publish excerpts from them here and on subsequent pages.

2. *The Achievement of William Faulkner* (New York, 1966), p. 63.

5. *MOSQUITOES*

The Real People behind the Characters

Joseph Blotner has provided a rather elaborate key to the actual people who lie behind the characters met with in *Mosquitoes* (see his *Faulkner,* pp. 515–22). I shall here simply list his findings briefly along with my own comments upon some of them.

Gordon: William Spratling. But as I have indicated above, his ideas and attitudes are out of Rostand and Gautier.

Patricia Robyn: Helen Baird.

Theodore Robyn: Peter ("Josh") Baird, Helen's brother.

Dawson Fairchild: Sherwood Anderson. But see also pp. 141–44, 149–50, and 379–80.

Mark Frost: Samuel Louis Gilmore.

The Semitic Man (Julius Kauffman): Julius Weis Friend. See also pp. 376 and 379–80.

Mrs. Eva Wiseman: Mrs. Lillian Friend Marcus (sister of Julius Friend).

Major Ayers: Col. Charles Glenn Collins.

Dorothy Jameson: No identifiable real-life equivalent.

Jenny Steinbauer: No identifiable real-life equivalent.

Pete Ginotta: No identifiable real-life equivalent.

David, the steward: No identifiable real-life equivalent.

Faulkner: William Faulkner (mentioned once by Jenny Steinbauer).

Mrs. Maurier: The few names proposed as the person on whom Faulkner modeled Mrs. Maurier seem to me quite beside the mark. Mrs. Maurier is a rather broad caricature, and I daresay that she is an entirely composite figure who owes more to Faulkner's imagination and his reading than to any woman he ever met. But one aspect of her character may have come from Anderson's third wife. According to Julius Friend, "Elizabeth was quite the cultured lady and I think she figured that Sherwood was a barbarian with genius who could however with some effort be made acceptable to really important people like professors of English literature and social patrons of arts and letters." Mrs. Maurier knows that Fairchild is a well-known novelist, but she often cringes at what she feels to be his crude speech and behavior.

Ernest Talliaferro: Blotner sees him as cut from the same pattern as Eliot's Prufrock. I believe that this is to misunderstand Prufrock. Prufrock is well aware of his own limitations and uncertainties. He is a sophisticated and self-conscious man who knows what is wrong with himself and connects his own failure with a general failure in the culture around him. In Talliaferro, Faulkner has drawn a much coarser portrait of fatuous ineptitude. Prufrock is a civilized man—indeed, an overcivilized man. Talliaferro's cringing social posture ought not to blind the reader to his real aggressiveness. He is a real vulgarian who would use his devotion to "culture" as a means of self-promotion.

Julius Kauffman's Critical Judgment of Dawson Fairchild

I think that Faulkner had good reason to put these judgments in the mouth of Julius Kauffman, for the late Julius Friend, the person upon whom the character of Kauffman seems closely modeled, was thoroughly capable of uttering these sentiments, and it is possible that Faulkner actually heard him give utterance to them or to something like them. His papers, which Mrs. Friend has kindly allowed me to examine, reveal a man who was very well read in philosophy, history, and literature. He had obviously thought long and carefully on the nature and function of art and knew his own mind on aesthetic theory.

He was, Mrs. Friend tells me, much closer to Anderson than he was to Faulkner, and the Friends not only saw a good deal of Anderson in his New Orleans days, but later visited him after he had settled in Marion, Virginia. Yet for all of his personal warmth toward Anderson, Friend was capable of viewing Anderson's ideas and his relations with other writers quite objectively. His notes on Anderson's relations with Hemingway and with Faulkner show this. Friend says with reference to Anderson and Faulkner: "I think they were never very intimate. Sherwood was interested in Faulkner as a young man of talent. But Faulkner is not easy as an intimate. He would remain silent for hours at a time or talk without interruption for hours, mostly about himself and his ability." Friend goes on to say:

> Sherwood didn't care for competition in his own line. . . . It may explain his feeling toward Hemingway, Faulkner, O'Donnell. So long as these men were practically unknown Sherwood was interested in them. Later he felt that they had all accepted his help

and used him unworthily. Of course Hemingway did parody him in "Torrents of Spring" and Faulkner in that sad novel "Mosquitoes." (I too am one of the Mosquitoes, under the alias of Julius Weisman [*sic*]). But I think their main sin in his eyes was that they gained a more popular success than he—without acknowledgement of their indebtedness. This was ingratitude.

Friend shows a like quality of fair-minded detachment in his essay entitled "The Philosophy of Sherwood Anderson" which he contributed to the Sherwood Anderson number of *Story* (19 [1941]: 37–41). That essay is warm in tone and full of praise for Anderson's instinctive—even mystical—faith in the human heart and in its potentialities for goodness and growth, but Friend's is a measured praise that does not claim for Anderson intellectual virtues which simply were not his.

Mr. Albert Goldstein, another former editor of *The Double Dealer*, who knew Julius Friend well and for many years, has kindly heard me out as I set forth my interpretation of Kauffman's criticism of Dawson Fairchild, and tells me that he finds it consistent with Friend's views of Anderson. But this is not to say, of course, that Friend necessarily ever applied these comments specifically to Anderson as Kauffman is made to apply them to Dawson in *Mosquitoes*. Nor is it even to say that Faulkner acquired his critical estimate of Anderson from conversations with Friend. Perhaps Faulkner simply felt (or hoped) that his own estimate of Anderson's virtues and limitations was consistent with the views of so able and discriminating a man as he had found Julius Friend to be. But I think that at the least it is worth reporting what kind of talk could be heard from some members of *The Double Dealer* group when Faulkner was seeing them in the early months of 1925.

6. FIRST FORAYS INTO YOKNAPATAWPHA COUNTY

The Conclusion of "Miss Zilphia Gant"

The conclusion of this story is rather curious. The last paragraph of Section IV covers in capsule form the same events that are treated in Section V. The reader's first thought might be that after Faulkner had decided to treat the events in more detail by writing a Section V, he forgot to go back and cancel the now unnecessary paragraph that closes Section IV. There is, however, no manuscript or other evidence for this explanation. But if we assume that Faulkner intended the partial duplication, then it would appear that he was here experimenting with a rather tricky technical device.

The last paragraph of Section IV does indeed cover a great deal of ground in very cursory fashion. In it there is mention of Miss Zilphia's three years' absence from Jefferson and her habit of walking to and from school twice a day "with her daughter's hand in hers." But most of the paragraph is devoted to an account of Miss Zilphia's dreaming. Some ten years after her return to Jefferson, though her manner on the street was still "confident and assured," she reverted to her old habit of waking up weeping and of having disturbing dreams about Negro men. She tells herself that "something is about to happen to me." Then we are told that something did happen to her, and after that happening "She dreamed hardly at all any more," and when she did, the dream was about food.

There is no explanation, however, for the two important matters mentioned earlier in the paragraph—none, that is, until we get to the brief Section V. There, at last, we are told what Miss Zilphia did while she was away from Jefferson and how she came by the child. One would have supposed that this frustrated woman's getting what she had passionately yearned for—a child—would have calmed her spirits; and one gathers that it did have that effect when she first returned to Jefferson; but ten years later the weeping and the dreams begin to trouble her again. They stop only when "something" happens to her. The short Section V does clear up the matter of the child. She was not Miss Zilphia's child by any second marriage (p. 28), but, since little Zilphia's eyes were the color of "wood-ashes," like those of Miss Zilphia's husband, little Zilphia was *his* child by his second marriage. The reason for Miss Zilphia's three years' absence is thus accounted for.

What happened to Miss Zilphia, however, that ended her fits of weeping and the disturbing dreams? Why, for that matter, did they resume just ten years after Miss Zilphia's return to Jefferson? Little Zilphia was three when Miss Zilphia brought her to Jefferson. Ten years later she was thirteen, and we must suppose that her menstrual cycle began. It would have recalled to Miss Zilphia her own mother's stripping her naked when she was thirteen and inspecting her body periodically for signs of menstruation. For the cowed girl, under inspection of her mother's "cold mad" eyes, these experiences would have been traumatic. Miss Zilphia's old terror and apprehensions were revived by little Zilphia's having become a nubile woman (p. 13). What happened, then, to end the disturbing dreams? The menopause, the cessation of Miss Zilphia's own fertility. We are told on page 29 as the story ends, that Miss Zilphia was 42.

How long did the tearful awakenings and the distasteful dreams continue to trouble Miss Zilphia, once they had begun? Not very long. Faulkner has, as he so often did, built a very precise time-schedule into his story. It is easy to figure that Miss Zilphia was 27 when her mother drove away the young man Zilphia had just married. She must have been about 28 when she received news of little Zilphia's birth; 31, when she brought the child to Jefferson; and, in little Zilphia's thirteenth year, about 41. She had perhaps only a year to wait for the peace in which her few dreams were about food, in which she could dismiss the world of men, and get fat, her strange interlude being at last over. (It is immaterial that, statistically, 42 is early for the completion of menopause. The important thing is what Faulkner believed to be the likely age; and *Light in August* furnishes evidence that he believed it to be the early forties.)

Did Faulkner ever see Eugene O'Neill's *Strange Interlude?* We do not know, but it was much in the news. Everyone was talking about it; and since it opened in New York in January 1928, there is no chronological reason why it might not have influenced a story probably written in the latter part of that same year.

The reader may well ask: but isn't the hypothesis set forth just a little too tricky? My answer would have to be: yes, it's quite tricky, perhaps too much so to be justified. But is there any other hypothesis that will account for the "facts" in the story and also account for the way in which Faulkner has chosen to present them? Besides, the young Faulkner was at this period not only very much interested in psychology, particularly feminine psychology; he was also daringly experimental.

A Chronology for "A Rose for Emily"

At least six chronologies of this story have been produced.[1] Miss Emily's death is variously set at 1924, 1928, 1934, 1937, and (in two

1. Five of them have been conveniently printed together in M. Thomas Inge's *William Faulkner: "A Rose for Emily,"* The Charles E. Merrill Literary Casebook Series (Columbus, Ohio, 1970).

different chronologies) at 1938. But if Miss Emily died in 1938, how many Confederate veterans could have come to her funeral? A lad of fifteen who did not join the army until the last year of fighting, 1865, would in 1938 be eighty-eight years old. Men born in 1840, who were twenty-one when the war broke out, would, by 1938, be ninety-eight. The truth is that by 1938 there were very few Confederate veterans left in the entire South. A small town like Jefferson is unlikely to have had many even in the 1920s. Thus, some knowledge of history would support the supposition that Miss Emily died sometime in the 1920s.

Another factor must be taken into account. The "very old men—some in their brushed Confederate uniforms" who, at the funeral, talked "of Miss Emily as if she had been a contemporary of theirs, believing that they had danced with her and courted her" must have been a number of years older than she. If we set her birthdate at, say, 1852, then even the Confederate veteran who entered the war in 1861 as a lad of sixteen would have been seven years older, a significant difference in age when the girl is only nine.[2] Since Miss Emily is said to have died at seventy-four, she would have died in 1926.

The chronology that I print below follows closely that constructed by William T. Going (Inge, pp. 51–52), who has Miss Emily born in 1850, and that constructed by John V. Hagopian et al. (Inge, p. 83), in which her birthdate is set at 1854. The scheme that follows is indebted to both of these chronologies.

1852   Miss Emily is born.

1882   She is 30 and "still single" (p. 123).

(?) 1884   Her father dies when Emily is 31 or 32 (p. 123).

1884/85   Homer Barron appears "the summer after her father's death" (p. 124).

1885/86   Barron dies; the awful smell (pp. 122–23).

2. If, on the other hand, Miss Emily was not a contemporary of the Confederate veterans because she was a number of years *older* than they, then she would have had to be born at least before 1840, for Civil War veterans born in 1845 would be only twenty when the war ended in 1865. Yet if Miss Emily had been born in the late 1830s, the later events in her life would be completely out of kilter. For example, since the Grierson house was built in "the heavily lightsome style of the seventies" (*Collected Stories*, p. 119), Miss Emily would have been over thirty when the house was built. Yet a few years later she is said to have "got to be thirty" (p. 123), and a few more years have elapsed before we are told that she was now "over thirty" (p. 125).

1892	Emily begins to give lessons in china-painting (p. 118).
1894	Col. Sartoris has her taxes remitted (pp. 120, 128).
(?) 1901	Miss Emily gives up her lessons in china-painting (p. 128). But if we are to believe the statement on p. 120 that she had given up the painting lessons "eight or ten years before" the delegation called upon her, then this date should be 1904 or 1905.
1906/07	Col. Sartoris dies (p. 121).
1916	Emily vanquishes the deputation that calls on her about the taxes "just as she had vanquished their fathers thirty years before about the smell" (p. 121).
1926	Miss Emily dies (p. 128).

Give or take a year or so, and this chronology will account for the dates given or implied except for the one obvious discrepancy noted under the year (?) 1901.

Some Typical Misreadings of "A Rose for Emily"

A survey of the critical commentary on this story shows violations of history, aesthetics, and plain common sense as gross as those which disfigure half the chronologies set up for it. (See the preceding note.) Inge's *William Faulkner: "A Rose for Emily"* contains some useful and often sympathetic assessments of the literary value of this story. But the not least useful aspect of this little book is its testimony to the amount of nonsense that has been written about Faulkner's first published story.

The symbol-monger has been irresistibly attracted to "A Rose for Emily." The "analogy between Emily and the Old South" has been worked to death. "Her family connections, her home, the attitude of the townspeople toward her, her own tacit acceptance of a kind of patriotic homage—all point to Emily as a symbol of the Old South, of the tradition of chivalry and culture which that names evokes"—thus, one commentator remarks. But the clichés piled up in the sentence quoted emphasize the simplistic nature of the generalization. Which Old South does Miss Emily represent and what is *the* attitude of the townspeople toward her? Questions like these immediately arise.

In another comment quoted in Inge's collection, it is professed that Emily's necrophilia "suggests the necrophilia of an entire society that lived with a dead but unburied past." (Passing thought: Does the United States have a past, and if so, is it dead or alive? And if dead, should it be buried, the recent Bicentennial notwithstanding? What is the proper thing to do with a past, anyway?)

"Emily becomes Jefferson's sickness, its heritage from the past. . . ." What, then, should the town have done with Emily? Hanged her as a witch, Salem style? "The town harbored the decayed Grierson house, a symbol of the past. . . ." What should her fellow citizens have done with her house? Repaired and repainted it? Or bulldozed it down and put up a gasoline station or a fancy hamburger stand on the lot?

Another interpreter of the story manages to find out what no one else had succeeded in discovering, that Miss Emily had accomplices to help her hide away Barron's corpse in that upstairs bedroom. These accomplices were men who in the old days had paid court to Miss Emily. In order to protect her good name, they had helped her seal up the bedroom, a task said to be beyond a woman's strength. Why the faithful Tobe, who is said to know the "horrible secret of that upper room," could not have provided all the help needed, is not made clear. (In an earlier draft of the story, Faulkner makes it quite plain that Tobe was aware all along that Barron's corpse lay in an upstairs bedroom; see Michael Millgate's *Achievement of William Faulkner*, pp. 263–64.) But this enterprising commentator requires the existence of a group of dedicated ancient suitors for the sake of the story's true moral: though we are permitted to forgive Miss Emily's deed because she was after all a "crazed old lady," how can the reader forgive these "aged lovers" of hers, who have covered up her crime? That they could do so provides "a frightening comment on the moral fabric of the Southern social structure," even more frightening than Miss Emily's necrophilia.

The man who narrates the story is said to belong to this group of "secret protectors," who unlike Miss Emily, are "sane, deliberate, knowing." The group stands self-righteously and horribly amid the final debacle, "profferring to Emily . . . its loathesome rose of love." Their motive in helping Emily conceal her act was to keep "untarnished the honor and myth of the South," for Emily, as we are told over and over, is a symbol of the Old South. Yet if this was really their motive, why does one of them at the end of the story calmly watch the forcing of the door and the final exposure of Emily's guilt? If he and his cronies had really wanted to keep Emily's "macabre secret," they should have got Barron's corpse out of the house and disposed of it rather than "sealing" it up in the bedroom, or, had Miss Emily insisted on keeping it, they should have at least, right after her funeral poured a little

gasoline in the kitchen of her house and struck a match, and so destroyed the incriminating evidence.

Common sense must be allowed to raise its unhandsome head.
Literature is indeed symbolic, but a genuine symbolism has some
reference to the narrative context. If the symbols are simply concocted
and manipulated to humor the reader's private prejudices, he has
ceased to read the author's story and is replacing it with his own
fantasies. Drawing on common sense, one might begin by disposing of
a prejudice that seems to haunt so much of the critical writing on "A
Rose for Emily." It is the assumption that there is something peculiarly
—or at least appropriately—"Southern" about decayed corpses and
skeletons tucked away in locked rooms. But the only such actual happenings that have come to my own attention occurred elsewhere.

Some ten years ago, the British newspapers reported such a case. A
Londoner, a man of means and social position, one day suddenly
disappeared. His disappearance remained a complete mystery for ten
years until, quite by accident, a little-used room in the house was
opened and his skeleton was discovered seated in a chair. He had
apparently died of a heart attack while in his study. Curiously enough,
it had not occurred to anyone in the family to investigate this room—
and this was about as much point as the news story had. The reader's
response could hardly go beyond thinking that the dead man's family
couldn't have searched for him very hard; that maybe they had their
reasons. Or, how often did they clean the house? Or what happened to
their sense of smell?

In a more recent story, an Associated Press dispatch from a small
town in Massachusetts reported that a young man had turned himself
over to the police, saying to them: "My mother is in the house." There
indeed the police found her body, three weeks dead. Neighbors had
noticed her absence but had assumed that she was on vacation in
Florida or on Cape Cod. Whether or not the son was responsible for
killing his mother—she had been struck on the head with "a blunt
instrument"—and if so, what his motive was, were not stated in the
AP wire and are not of the same concern here as the two facts that
(1) the son, as he confessed to the police, had gone on living for
three weeks in the house that contained the dead body, and (2) the
villagers had not suspected the presence of the body in the house and
had not suspected the woman was dead.

Now for the third case, one somewhat closer to Miss Emily's. In the
mid-1970s, in Portland, Oregon, the body of a woman who had been

three years dead was discovered. An AP dispatch reported that a man had sealed up the body of his common-law wife in a back bedroom of the house in which they lived. The account tells us that

> The room looked the way it must have after she died. Nothing appeared changed. Magazines dated 1972 were scattered about. A bird lay dead in its cage. The remains of [the woman's] body, dressed in a red housecoat, lay on a bed, covered with a blanket. There was a heavy layer of dust in the room.

The newspaper account of the Portland case does provide a meager hint of the man's motivation. We are told that he loved the woman and "wanted to keep her even after she was dead." But the story does little to humanize the event or even to make it credible. We shake our heads at this poor deranged creature and go on to read Ann Landers or the stockmarket report.

Doubtless, research would turn up other cases. Just before this book was sent to the printer, someone put into my hands a copy of an AP dispatch datelined Albuquerque, New Mexico. It bore the headline: "Husband Put in Mothballs for 3 Years." The man's body had been concealed in a garage closet. Before the closet door had been nailed shut, the woman in the case, the dead man's divorced wife, had poured formaldehyde over his body and put mothballs in the closet. She told the police that her ex-husband had committed suicide when she refused his request for a reconciliation. But her conscience had bothered her for having concealed the fact of his death and so, after three years, she had gone to the police. The AP story contained one more curious and unexplained detail. When the police made their investigation they found the body of "a dog preserved in formaldehyde [concealed] in another closet."

In all these cases the news reports do no more than hint at what curious indifference, or what passions of love and hate, or what possessiveness and guilt, or what mental derangement accounted for what happened. A literary artist attempts to endow such brute facts with meaning. This is the essential difference between the sad little stories to be gleaned from the newspapers and Faulkner's masterful "A Rose for Emily."

So we come back to the question of what constitutes a proper interpretation of Faulkner's story. I have set forth mine in chapter 6, above, and the reader will decide for himself whether it seems convincing. Be that as it may, I could hope that all sensitive readers will agree that certain other interpretations are at odds with what Faulkner said he had in mind [1] and with what is far more important, the actual text of the story.

The various possibilities for misreading offered by this story have attracted the attention of at least one specialist in psychology and literature, Norman N. Holland, whose *5 Readers Reading* (New Haven, 1975) makes use of "A Rose for Emily" as its main exhibit. Since Professor Holland is primarily concerned with the prejudices, preconceptions, and blindsides that various readers bring to any work of literature, his choice of Faulkner's story makes very good sense. For the student of Faulkner, however, the principal merit of *5 Readers Reading* will be the light it throws on the stereotypes of the South and Southern culture that still flourish in the minds of our college students and others in the 1970s.

The Relation of FLAGS IN THE DUST *to* SARTORIS

As is generally known, *Sartoris* represents a somewhat shortened and altered version of a novel that Faulkner completed on 29 September 1927 and which he had meant to call *Flags in the Dust*. Nevertheless, it may be useful to set down here in summary form the principal differences between the two works and a brief history of how the differences came about.

In 1927 Faulkner entertained high hopes for his new novel. He was confident that it represented a great advance over *Soldiers' Pay* and *Mosquitoes*. But the publisher of these novels, Horace Liveright, emphatically rejected the new work. He told Faulkner that it lacked "plot, dimension and projection." He added, "The story really doesn't get anywhere and has a thousand loose ends."

Although Faulkner continued to believe in the book, a number of his friends to whom he showed it shared Liveright's judgment. At length Faulkner asked for his friend Ben Wasson's help in trying to place it with a publisher. Wasson did his best, but the novel was rejected by some dozen other publishing houses. At last Harcourt Brace agreed to publish it, but only on condition that it be substantially cut. Since Alfred Harcourt doubted that Faulkner could cut his own work, he offered Wasson a fee of fifty dollars to do the job, an offer to which Wasson at once agreed.

1. See *Faulkner in the University*, ed. Gwynn and Blotner, pp. 47–48, 184–85.

Wasson was evidently perfectly willing to have Faulkner's assistance with the cutting, if Faulkner wanted to help. Otherwise he would do it himself. Faulkner emphatically opposed cutting the book, and wanted no part in it; but he accepted the fact that the book had to be cut; for clearly there seemed no other way to get it published. Harcourt Brace was a reputable house, and they had offered an advance that he felt he could not refuse.

Faulkner's own vehement feelings in this matter are expressed in a manuscript note that has survived and is now preserved in the Beinecke Library at Yale. It was published in *The Yale University Library Gazette* for January 1973, with a brief introduction by Joseph Blotner. In this note Faulkner makes it clear that his strong impulse was to have nothing to do with any editing of *Flags in the Dust*.

The cutting was forthwith done, but more than cutting was involved, for some new material had to be inserted to bridge gaps, and certain passages had to be rewritten. George Hayhoe, in an article entitled "William Faulkner's *Flags in the Dust*," [1] provides a convenient summary of the nature of the changes, and since he believes that Faulkner did not work with Wasson in the cutting-revising operation, he offers some hypotheses to account for the revisions and additions.

> Aside from the obvious diminution of length and inclusiveness, *Sartoris* differs from the surviving typescript of *Flags* in several respects. Two passages were repositioned in *Sartoris*, most dramatically Will Falls's first reminiscence of the Old Colonel's Civil War adventures; a number of passages were added; several sections were rewritten (most of the changes being in style). Three hypotheses can be suggested to explain these differences. They may reflect Faulkner's revisions in another typescript which do not appear in the typescript which he kept in his files [and from which *Flags in the Dust* has been printed]; they may be the result of changes made by Faulkner in the galley proofs of *Sartoris;* or they may have been the revisions of an editor, a possibility which is not unlikely in view of the liberties taken by Smith as well as by Faulkner's other editors over the years. But no final conclusion can be reached since both the typescript which Wasson cut (and which served as setting copy) and the galleys are no longer extant.

1. *Mississippi Quarterly* 28 (1975) : 375.

Hayhoe (p. 370) quotes Faulkner as having written (or said) to Wasson in 1929: ". . . dont make any more additions to the script, bud. I know you mean well, but so do I." This sentence clearly indicates that Wasson did write additional material, and that Faulkner obviously did not approve of it. But is it possible that Faulkner redid some of it to suit himself and perhaps made further additions of his own?

Though Blotner writes in his *Yale Library Gazette* article that Faulkner wanted nothing to do with any changes in *Flags in the Dust*, Blotner does say (on p. 121) that, having accepted Harcourt's proposal, Faulkner "and Wasson both made revisions." On page 583 of his biography of Faulkner, however, I interpret Blotner as saying that Faulkner continued to remain aloof from the whole cutting-revision operation.

What were the principal changes made in editing Faulkner's original typescript into its *Sartoris* form? Blotner supplies a convenient summary. On page 584 of his biography, he writes:

> Ben [Wasson] deleted a long passage of Narcissa's reflections about Bayard as a boy and shortened Bayard's balloon ascent. He did the same thing with other passages in which Narcissa conveyed background material. Several scenes involving Byron Snopes, Virgil Beard, and Mrs. Beard were cut from the text. Long passages also went in which he had described Byron Snopes's twin torments: his anonymous lust for Narcissa and Virgil's blackmail. His final flight from Jefferson to Frenchman's Bend disappeared, as did the brief appearance of I. O. Snopes and his son Clarence. Horace's role was reduced: his one-time desire to become an Episcopalian minister, his sense of doom, his affair with Belle, a brief affair with her sister Joan, his prior involvements, his incestuous feelings toward Narcissa—all these were removed or drastically cut.

Wasson had told Faulkner that he had managed to get "about 6 books" into one novel and was trying to write them all at once" (Blotner, p. 584). Wasson's basic strategy, then, was to cut away the extraneous material and to make the novel tell one story only.

Whatever the soundness of Wasson's analysis and whatever the merits of the somewhat simplified novel that he managed to produce, the reader of the 1970s will probably prefer *Flags in the Dust* over

Sartoris. For his decision will scarcely be based on considerations of literary accomplishment alone, or even primarily. Neither the longer nor the shorter version of Faulkner's tale of the Sartoris family occupies a place among his great novels. The reader's primary interest will probably have to do with Faulkner's first considerable attempt to use Yoknapatawpha materials. In *Flags in the Dust* the reader will find *more* of Yoknapatawpha, including its sheer diversity. *Flags in the Dust* will provide him with a better sense of Faulkner's attempts to do justice within the confines of one novel to the landed gentry, yeoman whites, black people, and even the Snopeses.

Moreover, some values, it must be conceded, were lost in the cutting. If Horace Benbow is to constitute a real counterpoise to young Bayard Sartoris, we really do need to know more about him. We need to know more about even Byron Snopes in order to be able to regard him as a kind of romanticist, and thus to see that he too has his part in Faulkner's critique of the romantic hero in a disillusioned and unromantic age.

Faulkner's View of World War I

In arguing that Faulkner made a sharp contrast between the Civil War and the First World War, I do not mean to imply that he was not fully aware of the horrors of the bloody struggle between the North and the South. The casualties in that war were enormous, and the state of medicine and surgery in the mid-nineteenth century rendered the lot of the sick and the wounded terrifying. For the blockaded South, already short of medical supplies and all but unable to get more, the problem was compounded.

Faulkner was thoroughly aware of the suffering caused by the Civil War and was careful not to invest it with false glamor. He praised Stephen Crane for bringing honest realism to his treatment of the War. (See Michael Millgate's "Faulkner on the Literature of the First World War," *Mississippi Quarterly* 26 [1973]: 387–93.) Nevertheless, the characters in Faulkner's novels find, as Faulkner himself found, in the Civil War a certain disastrous glory. This quality is significantly absent from World War I as described in his short stories and his novels such as *Soldiers' Pay, Flags in the Dust,* and *A Fable.* The Civil War had scope for heroic action. The issues involved in that conflict were less abstract; the encounters, more concrete and immediately personal; the strategies of the commanders, more imaginative and adventurous. The Civil War was in fact essentially a war of movement and maneuver. Though the rifle fire was often murderously effective, the modern machine gun had not made its appearance. It was primarily the machine gun that was to condemn the troops engaged in World War I to the long stalemate of trench warfare, where they lived as troglodytes rather than as human beings.

One further important difference between the two wars is worth mentioning: in the Civil War the commanding generals were not remote from the troops in the field, not a distant and apparently inhuman force, far away from the firing line. This circumstance powerfully affected the attitudes of the men in the ranks toward those whose commands might well condemn them to death. Consider the following illustrations from the Civil War. The Battle of Franklin, in middle Tennessee, was not one of the great battles of the war, but it was one of the most fiercely fought. In this battle the Confederates lost six generals killed in action. Six more of their generals were wounded and another was captured. These major and brigadier generals were obviously not sitting out the battle in a bomb-proof dugout. Or recall what happened to the two most important subordinate commanders under General Lee, Jackson and Longstreet. They were both shot out of the saddle—and by their own troops—because, in these generals' eagerness to follow up the action, they had got so close to the fighting line that they were mistaken for enemy soldiers.

Faulkner was keenly conscious of this contrast between the Civil War and World War I. One notes, for example, the attitude taken toward the high command throughout *A Fable,* or the closing sentences of "Turnabout." After signaling for the release of his bombs on a French château known to be a German general staff headquarters, the American pilot of the bomber exclaims: "God! God! If they were all there—all the generals, the admirals, the presidents, and the kings —theirs, ours—all of them."

The shocking effect on the modern mind of the long stalemated warfare in the mud of the trenches has recently been set forth by Paul Fussell in *The Great War and Modern Memory* (New York, 1975). Another recently published book, *Voices of the Civil War,* edited by Richard Wheeler (New York, 1976), will be helpful to readers unfamiliar with the Civil War and hesitant to venture into the enormous literature on it that is extant. *Voices* is a collection of anecdotes, bits of description, and comments by representatives of both sides, from generals on down to privates and including journalists, both American and foreign. The excerpts printed make up a fair sampling of the ways in which that war was viewed by participants and by other first-hand observers. One is struck by the many tributes to gallantry, recognized in soldiers on the opposing side as well as one's own, and by the frequent, spontaneous expressions of admiration at the sight of regiments deploying or battle lines in motion: e.g., Pickett's advance at Gettysburg, "as grand a sight as ever a man looked on" (p. 318), ". . . came on in magnificent order, with the step of men who believed themselves invincible" (p. 319), ". . . muskets were raining death upon us. Still, on and up the slope toward that stone fence our men steadily swept, without a sound or a shot, save as the men would clamor to be allowed to return the fire . . ." (p. 320).

The Character of Young Bayard Sartoris

Bayard and his twin brother John differ noticeably in personality. They were both, to be sure, daredevils from the beginning, and both had an "air of smoldering abrupt violence," but Bayard's was a "sort of leashed violence," whereas John's violence "was a warmer thing, spontaneous and merry and wild" (*Flags in the Dust,* p. 64). Narcissa remembers, for example, that Bayard's face, unlike John's was "cold" and "arrogant" (p. 64). Even Narcissa's Aunt Sally, who disapproved of both boys, made a distinction: "John at least tipped his hat to a lady on the street, but that other boy . . . (p. 63).

When the carnival came to town and the balloon ascension was to be canceled because the man who was to go up in the balloon had been stricken with ptomaine poisoning, it was John who volunteered to substitute for him so that "the country people [who had come into town to see the exhibition] would not be disappointed. . . ."

Bayard also figured in an event that electrified the town. He "attached a rope to a ninety-foot water tank and, from the roof of an adjoining building, swung himself across the intervening fifty yards of piled lumber and freight cars and released the rope and dived into a narrow concrete swimming pool while upturned faces gaped and screamed" (pp. 64–65). But we are told that Bayard's act amounted to a display of "cold nicety of judgment and unnecessary cruel skill" (p. 65); that is to say, Bayard arranged matters so that his feat should appear more alarmingly dangerous than it actually was.

In personality, then, the twins were quite different. (One presumes that they were not identical twins.) Of the pair, it was John who more closely resembled the Civil War Bayard who rode back into the Yankee camp to pick up the anchovies. Yet this difference in personality between the two boys does not in itself account for Bayard's almost morbid sense of guilt for John's death. One grants that Bayard might well have felt a special grief, but he seems unnecessarily defensive in explaining why he failed to prevent his brother's being shot down by a German fighter plane. He actually seems quite irrational on this subject.

In an article entitled "Escape into Myth: The Long Dying of Bayard Sartoris," [1] John W. Corrington proposes an answer. "The root of Bayard's anguish is a fear and uncertainty of his own courage so profound that he finds himself driven by it to prove over and over again that he is in fact what he fears he is not: a Sartoris" (p. 40). Corrington goes on to say that this fear explains Bayard's

> coldness and cruelty, his lies and evasions and compulsive irresponsibility—even his repetitive nightmares and the need to retell over and over the last moments of Johnny's life and the fearless manner of his death. It is that hour in the sky near Amiens that has crippled Bayard. He has witnessed the meeting between his twin, his own image, the only person he has ever loved, and that death he fears so much. He cannot believe that he too is brave, can as easily and gracefully fulfill the demands of the Sartoris myth as did Johnny. [p. 40]

Johnny's way of accepting his death (see p. 170, above) was indeed a hard act to have to follow. Bayard, his memory etched by the sight of his brother kicking the plane aside and jumping, is obsessed by the idea of falling. From time to time he has a nightmare in which "he was a trapped beast in the high blue, mad for life, trapped in the very cunning fabric that had betrayed him who had dared chance too much, and he thought again if, when the bullet found you, you could only crash upward, burst; anything but earth" (p. 203 of *Sartoris*. It does not occur in *Flags in the Dust*). Because he is terrified of falling to his death, and yet still more terrified that he may not live up to the Sartoris standard of heroism, Bayard must prove himself over and

1. *Recherches Anglaises et Américaines* (Strasbourg, 1971), 4 : 31–47.

over again by riding the wild stallion, by driving at high speeds over the winding country roads, or by trying to fly the experimental plane.

This is the gist of Corrington's interpretation, though the article should be read in full by anyone interested in young Bayard's behavior and in the Sartoris code—what Corrington calls the "Sartoris myth." Can such an interpretation of young Bayard be brought into relation with the sense of postwar disillusionment that affected Bayard and many others—the kind of emptiness which we find in *Soldiers' Pay*? Corrington thinks so. Young Bayard has a twofold problem. If he fears that he cannot meet the demands of the Sartoris code, he is also aware that the modern world allows no real scope for anyone to live by it. The Sartoris code is deemed obsolete, "a game outmoded" (p. 369). Yet young Bayard has no other code with which to replace it—no other game that he has any wish to play.

7. *PYLON*

Chronology of PYLON

The dedication of the Shushan Airport (now the Lakeside Airport) at New Orleans occurred on Friday, 9 February 1934. The airshow which had been arranged to provide entertainment for the occasion was also keyed to the Mardi Gras festivities, for in 1934 Mardi Gras (Fat Tuesday) fell on 13 February. The theme of Rex, King of the Carnival, whose parade would be held on Mardi Gras day, was to be man's conquest of the air. When bad weather developed on Friday, it was decided to postpone the airshow until the day after Mardi Gras. Consequently, the events of the air show actually began on 14 February (Ash Wednesday) and ran through 17 February. Faulkner, who came down to see the airshow, arrived at the airport on 15 February.

When Faulkner addressed himself to the writing of *Pylon,* he decided to ignore the several days' postponement of the airshow, since he meant to make no use of those circumstances in his novel. So he had the dedication of the Feinman (Shushan) Airport take place on the first day of the airshow, that is, on the Thursday before Mardi Gras. Consequently, his reference (p. 77) to the night parade of the Krewe of Momus, the first of the three big night parades of the carnival season, which is always held on Thursday evening, makes perfect sense.

Faulkner's usual procedure was to make the present of his twentieth-century novels conform to the year of publication, not of composition, and he does this in *Pylon*. On the Saturday before Mardi Gras Faulkner has the Reporter date the promissory note 16 February *1935* (p. 207), presumably because 1935 was the year in which *Pylon* was published. But I have asked Professor James W. Webb to look at the MS of *Pylon* (now at the University of Mississippi) and he has kindly done so, reporting that the MS indicates that Faulkner has apparently superposed *1935* over *1934*. Whether or not he has done precisely that, the date *1934* is clearly legible in the MS. We may conclude that at the very least there is evidence to suggest that Faulkner hesitated over which year to choose.

Yet if the events of *Pylon* occur in 1935, then the chronology offered in the novel is in trouble. For Easter, of course, is a moveable feast, and in 1935 Easter occurred very late. It fell on 21 April. Mardi Gras consequently fell on 5 March, and if the Saturday on which the Reporter signed his promissory note was 16 February 1935, then it was not on a Saturday three days before Mardi Gras, but some sixteen days before it. Worse still, it is twelve days earlier than an event already described as in the past, the Thursday evening Momus parade.

Since Faulkner was writing fiction and not history, one may ask whether it makes any difference whether the year was 1934 or 1935, or 1929, for that matter? As for the precise year, it probably makes no difference. But it is proper to warn the reader who is trying to get the sequence of events staight, particularly a reader who knows something about the Mardi Gras season, of this inconsistency in the chronology. Then he can discount the importance of the confusion to suit himself.

Questions of consistency aside, it is interesting to note that Faulkner brings his story to an end before Mardi Gras day dawns. Clearly he had no wish to exploit whatever symbolism might lie in the fact that the morrow of penitence follows the traditional day of revelry. He gets Holmes and Laverne and the child out of the city by Sunday evening (p. 282).

The Air Races at Shushan Airport
(*14–17 February 1934*) and the Air Races in PYLON

Faulkner arrived at Shushan Airport on 15 February (Blotner, p. 833). The first serious accident had occurred the day before: Capt. W. Merle Nelson, who was a stunt pilot and had put rockets on the wings of his plane to provide a brilliant display for the evening performance, miscalculated his height, some thought blinded by his own rockets (New Orleans *Times-Picayune*, 15 Feb. p. 1; New Orleans *Item*, 19 Feb., p. 2), and crashed. The plane immediately caught fire and he was burned to death.

In *Pylon* (pp. 52 and 150–51) Faulkner retains most of the details of this incident. He renames the pilot Lieut. Frank Burnham, but, like Nelson, Burnham flew a "comet" plane, was thought to have been blinded by the rockets he had fastened to the wings, and so flew right into the ground (pp. 150–51), crashed, and burned.

The second bad crash, though nonfatal, occurred on 16 February. Harold Neuman, having to make a forced landing, failed to reach the runway, touched down on the grass, but hit a patch of muddy ground and his plane turned upside down. His wife, rushing from the grandstand through the crowd, was one of the first to reach the overturned plane. (*Times-Picayune*, 17 Feb., p. 1). The pilot suffered only very minor injuries, but the plane was badly damaged. Faulkner assigns this incident to Shumann, who, like Neuman, develops engine trouble, lands, but flips over, his plane's "undercarriage projecting into the air rigid and delicate and motionless as the legs of a dead bird" (p. 164). It is this incident that sends the Reporter looking for a new plane for Shumann to fly. Presumably, Laverne was present at the airport, but there is no account of her running to the scene of the accident.

The third bad crash occurred on 17 February. The pilot, Charles N. Kenily, was taking a veteran parachute jumper, Ben Grew, up for his scheduled jump. Something went wrong as Grew leaped. The lines to this parachute fouled the rudder and he dangled helplessly from the tail of the plane, which very quickly became unresponsive to the controls. The pilot was seen to leap out before the plane and the hapless Grew fell into Lake Pontchartrain. Both men perished, and though Grew's body was quickly recovered, Kenily's never was.

It is interesting to see how Faulkner adapted this incident to his purpose. He assigned it to Shumann. But Shumann comes to grief because of the tricky, unstable plane that he is flying. When the plane begins to break up, he flies it out over the lake before its final disintegration. As with Kenily, Shumann's body is never recovered, though a strenuous search is made for it. Faulkner made use of one more small detail. Kenily's hometown was Marion, Ohio; Shumann's becomes Myron, Ohio.

Kenily's wife and child were not in the grandstand and so did not witness his death. According to the *Times-Picayune* (18 Feb., p. 1), they were in Zanesville, Ohio, awaiting his return. Laverne and her little boy, of course, are present and do witness Shumann's death. Just as Harold Neuman's wife the day before had rushed toward her husband's wrecked plane, so Laverne races toward the seawall, beyond which Shumann's plane has gone down.

Faulkner borrows one more detail from an earlier event: Nelson had left a letter expressing his wish that, if he were killed, his body should be cremated and the ashes scattered from a plane over the field. Since Shumann's body cannot be retrieved, a like procedure, even had Shumann left a note requesting it, would be out of the question. But Faulkner does have a plane fly over the lake to drop a funeral wreath near the spot where Shumann had gone down.

Faulkner made use in *Pylon* of other episodes from the lakeside air show. Holmes, the parachute jumper, hurts his leg, having "been drifted by an unforeseen windgust over the stands and then slammed into one of the jerrybuilt refreshment booths when landing his parachute" (p. 164). Something very much like this happened to Jack Monahan on 14 February, when, about to drift over Lake Pontchartrain, he partially collapsed his parachute so that he "dropped quickly from about 35 feet, striking the inner edge of the seawall" and injuring himself (*Times-Picayune*, 15 Feb., p. 3).

Even Laverne's having been a parachute jumper in the past (though she does not jump at the Feinman Airport races) may just possibly have been suggested to Faulkner by the presence at the Shushan Airport carnival of a girl parachute jumper, Miss Eris Daniels, who made headlines on 17 February because she had had to be fished out of Lake Pontchartrain the day before when she misjudged the wind speed.

Several other real-life people who stand behind some of the incidents or characters in *Pylon* can be easily identified. *Pylon*'s Jules Despleins, the French aviator who performed aerial acrobatics, was obviously modeled on Michel De Troyat, who flew his plane at the air circus. Matt Ord has to be Jimmy Wedell, who was not only a fine racing aviator but a designer of planes, as is Ord in *Pylon*. With Harry T. Williams in the 1920s he formed the Wedell-Williams Air Corporation (the Ord-Atkinson Aircraft Corporation of *Pylon*). Their base of operations was Patterson, Louisiana, a little town some sixty miles west of New Orleans. Patterson is the Blaisedell of *Pylon* (p. 213).

Though Ord (Wedell) is not presented in *Pylon* as a daredevil courting danger, flying in the 1930s was a risky business and Wedell died in a plane crash near Patterson in 1934, not very long after his appearances in the Shushan air races. Two years later his partner, Harry T. Williams, was also killed in an air crash.

A. L. Shushan, always referred to as Abe Shushan, President of the Orleans Levee Board, gave his name to the Shushan Airport built in part on land reclaimed from Lake Pontchartrain. The airport building had the letter "S" worked into the decorations and appointments in myriad ways, much as in *Pylon* the letter "F" was used in the airport named for Col. H. I. Feinman, Chairman of the Sewage Board. The radio call signal for the airport was dot-dot-dash-dot, which the "green light above the beacon on the signal tower began to wink and flash . . . across the nightbound lake" (p. 40). Those familiar with the Morse Code will recognize that dot-dot-dash-dot signifies the letter "F." Faulkner was usually careful about little details like this.

What about the Reporter? Can he be associated with any real-life person? Not precisely. His preposterous name and his preposterous conduct, not to mention other matters, would suggest that he was largely made out of Faulkner's own head. Yet one or two details may have been derived from the veteran reporter on the New Orleans *Item*, Hermann Deutsch. Deutsch's by-line appears on a number of stories about the 1934 circus.

I first met Hermann Deutsch in the 1930s, though I saw him only infrequently. At my first reading of *Pylon* I was reminded of Deutsch by Faulkner's description of the Tall Reporter—his height, his thinness, but most of all his gait. In *Pylon* Faulkner has exaggerated the thinness—he makes the Reporter almost skeletal in appearance—and has rendered absurd his odd shambling kind of locomotion. Yet Faulkner had done no more than make a very broad caricature of a recognizable peculiarity.

In a conversation with Mr. Deutsch in 1974 I asked him whether he could have contributed anything to the portrait of the Reporter. He answered that he might have only in the sense that he was with Faulkner at the airport a good deal during the air carnival and that Faulkner might well have seen him walking about with a little boy belonging to one of the aviators riding on his shoulders (". . . the boy still riding on the man's shoulder," p. 22). But Deutsch modestly indicated that he couldn't hope to measure up to the Reporter's capacity, or even liking for, alcohol. Deutsch knew Wedell and the other local aviators well, and was one of the speakers at the memorial services held in 1936 for Wedell and Williams.

The Personality of Laverne

It is hard to place Laverne among Faulkner's women. She doesn't really fit with the "masculinized" women such as Drusilla Hawk Sartoris or Joanna Burden, each of whom in her own way is intensely traditional and unemancipated. She lacks the coyness and the coquettish manipulation of men, traits to be found in Cecily Saunders and Temple Drake. She is as ruthless—in her own terms, of course, and for her own ends—as Narcissa Benbow, but has almost nothing else in common with Narcissa. Perhaps she is closest to Charlotte Rittenmeyer. Both women are ruthless—with themselves as well as with others. Both live or try to live without reference to the future. But Charlotte is completely dedicated to an all-demanding dream, whereas it is very hard to discover what it is that Laverne lives for, except to meet the needs of her men. (Faulkner allows us to glimpse a residual domesticity in both women.) That is why it is difficult to regard her as an emancipated "new woman." In a sense, she is a primitive rather than a modern. In fact, the men in the troupe may best be regarded as primitives too. Instead of regarding them as machines "with cylinder oil for blood," as the Reporter would do, they might with more plausibility be regarded as a wandering tribe of savages, armed with more sophisticated throwing sticks and flint-flaked knives, feasting once in a while, but often going hungry as they follow the occasional herds of game, and in general experiencing the life of barbarous men which Hobbes long ago characterized as subject to the "danger of violent death . . . , solitary, poor, nasty, brutish, and short." *Pylon*'s emphasis on the airplane as a startlingly new and powerful machine should not distract us from the actual barbarity of their lives.

Place Names in PYLON

Many of the names in *Pylon* point to actual places: thus, New Valois is New Orleans and Francia is Louisiana. Grandlieu St. is clearly Canal St., and St. Jules Ave. is St. Charles Ave.; on page 87 it is referred to simply as "the Avenue." This is standard practice with St. Charles Ave. too). Lake Rambaud is Lake Pontchartrain.

The New Orleanians I have talked with are unanimous in making out Barricade St. to be Rampart St., which is the western boundary of the French Quarter, the Vieux Carré. But just possibly Faulkner had in mind Barracks St. The Terrebonne Hotel may very well be the Monteleone Hotel, in the Quarter. Alphonse's Restaurant is presumably Antoine's; Renaud's Restaurant, Arnaud's.

There is no street in New Orleans called Noyades (p. 184). I suspect Faulkner evolved the name in some such fashion as this: There is a Dryades St., named for the Greek tree nymphs. This probably suggested to Faulkner a hypothetical Naiades St., the street of the sea nymphs. But he may have decided to go Naiades one better by turning it into Noyades St.—that is, the street of the drowned. Faulkner probably remembered a poem by Swinburne entitled "Les Noyades." This is the only way that I can account for Hagood's translating the street name spelled out in the "chipped mosaic" letters set in the curb as "The Drowned" (p. 88).

Toulouse (p. 81) is the real name of a street in the French Quarter. Amboise is probably meant to be another street in the Quarter, but I have no guess as to its real equivalent, nor the real street represented by Bayou St. Lanier Ave. (p. 71), to judge from where it crosses Grandlieu (Canal) St., must be Claiborne Ave.

One of the more curious place names in *Pylon* is that of the Bienville Hotel. In *Pylon* it is situated on a side street and is shabby and rather raffish in atmosphere (p. 295). But in the 1930s there was in New Orleans an actual Bienville Hotel, not as prestigious as the St. Charles or as large as the Roosevelt, but new, clean, eminently respectable, and situated on St. Charles Ave. very near to Lee Circle. Faulkner was probably unaware that a Bienville Hotel actually existed. I suspect that he simply chose "Bienville" as a suitable name for a New Orleans hostelry. It is the actual name of a street in the Vieux Carré.

Faulkner's Attitude toward Fighter Pilots and Aerial Acrobats

Mention has been made above of the fact that the Reporter bears at least a faint resemblance to Hermann Deutsch. Be that as it may, the first draft of the Reporter's account of the dropping of a wreath over Shumann's watery grave—that is, the version that the Reporter crumpled into the wastebasket—might well have been written by

Deutsch himself. Compare the style of the Reporter's discarded account with the style of Deutsch's account of the sprinkling of Nelson's ashes over the waters of the lake. Here is the Reporter's first "literary" version:

> On Thursday Roger Shumann flew a race against four competitors, and won. On Saturday he flew against but one competitor. But that competitor was Death, and Roger Shumann lost. And so today a lone aeroplane flew out over the lake on the wings of dawn and circled the spot where Roger Shumann got the Last Checkered Flag, and vanished back into the dawn from whence it came.
>
> Thus two friends told him farewell. Two friends, yet two competitors too, whom he had met in fair contest and conquered in the lonely sky from which he fell, dropping a simple wreath to make his Last Pylon. [p. 314]

Here are the opening paragraphs of Deutsch's account as printed in the New Orleans *Item* for 19 February:

> A gay cavalier of the skies, whose whole life had been a carefree challenge to death, made his last gay gesture this morning through the hands of a friend and the power of man over the air.
>
> The ashes of Captain Merle Nelson, veteran of the war-time army air service and noted stunt flier, were scattered from the scudding clouds in a blast of wind that was the product of man and nature combined.
>
> Within less than an instant they had vanished from sight driving off in a gale as invisible particles almost as swiftly as the man of whose pulsing tissues they had once formed a living part had roared cloudward in the fine tingle of zestful living.

The Deutsch account is in the Reporter's mode—it is not the compendium of dry "facts" which the Reporter contemptuously strung together and left on his editor's desk (see p. 315 of *Pylon*). But the author of *Pylon* obviously rejected both modes. In a review of Jimmy Collins's *Test Pilot,* published only a few months after *Pylon* had appeared, Faulkner indicated what he thought of "sentimental journalese." Collins was a test pilot (and later died in the crash of a plane he was testing for the Navy), but he was also a "newspaper writer," as Faulkner is quick to observe; and Faulkner makes it plain that Collins's training as a journalist had injured his book.

In any case, Faulkner clearly did not see Shumann and Holmes as "gay cavaliers." *Pylon,* as it tells their story, brands any such characterization as false. Faulkner does not, to be sure, deny Shumann and Holmes courage, a sense of honor, and—Shumann at least—a real gallantry, but he is aware that to regard them as high-hearted cavaliers is to belie the whole context of their lives.

Was this also Faulkner's basic judgment of the fighter pilots of World War I? I do not forget that Faulkner as a very young man tried his best to become one of them. It may, therefore, be useful at this point to review this whole matter of Faulkner's attitude toward the fighter pilots of World War I, many of whom went on to become the racers and stuntmen and test piolts of the 1930s. Those who are interested in this topic should read in full Faulkner's review of Collins's *Test Pilot* and five of Faulkner's short stories: "Honor" (1930), "Death Drag" (published in 1936, but written in 1930), "Ad Astra" (written before March 1930), "All the Dead Pilots" (April 1931), and "Turn About" (written by January 1932). What I shall be saying in what follows represents my interpretation of these six items plus what Faulkner implies in *Soldiers' Pay* (1926) and *Flags in the Dust* (completed by late September 1927).

The closest that Faulkner comes to presenting one of his fighter pilots as a "gay cavalier" of the air, almost nonchalantly bidding life goodbye, occurs in *Flags in the Dust* (p. 239); quoted above on p. 170). John Sartoris makes a gallant gesture when his plane is hit, and he shows no trace of fear. He won't stay in the plane and burn; better to make a forthright clean ending by jumping. The act also has its ingredient of moral courage: cocking his snoot at his twin as much as to say: "Don't worry about me. I'm not afraid of dying. I'll make out."

John Sartoris is one of the drunken airmen in "Ad Astra" and a prominent character in "All the Dead Pilots." The impression that we get of him in these stories squares up well enough with the young man who chooses this gallant exit in *Flags in the Dust.* He is capable of anything. Plato would hardly call his daring anything like true courage; it scarcely amounts to a knowledge of what one should truly fear. Nevertheless, it is awesome—a truly devil-may-care zest for any outrageous action. Faulkner defines it for us in the last paragraph of "All the Dead Pilots," where the teller of the tale describes the quality in question: it is the "courage, the recklessness, call it what you will, . . . the flash, the instant of sublimation; then flick! the old darkness again. . . . It's too strong for steady diet. And if it were a steady diet, it would not be a flash, a glare." Like the intensity of first love, it is precious and wonderful, but it cannot be sustained. It would be foolish to expect it to last.

The description of such reckless courage in "All the Dead Pilots" has a close relation to Faulkner's account of the flyers in World War I, a judgment that Faulkner expressed several times in his fiction and in his interviews. These men, he holds, had burnt themselves out, exhausted their emotional energy. Even if they had not actually died in combat, they were, nevertheless, dead men—spent, drained, having to regard the rest of their lives as anticlimax. In "All the Dead Pilots" it is put this way: "Because they are dead, all the old pilots [those of 1914–18], dead on the eleventh of November, 1918" (Collected Stories, p. 511).

In spite of his recognition of such flashes of courage that light up the darkness, Faulkner's presentation of World War I is bleak with disillusionment. The war in the trenches was obviously horrible: witness the story "Crevasse"; but even the airmen found the war meaningless. Indeed, in one of the stories of the airmen, it was in its terrible waste of youth's reckless bravery that the war revealed its ultimate horror. Thus, at the end of "Turn About" the American officer commanding a bombing plane suffers so much indignation at the death of a young British torpedo boat officer that he takes desperate risks to assure a direct hit on a château used as a German corps headquarters. He wishes he could destroy all the commanders on both sides (see p. 392, above). It is the military machine itself that fills him with raging disgust.

"Honor" is a story about stunt flyers giving exhibitions after the war. The wingwalker has got into an affair with his pilot's wife and the pilot knows it and could easily have had a little "accident" that would have finished his rival. It is the old love-triangle story. But this terribly dangerous new machine, the airplane, takes the older tests of man's honor up one more notch of intensity.

The theme of reckless courage appears also in "Death Drag"; but here Faulkner has come at it from a new direction. The members of the team putting on daredevil aerial stunts live in circumstances even more straitened than does Shumann's troupe. But in "Death Drag" their story is worked out in comic terms—albeit comedy filled with absurdity and black humor. The stunt man is not the daredevil type. He is a desperate man, reduced to making his living by risking his life, but he is so enraged at the prospect of being cheated out of his full fee that he performs the most hair-raising feats as if he were scarcely paying attention to them. Certainly, he is no gay cavalier nor a self-conscious hero.

The introductory section of "All the Dead Pilots" ends with a very interesting sentence, and one that illuminates what Faulkner thought of his airmen. The English army censor who is the narrator says that the story he is to tell is "a series of brief glares" which reveal "the portent and the threat of what the race could bear and become. . . ." The "glares" to which he refers are those "flash[es]," "instant[s] of sublimation," moments of dazzling recklessness to which he will recur at the end of his story and to which I have already referred. Though these momentary glares cannot be sustained, they do reveal "what the race will bear." One notes, however, that this very perceptive censor of mails more than hints of something else: the "glares" also enable us to see the "threat of what the race could . . . become." In *Pylon* Faulkner duly honors man's capacity to take the flyer's risks and remain human, but he is also thoroughly aware of the threat of barbarism and the loss of humanity to which this kind of reckless life may lead. If the reader feels that I urge this latter point too strongly, I suggest that he read the conclusion of Faulkner's review of *Test Pilot*. There Faulkner imagines the possible development through specialization and even selective breeding of men trained from childhood to be precision pilots. If so, he hints, such pilots would show the impress of the machine. They would have been reshaped by the machine to the cost of their humanity.

From this notion he moves on to imagine what he calls a forthcoming "folklore . . . of speed," a folklore "peopled not by anything human or even mortal but by the clever willful machines themselves carrying nothing that was born and will have to die or which can even suffer pain . . . producing a literature innocent of either love or hate and of course of pity or terror, and which would be the story of the final disappearance of life from the earth." With the disappearance of love and hate, pity and terror, death and pain, humanity perishes. A literature "innocent" of such things might be read by a computer but not by a human being. The perfection of the machine might be the abolition of man.

The vision of men transformed into machines or perhaps simply displaced by machines foreshadows what Faulkner was to say on this subject in *A Fable*. See chapter 9, above.

8. *THE WILD PALMS*

Chronology of THE WILD PALMS

For a detailed chronology of both stories told in *The Wild Palms* volume, the reader is referred to Thomas L. McHaney's *William Faulkner's "The Wild Palms"* (Jackson, Miss., 1975), pp. 195–204. A curious feature of Faulkner's time scheme is his having the levee at Mound's Landing, Mississippi, break on 3 May 1927 whereas the actual break occurred on 22 April 1927. This is the more strange in view of the fact that except for postponing by eleven days the beginnings of the great flood on the lower Mississippi, Faulkner's account keeps quite close to historical accuracy.

Having in mind certain resemblances between Charlotte and Helen Baird, McHaney suggests that "perhaps the change of the flood from April to May" reflects the fact that the announcement of Helen Baird's marriage was made on 1 May 1927, the day on which (in 1937) "Harry and Charlotte leave New Orleans" together. (So says McHaney on p. 45, but in his Chronology, McHaney has Harry and Charlotte set out on 3 May, and this latter date must be right.)

The Title

A number of years ago James B. Meriwether pointed out that "an unnumbered title page" of the typescript setting copy of *The Wild Palms* bears "the cancelled title 'If I Forget Thee, Jerusalem,' typed in block capitals, with the published title pencilled in" (*The Literary Career of William Faulkner*, 1961, p. 69). As Meriwether also noted (on p. 28), the cancelled title is a fragment of verse 5 of Psalm 137. The problem has been: what did Faulkner mean by that title?

I think that I can now answer the last question and point to the specific book from which Faulkner took the cancelled title, Donn Byrne's *Messer Marco Polo* (1921). In chapter 2 above I quoted Joseph Blotner's statement that "bell imagery similar to that in [Faulkner's] letter to Helen Baird appears in Donn Byrne's *Messer Marco Polo*." The bell imagery in the letter actually comes from Rostand's *Cyrano de Bergerac* (see pp. 55–57, above), but Linton Massey, Blotner's informant on this point, may have known that Faulkner had read

Donn Byrne's book. At any rate, in that book there is a passage that suggests why "If I Forget Thee, Jerusalem" must have seemed a fitting title for the story of Harry and Charlotte.

In chapter VII we read of Marco Polo's audience with the Pope before he and his father and uncle set out for Cathay. The Pope feels an affinity with the young Marco. To the two older Polos, he has really nothing to say. It is to Marco that he wishes to speak, for, as he tells him, "My dear son, God has put wisdom in my head and beauty into yours." Marco is not really interested in the trip to Cathay as a great mercantile venture. He is going in order to realize a dream. So it is to him that the Pope gives counsel and his special blessing (p. 69):

> . . . never let your dream be taken from you. Keep it unspotted from the world. In darkness and in tribulation it will go with you as a friend; but in wealth and power hold fast to it, for then is danger. Let not the mists of the world, the gay diversions, the little trifles, draw you from glory.
> Remember!
> Si oblitus fuero tui Jerusalim,—If I forget thee, O Jerusalem,—
> Oblivioni detur dextera mea,—let my right hand forget her cunning—

In *The Wild Palms,* Jerusalem is the dream of the everlasting honeymoon that Charlotte says their union must always be. They must never forget it—never lapse from it. Indeed, what the Pope warns Marco Polo against as dangers to the dream are precisely those things which threaten the ideal love that Charlotte and Harry vow to maintain for each other.

Allusions to Hemingway

McHaney has a very interesting discussion of parallels between *The Wild Palms* and several of Hemingway's novels. Hemingway, too, has written a good deal about romantic love and the typical difficulties that impede it or beset it. In *The Sun Also Rises* there is the circumstance that renders impossible the sexual union of Jake Barnes and Brett—the war wound that emasculates him. In *A Farewell to Arms* the lovers are united, but after a few months of blissful happiness Catherine dies in giving birth to her first child. In *For Whom the Bell Tolls,* Robert Jordan and Maria, even amid the perils of the Spanish

War, enjoy perfect happiness, but on the third day after their first meeting, Jordan is dead. Thus, in these novels the problem of the woman dwindling into a mere wife, or the man "coming the heavy husband on" his beloved (*The Wild Palms*, p. 126) is sidestepped. Yet it could be argued that the brief space of time that Hemingway allows to his lovers suggests that he knew that the intensity of romantic love could not be sustained.

For perceptive comments on Faulkner's consciousness of Hemingway as a rival, the reader is referred to McHaney's chapter entitled "Anderson, Hemingway, and the Origins of *The Wild Palms*."

Faulkner's implied references to Hemingway on p. 97 of *The Wild Palms* touches on this matter, for it provides a clear indication that he had Hemingway in mind as he wrote the novel. In 1962 Melvin Backman (see the *Kansas City Review* for Spring 1962) first pointed out that the exchange between Charlotte and McCord on p. 97 refers to a passage in Hemingway's "The Snows of Kilimanjaro." Charlotte, speaking with a rather hysterical gaiety, is referring to their present financial position. Far from its having been rendered desperate, she asserts that "We've got forty-eight dollars too much. . . . Even the Armours haven't got forty-eight dollars too much. Drink up, ye armourous sons. Keep up with the dog." Since the scene is Chicago, the great meat-packing center, her reference to the wealthy owners of one of the meat-packing firms makes a kind of sense. "Armourous sons," however, seems rather pointless. "Amorous" sons? Or sons hungry for food—for the chops lying on the table before them? (Harry has just said for the second time, "Hadn't we better eat something?")

At any rate, McCord at once takes up the adjective and connects it with Hemingway. He says: "Yah. Set, ye armourous sons, in a sea of hemingwaves." McCord is here remembering the conversation in "Snows of Kilimanjaro" in which the wife of the dying writer remonstrates with him for his bitterness. She asks: ". . . do you have to take and burn your saddle and your armour?" Her husband relies: "Yes. Your damned money was my armour. My Swift and my Armour."

These rather far-fetched puns bring the crisis faced by Charlotte and Harry into focus. In the Hemingway story there was plenty of money but no love; for Charlotte and Harry, there is plenty of love but they are running out of money. The puns themselves are pretty terrible. Dramatically, however, they can be justified. Those in *The Wild Palms* at least are appropriate to the circumstances in which they are uttered. We are not told how many highballs had been drunk

when the puns begin to tumble forth, but one assumes several, and a
little later in the taxi, McCord is holding the "invisible dog" in his
arms—which perhaps argues for one or two more.

The Story of the Chops and the Iron Dog

When in Chicago Harry tells Charlotte that he has lost his job,
Charlotte says: "Well. And we haven't got a drink in the house. You
go down to the store and get a bottle while I— No, wait. We'll go
out and eat and drink both. Besides, we'll have to find a dog" (p. 96).
Harry is naturally puzzled, the more so when he sees Charlotte remove the two chops they had planned to have for supper and wrap
them up to take out with them. When Harry repeats "A dog" with a
question in his voice, her reply is "But certainly, friend. Get your
hat."

They start for the bar, Charlotte carrying the chops wrapped in
butcher's paper, and within a block they meet their friend McCord.
Charlotte greets him with the cryptic utterance: "We've lost our job.
So we're looking for a dog." In a few minutes Charlotte, Harry, and
McCord, with four of his friends, are "sitting about a table set for
eight, [with] an empty chair, an empty gap, the two chops unwrapped
now and on a plate beside a glass of neat whiskey among the highballs." They keep on drinking but they do not eat. Finally Charlotte
persuades Harry and McCord and two of the others to get into a
cab with her and they go looking for a proper dog. They drive all
the way out to Evanston in their search and there they do find one,
in someone's front yard—a "cast iron Saint Bernard with its composite
face of the Emperor Franz Josef and a Maine banker in the year
1859." Charlotte places the chops between the dog's iron feet and
returns to the cab.

The whole incident is drunkenly absurd: two people who have lost
their meal ticket (or at least a good part of it) decide to laugh it off
with their friends rather than mourn over it. As far as meals are concerned, they prefer drinking to eating. Such surely is the general import of the incident, but we still haven't accounted for the dog. I
suspect that Charlotte is building her fantasy on a joke that was
current in the period. I remember it, though I can't be sure of the
exact year in which it went the rounds.

A man comes into a restaurant, presumably one that will serve
liquor only if one orders a meal, and tells the waiter to bring him a

beefsteak, cooked bloody rare, a bottle of bourbon whiskey, and a bulldog. The puzzled waiter asks: "Why the bulldog?" The customer answers: "To eat the steak." It's not much of a joke, but it does provide some sort of foundation to an otherwise pointless story. It at least accounts for the dog, the cheerful abjuring of food—let the dog have it—and a celebration of the new state of affairs with a drunken party.

I think that I have seen the dog in question, or at least a reasonable facsimile of the dog described. It is a life-sized cast-iron Saint Bernard that lives in the front yard of a residence in the uptown section of New Orleans. The dog's face beautifully conforms to the graphic description that Faulkner has supplied on p. 98. The owner of this stately, iron-hearted beast has told me that years ago several other copies were cast in New Orleans. I wonder whether Faulkner may not have seen one of them.

Francis Rittenmeyer

Faulkner maintains a very even-handed justice in this novel. Charlotte Rittenmeyer's husband ought, by all conventional accounts, to be a perfect stick, a dull and completely conventional businessman who really cared nothing for his wife and who, out of pure spite, refused to give her a divorce when at last she met the man with whom she wished to share her life.

Rittenmeyer is a rigid man, wedded to traditional ideas, and unwilling, for religious reasons, to give Charlotte a divorce. Yet with her obvious distaste for marriage, did she seriously desire a divorce? One wonders. At any rate, Francis ought to be the obvious villain. But he is not. Though we learn very little about him, what we do learn is completely to his credit. He seems genuinely concerned about his wife. He makes provision for her return at any time she wishes to return. When he fails to get from her the regular monthly communication that she has promised, he hires a detective to check and make sure that she's not ill or starving or being mistreated.

When Harry is tried on the charge of murdering Charlotte, Rittenmeyer puts up Harry's bond and tries to persuade him to jump bond and escape to Mexico. When Harry refuses, he puts in a plea for him at the trial—and outrages the public by doing so. Finally, after Harry has been convicted and sentenced, he brings him the cyanide tablet to enable him to escape the tedious years of life imprisonment. All these efforts he makes, not out of liking for Harry, but because he had promised Charlotte that he would. He is the man of honor, a gentleman, a husband who had truly loved his wife. This last-mentioned fact seems inescapable. Indeed, Francis Rittenmeyer has to be listed among the victims of Charlotte's dream of romantic love.

What is Faulkner's final judgment of him? We are given a brief description of him after he handed Harry the cyanide: his face was "calm outrageous and consistent, the man who had been right always and found no peace in it" (p. 322). Harry starts to thank him, stops, and then, as Rittenmeyer prepares to leave the room, we get one last glimpse of his face: it is "consistent and right and damned for ever."

One wishes we had been told more about him. He turns out to be an interesting, complex character, almost challenging Harry's position as the tragic figure of the novel.

Love as a Transcendence of the Flesh and the World

In considering Harry's predicament, affirming a transcendence of the flesh which at the same time involves a dependence on the flesh, one might consider a few examples from the seventeenth century and from our own time.

Andrew Marvell in "The Definition of Love" makes it a virtue that the lovers can never expect to be united in the flesh.

> My love is of a birth as rare
> As 'tis for object strange and high:
> It was begotten by Despair
> Upon Impossibility.

The very impossibility of the union of the lovers gives to their love its special quality, and its intensity. Marvell's poem reflects a not uncharacteristic aspect of chivalric love. A modern poet, John Crowe Ransom, in his "Spectral Lovers," has treated the same basic situation, but the separation of his lovers is not forced by circumstance. It has been self-imposed—"For honor beat them back and kept them clear"—and the poet's tone is one of ironic pity for the lovers' self-denial.

In "The Ecstasy" John Donne resolves the problem in favor of physical consummation: spirit needs body for its full revelation.

> To our bodies turn we then, that so
> Weak men on love revealed may look;

411

Love's mysteries in souls do grow,
But yet the body is his book.

In another poem Donne has canvassed a related problem, the lovers' rejection of the world. In "The Canonization" the speaker of the poem knows that his pledged love to his mistress probably means the end of his career and a repudiation of all his worldly hopes. But he and the beloved woman cheerfully give up the world, each claiming to find a better world in the person of the other. Like Marvell's "Definition," this poem is witty and sophisticated. It celebrates an act done with full awareness of the consequences. The lovers proclaim that they can "die" if not live by their love. But though the speaker may be using "die" in its quite literal sense, the intellectual ambience of the poem suggests that he is also using "die" in a sense thoroughly familiar to his seventeenth-century readers, that is, meaning to experience the fulfillment of the sexual act. The supposition that this is the real, or at least an optional, meaning of "die" is not lessened by the analogies between romantic love and holy love that Donne exploits in the poem. After their death the faithful pair will be canonized as love's saints and, having ascended into their heaven, will be invoked to bestow on earth-bound lovers a "pattern" of celestial love.

Even in our own day, lovers are still occasionally represented as giving up the world and, if unable to live by love, willing to die by love. A few years ago the Swedish film *Elvira Madigan* depicted the story of a young cavalry officer who falls desperately in love with a girl who does a rope-walking act in a music hall. He abandons his career, his place in society, his wife and children, and takes the girl off to a rural hideaway. They have a blissful time until his small store of money runs out. They pawn their few possessions, but soon literally nothing is left. The officer cannot earn money, for the only jobs at hand are day-laborer's jobs, and his hands are too soft and white; no one will hire him. A few mornings later the lovers go out for a walk, and when the girl, though faint for lack of food, sees a butterfly and gasps with delight as she attempts to catch it, her lover puts a bullet through her head. The camera freezes on her facial expression and gesture in this moment of simple joy and holds it for perhaps two seconds. Then we hear a second shot. The officer has put a bullet through his own head and the screen becomes totally dark.

These references to lovers who defy society and count the world well lost for love, lovers who seriously mean to live (or else die) by love, are, of course, only a handful of what one could cite. A longer list would surely include Shakespeare's *Romeo and Juliet* and *Antony and Cleopatra* at one extreme and at the other, Villiers de l'Isle-Adam's *Axel*. It might also include one of Faulkner's favorite poems by Shakespeare, "The Phoenix and the Turtle." Those I have mentioned may suggest a sufficient historical context in which to place the story of Harry Wilbourne and Charlotte Rittenmeyer.

In *Elvira Madigan* and *The Wild Palms,* however, there is no sense of an objective transcendental world such as buoyed up the neo-Platonic lover of the Renaissance or, in the late Middle Ages, provided a sense of a quasi-Christian heaven for the Gnostic chivalric lover. For Harry and Charlotte nothing really exists beyond the natural world. There is only, as Harry says, over and over, the old mammalian meat. And so this massive and even transcendent dream of a unique and precious experience—an experience that can torment the poor body itself, not merely with passion but with a hungering for food, this corrosive dream which demands so much of the hard-driven flesh and sometimes denies the flesh its own simple pleasures, floats upon nothing more solid than that frail and transient flesh itself. Once the flesh becomes only so much carrion, the dream of transcendence winks out like a snuffed candleflame.

Such is the built-in contradiction that has become so acute for modern man generally. He has not, at least up to this point, been willing to give up completely such transcendent experience as has filled the imagination of his forebears, even though he believes that his naturalistic world view insists that he conscientiously deny everything that claims to transcend nature. It would seem that if Harry (and Charlotte, too, for that matter) felt compelled to put so much trust in the flesh, they might have given it a little more consideration, been willing to feed it, been willing even to pamper it a bit, in view of what precious freight (their consciousness of each other) it bears. But they hesitate to take the body's needs seriously, lest they compromise the erotic dream it supports. Perhaps the romantics generally and not merely Faulkner's romantic lovers have been caught in such a contradiction. Yet with Harry and Charlotte, the contradiction is exposed quite nakedly: the actual Donne and Marvell and the mythical Tristan and Isolde did believe that the body contained a soul that was distinct from and separable from the body.

9. *A FABLE*

The Mutinies in the French Army

Faulkner's *A Fable* does not follow very closely what actually happened in 1917 on the Western Front; and there is no compelling reason why a fiction writer should stick close to historical fact. He may have very different purposes. After all, he is writing a novel, not documented history. Faulkner certainly did not claim that *A Fable* was in any way an account of an actual mutiny. Nevertheless, there are some interesting parallels between some of the things that are made to happen in *A Fable* and what actually did happen in France in 1917.

There was a mutiny in the French Army in the spring of 1917, and by early summer the French Army was riddled with untrustworthy and sometimes actually rebellious battalions and regiments. The first refusal of an army unit to obey the command to move up to the front occurred on 29 April 1917.[1] The Second Battalion of the 18th Infantry Regiment had made an attack on the German trenches and had been reduced from nearly 600 to 200 uninjured men. After being reorganized and brought up to strength by replacements, the soldiers of the battalion had been told that they would be sent to a quiescent part of the line. When later they learned that they were to be employed again as an attack force, they refused to go. Their mutiny was, however, temporary. After some hours they were persuaded, most of them at least, to obey orders and move into the front lines. But an example had to be made, and a number of the men were charged with having incited the others to refuse to obey orders. These were court-martialed, all found guilty, and sentenced to imprisonment in French Guinea, except for five who were to be executed.

A Corporal Cronau had been arrested because of a report that "a big blond corporal" had been one of the ringleaders in the mutiny.

1. I rely here and subsequently on Richard M. Watt's *Dare Call It Treason* (London, 1964). It is a well documented account of why the mutinies began, the grave danger that they presented to the success of the Allied cause, and how morale and discipline was finally restored. For reasons easy to guess, the citizens of the United States in 1917 were told little or nothing about the mutinies. Few Americans know much about them even today. How much Faulkner knew about the near collapse of the French Army, I cannot say.

When it was ascertained that he had actually been in hospital at the time of the mutiny, the investigators seized on another corporal, Moulia by name, though Moulia had an excellent battle record. Apparently, the authorities felt that they had to have a corporal. Ironically, when the executions took place, Moulia alone of the five escaped. Just as he was being led before the firing squad, the Germans let down an artillery barrage, and he broke away and fled into the woods. He was never recaptured. The point is not important. I mention it only to show how life imitates art or, in this incident, anticipates art. Here is Faulkner's Corporal, that strange and elusive person who could not be fully abolished, try as the French military organization might.

It was not because the Second Battalion of the 18th Infantry Regiment had been infiltrated by Communists that it mutinied; nor had it been seduced by the leaflets urging peace (though they were continuously being distributed); and certainly it did not mutiny because some mysterious corporal had told these soldiers that all men were brothers. The soldiers of the Second Battalion were simply men reduced to despair. They had learned that you could not break through the German entrenchments. They were tired of dying on the barbed wire after being riddled by machine gun fire. They had learned from sad experience that the highly touted plan developed by the French Commander-in-Chief, Robert Nivelle, had failed, and they had completely lost confidence in him and in the whole general staff. Because such despair had become pandemic—after all, this was the third year of the war and the French losses had been frightful—other mutinies were bound to take place, and they did.

On 3 May, there was a mutiny in the Second Division of the Colonial Infantry. When ordered up into the front line, the men refused to pick up their rifles, telling their officers, "We're not such fools as to attack against uncut barbed wire or unshelled German trenches." Most important of all, the troops speedily learned that if enough of them refused to obey orders, there was little that their officers could do about it. The revolt against authority quickly spread throughout the whole Second Division. The French Command soon found that "To court-martial two thousand men is ridiculous and impossible, to contemplate shooting two thousand mutineers is unthinkable" (*Dare Call It Treason,* p. 161). *Pace* General Gragnon, the rest of the French generals in *A Fable* know better than to do this, and they act precisely as did the French generals in World War I. Yet the French did throw two-thirds of the mutinous 310th Regiment into a stockade (cf. pp. 13–14 of *A Fable*) though out of the whole regiment only sixteen soldiers were sentenced to death.

More and more serious mutinies occurred throughout May and June of 1917. The situation was critical. Paris was only sixty miles away from the nearest segment of the battle line, and at one point, according to Watt, the French had between Paris and the battle line only two divisions on whose implicit loyalty they could count. If the Germans had known this and had launched a major attack, they would speedily have been in Paris. According to Watt, it was Pétain who carried out the reforms necessary to restore morale and rehabilitate the troops into an effective force once more. Curiously enough, just as in *A Fable*, the Germans did not attack during this period. No one seems to know why not. Perhaps they were exhausted too. Perhaps their general staff at this time was no more imaginative or intelligent than the French general staff.

Watt, by the way, is about as hard on the quality of the French generals as Faulkner is in *A Fable*. Watt stresses the point that many of the French troops felt that the high command had lost all touch with them and their interests, was willing to sacrifice them cold-bloodedly for its own glory or personal advantage, and that it lived in a world of its own, far removed from the mud of the trenches and from the men who, when an attack was called for, had to face murderous gunfire. Such also is the basic attitude of the common soldiers as depicted in *A Fable*. There is, of course, nothing extraordinary about this parallelism between history and Faulkner's fiction; the literature of World War I very early began to reflect such a situation, and it is a view that Faulkner would have encountered not only in his general reading about the war but in his conversations with returned American infantrymen.

The Old Marshal's Military and Political Ideas

For some reason, the Marshal-to-be left the army, dropped completely out of sight, and spent some thirteen years in a Tibetan lamasery. We are given little more than the bare facts, and yet the inference is plain: he had retired from the world to meditate and to come to terms with reality. He was disciplining himself—preparing himself for some great cause. That cause, we are told, proved to be the salvation of France in her hour of need and, with her, the salvation of the civilization of the West, of which Paris is seen as the cultural capital.

The Corporal's great adversary has, thus, been carefully groomed for the contest, and is allowed to approach it with considerable fanfare. But how does he go about saving the West? Apparently simply by having the Corporal shot. If other French generals could have handled the situation in the same way, the Old Marshal's role shrinks to something quite ordinary. One might remark that another general in the novel, Charles Gragnon, a mere division commander, would have attended even more promptly to this matter; Gragnon tried his best to have his whole division of six thousand men executed when they refused to go over the top.

The Quartermaster General sees in his old friend, the Marshal, an almost godlike man. Providence has not only endowed him with special inborn virtues, but he also has carefully prepared himself through his whole lifetime for his lofty and arduous task, the salvation of France. But in fact he exhibits no extraordinary powers and accomplishes only what the French generals like Foch and Pétain (see the preceding note) did accomplish in history—not significantly more.

By 1917, if not perhaps earlier, the Marshal had come to see quite clearly what kind of war it was. There was no hope of breaking out of the long stalemate of trench warfare. The war was one of attrition, and the task of any commander on the Western Front was simply to hold the defensive line, maintain morale, and wait until the United States was ready to bring to bear its full industrial might. This task had great importance, but it scarcely required military genius, and in spite of the Quartermaster General's laudations of his friend, no military genius is ever displayed by the Marshal.

As far as the salvation of France and of Western civilization is concerned, it is now generally agreed that World War I, far from saving Western civilization, was really a suicidal war, which seriously weakened Western Europe and as a consequence brought on the even more debilitating World War II. The Marshal does not voice such a prophecy, though such an interpretation is clearly implied. But the Marshal does indicate that among the European powers no real victor can come out of this war. He foresees that in the future war can even "become the last refuge from bankruptcy," and prophesies that if the Corporal decides to keep his life, the Corporal may see the day arrive "when a nation insolvent from overpopulation will declare war on whatever richest and most sentimental opponent it can persuade to defeat it quickest, in order to feed its people out of the conqueror's quartermaster stores." The Marshal goes on to remark that fortunately, since in this war France and Britain are allied with the ultimate

417

victor (the U.S.A.), they will "find [themselves] in the happy situation of gaining almost as much from [their] victory as the German will through his defeat" (p. 345).

Faulkner here is obviously allowing his French general hindsights gained from the post–World War II period. Yet, whatever the source, Faulkner has endowed the Old Marshal with sufficient prophetic vision to realize that France will come out of the World War I with not much more than a token victory. His statement makes it all the more difficult to see why, now that the United States has come into the war, it matters very much to the Marshal whether it is the Allies or the Central Powers that become the technical victors.

It might be argued that such recognition on the Old Marshal's part accounts for the fact that the military leaders on both sides need to be in league with each other to keep the war going. Whether Germany or the Allies win has come to be quite secondary to the maintenance of the international military machine and the grip of the generals on their own countries. (Here, of course, the novel goes much further than any revisionist historian has yet gone.) Such an argument comes to grief, however, the moment that the Marshal proposes either making the Corporal the head of a world state or else shooting him dead. If the latter course can accomplish what the former course would also accomplish, why hesitate to order the Corporal's execution? It is simpler, quicker, and easier. For it is never made clear that an international military establishment requires the Corporal as a sort of linchpin to hold it together. The fact that the Marshal foresees the United States as the real victor makes it the less likely that an obscure middle-Eastern peasant with a French passport would be accepted as a world overlord, with Paris as his capital. In his conference with the Corporal, did the Old Marshal suddenly lose all his realism and political sagacity? Or was he simply having the younger man on?

Yet, if the Marshal did really believe that the military men of all nations could be brought into a sort of supernational directorate to keep the peoples of the world in order, then he was a very poor prophet. In almost no time, Fascism was afoot in Italy and Hitler was soon to come to power. Russia had already gone over to the Bolsheviks who had begun the process of creating their own revolutionary army.

Not the least surprising aspect of the Old Marshal's character is his hatred of machinery. One would scarcely have suspected it, for military men from the dawn of history have seen the enormous advantage to be gained from more sophisticated weapons. But the Marshal names as the most ominous threat to man's survival "his enslavement to the economic progeny of his own mechanical curiosity" (p. 352). The Marshal makes a more savage attack on the automobile than is made even in *Pylon* (p. 87). He predicts that it will eventually destroy the home so entirely that the very word will vanish "from [the] human lexicon."

There follows a page and a half of apocalyptic vision in which men live their whole lives like terrapins enclosed in monstrous steel shells, trundling over "an expanse of concrete paving" from which protrudes not a single "tree or bush or house." In this nightmare world, wars will abound: every man will need to stay inside his steely shell, which will serve as a shelter "from the hail-like iron refuse from his wars." He will have had to build "tanks bigger and faster and more impervious and with more firepower than any before" and to build bigger and more destructive aircraft. One might have expected that a man like the Marshal, who apparently believes in perpetuating the military establishments of the world, might take some comfort from thinking that wars would never cease.

The Marshal even invokes the "Frankenstein" image. Like Mary Shelley's too inventive scientist, mankind will have created a monster more dire than any human enemy. The slave that Man has devised will thus prove the real threat to the existence of his begetter. Perhaps the last great battle will be a contest of rival mechanisms, an Armageddon fought by the "final two" of the mechanical monsters Man has constructed. The Marshal imagines the final pair of them "engaged in the last gigantic wrestling against the final and dying sky[, a sky] robbed even of darkness and filled with the inflectionless uproar of the two mechanical voices bellowing at each other polysyllabic and verbless patriotic nonsense" (p. 354).

I call attention to these dire prophecies and to the terms in which they are phrased, not because they are particularly new or because the Marshal's rhetoric is more impressive than that of other such prophecies delivered in our time, but because it is the Marshal who speaks them. The Marshal, head of a great military machine which employs in its warfare the most sophisticated machines that the age had been able to produce, stands as a curious champion of the forces condemning mechanism. It is simply one more of the contradictions to be found in this most puzzling of Faulkner's characters.

Faulkner's Own Conception of Man's Ability to Endure

What does the Old Marshal mean when he tells the Corporal that man and his folly will endure—and prevail? What, for that matter, does the Corporal mean by "endure"? An answer to these questions is further complicated by the prophecy of man's endurance as proclaimed in Faulkner's Nobel Prize Speech.

In that speech, Faulkner said that he refused to accept "the end of man" and went on to declare: "I believe that man will not merely endure: he will prevail. He is immortal, not only because he alone among creatures has an inexhaustible voice, but because he has a soul, a spirit capable of compassion and sacrifice and endurance." The task of the literary artist, Faulkner said, was to use his gift of language "to help man endure by lifting his heart, by reminding him of the courage and honor and hope and pride and compassion and pity and sacrifice which have been the glory of his past." The poet's voice can indeed be "one of the props, the pillars to help him endure and prevail." [1]

So Faulkner put matters on 10 December 1950. Some months later (28 May 1951), in addressing the graduating class of the University High School at Oxford, Faulkner again referred to "man's capacity for courage and endurance and sacrifice." But his emphasis in this speech was, quite properly, not on the poet's voice or on what the literary artist could do, but on the task of the individual human being. "It is not men in the mass who can and will save Man," Faulkner told the students. "It is Man himself, created in the image of God" and possessing the capacity and the responsibility to choose between right and wrong. The emphasis here is on man's ability to distinguish right from wrong and his responsibility to make proper choices in his actions. Nevertheless, once again Faulkner cites "endurance" as one of man's prime virtues, ranking it with his capacity for courage and sacrifice.

How does the Marshal's view of man as expressed in *A Fable,* published in 1954, differ from Faulkner's own views? The Marshal, one notes, stresses man's voice, though he does not refer to it as speaking encouragement to man through a poet's lips and reminding man of the deeds of courage and honor and hope and "compassion and pity and sacrifice which have been the glory of his past." Though the Old Marshal makes use of Faulkner's own adjective for man's voice, "inexhaustible," he adds to it the adjective "puny," and for the Marshal this puny voice is not reciting the roll-call of man's deeds of valor,

1. For this and the other two speeches discussed in this note, see *Essays, Speeches, and Public Letters by William Faulkner,* ed. James B. Meriwether (New York, 1965).

sacrifice, and compassion. Instead, it is "still talking, still planning."
And what is it planning? "To build something higher and faster and
louder; more efficient and louder and faster than ever before. . . ."
Furthermore, the Old Marshal does not credit man with possessing a
soul. He is "ten times prouder of that immortality which [man] does
possess," his old "primordial fault" of which he can never be rid,
than ever man ought to "be of that heavenly [immortality] of his
delusion. Because man and his folly—" And when the Corporal
breaks in with "Will endure," the Old Marshal "proudly" replies
that they "will do more. They will prevail."

I suppose that there is a distinction to be made here. To say that
man and his folly will endure is to express realism, sound enough
stoicism, and, just possibly, orthodox Christianity.

Rather surprisingly, the Corporal apparently accepts the Marshal's
linking of man and his folly. Should we interpret his statement, "They
will endure," as a laconic way of saying: "Yes, man's folly will endure;
nevertheless, man will survive in spite of it"? Whatever the Corporal
meant to say, the Marshal's meaning comes out clearly enough. Interpreted in the light of his preceding statements (pp. 352–54), he is
saying here the endurance of man's folly is the very guarantee of man's
own endurance. I interpret him in this way: If man had more sense—
if he were ever to become truly wise—he would see that he hadn't a
chance and would give up the struggle. But wedded as he is to his
folly, he won't give up, and the Marshal predicts that in the struggle
he will come out with better than a dogfall. He will actually win.
This is what I make of his concluding prophecy: "They [man and
his folly] will prevail."

Prevail over what precisely? It isn't clear. Perhaps the Old Marshal
is simply being rhetorical, and his prophecy of a vague, quite un-
specified victory is simply a way of adding a further flourish to his
sardonic praise of man's incorrigibility. In his Nobel Prize Speech,
Faulkner is saying something quite different from what the Old
Marshal is made to say—and different, one is constrained to add,
from what even the Corporal is made to say. Indeed, the Corporal's
faith in man, I have to repeat, is not remarkably different from
Jurgen's. The Corporal seems to have no more theology than Jurgen.
His confidence in himself is something that he simply feels in his
bones.

Since some readers will be more interested in Faulkner's personal
beliefs than in the Old Marshal's or even the Corporal's, I shall turn

now to Faulkner's and attempt a few further comments. Even though in the Nobel Prize Speech Faulkner founds man's "immortality" on his possession of a soul, I regard the speech as basically a humanistic document, even though in virtue of its language it possesses Christian overtones. In his address to his high school audience, these Christian references become more explicit, though I am far from certain that Faulkner meant them to be taken in their literal and orthodox meaning.

Though Faulkner tells his high school students that man is created in the "image of God," the responsibility he stresses is a human responsibility to choose between justice and injustice, courage and cowardice, etc. Man is to be responsible for saving himself. His enterprise is essentially one of self-salvation. This emphasis on man's moral and spiritual responsibility to correct abuses and thus save the world is also to be found in Faulkner's "Address to the Graduating Class of Pine Manor Junior College" (8 June 1958). The name of God is again invoked, but the task of dealing with what is wrong with the world and, indeed, "completing" the world is left up to man, not to God. In creating the world and a creature capable of coping with the world, God has done enough. For God, Faulkner declared, "didn't merely believe in man, He knew man. He knew that man was competent for a soul because he was capable of saving that soul and, with it, himself."

God's further purposes will thus be brought to conclusion not directly, but through his agents. In this enterprise of completing the world, God has found a use for even that "splendid dark incorrigible" angel, the rebellious Lucifer. Instead of simply casting Lucifer "shrieking out of the universe," God permitted him to exist so as to "remind us of our heritage of free will and decision." God uses the "poets and philosophers to remind us, out of our own recorded anguish, of our capacity for courage and endurance. But it is we ourselves," Faulkner exhorted his audience, "who must employ them."

This speech probably represents Faulkner's closest approach to a kind of theism, though again, we cannot be sure how literally we ought to take terms like "God" and "angel." But there need be no doubt that this speech does represent Faulkner's deep-seated beliefs about man, his capacities, his responsibilities, and his role in the world.

Curiously enough, Faulkner's general position reminds me very much of John Milton's own somewhat eccentric version of Christianity. Like Faulkner, Milton does not have much to say about man's need for grace: man can save himself if he will only sincerely strive at the task. There is the same stress on man's free will, and the responsibility that free will entails. There is, also, the same stress on God's refusal to suppress the Devil or protect mankind from his assaults. The wayfaring Christian has to be tested. He must not expect to be sheltered from the temptations of the world, the flesh, and the devil. No more than Milton could Faulkner approve of "a fugitive and cloistered virtue." Finally, both Faulkner and Milton were often irked by the follies and insipidities of organized religion. In fact, neither seemed to have much regard for the Church or to feel much need of institutional spiritual support.

APPENDIX B

A Further Note on the Narrative Sequence of ABSALOM, ABSALOM!

John C. Hodgson has attempted to work out the scheme in accordance with which Faulkner uses double quotation marks, single quotation marks, italics, parentheses, etc., in this novel.[1] The scheme devised seems to work very well for much of the novel (though Hodgson has to concede some inconsistencies here and there). But I think his application of it with reference to chapter v is forced and arbitrary, and that it breaks down utterly with reference to chapter III. Hodgson argues that the break with his code in chapter III was used by Faulkner "to denote a significant temporal distinction." The distinction of which he speaks is more than significant. It is drastic, for it involves shifting the conversation between Mr. Compson and Quentin (which occupies chapter III) from the evening before Quentin rode out to Sutpen's Hundred (the time of the chapters that flank it, II and IV) to some time *after* Quentin had returned, presumably the next day.

Such a shift is too radical to be "proved" merely by a hypothetical change in typography. What are the more substantive matters that Hodgson believes justify placing it in the sequence of events after chapter v?

1. "Logical Sequence and Continuity: Some Observations on the Typographical and Structural Consistency of *Absalom, Absalom!*" *American Literature* 43 (1971): 97–107.

(1) On page 62 (of chapter III) Mr. Compson tells Quentin that Sutpen "named Clytie as he named them all [i.e., his children], the one before Clytie and Henry and Judith even. . . ." Hodgson thinks that his passage indicates that Mr. Compson at this point knows that Bon was Sutpen's son, something which he did not know until after Quentin had returned from Sutpen's Hundred. But if Mr. Compson knew that fact when he spoke the sentence in question on page 62, why didn't he say ". . . named Clytie, as he named them all, Henry and Judith and Charles Bon, even. . . ." In his excitement at having just learned from Quentin that Charles Bon was indeed Sutpen's son, it would be incredible that Mr. Compson would have left his name out of the list and simply referred to him as "the one before Clytie and Henry. . . ." When Mr. Compson addresses himself to the subject at a time in which he did know that Bon was Sutpen's son (p. 265), he mentions Bon by name.

(2) Hodgson adduces as further evidence of his thesis Mr. Compson's allusion "to Jason and the dragon's teeth." But the name *Jason* does not occur in *Absalom, Absalom!*, though there are references to Sutpen's "fecundity of dragon's teeth" (p. 62) and "fecundity of dragons' teeth" (p. 266). Is Mr. Compson referring to the story of Jason or merely to the story of Cadmus? Both Greek heroes sowed dragon's teeth—Jason's supply actually came from the dragon that Cadmus slew—and in both cases, the harvest was of armed men. Hodgson, who, by the way, makes no allusion to the story of Cadmus, believes that the "allusion to Jason" supports his case because the "story of two brothers destroying each other at the instigation of the very man who has sired them provides a striking parallel to the Jason myth, but the story of Henry and Bon could have borne no resemblance to the myth in Mr. Compson's eyes had he not known that they were indeed brothers."

But how many striking parallels are there in fact to be found between the Jason myth and the Sutpen myth? Jason did have a half-brother, Pelias, who held the throne to which Jason thought he had an equal or better claim, and Pelias persuaded Jason to undertake to bring back the Golden Fleece in the hope that Jason would not survive that perilous adventure. But here we have brother plotting against brother, not their father setting them against each other. (Actually they had *different fathers,* though the same mother.)

As for sowing dragon's teeth in the sense of taking an action that may have dire results—the usual way in which the saying is used—

that meaning will work for the story of Cadmus as well as for the story of Jason. So will the hero's mitigating the peril to himself by causing the armed men to fight among themselves. The parallels between either of these stories and that of Sutpen would amount to no more than that Sutpen, in begetting children (sowing the field), is unwittingly raising up dire problems for himself (the teeth turn into armed men). Such seems to be all that Mr. Compson means by the allusion in the passage on page 266, where we can be sure that Mr. Compson *does* know that Bon is Sutpen's son. There he speaks of "the Charles Goods and the Clytemnestras and Henry and Judith and all of them— that entire fecundity of dragons' teeth. . . ." Note that here Judith and Clytie are called dragon's teeth too. In the Jason and Cadmus stories, the hero, by hurling a stone into the midst of the armed men, causes them to fight among themselves, but Mr. Compson, by pointedly including Clytie and Judith among the dragon's teeth, renders this aspect of the Greek myth inapplicable to the Sutpen story. He does not limit the term to the boys, Bon and Henry, who quite obviously did *destroy* each other. Mr. Compson sees Sutpen's "entire progeny" as "dragon's teeth." If such is all that he meant, then we can turn back to page 62 (in chapter III) and include the unknown one, "the one before Clytie," along with the girls. For Mr. Compson, all Sutpen's children were a threat to their father.[2]

The decisive reason, however, for regarding the conversation recorded in chapter III as having taken place before Quentin rode out to Sutpen's Hundred rather than after his return is a reason urged by common sense. Can one imagine Mr. Compson, now that the secret of Bon's parentage has been made clear to him, not making some reference to it? In chapter III he talks, page after page, with almost no mention of Bon. In fact, the chapter has largely to do with Miss Rosa and the Coldfields, a topic appropriate enough under the

2. One cannot confidently penetrate Mr. Compson's mind or assign precise meanings to some of the rhetorical tropes, but here is a try. Judith proves disastrous to her father by insisting upon marrying Bon and thus causing Henry, her father's only male heir, to kill Bon and flee the country. The unknown child, born in Haiti, has been responsible in some way for his father's having to pull up stakes and come to another country to start over. As for Clytie, Mr. Compson has himself given a hint as to why he has included her: she was at least "the presiding augur of his own disaster." This may not seem an impressive reason, but that very fact makes for my case: if Mr. Compson can call even Clytie a "dragon's tooth," almost any child of Sutpen's can qualify, including the one in Haiti about whom Mr. Compson (p. 62) at this point knows next to nothing.

circumstances since Quentin has been listening to Miss Rosa for several hours, and as soon as it becomes dark he will call for her to humor her absurd request.

Chronology of LIGHT IN AUGUST

Scholars have for a number of years pretty well agreed that the "present" of *Light in August,* that is, the year in which Joe Christmas and Joanna Burden die and the novel ends, is 1932. This accords with Faulkner's tendency to make the "present" of one of his novels coincide with the year in which the novel was published. The most detailed chronology of *Light in August* that I know of is that worked out by Sally Page Wheeler (see *The Southern Literary Journal* 6 [1973]: 20–42), who also finds 1932 to be the year in which the story comes to an end; the way in which the various datings in her chronology mutually support each other gives one confidence in her dating of the various items. But I want to adduce more specific evidence to justify 1932 as the correct year.

The most precise evidence for that date can be summarized as follows: On page 443 we learn that when Hightower's father returned from the war "in '65," Mrs. Hightower took the coat that her husband had worn through the war "and put it away in a trunk in the attic. It stayed there for twentyfive years," that is, until their son, Gail Hightower, a boy of eight, opened the trunk and took the coat out to look at it. By this calculation, the year in which the boy opened the trunk would have been 1890 and the boy would have been born in 1882. In the year in which the novel ends, Hightower is referred to as a "fifty-year-old outcast" (p. 44). Hence the year in question must be 1932.

These dates given on pages 44 and 443 are quite specific. The number of years that Faulkner on page 44 assigns to Hightower, precisely "fifty," does not appear to be a rounded-off number. For on page 465, when Hightower reaches his moment of truth, he says to himself, "I know that for fifty years I have not even been clay: I have been a single instant of darkness in which a horse galloped and a gun crashed." That is to say, he had never lived at all, being no more than his "dead grandfather on the instant of his death. . . ."

If the year of Joanna Burden's death is 1932, then, since the month is clearly August and Faulkner has even given us the day of the week and the time of the day—shortly past midnight on a Saturday morning—it may be possible to determine which of the four possible Saturdays in August of 1932 is the one in question. Granted that specifying the Saturday is not important in itself, it is nevertheless tempting to try to see how far Faulkner's remarkably detailed and coherent chronology can be extended. In any case, there would be a very practical gain for the reader in being able to refer to calendar dates as he tries to follow the complicated shifts in time that Faulkner employs, or as he tries to keep straight the later events of the novel, all of which Faulkner has carefully keyed to the date of the murder. Thus, it is less confusing if the reader can say to himself that on 9 August Joe asked a farmer's wife to tell him the day of the week, rather than to be forced to say that Joe did so on the Tuesday following the murder; or that Joe was killed on 15 August, rather than on the second Monday after Joanna's murder.

The prime clue for ascertaining the date of Joanna's murder is to be found on page 405. There we learn that Brown had lived in the Burden cabin with Joe "for four months." Brown ended his residence there, of course, on the Saturday in August when Joanna's body was found. It can be determined that he first moved into the cabin late in March or in the first few days of April. A careful reading of pages 252–56 shows the following succession of events.

One evening in February 1932, Joe found a note from Joanna asking him to see her (p. 252). He did so, but this was the last time that he talked with her within "the next two months" (p. 254). The only exception was a meeting that occurred in March—the one time that he had seen her "since February" (p. 255). The two-month period that began with the February meeting would come to an end in April, when Joe received another summons from Joanna and went to her house to talk with her. Moreover, this April meeting, we learn (p. 256), occurred "over a month" after the meeting in March in which Joe told Joanna that "Brown was coming to live with him in the cabin" (p. 255).

Joe had first met Brown when the stranger turned up at the planing-mill where Joe worked, "one day early in the spring" (p. 255)—presumably early in March. Joe evidently took some time to look Brown over (p. 255) before deciding to take him into his whiskey business and into his cabin as a roommate. If Brown had taken up residence in the cabin in early or even in mid-March, we should have to stretch the period of his residence there far beyond "the four months" (p. 405) in order to make it terminate in August.

It was on a Sunday (p. 255) that Joe informed Joanna that he was bringing Brown into the cabin. If we assign that meeting to the last Sunday in March of 1932, the 27th, the date will fit very well. Presumably, the feckless Brown would have needed no urging to accept Joe's invitation. One supposes that he would have moved in at once or within a few days thereafter, that is, just about four months before 6 August.

But did he? How do we know that Joe did not put off his invitation until April and that it was still later that he told Joanna that he was bringing Brown into the cabin—say, in mid-April—a date that would make the four months of Brown's sojourn in the cabin end, not on 6 August but on 13 August or even on 20 August?

We can discount this last possibility for the following reasons. When, some two months after their February meeting, Joe was summoned by Joanna to come to her house, Brown was already living in the cabin (pp. 255–57) and presumably had been living there for over a month. For we learn that Joe had been apprehensive "for over a month now" because Joanna "had done nothing, [had] made no move" (p. 256). Why was Joe apprehensive? Because he feared that she might visit the cabin unannounced and thus allow Brown to come to suspect what his relations with Joanna were. Thus throughout this period, Joe would "trick and avoid Brown in order to reach the cabin first" (p. 256) to forestall a meeting between Brown and Joanna. Brown, then, would seem to have been living in the cabin since late March; for if we date the February meeting of Joe and Joanna as late as possible (on 29 February), Joanna's summons to Joe (which came two months later) would still fall within the month of April, and the period of Joe's apprehension, which lasted for "over a month" (p. 256), would still have to stretch back into March. In short, if we date Brown's coming into the cabin too early in March, his four months of residence will not stretch into August as it must; on the other hand, if we date it much beyond the first few days of April, the two-month interval between the last possible date for a February meeting and the April meetings of Joe and Joanna will have to be stretched too far.

Granted that Faulkner's period of "four months," "two months," and "a month and more" are not to be interpreted as strictly accurate, nevertheless we must not extend them until they are meaningless. Besides, one gains confidence in the basic soundness of these references from observing what close mutual support they afford each other—and how well the chronology they determine accords with the dates suggested by the pages (257–63) that immediately follow.

Thus, after Joe found the note that Joanna had left for him in the cabin—toward the end of April ("over a month" after his meeting with Joanna on 27 [?] March)—such notes continue to arrive at the cabin and Joe continues to go to Joanna's house. Presently, he is traversing "the late twilight of May" on his way there (p. 263). On an "August night three months later" (p. 264) he will hear the clock strike midnight and mount the stairs to kill her.

There is one more bit of evidence which, if it counts for anything, again points to 6 August as the date of the murder. In his University of Virginia question-and-answer sessions, Faulkner was asked about the meaning of the title *Light in August,* and explained it in this way: ". . . in August in Mississippi there's a few days somewhere around the middle of the month when suddenly there's a lambence, a luminous quality to the light. . . . It lasts just for a day or two, then it's gone. . . . And that's all that [my title] meant, just that luminous lambent quality of an older light than ours." [1]

The one passage in the novel where Faulkner describes the August light in precisely these terms occurs on page 465. It is in "the lambent suspension of August" that the wounded Hightower has his vision. The date—provided we date the murder 6 August—is 15 August, and that is about as near the middle of the month as one could get. One should not, of course, insist on exactitude here: Faulkner's special quality of light obviously does not strictly follow the calendar. Yet the evidence, for whatever it be worth, again points to 6 August as the date of Joanna's death.

CONTENTS OF *THE YOKNAPATAWPHA COUNTRY* AND *TOWARD YOKNAPATAWPHA AND BEYOND*

The chapters of the two volumes are listed here in the approximate order of the composition of the works with which they deal, in the interest of readers who wish to take up the discussions in chronological sequence.

---

1. The passage in its entirety can be found in *Faulkner in the University,* ed. Gwynn and Blotner, p. 199.

Index

435

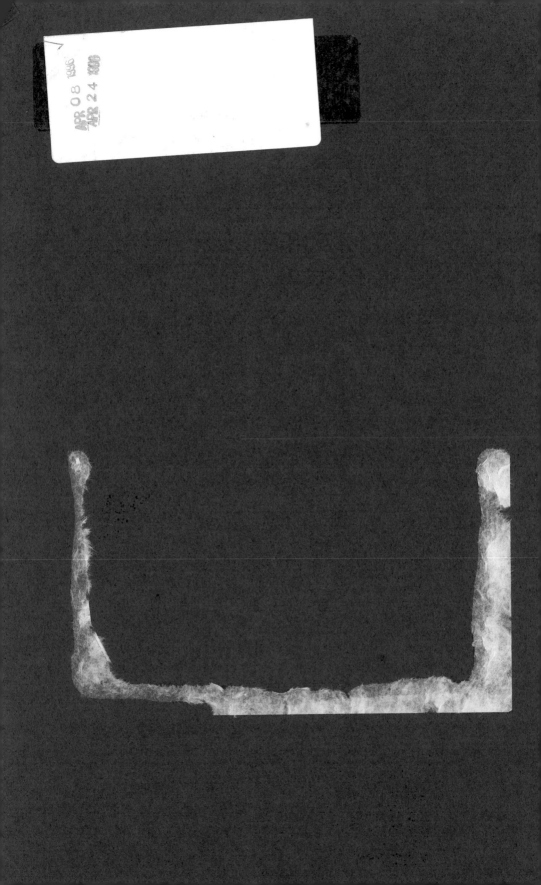